Discourses of Denial

Yasmin Jiwani

Discourses of Denial
Mediations of Race, Gender,
and Violence

UBCPress · Vancouver · Toronto

15 14 13 12 11 10 09 08 07 06   5 4 3 2 1

Printed in Canada on ancient-forest-free paper (100% post-consumer recycled) that is processed chlorine- and acid-free, with vegetable-based inks.

Library and Archives Canada Cataloguing in Publication

Jiwani, Yasmin
 Discourses of denial : mediations of race, gender, and violence / Yasmin Jiwani.

Includes bibliographical references and index.
ISBN-13: 978-0-7748-1237-5 (bound); 978-0-7748-1271-9 (pbk.)
ISBN-10: 0-7748-1237-0 (bound); 0-7748-1271-0 (pbk.)

 1. Women immigrants – Canada – Social conditions. 2. Minority women – Canada – Social conditions. 3. Sex discrimination against women – Canada. 4. Violence – Canada. 5. Violence – Press coverage – Canada. I. Title.

HN103.5.J59 2006   305.48′8′00971   C2006-900046-8

Canadä

UBC Press gratefully acknowledges the financial support for our publishing program of the Government of Canada through the Book Publishing Industry Development Program (BPIDP), and of the Canada Council for the Arts, and the British Columbia Arts Council.

This book has been published with the help of a grant from the Canadian Federation for the Humanities and Social Sciences, through the Aid to Scholarly Publications Programme, using funds provided by the Social Sciences and Humanities Research Council of Canada.

UBC Press
The University of British Columbia
2029 West Mall
Vancouver, BC V6T 1Z2
604-822-5959 / Fax: 604-822-6083
www.ubcpress.ca

In memory of
    my grandfather, Sultanaly Contractor
  my great aunt, Gulbanu Rattansi
    my colleagues, Amanda Ocran and Bob Everton
  my student, Nawaf al Rufaie

Contents

Acknowledgments

Presenting a paper on imperial feminisms at a recent conference panel on mediating inclusions and exclusions, I was struck by a comment from one of the few attendees at the session, a well-established White scholar. His question centred on why we, the panellists, had decided to talk about race as if it were a "real" category. His language was somewhat more sophisticated, but his basic argument was that in making race real, we were dangerously close to essentializing a category that is fluid and socially constructed. This is an argument often articulated against those who talk and teach race. My response to that comment was and is that race is real to me. It marks me just as gender does, but the confluence of race and gender interlocks in ways that shape every facet of my life, determining the choices I make, the paths I travel, and the roads I am prohibited from travelling.

Later that day, my co-panellist, also a White man, commented on the nature of the question we were asked on the panel. Having just observed questions that were directed at me in a consecutive panel, he noted that doing any kind of work on race seemed like a constant battle, that I was always being challenged and my views contested. Speaking of the earlier panel in which he had participated, he commented that the man asking the question was White like himself. Whereupon he remarked that such a question was possible because the questioner, like himself, could always opt in and out of the struggle. I cannot opt in and out of the struggle. In fact, the struggle is an ongoing challenge in which the task is one of explaining race, showing its intricacies, and suffering its consequences. Nevertheless, as Sherene Razack cautions us, none of us is innocent in the story of race. Rather, we all have privileges and penalties that accrue from our particular positioning in the raced and gendered hierarchies that contain and define us. This book, then, is part of that constant challenge in talking race, but it also reflects the privilege in being able to tell this story, for not everyone has the opportunity to do so.

No work stands in isolation, and this book is no different. I would especially like to acknowledge the volunteers at the FREDA Centre and most particularly Bruce Kachuk. As well, my sincere thanks to Jo-Anne Lee, a friend and a colleague, who persuaded me to take on this task of integrating the various researches I have conducted. A special note of appreciation to Linnett Fawcett, whose friendship and solidarity will always be valued and who spent countless hours trying to put order to a disorderly array of thoughts and texts; Felix Odartey-Wellington, who has been more of a colleague than a student and whose last-minute searches and careful reading saved the day; and Ya Ting Huang, who spent many hours putting together what seemed like a never-ending reference list; Candis Steenbergen for her wise comments and encouragement throughout; Christian Bertelsen for his thought-provoking reflections and critical reading; Ross Perigoe for his comments on an earlier draft; and to Tanisha Ramachandran, who was always there. I am immensely grateful for her friendship, companionship and solidarity. However, my deepest thanks are for Marie Claire MacPhee and Trish McIntosh, who stood beside me at the most trying of times, giving me critical feedback and sharing invaluable insights. Most of all, I want to acknowledge my partner in life, Iqubal Velji, who nurtured and sustained me through intense and often frustrating periods of work; my mother and father, Goolzar and Mansuralli Jiwani, to whom I owe so much of what I am today; my sister Sarah for her pragmatic attitude and continuous encouragement, and my sister Nazlin for being there. The inspiration for this work comes from my grandfather, Sultanally Contractor and my great aunt Gulbanu Rattansi, may their souls rest in peace.

I owe an intellectual debt to my mentors and colleagues and would especially like to recognize Helene Berman, Lorraine Cameron, Parin Dossa, Paul Heyer, Amin Al-Hassan, Agnes Huang, Fatima Jaffer, Sherry Jamal, Jo-Anne Lee, Minelle Mahtani, Amin Merchant, Shelley Moore, Nancy Janovicek, Sherene Razack, Zool Suleman, and Sunera Thobani. Their work, insights, encouragement and solidarity have made my life much richer and my convictions stronger. Last but not least, I would like to acknowledge my colleagues in the Department of Communication Studies at Concordia University, who have offered me an intellectual space and a sense of belonging, and to Emily Andrews and Ann Macklem at UBC Press for their assistance throughout this process.

Funding is a crucial reality for academics and community researchers alike. Much of the research presented here was supported by grants from the Social Sciences and Humanities Research Council's Standard Research Grant (#410-2004-1496) and the Social Cohesion Strategic Theme Grant (829-1999-1002). As well, Status of Women Canada provided much of the funding for the research on racialized girls and young women, and the Vancouver Foundation with Status of Women Canada and the BC Centre for Excellence for Women's Health provided the funds for the research on racialized women and their encounters with the health care system.

I would also like to acknowledge Taylor and Francis (http://www.tandf.co.uk) for granting me permission to reprint my essay "Gendering Terror," which first appeared in *Critique: Critical Middle Eastern Studies* 13, 3 (2004): 265-91; to Sage, for permission to reprint an article which was published in *Violence against Women* 11, 7 (2005): 846-75; to Wilfrid Laurier University Press for allowing me to reproduce several pages of my article from *Canadian Cultural Poesis*, edited by Garry Sherbert, Annie Gerin, and Sheila Petty (forthcoming 2006); and Thomson Nelson for permitting me to reproduce sections of my article from their second edition of *Mediascapes: New Patterns in Canadian Communication*, edited by Paul Attallah and Leslie Shade (2005).

The strength of this work comes from the voices and experiences of the girls and women who shared their lives and realities. I thank and acknowledge them for sharing their truth. This book is dedicated to their efforts, survival and success in this land we have come to call "home."

As always, any shortcomings are entirely due to me.

Introduction

Denials of racism are the stock in trade of racist discourse.

— Teun van Dijk, *Race and Ethnic Relations*

Canada suffers from historical amnesia. Its citizens and institutions function in a state of collective denial. Canadians have obliterated from their collective memory the racist laws, policies, and practices that have shaped their major social, cultural, political, and economic institutions for 300 years.

— Frances Henry et al., *The Colour of Democracy: Racism in Canadian Society*

Race, gender, and violence continue to be topical issues in contemporary Canadian society. From public perceptions of increasing girl gang violence to the supposed importation of terrorism, the "imagined" Canadian nation has had to not only grapple with a changing "complexion" but also face the pervasive and deeply entrenched nature of violence interwoven in its history and informing contemporary social concerns – from intimate, domestic violence to international state-supported violence. This book deals with these issues, but does so from a critical anti-racist and feminist framework.

As reflected by my titling of the book – *Discourses of Denial: Mediations of Race, Gender, and Violence* – my intent is to demonstrate how the various issues of racism and sexism constitute forms of violence. Their separation in daily thought and talk serve strategic purposes – namely, in obfuscating links that could facilitate analysis and, more importantly, coalition building. Sexist violence and racist violence share the common denominator of being structured in a larger culture of power – a culture mediated by institutions structured in dominance. In focusing on discourses of denial, then, my aim is to explicate the links between different forms of structural violence as well as demonstrate how discursive fields – the parameters defining a particular subject matter in terms of how it is thought of and talked about – operate in different realms of social life. These are the mediations I refer to in the book's title, for it is in their communicative expression, their continual reinforcement of a particular common-sense view of the world, that separations between structural and more interpersonal forms of violence are maintained. It is these discursive strategies and moves by which one kind of violence gets recognized and another erased, trivialized, or contained within categories that evacuate the violation of violence that I attend to in this book.

My focus is on the intersecting and interlocking influences of race, gender, and violence as they contour and texture the Canadian public imagination and, more specifically, as they inform the lives of immigrant girls and women of colour. Drawing from academic and activist work, these chapters map the terrain of race, gender, and violence in different spheres of social life: from mediated representations that advance a particular definition of racism and racialized groups in the language of culture, to the intertwining, layered, and complex relations between racism, sexism, and violence in everyday life. I trace the ways in which the violence of racism and sexism is framed, communicated, and experienced – in their encounters with the health care system, in the school system, and in representational discourses offered by the dominant media.

The notion of mapping evokes associations with geographers and mapmakers who chart the contours of particular terrains, identifying the rifts and valleys, the sites of excavation and danger. Sherene Razack (2002) draws attention to this task of mapping as being central to the process of colonization and so positions her work as an "unmapping" of the spatialization of gendered racial violence. In her unmapping, Razack seeks to strip the colonial mantle and organizational structure that has constituted this spatialization. My task here is slightly different. My aim is to map the discursive fields that govern the discourses of raced and gendered violence, not so much in a spatial sense but in terms of highlighting the inundated and uneven landscape of these multiple and interweaving structures of domination. In this sense, my mapping is situated from a vantage point outside these dominant discourses insofar as it is grounded in the subjugated knowledges that I share with those who are in the interstices of converging oppressions. But it is also situated within this very terrain of multiple, competing, and hierarchized discourses. Thus, my focus is on the tips of the icebergs, so to speak, that emerge from the subterranean deposits of accumulated knowledge, knowledge grounded in a legacy of colonialism. Those tips that I look at represent the institutionalized structures and systems that embody in explicit and tangible forms some of the valuations and rules encoded in these subterranean archives of knowledge.

Consequently, in mapping these terrains, I pay specific attention to two sensational cases that were widely reported in the media in order to illustrate the ways in which the discourses of race and racism are translated in the language of dominance. I juxtapose these mediations with empirical studies that examine the realities of girls of colour and recount the myriad ways in which they struggle to negotiate a sense of identity and belonging. I extend this analysis to the domain of health care, detailing the findings of a qualitative study highlighting the voices of immigrant women of colour who have experienced violence and recount their interactions with health care professionals in settings such as hospitals and emergency rooms. From the rather private context of the health care encounter, I return to the mediated nature of our stock of common-sense knowledge, directing the focus this time to an exploration of the gendered nature of terror – how the media represented the events of 9/11, with specific attention to the racialized discourse of that coverage.

In deconstructing the discourses of power that form and inform social life, I am keenly aware of the constantly shifting and somewhat tenuous nature of legitimization as a process by which dominant institutions obtain consent from those they govern. In other words, while I focus on structures of power and the discursive devices used to maintain them, I also direct my attention to the sites of intervention where such power can be challenged, transformed, or diverted in the interests of privileging subjugated knowledge(s) (Foucault 1980a, 82), even if these ruptures are only momentary. Consequently, I end certain chapters in this book with possibilities and suggestions for interventions within the existing matrix of institutional and informal power bases – the matrix of domination (Collins 1990). As Foucault (1980b, 95) has noted, where there is power, there is resistance.

In examining the ways in which race, gender, and violence are mediated through everyday talk and text, I argue that three ideal types (using Max Weber's [1958] conceptual category) emerge: the reasonable person, the preferred immigrant/conditional Canadian, and the preferred patient. These ideal types implicitly describe and prescribe the ideal typical Canadian. As a reasonable person, especially within the context of law, the ideal typical Canadian is the law-abiding, rational, White; middle-class person who speaks the dominant language and embodies national mythologies that are then performed accordingly. Much has been written about the reasonable person test in law, particularly from a feminist standpoint (Bhandar 1997; Devlin 1995).[1] The notion of a reasonable person, especially as derived from the national mythology of Canada as a peaceful kingdom, rests on the assumption that such a person makes few demands, pays her/his taxes, and lives out her/his life in a linear trajectory that begins from humble origins and rises to the pinnacle of economic and social success. Such a person cares about her/his society, contributes to its well-being, and participates in the

active maintenance of the social order through citizenship. This hypo-
thetical person does not complain about injustices, does not play the race
or gender "card," and does not make unceasing demands on the state or on
others. Instead, benevolence marks her/his attitude toward others who are
less fortunate. Ultimately, however, the reasonable person perceives everyone as equal and enjoying the right to make what they will of their lives.
This is the ideal Canadian. For the purpose of clarity and generality, I do
not draw the gendered distinctions here, though they undoubtedly bear on
who constitutes the ideal Canadian woman or man. Rather, what I wish to
underscore are the hegemonic notions of masculinity and femininity that
are raced, classed, sexualized, and able-bodied.

The preferred immigrant fits the mould of the reasonable person. But,
unlike the reasonable person, who is most likely to be born in the country
and who is White, the preferred immigrant tends to be a person of colour.
This person does not bring conflicts over from her/his ancestral lands of
origin. In other words, such a person shows patriotic loyalty to Canada, a
land that has provided many opportunities and for which s/he is grateful.
At the same time, the preferred immigrant also believes in the system, adhering to the same liberal beliefs as those of the reasonable person. S/he too
believes that all can succeed if they just try hard enough. Success is seen in
economic terms. The preferred immigrant, also law-abiding and polite, as-
similates into the dominant society. The preferred immigrant leaves her/his
culture behind or retains only those aspects of it that are not problematic or
that can be periodically celebrated outside the closet of family and community (Mahtani 2001) or kept within it (Peter 1981). S/he is the model minority. Within the context of an encounter with the health system, s/he becomes
the preferred patient, neither demanding nor complaining but simply abid-
ing by the rules and the normative standards of the institution. These ideal
types are not mutually exclusive; rather, they shade into one another and
are invoked in different contexts. Primarily, they are implicit standards
against which Others are evaluated. However, though shrouded in the layered veils of the collective common-sense stock of knowledge, these ideal
types, I suggest, are consistently circulated through media portrayals of Others who do not "fit" and who transgress these normative rules. They become the less preferred. In the privileging of a hierarchy of preferred persons,
the violence of dominant structures of power is erased.

This book, then, maps out an important but often neglected labyrinth of
social relations, providing a historical background to present-day inequalities and shedding light on how their institutionalization impacts on the
current context in which we live.

Situating This Work
Although various chapters in this book were conceptualized and some writ-

ten at different times and delivered to diverse audiences, they nonetheless cohere around the central theme of denial – how denial is expressed and how discourses of denial contribute to the erasure, containment, trivialization, or dismissal of racism as a form of violence. In bringing these pieces together, and reflecting on the common themes underpinning the analyses presented, my intent is to demonstrate the discursive violence through which this denial is accomplished. Throughout this body of work, I constantly reiterate the extent to which Canada, as a nation, practises denial when it comes to issues of sexism, classism, and especially racism; how this tendency to cover up – to conveniently turn a blind eye – manifests itself at the macro and micro levels of social reality. In the first part of the book, I trace these manifestations through general mappings of the key concepts of race, gender, violence, and the role of the media. In Parts 2, 3, and 4, the ways that such denial – be it personal, institutional, or governmental – plays itself out in very real terms at the micro level are illustrated by focusing on a number of case studies and research projects in which I have been directly involved. As notions such as common sense, the reasonable person, and normative values are repeatedly picked apart and revealed for what they are – arbitrary standards set by the dominant culture to reinforce that culture's sense of superiority and position of power in society – my hope is that the reader will confront her/his *own* common-sense values and practices, and reconsider Canada's official rhetoric on these and other issues through more critical lenses.

An equally strong thread throughout this book is the issue of the media's complicity in institutional racism and sexism. Be it in their reporting of the violence experienced by immigrant girls and women (Parts 2 and 3) or the spectre of terrorism post-9/11 (Part 4), I demonstrate how the media act as crucial agents in the promotion and safeguarding of the dominant culture's values, biases, and expectations. I also show how contemporary media coverage of people of colour is rooted in, and conveyed to us through, colonially inscribed filters.

In bringing together a discursive analysis of such seemingly diverse issues as media representations, encounters with the health care system, and the experiences of racialized girls and women of colour, my purpose is to raise awareness of the everyday violence resulting from such structured inequalities that is occurring in Canada today, and to highlight its tragic consequences. These daily enactments of violence, I maintain, are all the more insidious because they are kept in the dark – carefully concealed beneath our much lauded and highly celebrated official policies on multiculturalism, gender equality, and human rights. When these violations on occasion surface – are brought, via the sensation-seeking media, into the cold light of day – they send shock waves into our normally complacent public consciousness but fail to provoke useful reflection upon the root causes underpinning such tragedies. In locating these individual instances of violence within a larger framework, my aim is to bridge the gap between theory and practice – between conceptual frameworks and their influence and expression in everyday reality.

This desire to bridge the gap between theory and practice is rooted in my own experience as an immigrant woman of colour, officially a Canadian citizen but unofficially an Other, an identity that, as a Muslim, has gained increasing salience since 11 September 2001. It also comes from my own experiences as an activist, a cultural worker, and now an academic and draws from my confrontations and negotiations with, as well as resistance to, the dominant inscribed standards, values, and attitudes that contour the lives of people of colour.

Much of the work I draw on in these chapters is grounded in my experiences and the opportunities I have had in collaborating on participatory research projects with grassroots community organizations and advocacy groups over the last decade. As the principal researcher and coordinator at the FREDA Centre, one of the five Canadian centres dedicated to researching violence against women and children, I was able to bring an anti-racist perspective to issues of gendered violence. This allowed me to engage in and conduct participatory action research on gender-based violence with marginalized groups and communities. In these instances, the role of research was critical not only in legitimizing the experiential reality of all those who endure racist and sexist violence but also in attempting to bridge the gap between the expertise and experience of community and academic knowledge. It is the viability and continued existence of this bridge that motivates me to undertake this work. Activism and academia can sustain each other, both as an attempt to articulate, legitimize, and make sense of the experiential realities of oppression, and as enabling strategic interventions by which to draw attention to and dismantle the structures of domination. As I outline in the chapters that follow, the legitimizing power of academic writing, access, and institutional resources can be harnessed in the interests of social change even though such attempts are amenable to cooptation by those in power. Nonetheless, as potential sites of intervention, such structures of legitimation as the academy are a useful and resourceful site for those committed to social change, especially in terms of challenging or contesting national mythologies that seek to advance images of Canada as a harmonious, progressive, and liberated state.

My work at the FREDA Centre also foregrounded, both experientially and academically, the interconnections between racism and sexism. As a Brown woman in the feminist anti-violence movement, and as an academic among front-line workers, my presence signalled the tension between the political need to advance a universal construction of woman as victim of sexist violence and the specificity of racialized sexism as manifested in the situation of women of colour advocates, service providers, and survivors of violence, a difference I discuss in this book. This tension was exacerbated by the legitimate suspicion that academic expertise did nothing other than hijack, through appropriation, the lived experiences and grounded expertise of frontline workers, many of whom had either experienced or witnessed gendered violence first-hand. Yet, as I demonstrate, racialized and gendered violence are interconnected and interlocking. When one is privileged as an explanatory framework, it is often at the expense of the other, and vice versa. Further, these interlocking structures of domination certify that the ensuing violence is framed, understood, and responded to differently, all in the interests of retaining the basic structure of power and privilege of White dominance.

The overall strength of this body of work – and hence its critical importance to scholars, activists, service providers, and the general public – lies in its mapping of the invariably complex and often troubling social, political, and economic terrains in which Canada's subtle yet highly toxic forms of racism are evident. I anticipate that these mappings will prove insightful and informative, that they will fill in many gaps, and that they will provoke thought and incite action. I seek both to explain why things are the way they are and to suggest ways that we can fight for and effect social change. Through the frequent invoking of the voices of those who endure these realities daily, I strive to make explicit the experiential impact of racism, sexism, and classism in people's lives, as well as foster an awareness of how these forces intersect and operate at a number of levels.

By disturbing these complacencies – the taken-for-granted and normative prescriptions that texture a sense of normalcy and routinize the violence of racism, sexism, and classism – my hope is to uncover and lay bare the conditions by which a truly organic solidarity can be forged – a solidarity that validates the experiences and feelings of those who are subordinated and that embraces and promotes their agency in transforming a system structured in dominance.

Defining the Audience
When writing this work, I was confronted with the question of defining my ideal audience. In reflecting upon this question and dwelling on the terrain I intended to chart, I quickly came to the conclusion that this book is not meant for experts. In fact, those who are well versed in high theory will undoubtedly be left unsatisfied. On the other hand, for those who travel along multiple and interdisciplinary boundaries, this book might afford them a better insight into the ways in which systems of dominance are interconnected and how the resulting confluence shapes social reality. Primarily, though, this book is intended for those who are attempting to make sense of the violence of racism. They include the young women of colour whose voices inform the various chapters, the immigrant women whose experiences

form the basis of the investigations outlined here, and the front-line workers and advocates in the feminist anti-violence movement, the anti-racism movement, and other social movements aimed at ending poverty, criminalization, and inequality in all its multiple forms. As well, my hope is that this book will serve to inform students, teachers, and policy makers who are invested in making progressive social change.

A Note on Terminology

Although much of the writing on race has underlined its constructed nature by placing quotation marks around the word, I have decided not to do so for the simple reason that the reality of race in shaping the lives of people of colour cannot be disputed. As George Dei (1999) argues, we do not place quotation marks around the words gender, age, class, sexuality, or ability, even though each of these categories is socially constructed. Yet, we tend to construct race as if it were a dubious category. Here, I am not proposing a genetically deterministic notion of race, an interpretation that has increasingly surfaced on the part of pharmaceutical companies to profit by producing tailor-made, race-specific drugs. Rather, it is the socially constructed nature of race that I wish to underscore. For my part, the terms race, raced, and racialized refer to the social construct of race and the processes of racialization by which the construct is imbued with negative valuations, valuations that are designed to Other, inferiorize, and marginalize groups and individuals who are different from the ideal type or norm. At the same time, I do not wish to advance an essentialist notion of race as constituting some fixed and essential attribute. Instead, my argument is that, in contemporary society, the salience of race as a category for regulating power and access and for maintaining a hierarchy cannot be contested. Thus, rather than denying it, the critical aspect is to examine conditions that contribute to the ways in which race is strategically used to define, implicitly and explicitly, the hierarchies of preference that underpin and reinforce structures of domination.

I use the term racialized women of colour throughout this book, bearing in mind that this terminology is rather context specific. In Britain, women of colour are commonly referred to, in academic writing at least, as Black women. The designation of Black has different meanings in the United States and Canada. In speaking about racialized women of colour, I am cognizant that Aboriginal women and White women are also racialized. However, Aboriginal women have a different history, as indigenous peoples of this land. My position as an immigrant and an Other makes me painfully aware of how immigration itself was structured in the interests of forging the Canadian nation and grounded in the displacement and genocide of Aboriginal peoples.

In using terms such as Black and White, I have deliberately chosen to mark these words by capitalizing them. My intent is to draw attention to their constructed nature: the technique of capitalization ruptures the normativity associated with these words.

Organization

I have divided this book into four parts, each of which deals with a specific facet of the overall themes of race, gender, and violence. I locate the confluence of these themes in different domains, paying particular attention to the discourses of denial operating within each of the contexts being examined. An organizing principle underlying the chapters is the implicit contrast between the mediated representations of violence as these are communicated in the mass media, notably print media, and the experiential realities of those directly affected by the violence of racism. Thus, while the first two chapters lay out the theoretical scaffold on which the rest of the work hangs, the subsequent chapters juxtapose this contrast between mediated representations and experiential realities. In the last chapter, I return to the mediated representations, this time drawing out their material implications for those most affected by the coverage. Implicit in the organization is the link between public and private aspects of violence. In other words, what appear as public texts in the mass mediated world are indelibly linked to the occurrences that texture the private realm of experience. However, these private experiences are not simply reflected but refracted in the mediated accounts.

Part 1: Laying the Terrain

In the introductory chapter, "Reframing Violence," I lay out the conceptual framework for the book and make an argument for examining various domains of inquiry through a raced and gendered perspective. Key terms are defined and elaborated. I draw particular attention to the hierarchical nature of Canadian society, pointing out its history as a colony and a colonizing nation. I situate the interlocking influences of race, gender, and class, highlighting the ways in which the dominant culture of power maintains its hegemonic control. I link the hierarchical nature of Canadian society to the dimensions and realities of structural violence, emphasizing the particular factors that shape and contribute to the marginalization of racialized women of colour. The resulting vulnerabilities, I argue, are anchored in structures of dominance, which define the standards by which racialized people are assessed and treated in ways that influence their lived realities and autonomy.

In the second mapping of this part – Chapter 2, "Mapping Race in the Media" – I elaborate on concepts introduced at the beginning of this book –

concepts such as culture, racism, and sexism – and insert the media into the picture, suggesting not only how the media play a major role in shaping public opinion but how the strategic use of the media is one of the primary ways that those in positions of power justify, legitimize, and gain support for the actions they take. The media, as Stuart Hall (1980a) has argued, are structured in dominance. They make up a powerful institution populated and controlled by the elite, who then liaise with other elites to maintain the status quo (van Dijk 1993). The media, as institutions, are among the wealthiest organizations in this society. They constitute a monopoly of knowledge, and through their practices of selection, editing, and production determine the kinds of information we receive about our culture, nation, and the rest of the world. How race is represented in the dominant media is indicative of the place accorded to racialized groups in the symbolic landscape of the nation, and further, of how they are perceived in terms of belonging to the imagined community reflected by the media.

Part 2: Sensationalized Cases

Chapters 3 and 4, in Part 2, examine the murders of Reena Virk in Victoria, and members of the Gakhal and Saran families in Vernon, British Columbia. Both these cases were widely reported in the provincial and national media. Through these case studies, I illustrate the ways in which specific definitions of culture are used and in some instances evacuated from the kinds of explanatory frameworks offered by officials such as court judges and the media. As with official government discourse, the media tend to identify culture as that which is visible and different from the norm. The norm remains invisible in the background but nevertheless is a benchmark by which to assess and evaluate the differences of those whose cultures are considered to be Other. In the case of the Vernon tragedy, the cultural signifiers used throughout the reportage clearly position the murders as arising from a cultural practice of arranged marriages and women's supposedly subordinate status within the Sikh religious tradition. The analysis of the murder of Reena Virk, however, points out how a cultural explanation is explicitly avoided in order to divert attention from issues of racism and the consequences of racialized difference, and to privilege a definition of the situation as emerging from girl violence and bullying. In the last instance, the emphasis on girl violence and bullying serves to legitimize the dominant frame of girl-on-girl violence. This, I argue, fuels an ongoing backlash against feminism.

By juxtaposing these two cases, I show how race is conveniently erased when it suits the public imagination and the media's agenda, and conversely, invoked in a culturalized form (to the exclusion of almost all else) when deemed necessary. Hence, the killing of Reena Virk is framed as a generic girl gang violence phenomenon, while the Vernon murders are attributed to a culturally specific ethnic phenomenon.

Part 3: Voicing the Violence

As I suggest above, there has been increasing media focus and public attention devoted to the issue of violence against girls, especially in cases where that violence is perpetrated by other girls. Within Canada, this attention has often been couched in the media as an emblematic sign of gendered equality – namely, that girls have become *just like* boys, in other words, *as violent* as boys. Using this debatable proposition as a jumping-off point to interrogate what is really going on out there in the world of girls and young women, I examine in Chapter 5, "Racialized Girls and Everyday Negotiations," the particular susceptibilities to violence experienced by young women of colour. Drawing on research data gathered using a participatory action research framework, I focus on the heightened risks faced by these young women as a result of their social location in a hierarchically raced and gendered society, and highlight the particular ways in which systemic and intimate forms of violence intersect and interlock in their lives. I also outline some of the methodological issues involved in conducting research with communities that are marginalized because of their immigrant and racialized status.

By combining my voice with those of the girls in this study who courageously spoke out about their lives, I emphasize the subtlety with which racism is communicated and naturalized, and how it intersects and interlocks with sexism to influence the lived realities of racialized girls and young women of colour. The particular and often conflicting dynamics at play for girls who find themselves dealing with a confluence of patriarchal powers within and outside their communities are also examined.

Chapter 6, "Gendered Racism, Sexist Violence, and the Health Care System," examines the issue of immigrant women of colour and their experience of violence, and their subsequent encounters with and access to the formal health care system. By "health care system" I am referring to physicians' private practices, walk-in clinics, and hospitals where women are likely to seek services for violence-related health issues. After reviewing some of the current literature in the area and identifying key variables that contribute to immigrant women's vulnerability to violence and lack of access to health care, I introduce the voices of immigrant women of colour and service providers who participated in research conducted in British Columbia. Bringing these voices into concert with those studies cited in the first part of the chapter, I conclude by arguing for a socio-ecological model of health care that recognizes the power inequalities and imbalances imbricated in the medical encounter between immigrant women of colour and the medical professionals who serve them.

Part 4: Mediations of Terror

Although the medical encounter constitutes one site in which gendered racism and sexist violence are understood and reproduced in a specifically hegemonic sense, the circulation of mediated images that feed into and retrench stereotypes of racialized Others is the base from which, I argue, preconceptions about preferred patients and immigrants actually emerge. Thus, in the final chapter, "Gendering Terror Post-9/11," I return to the media's representation of these very issues, this time focusing on race, gender, and violence as symbolically communicated through representations of the Orientalized body. In this final chapter, I interrogate the notion of terror and its gendering in the press coverage following the events of 11 September 2001. I begin by outlining the discursive structures of Orientalism as defined by Edward Said (1979) and go on to examine their resonance and continuity in stories covered by the *Montreal Gazette*. This newspaper's peculiar location and status as the major English daily in Montreal, a Québécois landscape that contains a sizeable Muslim population, makes it a valuable object of inquiry. An analysis of the *Gazette*'s coverage demonstrates the ways in which the media rework and refract dominant discourses of racism and sexism. The consequences of being constructed as threatening Others are then explored from a gendered and raced perspective.

Conclusion

In the Conclusion, I draw together the threads that have been woven throughout the parts. I ground this approach in a strategy that seeks to rupture dominant frames of meaning by strategically inserting alternative viewpoints and presenting alternative explanations. For it is in disturbing the complacencies that we get a glimpse of the alternatives – alternatives which, when applied, might serve the task of dismantling structures of domination and creating a more egalitarian society.

This book is written from an interdisciplinary and multidisciplinary perspective. As an intellectual bricoleur, I traverse various terrains seeking out different insights in order to name and make sense of the structures of domination that contain, constrain, and erase the lives of those on the margins. I do not profess expertise in all these realms of knowledge, each of which is accompanied by its own specialized stock of knowledge. Instead, in the tradition of bricolage, I seek to assemble and link those insights that can help make sense of our existing realities and that can rupture the seemingly smooth surface of our collective common-sense stock of knowledge. In drawing attention to the fissures and ridges in this stock of knowledge, I am reminded once again of my own standpoint, both as a woman of colour and as an activist-scholar. But rather than relativize the insights offered here as merely stemming from one standpoint among many, I prefer to situate them within the larger tradition of critical anti-racist and feminist work, acknowledging the debt I owe to those who have initiated and who continue this struggle in diverse ways and on multiple fronts. My hope is that this work will fulfill what Sherene Razack (1998a, 16) has so eloquently articulated, in that, "if we can name the organizing frames, the conceptual formulas, the rhetorical devices that disguise and sustain elites, we can begin to develop responses that bring us closer to social justice." This work is offered as one small contribution toward that end.

Part 1
Laying the Terrain

1
Reframing Violence

Viewing the very definition of violence as lying *outside* hierarchical power relations of race and gender ignores how the power to
define what counts as violence is constitutive of these same power
relations.

> – Patricia Hill Collins, "The Tie That Binds:
> Race, Gender and US Violence"

Our societal definition of violence must include the direct results
of poor medical care, economic inferiority, oppressive legislation,
and cultural invisibility. By broadening our definition of violence,
we combat the minimalization of our experiences as women of
colour by the dominant culture. We must name the violence, or
we will not be able to address it.

> – Chezia G. Carraway, "Violence against Women
> of Colour"

The two epigraphs above underline the necessity to broaden existing definitions of violence so they encapsulate the complex dynamics of interlocking forms of oppression. Many of these forms are structurally rooted and it
is this quality of embeddedness that needs to be deconstructed if we are to
unmask the discourses of denial operative in Canadian society. In this chapter, I focus on the ways in which violence is commonly understood and
how its common-sense definitions occlude structural factors. In pursuing
this line of inquiry, my intent is to underline the ways in which violence is
structured in dominance. I begin by defining the structures of power that
underpin, inform, and regulate social relations, including those around gender and race. I argue that the society in which we live is deeply anchored in
a history of violence and in that respect replicates a pattern of dominance

derived from and inscribed within a colonial legacy. Drawing from critical anti-racist feminist frameworks, I discuss intersecting and interlocking hierarchies of power that maintain inequalities structured on the basis of race and gender. The invisibility of these structures of power and the attendant discursive economy of violence are communicated through institutions of legitimation, including the mass media, a topic I explore in the following chapter. However, this discursive economy of violence is also rendered legitimate through the very definitions employed to define and describe violence. I trace these definitions, highlighting the role of common sense, as grounded in structures of White dominance, and the resulting explanatory frameworks that are deployed to explain violence as experienced by racialized women of colour. My point of departure necessarily begins with a contextualization of race and its relationship to White structures of dominance.

Contextualizing Race within the Power of Whiteness

Scholars have repeatedly pointed to the history of Canada both as a colonizing and colonized country (see Bannerji 2000; Thobani 2002a; Razack 1998a, 1998b, 2002). This dual and somewhat contradictory historical formation has undoubtedly shaped the way in which the state continues to stratify groups in the interests of maintaining a hierarchical structure of power and privilege. Violence is one effective way by which particular groups are kept in their place. But rather than espouse a limited definition of violence that tends to be ingrained in our common-sense stock of knowledge, the definition of violence I adhere to in this chapter encompasses the spectrum of coercive, physical, and institutional power – in other words, it subsumes the very character, instruments, and goals of domination.

A crucial way in which power is naturalized and communicated is through structures of dominance. These structures are grounded in predominant "ways of seeing," to borrow a phrase from John Berger (1972). The latter derive from and reinforce the dominant common-sense stock of knowledge – that which is taken for granted, assumed, and reproduced over time. Stuart Hall (1990a) argues that a society's common-sense stock of knowledge is never homogeneous or monolithic. Rather, it is filled with contradictory bits and pieces of knowledge that are acquired, transformed, and reproduced over time. Drawing from Gramsci, Hall (1979, 325-26) reasons, "It is precisely its 'spontaneous' quality, its transparency, its 'naturalness,' its refusal to be made to examine the premises on which it is founded, its resistance to change or to correction, its effect of instant recognition, and the closed circle in which one moves which makes common sense, at one and the same time, 'spontaneous,' ideological and unconscious. You cannot learn, through common sense, *how things are:* you can only discover *where they fit* into the existing scheme of things." It is the commonalities inherent in the shared language of power, through which consent is obtained, that become the crux of any inquiry that seeks to decode how power is discursively produced and reproduced. In other words, the focus is one of deciphering the types of discursive devices and strategies and the ways in which they are used to explain violence in the mass media, in the courts, in hospitals, and in the everyday lives of racialized girls and women of colour. What do these strategies have in common? And how do they shape the lives of racialized girls and young women of colour? How are they naturalized and made recognizable? In other words, what makes them pass as common sense such that one simply takes them for granted?

In *Whitewash*, John Gabriel (1998, 13) argues: "The power of whiteness lies in a set of discursive techniques, including *exnomination*, that is the power not to be named; *naturalization*, through which whiteness establishes itself as the norm by defining 'others' and not itself; and *universalization*, where whiteness alone can make sense of a problem and its understanding becomes *the* understanding." Exnomination, naturalization, and universalization become the tools by which racialized groups are differentiated from the dominant White elites, with the basis of that difference being naturalized in the language of common sense. While elite power remains unnamed, the profile of racialized groups is heightened in contrast, and while the dominant power remains invisibilized, the stigmatization and Othering of racialized groups is rendered more visible and necessitated on the grounds of perceived and assumed difference; similarly, through universalization, racialized groups are wittingly and unwittingly compared with those who are considered normal, where normalcy is defined according to dominant criteria of the good, law-abiding citizen or the reasonable person.

In his illuminating work on fantasies of White supremacy, Ghassan Hage posits that such fantasies are foundational to nationalism in White settler societies. As such, they derive from and feed into a field of Whiteness. He suggests (2000, 58) that

> "Whiteness" is an everchanging, composite cultural historical construct. It has its roots in the history of European colonisation which universalised a cultural form of White identity as a position of cultural power at the same time as the colonised were in the process of being racialised. Whiteness in opposition to Blackness and Brownness, was born the same time as the binary oppositions colonizer/colonized, being developed/being underdeveloped, and later First World/Third World was emerging. In this sense, White has become the ideal of being the bearer of "Western" civilization. As such, no one can be fully White, but people yearn to be so. It is in this sense, that Whiteness is itself a fantasy position and a field of accumulating Whiteness. It is by being qualified to yearn for such a position that people can become identified as White. At the same time, to be White does not mean to yearn to be European in a geographical sense.

In referring to the simultaneous construction of Whiteness and the racialization of people of colour, Hage draws attention to the legacies imparted by colonialism. In its simplest term, racialization refers to the process whereby groups are marked on the basis of some kind of real or putative difference – whether this is skin colour, culture, religion, language, or nationality (Miles 1989, 74). Although such a broad definition captures the relations of power inherent in racialization, it fails to inflect the violence of racialization – a violence poignantly captured in Franz Fanon's (1967) work. For Fanon, the violence of racialization was directly linked to colonization and manifested in the corporeality of the body. Skin colour assumes a heightened significance in this regard, as it becomes the site and repository of discourses of difference – discourses highly damaging to the psyche and development of the racialized Other (see Barot and Bird 2001). For the Black body to be constructed as different and inferior means that the White body retains its pristine, innocent, and valorized status. Thus, racialization is a dialectic process. It rests on the centrality of Whiteness – its normativity and invisibility.

The hierarchical nature of contemporary Canadian society is part of our taken-for-granted, common-sense stock of knowledge. It remains invisible (in terms of its dominance) yet transparent in the economic and cultural privileging of certain groups over Others. It also communicates the positioning of different groups. Hence, how groups and individuals are seen becomes crucial in terms of where they are placed in the social order. And how they are perceived is itself contingent on the historical stock of knowledge underpinning the contemporary social order. Further, how they are regarded, and how they in turn perceive themselves, influences the kinds of actions that are directed against them, as well as the actions they themselves undertake (S. Hall 1992).

As with the positioning and perception of different groups in society, the shared language of power as it is discursively communicated by dominant institutions (such as the media, the medical system, the justice system, and the education system) influences the categories by which the world is defined. Hence, certain definitions of violence are normatively enshrined – they are taken for granted and influence the ways in which violence is understood in everyday thought and talk. In other words, they shape the cognitive and social "maps of meaning" (Morley 1980) that make categories such as violence intelligible and, in the process, define those aspects of violence that are sanctioned and those that need to be defused or punished.

Violence and Hierarchies of Power

It has been suggested that we live in a violent society and that the violence which takes place within the intimate context of the family mirrors the violence that surrounds us (Lynn and O'Neill 1995). Although this view has some legitimacy, particularly if one observes the ways in which violence is accepted, glorified, and normalized in certain contexts, it fails to address the complexity of social relations and institutions that tolerate and sustain violence and those that prohibit the use of violence. Nor does such a view take into consideration the factors that contribute to the increased vulnerability of some groups of people to violence and that promote the differential valuations attached to specific forms of violence such that some forms of violence are invisibilized and others rendered more apparent. Moreover, this approach invites the question of how certain forms of violence benefit some people at the expense of others, and further, how they inform society's attitudes toward particular forms of violence.

Dictionary definitions of violence embrace its physical, psychological, and discursive dimensions and underline the use of force and the abuse of power inherent in all forms of violence. What they fail to capture are the levels at which violence occurs and the differential treatment of various kinds of violence. Violence occurs within intimate relationships, between peers, at the societal level, within institutions, and within and between states. Some forms of violence are sanctioned, others more indirectly endorsed, and some are just not tolerated. Until recently, for instance, violence in ice hockey was considered part of the game. That view has been contested and there is increasing opposition to open displays of violence on the ice. Nonetheless, sports such as wrestling depend on violence or stylized violence for their appeal. Video games, television shows, and popular sports all embody forms of violence that are celebrated as testaments of strength, endurance, and power. State-imposed violence is yet another example of the use and abuse of power. Slavery, indentured labour, the internment of particular groups of people during specific historical periods, and the ongoing genocide and containment of Aboriginal peoples on reserves are just a few examples of state-imposed violence. More recent examples include the detention of immigrants and refugees, and the imposition of welfare laws that exercise punitive measures on specific groups of people. As Collins (1998, 922) maintains, "Definitions of violence lie not in acts themselves but in how groups controlling positions of authority conceptualize such acts."

In contextualizing contemporary violence, it is imperative to recall the violence inherent in the very process of nation building, the creation of the Canadian state through colonization. As Thobani (2000a, 283) asserts: "The nation that was 'imagined' by British, and later by Canadian, ruling elites was a White one, and what we have come to know today as the Canadian nation was founded through the colonization of Aboriginal peoples, the subordination of their sovereignties, the appropriation of their resources, and the settlement of Europeans on Aboriginal lands." The subsequent hierarchies of power that were installed to create and solidify the boundaries of the Canadian state were themselves embodiments of violent struggles waged in the interests of gaining control. As Thobani notes, there were more than five hundred Aboriginal cultures residing on Turtle Island, the name that Aboriginal nations use to call what is now known as Canada. Their containment on reserves, and assimilation through measures such as the residential school system, displacement, and genocide, contributed and continues to contribute to the formation of Canada as a nation-state. This hierarchical structure of power is not monolithic or homogeneous. Often, torn apart by internal tensions, competing interests, and diverging loyalties, its tenuous hold is maintained through economic, cultural, and political dominance (see also Huttenback 1976).

The reality of colonization is evident in its enduring legacy. As Edward Said (1979, 41) observes, by 1914, the European powers had colonized 85 percent of the world. In effect, colonization entailed the destruction of indigenous economies, the indigenous knowledge base (composed of spiritual beliefs, social and normative values, and juridical and political governance structures), and modes of knowledge transmission (L. Smith 1999). Colonization, in other words, transformed the world as it existed (Wynn Davies, Nandy, and Sardar 1993). It privileged a hierarchy whereby White, able-bodied, heterosexual (by and large) males remained at the helm of colonial enterprises. As Anne McClintock (1995, 6) suggests, "The vast, fissured architecture of imperialism was gendered throughout by the fact that it was white men who made and enforced laws and policies in their own interests."

In the interests of colonizing, the reigning elites in Canada, as in other colonies, selectively chose particular groups by which to accomplish the task of nation building. Through preferential structures, specific groups were privileged over others. Some were brought in as cheap, indentured labour to be used and then returned to their countries of origin, others were encouraged to settle the land, and others still were confined to pieces of lands they once possessed. The end result was a vertical mosaic, a mosaic in which the pieces were kept apart and arranged in a manner that secured the power and privilege of the ruling elite.[1]

The notion of Canada as a vertical mosaic was subsequently fleshed out by John Porter (1965), and although the specificities of his model have been critiqued, its relevance lies in making visible the hierarchical nature of Canadian society (Bolaria and Li 1988; Calliste and Dei 2000; P. Li 2003). Today, this hierarchy is regulated economically by a preference for "Canadian experience" and Canadian credentials, and undergirded by symbolic preference structures regarding who constitutes a real Canadian (see Folson 2004). Roberta Hamilton (1996) has extended this concept to include the gendered dimension of Canadian society, emphasizing the exclusion of women's concerns and the differential allocation of societal rewards, as well as the exercise of punitive measures on different groups of women (see also Razack 2002).

Clearly, any hierarchical system sustains itself through the deployment of categories whereby groups can be defined and ranked in terms of their access to varying degrees of power and privilege. This is where the concepts of racism, sexism, ableism, ageism, classism, and homophobia become articulated with other concomitant social institutions to advance and legitimize criteria of inclusion and exclusion. As instruments of power, these structures of domination define the social order, producing and reproducing social inequalities through articulating and prescribing differential values to these differences. But these structures are themselves deeply rooted in the violent exercise of power – whether such power is communicated through coercion or explicit brutality. Their power resides in the discursive formations that have evolved in conjunction with the need to maintain and legitimize the power and privilege of elites.

A discursive formation, as David Goldberg (1990, 297) argues, "consists of a totality of ordered relations and correlations – of subjects to each other and to objects; of economic production and reproduction, cultural symbolism and signification; of laws and moral rules; of social, political, economic, or legal inclusion and exclusion. The sociodiscursive formation consists of a range of rules: 'is's' and 'oughts,' 'do's' and 'don'ts,' 'cans' and 'cannots,' 'thou shalts' and 'thou shalt nots.'" Such formations are circulated through what Foucault (1980a) refers to as "regimes of truth." As Foucault (1980a, 131) notes, the effectiveness of these discourses is apparent in their "organizing and regulating relations of power," such that that power becomes normalized. Hence, how violence is understood, experienced, and responded to is indicative of a discursive formation that defines and regulates its meaning such that this meaning is consonant and articulated with the needs and ideologies advanced within different social domains, but which can yet be harnessed by the dominant powers.

It is the normalization of violence that renders it invisible, or visible only under certain conditions and within prescribed definitions. Hence, the violence of colonialism, of nation building, are made invisible. Similarly, the violence of racism, sexism, ableism, and other structures of domination are veiled from view, leaving only the most explicit traces of victimization, which are subsequently subsumed and marginalized in the subjugated discourses of the communities so affected. Himani Bannerji (2000, 47) eloquently summarizes the situation when she states: "This story of neo-colonialism, of exploitation, racism, discrimination and hierarchical citizenship never gains much credibility or publicity with the Canadian state, the public or the media."

Legacies of colonialism and Orientalism (Said 1979) form a backdrop against which contemporary policies and practices are articulated and which informs and underpins the construction of racialized peoples and communities. Regulatory practices such as immigration admission criteria, legislation concerning crime and deviance, social practices, and stereotypical judgments about peoples of colour are some of the ways in which particular groups are racialized and constructed in the Canadian landscape. They constitute the grid through which racialized peoples are perceived and subjected to differential treatment through strategies and tactics of exclusion, annulment, stigmatization based on disavowal, and conditional acceptance based on exoticization, assimilation, and the ideology of democratic liberalism.[2]

In Canada's history, it is evident that racialized women were used to consolidate the nation as a White settler society (Abu-Laban 1998; Bannerji 2000; Thobani 1999a). Regarded as moral and social threats, women of colour were feared as transmitters of sexually communicated diseases and for their presumed fecundity. Early suffragists argued that women of colour should be denied entry so that their offspring could not in any way pollute the purity of the nation and, by corollary, diminish the value and stature of White women. Early laws, as Backhouse (1999) demonstrates, were formulated to impede the migration of people of colour, especially women, and prohibit any engagement between men of colour and White women (see also Walker 1997). These men were not allowed to employ or engage in relations with White women (see also Park 2004). Unable to bring their wives and children with them, many formed bachelor communities in ghettoized neighbourhoods (Chan 1981; Wu 2003).

It can be argued that the continuity between first generation and subsequent generations of people of colour in White settler colonies lies in the existence of colonial traces that contain and define their representations and mediate their daily realities. In this regard, the bodies of women of colour were and continue to be regarded as requiring control and containment. Although their sexuality was once viewed as a boon to service the men of Empire, now women of colour are most likely to be constructed as able-bodied subjects, whose labour, sexual or otherwise, can be exploited for the benefit of the nation. These representations are most evident in the racialized hierarchies of preference and privilege structuring contemporary Western societies.

Racially based internal hierarchies of power and privilege are, then, a structural feature of White settler societies such as Canada. Within such a framework, diverse groups occupy correspondingly different positions in the hierarchy, their positionality secured through complicity and compliance. The social practices of such a vertical mosaic translate into daily occurrences through which racialized groups not only are relegated to the bottom of the hierarchy (through differential degrees of exclusion and inferiorization) but also, through internalization, enact those very practices within their own peer groups.

Multiculturalizing Race

A broader discussion of these race-based hierarchies needs to be grounded in the context of contemporary multiculturalism, given that it remains a dominant ideology, organizing relations of power between groups in society. Critical analyses of Canadian multiculturalism suggest that it was a policy founded on the myth of two charter groups – the English and the French – and designed to appeal to both while simultaneously appeasing the needs of the "third force" – the German and Ukrainian population situated on the Prairies and the west coast of the country (Moodley 1983; Peter 1981). Legislated into law in 1988, the policy has since evolved from one of political containment, especially aimed at neutralizing Québécois nationalism, to a celebration of culture and heritage and, more recently, to a policy designed to gain equity for groups that have and continue to be excluded from the dominant spheres of society. Fleras and Kunz (2001) offer a useful breakdown of the policy, demonstrating its evolution from its inception to its current application. They argue that in the 1970s, when the policy was first formulated, it basically focused on ethnicity. More recently, the focus has shifted to a civic multiculturalism in which the emphasis on "constructive engagement" with the aim of facilitating inclusion and belonging (16) are defined as the predominant goals. However, as Das Gupta (1999) points out, the rhetoric of inclusion and belonging does not have a material, economic basis, given the cuts in funding to organizations that mobilize around the provision of anti-racist services and advocacy.

In practice, however, the initial emphasis on culture continues to confound and conflate with issues of race. First, the policy as it has been articulated basically translates the historical violation of colonization into one of cultural coexistence. In other words, how the Canadian state was formed is mythologized as an outcome of two "founding" nations. Aboriginal peoples and the violence of colonization are carefully erased from this cultural conceptualization (Thobani 1998). Second, the policy is riddled with contradictions that on the one hand acknowledge individual and group rights, especially with regard to representation and participation, but on the other translate these rights into the language of culture. Thus, representation becomes an act of cultural representation in the cultural arenas of production, and participation is defined in cultural terms – that is, the particular collective's right to participate in the cultural spheres of society. The recent emphasis of the policy on issues of inclusion of visible minorities throws into relief the central contradictions inherent when culture and race are conflated. For one, the policy in practice tends to equalize all cultural groups so that distinctions between more established cultural communities that are no longer racialized in the same way as communities of colour are collapsed. Thus, second-, third-, and fourth-generation Irish are regarded in the same way as more recent racialized communities – the Somali-Canadian community, for example. The net effect is one of erasing the degree and type of racism directed at the Somali community but also of discounting the lack of cultural capital and resources within this community as compared with the Irish community. I do not mean to suggest that the Irish have not been racialized and did not suffer historically from exclusion and stigmatization. Instead, as the historical context in the United States demonstrates, there was a "Whitening of the Irish" resulting from the political alliances they forged with the Southern planters (Bhattacharyya, Gabriel, and Small 2002). What I wish to underscore here is the relevance of race as a salient marker of identification in particular contexts and at given historical moments. As well, where the Irish are positioned vis-à-vis the Somalis in a hierarchy of preferred immigrants is extremely relevant. Further, skin colour as the basis of identification also suggests the degree to which one can pass or is unable to pass into dominance. Thus, while the Irish were Whitened at that particular historical juncture in the history of the South, can the Somalis be so Whitened today? I would argue no, and here I base my rejection on the history of colonialism, the corporeality of race as a marker of identification that is visible and, through its visibility, used strategically and tactically to maintain White dominance. However, and undoubtedly, the penalties associated with race can be and often are mitigated by class privilege. Nonetheless, the connotations of race ensure that, even with class privilege, one is likely to encounter certain barriers rooted in systemic structures of domination.

I suggest that when race and ethnicity come together, ethnic identification becomes more potent as a political basis of identity and as a signifier of power relations than in those situations where such identity simply reflects affective ties or a symbolic recuperation based on nostalgia (Gans 1979). As Rumbaut (1994, 754) observes, "Ethnicity may for some groups become optional and recede into the social twilight, as it did for the descendants of the white Europeans or it may become for others a resilient resource or an engulfing master status." He further suggests that discrimination and disparagement are factors that contribute to a heightened attachment to ethnic identity. Contextual factors are, then, critical in determining how Whiteness is defined and, by corollary, how the status of Otherness is defined. But ultimately, these contextual factors point to the persistence of a hierarchical system of preferences that inflects and deflects differences in the interests of power.

That aside, the translation of equity and access into the language of culture ensures that the production and consolidation of group and community-based identities are defined on the basis of an adherence to and practice of particular cultural traditions. Funding adjudicated on the basis of belonging to defined and cohesive cultural groups facilitated the conversion of loose cultural affinities into bounded and discrete cultural entities irrespective of the reality that cultures are not frozen in time nor homogeneous in interpretation. Supplementing this externally imposed condition were internal forces which cohered groups into a defensive retreat against the hostility and exclusion they experienced from the dominant society. As Himani Bannerji argues:

> Things are different with us, that is, non-white immigrants – even if we are conversant in English or French, which people from South Asia, Africa, and the Caribbean generally are. With them the process is reversed, since they come as individual migrants and slowly harden into the institutional form of the community. The reason for this, I am afraid, is not what is inside of them, but rather in their skin. Their skin is written upon with colonial discourse – which is orientalist and racist. Thus memories, experiences, customs, languages, and religions of such people become interpreted into reificatory and often negative cultural types or identities. The political process of minoritization accompanies this interpretive exercise, and together they lead to the formation of communities. When we speak of "diversity" it is this set of reified and politicized differences that we are invoking, and they provide the basis for ethnocultural identity and politics of representation. (2000, 160)

Communities, then, become a focal point of the policies, despite the reality that these communities are, as Bannerji (2000) reminds us, not natural constructions but social constructions mediated out of a necessity to respond to particular state policies. In turn, these communities are harnessed by these policies to better serve the status quo and thereby utilized to maintain a hierarchical racialized structure of power. Such communities are reified as embodiments of particular cultural formations even though what they may be representing is a graft of a culture, specific social classes within that cultural formation, and particular interpretations of cultural traditions. Patriarchal and economic elites maintain the boundaries of these so-called cultural communities, ensuring compliance and cohesion. However, as Bannerji remarks, this is not only a top-down imposition but also a bottom-up response, based on the racism, exclusion, and hostility from the dominant society faced by these groups. Within the context of these communities, power is naturalized and rendered normal through the recuperation and reification of tradition.

Bannerji calls our attention to a key element of multiculturalism, namely, the connection between race and culture. Racialized communities are minoritized and interpreted as primordial cultural entities rather than as entities formed through state measures. Further, these cultural labels are not neutral but carry Orientalist and racially inscribed connotations of inferiority, positioned as they are in opposition to a construction of Western society that represents itself as progressive, emancipatory, and democratic. Racial differences become encoded as cultural differences, and race itself is culturalized (Razack 1998a). A corollary to this is that Whiteness has no culture, but culture becomes the signifying badge of difference for people of colour. Drawing from Essed (1990), Amita Handa (1997) argues that the emphasis on culture evacuates concepts of race and racism, so that cultural tolerance comes to replace the need for racial tolerance (see also Bannerji 2000).

To tolerate, as Mirchandani and Tastsoglou (2000) remark, is to "put up with" and not necessarily to embrace difference. Indeed, Hage (2000) suggests that the call for tolerance can be exercised only upon those who are intolerant. In other words, those who need to be tolerant are simply those who are capable of being intolerant. Referring to multiculturalism in the context of Australia, Hage observes that "multicultural tolerance, like all other tolerance, is not, then, a good policy that happens to be limited in its scope. It is a strategy aimed at reproducing and disguising relationships of power in society, or being reproduced through that disguise. It is a form of symbolic violence in which a mode of domination is presented as a form of egalitarianism" (87).

The violence of racism is shrouded by discourses of denial, discourses predicated on the categorization of racism as something other than what it is; on the tactics of individualization; and the conversion of racial difference into categories that demonize, trivialize, compartmentalize, exoticize, erase, or contain that difference in ways that suit the interests of a dominant, hegemonic power. In part, this is achieved through a systemic blanketing or "whitewashing" of racist sexism as well as through the use of coded language to refer to racialized differences. Bannerji (2000, 47) summarizes it succinctly when she says, "There is not even a language within the state's redress apparatus to capture or describe the racist sexism towards third world or non-white women or men." What language does exist is that which utilizes coded signifiers such as "culture," "diversity," "tolerance," "difference," thereby bracketing any notion of systemic and symbolic violence of race and racism (see also Karim 1993a, 1993b; Mirchandani and Tastsoglou 2000). Concomitantly, most discourses on race utilize coded words such as "immigrant," "refugee," "alien," "terrorist," and the like to refer to people of colour. Such words cover up and obfuscate the central defining and regulating relations of power and reify these categories as authentic absolutes against which the normative Canadian is implicitly defined as the White, law-abiding, citizen of the nation.

Gendered Racism and Sexist Violence

Within scholarship on gender-based violence, the feminist movement in Canada has been particularly successful in highlighting the power of sexism as a systemic form of violence underpinning and influencing the lives of women and girls (Duffy and Momirov 1997; H. Johnson 1996; McKenna and Larkin 2002). It has in fact succeeded in bringing a subjugated knowledge (women's experiential realities of violence) to the centre and, through institutionalized power, legitimizing both this experiential knowledge and the advocacy it has generated (see Faith 1993; Taylor, Barnsley, and Goldsmith 1996; Timmins 1995).

Hence, the argument that gender-based violence is made possible by the ideology of sexism in which women are perceived and treated as less worthy than men is more readily and overtly acknowledged within certain domains (see also Richie 1996). Sexism is recognized as a system of beliefs and attitudes based on the alleged inferiority of women, inferiority that translates into attitudes that women cannot be believed, that women are incapable, and that women are inherently subordinate to men (Browne 1997; Duffy 1995). Within an institutional framework, sexism translates into policies and practices that deter women's advancement, justify inequality in wages, and make women vulnerable to violence such as sexual harassment, rape, and murder (DeKeseredy and Kelly 1995; Ferraro 1997; L. Kelly 1987; Lakeman 2000). In the context of the criminal justice system, sexism is evident and documented in the ways in which women are disbelieved, have their concerns trivialized or dismissed, and are revictimized (Bonnycastle and Rigakos 1998; Martin and Mosher 1995). As Walter DeKeseredy and Linda MacLeod (1997) have argued, gender-based violence is sexist violence.[3]

For racialized women of colour, the exposure to patriarchal structures is refracted through their positioning in subordinate roles within the larger society, as well as within their particular communities. This is not simply a situation of a double dose of patriarchy. Rather, how the dominant society constructs racialized communities has implications for the gendered dynamics within communities. Black feminists such as Angela Davis (1983), Patricia Hill Collins (1998, 2000), and bell hooks (1982, 1990), to mention only a few, have drawn attention to the complex intersecting and interlocking influences that have shaped Black women's lives in the United States. Patricia Hill Collins (1998, 919) suggests that "while violence certainly seems central to maintaining *separate* oppressions – those of race, gender, social class, nationality/citizenship status, sexual orientation and age – violence may be equally important in structuring *intersections* among these hierarchies. Rather than viewing violence primarily as part of distinct social hierarchies of race and gender, violence may serve as the conceptual glue that binds them together." If violence is the glue that binds them together, then how is violence against racialized women of colour framed and understood?

Intersecting and Interlocking Violence(s)

In contrast to the heightened awareness of sexism as violence, the intersectionality of racism and sexism, or what Bannerji (2000) has termed "racist sexism," has only begun to be uncovered in the same way and with the same institutional force as has mediated mainstream feminist scholarship (see Razack 2002, 2004). Intersectionality is a key concept navigating this maze of crosscutting, intertwining, and intermeshing conduits of domination. As Kimberle Crenshaw (2000, 8) elucidates, intersectionality "addresses the manner in which racism, patriarchy, class oppression and other discriminatory systems create background inequalities that structure the relative positions of women, races, ethnicities, classes and the like" (see also Crenshaw 1994). However, critical anti-racist feminists have argued that these social forces – far from remaining as background features – interlock so that the construction of identity is itself contingent on the particular nexus of interlocking factors operative in a given context. Sherene Razack (1998a, 13) defines it most clearly when she states: "Interlocking systems need one another, and in tracing the complex ways in which they help to secure one another, we learn how women are produced into positions that exist symbiotically but hierarchically."

In part, the difference between the mainstream feminist agenda and the critical anti-racist perspective on violence has to do with a discourse of denial surrounding the acknowledgment of explicit and pervasive racism against women of colour within the academy, the women's movement, and the wider society. This is achieved through the promotion of a universalized category of woman that collapses differences between women.[4] In speaking to this issue, Linda Carty (1991, 31) comments, "As Black women we experience our femaleness and Blackness together, always at the same time, and we challenge whether it is possible for white women to be white or female because we see them as white *and* female."

Spelman (1988) has similarly argued against an essentialist construction of gender. In a hierarchical society, the power and privilege attached to one level is predicated on the lack of power and privilege of those belonging to a lower level (Razack 1998a). For instance, in the plantocracies of the southern United States, the status, power, and privilege accorded to the White woman placed her apart from and at a higher level than the Black slave woman. The chastity, femininity, and purity of the White slave owner's wife contrasted with dominant conceptions of the slave woman as a Jezebel or an Aunt Jemima (Davis 1983; Jewell 1993). The one set of norms raised the status of the White woman, while the other inferiorized the slave, a violent process in and of itself, as well as making her vulnerable to other kinds of violence and violations. However, the moral regulation of White women's bodies was also confining in the sense of limiting their agency and power, rigidly subordinating them to White patriarchal domination. In contemporary times, the interlocking structures of power and privilege are evident in the differential use of women of colour as labourers and domestics that makes it possible for White women to be employed outside the home (see Arat-Koc 1995; Mohanty 1991b; Ng 1993a). The exploitation of one group of women makes the liberation of another group of women possible (Bhattacharyya, Gabriel, and Small 2002). Yet, in the universalizing language of dominance, all women are seen as being liberated, as all can participate in paid work outside their own homes.

Pointing to Catherine McKinnon's argument about the traumatic impact of rape on all women, Angela Harris (1997) demonstrates how, historically, rape against Black women was not even considered rape by the dominant society. There were no laws against the rape of Black women, even though the rape or alleged rape of White women often resulted in the lynching of Black men. Her analysis demonstrates the unequal application of laws, the differential construction of women, and the ways in which the rape and lynching were interrelated. In analyzing these interlocking systems, Harris offers an insightful critique of what she describes as the dominance theory, a theory that coheres around the notion of a universal woman. She posits: "First, in the pursuit of the essential feminine, Woman leached of all color and irrelevant social circumstance, issues of race are bracketed as belonging to a separate and distinct discourse – a process that leaves black women's selves fragmented beyond recognition. Second, feminist essentialists find that in removing issues of 'race' they have actually only managed to remove black women – meaning that white women now stand as the epitome of Woman" (13). She further contends that in ameliorating the essentialist framework, feminists often try to use a "nuanced approach." In the latter, diverse women's experiences are recognized, albeit in "footnotes" supplemental to the main text, and then attributed to a matter of context. The more problematic aspect of a nuanced approach is that it leaves undisturbed the central yardstick by which all women's experiences are measured, namely, the normativity of White women's experiences.

These critiques are still relevant to much of the work that has been undertaken on issues of violence against women in Canada. The landmark Canadian Panel on Violence against Women (Marshall and Vaillancourt 1993, 7) put forth the following categories to define the kinds of violence that women and girls experience: physical, sexual, psychological, financial, and spiritual. While the panel members were cognizant of the realities of women of colour – a reality forcefully brought to their attention by the advocacy of women of colour to have representation within the panel – the actual recognition of racism as a form of violence, and of the alliances between patriarchal powers within communities of colour and the dominant society, remains a mute observation, confined to those pages of the panel's report that specifically address women of colour (see Chapter 11 of the panel's report, "Women of Colour," in Marshall and Vaillancourt 1993). Ostensibly, the panel's focus was on foregrounding sexist violence so that so-called background inequalities such as racism are not privileged in the same way. Nevertheless, relegating these systemic inequalities to the backstage only reinforces dominant definitions of violence that strategically deflect attention away from how and why such forms of violence are extant in the first place, or the forces that sustain their continued power. In other words, by focusing on some kinds of violence rather than others, the tendency is one of evacuating an analysis of the power hierarchies that lie at the foundations of a racist, sexist society. It conforms to what Harris (1997, 14) describes as the "nuance theory" of gender oppression.

The invisibility of structures of domination is reinforced by announcements pertaining to the declining levels of violent crime, spousal murders, and homicide in general. But the mapping of the terror that results in ongoing harassment, racial profiling, deportations, and other structural and coercive forms of violence designed to keep certain groups and individuals in "their place" receives scant attention in the official documentation of the state and is, by and large, unreported in the dominant media. If it is at all made manifest through a few unroutinized interruptions, it is referred to in the language of power – in the dominant discourse – as pertaining to an exception or more likely to the actions of undeserving, overly demanding, hypersensitive, over-reacting, transgressive minorities or their barbaric cultures (Razack 2004) that need to be excised from the social body. Instead, the tendency of this dominant discourse is to celebrate conformity by valorizing individual will or the innate "cultural" traits of a particular group to transcend barriers by successfully negotiating, surviving, and thriving against all odds. The latter representation works to neutralize any charge of systemic violence or terror and focuses instead on the model minority, as evidenced in cases of individual success, such as the appointment of a governor general, a member of parliament, a business magnate, and so forth, all of whom have "foreign" origins but who have nonetheless transcended their cultural inheritances and climbed up the ladder of power and privilege.

Embracing an intersectional and interlocking framework involves a further examination of the ways in which different systems work in concert with each other to engender particular forms and expressions of violence. In shifting the focus away from a universalized construction of sexist violence, I do not mean to suggest that racialized women of colour do not experience gendered violence. Rather, the particular instantiation of such violence is contextual and relational – it depends on the forces operating in a given historical moment, as well as whether such violence is recognized as violence, and whether it is privileged as a kind of violence deserving of societal intervention and resolution. This, of course, raises the question as to what kinds of interventions are deemed necessary and by whom.

In delineating the particular vulnerabilities and susceptibilities of different groups of women to violence, what stands out are the systemic forms of violence at each site where they interconnect and interlock with intimate and interpersonal forms of violence. Factors such as isolation, dependency, marginalization, and stigmatization that are part and parcel of making an individual or group susceptible to violence are occluded, negated, or erased in accounts of violence against specific groups of people. Thus, when the group or individual constitutes a historically excluded minority, a minority whose realities are deeply shaped by structural forces mediated through everyday exclusion, marginalization, ghettoization, and coercive assimilation, the violence of these actions is absented from descriptive accounts, which tend to focus on the cultural peculiarities of these groups, their presumed proclivity to violence, or their "risk" to violence. Such accounts fail to take into consideration factors that put these groups at risk in the first place and at risk particularly from discursive and material violence exercised by the dominant society. How are specific groups of women isolated, impoverished, made dependent, and excluded through racism and sexism?

Situating Women of Colour

In speaking of racialized women of colour, the tendency is often to conflate their status with immigrant status. Indeed, in the Canadian popular imagination, most women of colour are defined as immigrants, and as immigrants, they occupy a particular range of representations. This conflation derives in part from the erasure of women of colour in the official histories of the nation, and in part from the barriers imposed to prevent women of colour from immigrating to the nation (Agnew 1996; Dua 1999). However, since the liberalization of immigration laws in 1976, the number of women of colour who have immigrated has increased. Das Gupta (1999, 191) observes that "over half the immigrants who arrived in Canada since the 1970s and three-quarters of those who came in the 1990s are visible minority members"; these numbers indicate that traditional and preferred source countries of immigrants have dried up.

One consequence of this link with immigration has been the continual identification of women of colour as perpetual outsiders to the nation. Das Gupta notes that

in everyday discourse, the phrase ["immigrant women"] is used interchangeably with the phrase "women of colour" by most Canadians, whether they are "of colour" or "White." This particular usage is underlaid with a notion of who a "Canadian" is or what a "Canadian looks like." The implication is that a Canadian is White, middle or upper class and Anglo or Francophone. Anybody who deviates from this stereotype – someone who is a person of colour, has a non-dominant accent, wears a "different" dress or headgear, coupled with a working class occupation – would be referred to as "immigrant" or non-Canadian, even though they may be holding Canadian citizenship. (1999, 190)

I deal with the implications and entrenched nature of this association in Chapter 5. Here, I wish to underline this association given its slippage into research dealing with race, gender, and violence. Existing Canadian studies focusing on racialized women of colour and their experiences of violence have tended to focus on them as immigrant women. This stems from the fact that many high-profile cases have involved immigrant women and that community-based advocacy and service organizations have mobilized around the issue of immigrant status in order to address the lack of available services for women of colour who have experienced violence (Agnew 1996, 1998; Dosanjh, Deo, and Sidhu 1994; Razack 1998a). This focus on immigrant origins is particularly evident in studies concentrating on specific and cultural forms of violence exhibited by women from racialized immigrant communities.

Thus, in contrast to the universal construction of gendered violence, which erases all differences between women or confines them to a footnote, this second and related perspective heightens differences between women, locating these differences in the realm of culture. In both cases, however, the accentuation and levelling of difference functions strategically to underscore White superiority and power (see, for instance, Lorde 1983). Uma Narayan provides a succinct analysis of this latter cultural approach when she states:

In thinking about issues of "violence against Third-World women" that "cross borders" into Western national contexts, it strikes me that phenomena that seem "Different," "Alien," and "Other" cross these borders with considerably more frequency than problems that seem "similar" to those that affect mainstream Western women. Thus, clitorodectomy and infibulation have become virtually an "icon" of "African women's problems" in Western contexts, while a host of other "more familiar" problems that different groups of African women face are held up at the border. In a similar vein, the abandonment and infanticide of female infants appears to be the one gender issue pertaining to China that receives coverage. These issues then become "common topics" for academics and feminists, and also cross over to a larger public audience that becomes "familiar" with these issues. It is difficult not to conclude that there is a premium on "Third-World difference" that results in greater interest being accorded to those issues that seem strikingly "different" from those affecting mainstream Western women. (1997, 100)

The iconic representation of specific forms of violence is, then, just as problematic as an approach that erases all differences. But here, in particularizing these kinds of violence as endemic of Other cultures, the implicit assumption is that the gendered violence of "our" culture (read North American culture) is more legitimate because it is normalized and less apparent. However, in the enhanced recognition of difference, acts of violence are construed as signs of the peculiarities of Other cultural traditions, peculiarities that reflect the traditional, barbaric, and inferior constructions of the cultures of Others.

Bordering the Nation, Bordering Communities

> When the terrain is sexual violence, racism and sexism interlock in particularly nasty ways. These two systems operate through each other so that sexual violence, as well as women's narratives of resistance to sexual violence, cannot be understood outside of colonialism and today's ongoing racism and genocide. When women from marginalized communities speak out about sexual violence, we are naming something infinitely broader than what men do to women within our communities, an interlocking analysis that has most often been articulated by Aboriginal women.
>
> – Sherene Razack, *Looking White People in the Eye*

As I have maintained elsewhere (Jiwani 2005c), part of the problem of speaking about violence against women of colour is the racialization of these communities as deviant, traditional, backward, and inherently oppressive (see Chapter 6). Thus, to speak about violence is, as Flynn and Crawford (1998) have argued, to commit "race treason"; it is to betray "racial loyalty" (Richie 1996). Indeed, the fallout of stereotypes of immigrant communities as violence-prone has been one of silencing women from within these communities (Bannerji 2000). In a call to break the silence, Angela Davis (2000, 2) has consistently argued that "we must also learn how to oppose the racist fixation on people of colour as the primary perpetrators of violence, including domestic and sexual violence, and at the same time to fiercely challenge the real violence that men of colour inflict on women." This is a difficult task, particularly given the social climate, in which calling attention to abuse can result in the deportation of the sponsoring "head of household" and children, putting the family in further jeopardy; or it can lead to the imprisonment of the sole person who is the breadwinner; or alternatively, it can result in the stigmatization and marginalization from a community with which one otherwise identifies. In other words, breaking the silence has a cost, yet it is a cost that untold numbers of racialized women of colour have borne and continue to bear on a daily basis.

Although the history of immigrant women of colour is an important one and one that is continually being recovered by critical anti-racist feminists, my intent here is to demonstrate the ways in which particular explanations of violence against women of colour are privileged. In doing this, I situate my point of departure in Anthias and Yuval-Davis' (1992) analysis of gender and nationalism, an analysis also embraced by McClintock (1995) in her extensive study of race, gender, and imperialism. For Anthias and Yuval-Davis, women's bodies constitute the site on which the discourse of nationalism is inscribed. At the same time, women are, as McClintock (1995) argues, implicated in the process of nationalism. As reproducers of the nation, both biologically and socially, and as "transmitters of culture," women's bodies are used "as signifiers of ethnic or national differences, as a focus and symbol in ideological discourses used in the construction, reproduction and transformation of ethnic or national categories" (Anthias and Yuval-Davis 1992, 115). However, this use of women's bodies is, as Himani Bannerji (2000) notes, a form of dehumanization. It objectifies women as no more than "handmaidens of god, priest, and husband" (169).

Within the context of the Canadian nation-state and its historic and contemporaneous racialization of difference, women's bodies are similarly marked. "Good" women are those who represent and conform to a hegemonic construction of femininity that is itself bound to notions of nationness, or the identity and reputation of the community. "Bad" women deviate from such an ideal. However, there are degrees of goodness and badness, as exemplified in what happens to women who deviate and the extent to which they depart from the normative constructions of femininity (see Faith and Jiwani 2002). As well, notions of goodness and badness are context based. In other words, it depends on who is defining the boundaries and the power they possess to enforce such definitions. As suggested by Whitehead, Bannerji, and Mojab (2001, 4), "Notions of propriety and respectability, are in turn, linked to the nationalist construction of ideal gender identities."

These hegemonic notions of femininity seal particular definitions of the imagined community (B. Anderson 1983) that is the nation. They symbolize how the nation views itself and how the women within it view their role as reproducers of the nation. Thus, honour, morality, sexual purity, and religiosity are standards by which women are often judged as signifiers of the nation. However, much depends on which groups of women are considered worthy of bearing this burden of signifying the nation. Some deviations are tolerated – if not encouraged – in the interest of maintaining a hierarchy of those who best fit the national imaginary and those who do not. Some kinds of deviations were and are normalized at given historical moments. Historical examples indicate how First Nations and Metis women were often positioned as so-called country wives, used to service White male colonizers until the arrival of marriageable White women (see also Leacock 1980). Similarly, as Razack (1998b) reminds us, bodies of Third World women were and are often used as sexual commodities to service the needs of White male tourists frequenting parts of Asia. As well, racialized women from different areas of the world were and continue to be trafficked in as prostitutes and mail-order brides (Perez 2003; Narayan 1995). As deviant bodies, racialized women of colour occupy a "zone of degeneracy" in contrast to those who fit the national imaginary of hegemonic femininity (Razack 1998b). The latter group of women occupy the zone of "morality."

Occupying a zone of degeneracy, as Razack (2002) notes, makes the bodies of women of colour all the more susceptible to certain forms of violence – violence imposed on them by the dominant society and articulated through White patriarchal power. Such violence is predicated on discourses of exotica, innocence, and the premise that masculinities may be experimented and exercised upon the bodies of these Others (Said 1979). Nevertheless, women of colour are also subjects of violence from within. And it is the convergence of these internal and external patriarchies that demands scrutiny.

Gender-based violence is an issue common to all women and girls.[5] However, its framing and expression have much to do with the historical and contemporary context in which women live. For racialized women of colour in Canada, gender-based violence has been and continues to be a relevant and topical issue, but its articulation from within and outside the community frames it in particular ways. It is this definition that I am particularly interested in exploring, especially since definitions and categories are most often articulated in the interests of hegemonic powers and with the intent of reinvigorating, through resonance, sedimented stocks of common-sense knowledge.

Situating Culture Talk
It has been argued that within racialized minority communities, moral prescriptions are transmitted in the language of culture. American studies of racialized women of colour and their experiences of violence include those pertaining to South Asian women (Dasgupta and Warrier 1996), Korean families (Choi 1997; Rhee 1977), Chinese out-of-town brides (Chin 1994), Mexican-Americans (Champion 1996), Asian-American communities

(Huisman 1996), and Latino women (Aldarondo, Kaufman, and Jasinksi 2002; Perilla, Bakeman, and Norris 1994). All of these underscore the salience of cultural traditions in prescribing and describing women's and girls' positions in these communities (see also Raj and Silverman 2002). These studies further contend that the cultural scripts encoded within these communities account for the type and incidence of gendered violence. For example, Perilla, Bakeman, and Norris (1994, 325) argue that "emotional and physical abuse of Latinas by their male partners is deeply woven into the tapestry of Latino culture in the United States." They elaborate: "Cultural scripts such as these ('machismo'/'marianismo,' dominance/submission) support an imbalance of power in traditional Latino families and provide an environment ripe for the occurrence of domestic violence" (326). What makes these particular scripts salient at given historical moments is left unstated, though the authors, as in the previously mentioned studies, do make note of structural considerations such as immigration status, under- and unemployment, isolation, lack of English-language fluency, and marginalization through racism. However, the resulting impression one gets is that racialized women of colour are particularly prone to what Uma Narayan (1997) has termed "death by culture." This cultural gaze also reinforces the notion that racialized communities of colour are tradition-bound and frozen in time, not to mention inherently violent. Such "culture talk," as Razack (1998a) defines it, is strategic – it serves a useful end, both in the sense of deflecting attention away from commonalities and, more to the point, of defining which groups are acceptable and unacceptable – which fit the criteria of preference of the imagined Canadian nation. Razack offers a succinct and eloquent summary of the dangers involved in using culture as an explanatory vehicle for defining violence against racialized (and immigrant) women of colour. As she puts it (1998a, 58-59):

> Both within our communities and outside of them, the risks Aboriginal women and women of colour encounter when we talk about culture in the context of sexual violence are manifested on several levels. First, many cultural communities understand culture and community in ways that reflect and leave unchallenged male privilege. Indeed, the notion of culture that has perhaps the widest currency among both dominant and subordinate groups is one whereby culture is taken to mean values, beliefs, knowledge, and customs that exist in a timeless and unchangeable vacuum outside of patriarchy, racism, imperialism, and colonialism ... Second, when we bring sexual violence to the attention of white society we always risk exacerbating the racism directed at both the men and the women in our communities. In this way, we risk being viewed by our own communities as traitors and by white society as women who have abandoned our communities because they are so patriarchal. Third, as communities of colour, we need to

understand sexual violence as the outcome of both white supremacy and patriarchy; culture talk fragments sexual violence as what men do to women and takes the emphasis away from white complicity.

Yet, if we are to locate and understand gendered violence as it is manifested and expressed within racialized communities without resorting to cultural pathologies or "death by culture," we need to situate the discourses through which this violence is made possible. In mapping the ways that gendered violence in racialized communities of colour is framed, exercised, and communicated, I suggest that a central and organizing motive is that of regulation – the regulation of morality and mobility. The regulation of morality suggests boundaries defining the limits of acceptable sexual, social, and representational behaviour, and the regulation of mobility can be defined as the imposition or exercise of limits within which one can physically leave a violent situation or, alternatively, the ways in which one is forced, through persuasion or punishment, to remain within a given situation. Alternatively, mobility can be understood as that which defines a person or group's ability to cross borders and boundaries. For racialized peoples, mobility is severely restricted by the constraints imposed on them by the state through immigration criteria and the like, as well as by constraints imposed on them by economic conditions.

Morality and mobility are not mutually exclusive categories; they shade into and inform one another. In proposing that these categories are anchored in the regulatory practices governing women's lives, I draw from Sherene Razack's (2002) work on race, space, and the law, and from Whitehead, Bannerji, and Mojab's (2001) introduction in *Of Property and Propriety*. While Razack calls our attention to the spatial organization that is part of the legacy of colonization, a spatialization that clearly defines zones of degeneracy where all Others are *contained*, Whitehead, Bannerji, and Mojab underscore the notion of propriety, emphasizing the moral regulation of women's and girls' bodies and the constitution of these bodies as property in the language of patriarchy.

In her insightful and nuanced analysis of the murder of Pamela George, an Aboriginal woman from the Sakimay Reserve of the Saulteaux First Nation in Regina, Razack (2002) demonstrates how racialized gendered violence is rendered permissible because of the *containment* of its subjects in categories of degeneracy and as spatially located outside the boundaries of normative society. Pamela George was assaulted and murdered by two White men. The city of Regina, as Razack describes it, was historically divided. It was a place where relations between the dominant Whites and the subordinate Natives were structured legally and spatially and were underpinned by economic, sexual, and racial violence. Citing the work of Sarah Carter, Razack (2002, 131) points out how, historically, Aboriginal women's mobility was regulated through the introduction of a pass system and how "government agents sometimes withheld rations to reserve communities unless Aboriginal women were made available to them." The legislative mechanisms imposed on Aboriginal people were also gender specific.[6] Aboriginal women were denied Indian status if they married outside the reserve. Yet, Aboriginal men could retain status even if they married a woman from outside their reserve; their wives would acquire Indian status. This form of regulation constituted a foundation upon which subsequent relations were and continue to be enacted. In linking the murder of Pamela George to this colonial foundation, Razack demonstrates how daily exchanges of violence are tolerated on the basis that they invoke resonances with the representation of Aboriginal women as "sexually licentious and bloodthirsty" (130).

In analyzing the details of the court case involving the two accused White men, she notes that the violence done to Pamela George was normalized and naturalized, reflecting hegemonic notions of White masculinity. Commenting on the impunity of the two accused White men and their trivialization of the violence they had committed, Razack (2002, 136) remarks that "the subject who must cross the lines between respectability and degeneracy and, significantly, return unscathed, is first and foremost a colonial subject seeking to establish that he is indeed in control and lives in a world where a solid line marks the boundary between himself and racial/ gendered Others. For this subject, violence establishes the boundary between who he is and who he is not." Violence, then, is an instrument of power and self-definition. However, its exercise depends on what the discursive formations and regimes of truth – to use Foucault's term – define as the zones of degeneracy, and which bodies are perceived to be degenerate and can be subjected to violence with impunity. Thus, Pamela George as an Aboriginal woman and a sex trade worker was, within the construction of White hegemonic masculinity and its institutions of power such as the court, defined and described as occupying the zone of degeneracy. Because hers was perceived as a degenerate body, the violence done to her was trivialized and its impact erased. Here, violence acts as a way of reinforcing White hegemonic masculinity and reinscribing spatial and social relations of power.

Morality and mobility are clearly evidenced in the case of racialized established, immigrant, migrant, and diasporic communities. For here, moral regulation becomes, as Bannerji (2000) suggests, a way of controlling women and girls. Since women's and girls' bodies are emblematic of culture and marked as signifiers of tradition, their containment through strict moral regulations also impedes their mobility into areas that are defined as contrary to "cultural" traditions. I frame "culture" in quotation marks because which aspect of culture is defined as *the* culture and which traditions are invented or inflected very much depends on the power hierarchy extant within these constructed communities. Regulations governing mobility are introduced and sustained through both state power (as in immigration criteria, deportations, border controls, security certificates, and the like), as well as through social and normative sanctions against those who trespass into given areas. But limitations on mobility also derive from within communities, as these provide girls and women the boundary markers indicating where they can go, and inversely, where they cannot go. Moral prescriptions define who they can interact with, how they can interact, and the rules governing their comportment.

Recent studies employing an intersectional analysis offer more complex insights into the structures of violence, as these are articulated with notions of discourses of femininity and masculinity, and enacted through the regulation of morality and mobility. In her study of Filipino youth in the United States, Espiritu (2001) notes that girls' sexuality and behaviours are highly regulated in response to what is perceived to be a failing of the dominant society. Thus, while girls and young women in the White, dominant society are regarded as being sexually promiscuous, lax in moral behaviours and values, Filipinas are supposed to signify the opposite – the superior morality of the community as reflected in chaste behaviour and restricted sexual expressions. Espiritu (2001, 436) observes that "the immigrant community uses restrictions on women's lives as one form of resistance to racism. This form of cultural resistance, however, severely restricts the lives of women, particularly those of the second generation, and it casts the family as a potential site of intense conflict and oppressive demands in immigrant lives." Racism and sexism, then, structure discourses of femininity, fixing girls and women as signifiers of culture from within and as emblematic symbols of that community to the outside world. Similarly, they restrict girls' and women's mobility in terms of their ease of movement from within to the outside and from outside to the inside – in other words, being able to walk freely between worlds rather than constantly having to negotiate the tight interstices between different cultural arenas and expectations (an issue I explore in greater detail in Chapter 5). In highlighting this interplay of internal and external influences, Abraham (1995, 452) remarks: "Ethnicity becomes the basis for group identification and solidarity in an alien country. At the same time, specific physical features and cultural habits remind the dominant group and the immigrant group of their foreign background – regardless of their previous socioeconomic class – thereby stereotyping, boundary marking, and restricting total acceptance of the immigrant by the mainstream (Ngan-Ling Chow 1993). The social situation is frequently manifested in the dominant group forming the core and the subordinate group being allocated a peripheral position in the social, economic, and political structure of the setting."

Both morality and mobility are regulatory discourses that prescribe and describe the discourses of femininity defining the lives of girls and women from racialized communities of colour, communities often located in the peripheries of the nation. However, the boundaries of these discourses are somewhat permeable in the sense that, although structured in the dominance of race, they are not fixed but, rather, socially constructed. There are "proper" ways of breaking the rules and "improper" ways of doing so. So, for instance, through assimilation, one can break the limits imposed by the moral discourses of a community. Such a move signals liberation from the strictures of a traditional society and an embrace of the supposedly modern, egalitarian ethos of the dominant society. It allows for a greater degree of mobility but it also defines that mobility in terms of where and how young women of colour are allowed in, the degree to which they will be accepted, and the kinds of violence to which they will be subjected. As exotic and assimilated Others, they may gain entry into the dominant society, but their exoticized representation will also categorize them as Others, thus rendering them susceptible to different forms of violence.

Assimilation also offers, especially through class privilege, a greater degree of mobility. On the other hand, the deeply racialized nature of identity, both group and individual based, limits such latitude in the sense that no matter how rich or assimilated a person of colour is, where s/he can go is undoubtedly curtailed by elite structures of power. "Fictions of assimilation" – what Melinda de Jesús (1998) describes as the illusory promises of fitting in and belonging provided one buys into the trappings of so-called normalcy and normative behaviour – are just that – fictions – when they run headlong into the reality of race and racism. For the present, what I wish to underscore is that such fictions exist and as such they exert influence on naming who and how one can exercise power and mobility. Again, all of this needs to be contextualized within the realm of the nation as a vertical mosaic. In a hierarchy structured in dominance, the ideological labour involved is one of keeping each group "in its place." This includes racialized people of colour whose confinement at a particular level of the hierarchy ensures that those above can maintain their power and privilege.

Conclusion

In reviewing how violence against racialized women of colour is understood and articulated, it is apparent that both the discourse of sameness (as in the universal woman) and the discourse of difference (as in "death by culture") fail to encapsulate the complex ways in which race and gender intersect and interlock. Moreover, they evacuate histories and subjectivities by focusing on a single dimension of either culture or the common vulnerabilities ascribed to gender as it is framed and articulated within patriarchal structures. Nevertheless, as regimes of truth, these paradigms have the power to privilege certain forms of violence, while erasing other forms whose implications are just as violently searing on the individual and collective psyche. The central organizing discourses that govern and regulate bodies of racialized women of colour – morality and mobility – contribute to girls' and women's vulnerabilities to sexist and racist violence. The question remains as to the conditions in which these discourses are invoked and how they play out in the arena of minoritized racialized communities that are attempting to define a sense of identity in the face of a hostile, exclusionary milieu. Further, how do these discourses structure understandings of violence within racialized communities confronted with assimilation as the only avenue by which to gain a sense of acceptance and belonging, even though the latter is continually tenuous and conditional? These are questions I seek to address in the next few chapters, beginning with an analysis of the dominant media's representation of racialized people of colour. As institutions structured in dominance, the dominant media, I argue, play a crucial role in racing the nation by reflecting an imagined community, its hegemonic ideals, and its fictions of assimilation. In erasing the violence of race and racism, the dominant media indelibly engage in discursive violence. Thus, in representing Others as prone to violence, criminality, and as culture-bound, traditional, and fixed entities, the media maintain an image of the nation as a peaceful haven marred only by the importation of deviance by Others.

2
Mapping Race in the Media

If the media function in a systematically racist manner, it is not because they are run and organized exclusively by active racists; this is a category mistake. This would be equivalent to saying that you could change the character of the capitalist state by replacing its personnel. Whereas the media, like the state, have a *structure*, a set of *practices*, which are not reducible to the individuals who staff them ... What is significant is not that they produce a racist ideology, from a single-minded and unified conception of the world, but that they are so powerfully constrained – "spoken by" a particular set of ideological discourses.

> – Stuart Hall, "The Whites of Their Eyes,
> Racist Ideologies and the Media"

As Stuart Hall reminds us, racism cannot simply be attributed to individual intent and desire, though of course this is an important area of consideration. Rather, institutional practices, routinized behaviours, and normative values work in concert to structure the ways in which media institutions, like other institutions in society, privilege particular interpretations. Hall makes a distinction between active racists and passive racists that I find extremely useful. I associate passive racism with silent racism: a form of racism which, Barbara Trepagnier (2001, 151) argues, "contributes to a culture of denial, a social condition that results in the persistence of the racial status quo." Passive racism, I contend, is just as violent as overt or active racism. But more importantly, it is the structures of power that enable racism, both in its passive and active form, that require interrogation.

Violence, as I suggest in the previous chapter, is a mechanism by which individuals and groups impose or maintain a position of power in a hierarchy structured in dominance. In decoding discourses of power and the discourses of domination (Henry and Tator 2002), the media become a central site of inquiry, in terms of both the particular kinds of representations they deploy and the discursive devices they use to communicate the common-sense stock of knowledge. I propose that it is only by scrutinizing the power and powerful messages of dominant media institutions that we can begin to understand the ways in which representational discourses of race and racism are used to maintain and perpetuate hierarchies of power.

In this chapter, I offer a primer of sorts on race and the media. Although by no means an exhaustive overview of the now burgeoning Canadian literature dealing with the issue, the chapter is intended to offer insights into how racialized women and men of colour are represented in the Canadian mass media. I begin by outlining the historical reservoir of representations that form and inform contemporary representations of racialized groups in the media. I then discuss the coverage of racialized people of colour by the news media, the providers of supposedly factual reportage. In examining this reportage, I emphasize the routine narratives and practices of the media that result in stereotypical portrayals of racialized people of colour. I also emphasize the particular definitions of race and racism that the media tend to advance. My intent in traversing this terrain is to underscore the violence of mediated racism as evidenced in the representational discourses pertaining to racialized people of colour. This symbolic violence is, I maintain, critical in reproducing common-sense notions of difference whereby difference is constructed as that which deviates from the invisible, normalized, and taken-for-granted background of White dominance.

Historical Dimensions: Locating the Grammar of Race

In attempting to situate contemporary representations of racialized people in the mass media, a significant point of departure is the currency and range of representations that were generated during the colonial period. As critical vehicles disseminating dominant ideologies, the mass media circulated images of the colonized that served the interests of the Empire (Said 1979; M.L. Pratt 1992; Grewal 1996; Shohat and Stam 1994). Contemporary discourses on race bear "traces" of these "past articulations" (S. Hall 1990a, 11) and, hence, examining these historical representations is instructive insofar as doing so sheds light on contemporary portrayals.[1]

As powerful institutions structured in dominance, the media's messages and constructions inform the public imagination – influencing the lives of racialized minorities. However, the media do not operate in a vacuum. They work in concert with other dominant powers to present a hegemonic view of social reality and the particular positioning of groups within that reality. This ideological labour is not without contestation, as hegemony requires continually obtaining the consent of the governed. Yet, despite the challenges and contestations, the hegemonic power of the media cannot be under-estimated. For as capitalist institutions, the media are owned by Western conglomerates, which in turn exercise particular influences on the kinds of images and stories about Others that are disseminated locally and globally (Herman and Chomsky 2002; Herman and McChesney 1997; Winter 1997, 2002). As Stuart Hall (1990a, 14) notes, "the 'white eye' is always outside the frame – but seeing and positioning everything within it." It is this normative White standard that determines the categorization of racialized minorities within the social order and that ultimately influences how they are perceived and treated by others. The White eye, then, is the power of Whiteness communicated through the discursive strategies of exnomination, naturalization, and universalization that I discuss in the previous chapter.

However, by reiterating the issue of Whiteness, I am not advocating an essentialist interpretation. Rather, I agree with Fiske (1996, 42) when he argues that Whiteness is best understood as a "strategic deployment of power," and further, that:

> It comprises the construction and occupation of a centralized space from which to view the world, and from which to operate in the world. This space of whiteness contains a limited but varied set of normalizing positions from which that which is not white can be made into the abnormal; by such means whiteness constitutes itself as a universal set of norms by which to make sense of the world. When faced with a crisis – that is, a situation which demands solution – whiteness can withdraw into its self-constructed normality and never question its assumption that the abnormal – that is, that which threatens whiteness – is what must change in order to resolve the crisis. Constructing and occupying the space of whiteness, then, is simultaneously constitutive of the viewer-occupier, the process of viewing, and that which is viewed.

In constituting Whiteness as "a field of power" (Hage 2000, 55), Fiske delineates how the power to define the abnormal in opposition to an unstated and implicit normality establishes and legitimizes the self/Other dichotomy as, drawing from Foucault, a regime of truth. In other words, it is not a matter of an empirical, material, and absolute truth (for there are many truths) that we need to attend to as a formula for defining an essentialized abnormal but, rather, how certain truths are installed as truths and used in the interests of sustaining and reproducing unequal power relations.

In a liberal democracy, the media can function legitimately only if they are able to convince us that they represent our interests (Hackett et al. 2000; Hackett and Zhao 1998). Thus, rather than it being the reality or unreality of particular representations that is debated, the key point that needs to be addressed in terms of race and representation is, in whose interests are particular kinds of representations being deployed? And further, what do they indicate about the social status ascribed to that specific group or individual? In other words, how do these representations work to make sense of social reality, and what kind of actions are these representations legitimizing?

If we go back to the height of imperialism and colonialism, it is apparent that the reservoir of representations about Others that were formed and circulated at the time helped to solidify a sense of the European self. In that sense, the Other was defined as being excessively sexual, physically different, inferior in mental and social capacities, threatening, alien, savage-like, dirty, ignorant, primitive, and beyond the pale of civilization. However, the Other was also defined inversely as exotic, erotic, mystical, innocent, majestic, and a noble relic of a bygone era (McBratney 1988; Greenberger 1969; Hammond and Jablow 1977). Stuart Hall (1990a) and Homi Bhabha (1983) argue that this tension and ambivalence between the two diametrically opposite sides of these representations is inherent to all colonial stereotypes. For Bhabha, these polarities reflect the ambivalence between desire on the one hand and disavowal on the other, or, between the recognition of sameness and the demonizing of difference. Hall (1989b, 14) defines this ambivalence as constitutive of the "doubling syntax" of a grammar of race, whereas McBratney (1988) refers to this ambivalence as a "doubling discourse."

According to Hall (1990a, 15), these dominant representations of colonized peoples formed the "base images of a 'grammar of race'" – a grammar that cohered around the following power coordinates inherent in the dominant discourses of the day. As Hall (1990a, 14) states:

(1) Their imagery and themes were polarized around fixed relations of subordination and domination. (2) Their stereotypes were grouped around the poles of "superior" and "inferior" natural species. (3) Both were displaced from the "language" of history into the language of Nature. Natural physical signs and racial characteristics became the unalterable signifiers of inferiority. Subordinate ethnic groups and classes appeared, not as the objects of particular historical relations (the slave trade, European colonisation, the active underdevelopment of the "underdeveloped" societies), but as the given qualities of an inferior *breed*. Relations, secured by economic, social, political and military domination were transformed and "naturalised" into an order of *rank* ascribed by Nature.

In projecting onto the colonized traits that were considered excessive (sexuality, immorality, emotionality, fecundity, and so on), the colonizers were able to construct an image of themselves as intelligent, rational, superior, moral, and controlled. Within the base images of this grammar, even so-called positive representations become problematic because they reaffirmed the superiority of the colonizing force against the imputed inferiority of the colonized. The noble savage of a bygone era is none other than a relic of a stagnant civilization that has remained frozen in time as compared with the dynamic and progressively evolved culture of the Western colonizer (L. Smith 1999). Not only does the construction of the noble savage stereotype buttress White superiority but it allows for the expression of benevolence and rationalizes the containment of these relics in museums as emblematic signifiers of a lost past.

The opposition of the noble versus the barbaric savage is reflective of the two-sided nature of these stereotypes and indicative of the tension and ambivalence inherent in these constructions. This "doubling syntax" facilitates the strategic use of the discourse to legitimize interventions by the dominant powers. As innocent children of the past, Natives can be controlled and guided on the path to progress. But, their very proclivity toward savagery needs to be contained through subjugation. Such sentiments come through clearly in the writings of White explorers who set out to chart and colonize others and their lands. To exemplify the kinds of representational discourses that were being circulated about Africa and Africans, Hammond and Jablow (1977, 54) quote John Hanning Speke, who set out in 1857 to "discover" the source of the Nile River. Speke wrote: "How the negro has lived so many ages without advancing, seems marvellous, when all the countries surrounding Africa are so forward in comparison; and judging from the progressive state of the world, one is led to suppose that the African must soon either step out from his darkness, or be superseded by a being superior to himself. Could a government be formed for them like ours in India, they would be saved; at present the African cannot help himself." In a strategic sense, these base images allow for and legitimize a measure of social distance whereby *they* become the repository of all that *we* are not, and conversely, *our* superiority is affirmed through *their* inferiority. This *us* and *them* distinction is central to how the popular and news media represent racialized groups (see van Dijk 1992, 1993). More critically, the relations of power communicating the superiority of the colonizers in relation to the inferiority of the colonized that were circumscribed and inscribed within these representational discourses engendered particular kinds of responses. In the above tract by Speke, one can see both the benevolence so typical of imperial powers and the motives that necessitated or legitimized actions based on benevolence: rescue can be implemented only if the target of the rescue is considered to be deserving and rescuable.

The theme of rescue through benevolence underpins power relations and gives expression to those relations in ways that "make sense." Thus difference, which is threatening, can similarly be recuperated through its conversion into exotica, or its neutralization through containment. In speaking of the exotic, it is apparent that imperial literature was replete with representations constructing women from the East and other parts of the world as exotic Others who needed to be unveiled so that their hidden natures could be consumed by the colonizers (see Chapter 7). Alternatively, as Mohanty (1991b) demonstrates, the dangers of exotic Others had to be contained, if not eliminated, in the interests of the Empire.

These colonially inscribed images are not so far removed from the realm of popular culture now, where their contemporary manifestations have been reworked to suit current tastes. Stuart Hall (1990a, 16) remarks, "The scheming villains and their giant-sized bully boys in the world of James Bond and his progeny are still, unusually, recruited from 'out there' in Jamaica, where savagery lingers on. The sexually-available 'slave girl' is alive and kicking, smouldering away on some exotic TV set or on the covers of paperbacks."[2] Recent popular films such as *Catwoman*, *The Last Samurai*, and *Kill Bill* bear traces of this grammar of race and contain the double syntax of representations dealing with the Other (see also hooks 1992, 1994). The widespread currency of these images is also apparent in fiction adventure stories, comic strips, and even literature selected as part of school curricula.[3] However, in contemporary popular culture, the ambivalence or doubling syntax of these pitiable and pejorative, or exoticized and threatening, representations has been somewhat bridged through the introduction of cultural and racial hybrids who symbolize a conjoining of the best of the West and the East but whose presence is clearly designed to reaffirm White superiority (see Jiwani 2005b; Minh-ha 1989b; Palumbo-Liu 1999). This form of containment serves to tame the savages, enabling their recuperation for consumption.

Such taming and consumption of the exotic also takes the form of appropriation whereby symbols and fashions from other cultural traditions are stripped of their original meanings and reused in a White context. In her discussion of the Western appropriation and use of South Asian symbols of femininity, Meenakshi Gigi Durham (2001, 213) remarks: "The U.S. mass media's presentation of Indian femininity as a substructure for white female sexuality serves to legitimate the hegemonic construction of Western superiority over Asian culture. In a sense, it inverts the traditional objectification and exoticization of the Oriental female body – here, the South Asian body is not represented as sexually exotic; rather, it is used to supplement white female sexuality through a system of pastiche." The homogenization of difference is another strategic move by which racialized Others were and often continue to be represented as hordes, having little or no individuality, and as being highly interchangeable (JanMohamed 1985): an Asian woman is like any other Asian woman (Hagedorn 1997; Jiwani 2005b; McAllister 1992). As hordes, the colonized are colourful backdrops to the exploits of contemporary celluloid heroes such as Indiana Jones and James Bond. In writing about Hollywood's depiction of American Indians, Bataille and Silet (1980, 40) emphasize this notion of homogenization, noting that "Hollywood created the instant Indian: wig, war bonnet, breechclout, moccasins, phoney beadwork. The movie man did what thousands of years of social evolution could not do; Hollywood produced the homogenized Native American, devoid of tribal characteristics and regional differences. As long as the actor wore fringed pants and spoke with a halting accent, he was Indian." The colonized came to be represented in particular ways – as savage hordes, exotic women, and dangerous Others – so as to further the goal of Empire, whether that was through its various "civilizing" missions, or throughout outright invasion and conquest.

Although the most obvious stereotypes within these representational discourses have and continue to be contested, the reality is that such stereotypes persist and inform much of our culture. The recurrent use of the Arab terrorist stereotypes as evidenced in popular television shows such as the series *24* or films such as *The Siege* (Wilkins and Downing 2002) is reflective of the long-lasting power of these representations and the persistence with which they are used to continually reconstitute Whiteness as dominance and to reinscribe relations of superiority and inferiority. Cast as threats to "civilization," these stereotypical representations of the Arab terrorist serve the purpose of demonizing an enemy "out there" or "over here" in the nation and thereby provide ample justification for the invasion of their lands, the passage of draconian laws forbidding their entry, and their criminalization once inside the nation. As shorthand devices, stereotypes work to communicate in a condensed fashion what would otherwise be unfamiliar to a mass audience (Nichols 1990-91). Nonetheless, by collapsing differences between and within groups, by exoticizing and demonizing the Other, the media dehumanize and objectify particular groups, and in so doing, contribute to their marginalization and naturalize inequalities.

The News

The seepage of colonial representations of Others is not simply confined to popular media. It also influences the structure of stories covered by the contemporary news media. It is in the latter context that these representations assume a heightened significance – a significance imbued by the aura of the news media as providers of objective, impartial, and balanced public accounts of the world (Molotch and Lester 1974) and as contemporary bards reproducing collective myths of identity and belonging (Fiske and Hartley 1978; see also Lule 2002). News stories embody narratives that are themselves grounded in the historically sedimented stock of knowledge – the reservoir of images described above. In so doing, they activate a whole chain of signification. Stuart Hall (1984, 5) observes, "We mainly tell stories like we've told them before, or we borrow from the whole inventory of telling stories, and of narratives" (see also Bird and Dardenne 1988; Darnton 1975). In other words, the narrative structure activates previous representations, which then ground and inform the meaning of current representations. In this way, a series of associations is invoked. Van Zoonen (1994, 38) points out: "The bardic function has inherently reactionary tendencies since it needs to rely on familiar meanings and interpretations. What falls outside an already existing consensus is hard to make sense of, except as 'otherness' or 'deviance.'" As public texts (Connell 1980), media representations highlight the often invisible but dominant consensus that shapes the boundaries of acceptability (Gitlin 1986).

In an examination of the violence of race in the news media, the latter's role in transmitting hegemonic ideology needs to be elaborated. First, the news media shape public opinion by defining issues, setting the agenda, framing the parameters of debate, and providing us with the very categories of language by which to make sense of the issues. Second, as representative public texts, the news media influence policy makers by presumably presenting the people's view. Third, the media impact socialization – in fact, they are a powerful instrument of socialization by "prescribing and describing" (Bannerji 1986) the world and the social rules governing that world. Through the media, we learn where we fit in the social order and, moreover, how to increase our chances of fitting in, the latitudes of freedom which we can exercise, and the penalties that may accrue from transgressing these limits. In that sense, the media clearly privilege and communicate the dominant discourses of morality and mobility (see Chapter 1). Fourth, the media sell audiences as potential consumers to advertisers (Hackett et al. 2000; Winter 1997). As profit-making industries, the media attempt to provide a fare that audiences are likely to consume, a fare that rests on audience familiarity and resonance.

The news media work with other dominant media to represent a symbolic image of the nation. Hence, if particular groups are consistently underrepresented or represented in stereotypical ways as abnormals – criminals, unassimilable immigrants, undeserving Others, those who don't fit the ideal normative standards, and those who do not belong to the nation – then it follows that the ruling powers are likely to use these representations as justification for imposing measures that effectively curtail the rights of these groups in entering or remaining within the nation. Representations of racialized minorities in the dominant media of a nation are, then, indicative of how that nation perceives itself and the groups within it. The association between representation and violence lies in the way in which groups are objectified, dehumanized, and inferiorized in the media. In this sense, media discourses can and do exert a form of symbolic violence. As Michel Foucault (1981a, 67) posits, "We must conceive discourse as a violence which we do to things[,]" and the act of representation bears that burden, particularly when it is exercised from a position of power and in the interests of maintaining that dominance.

News is also a complex of culture and commodity. It has to be intelligible to make sense, and it has to have an inherent structure of appeal in order to capture a market. Hence, through the selection of stories presented and the manner in which they are communicated, the news draws from and reinforces the common-sense stock of knowledge. Connell (1980, 140) suggests: "The explanations proffered by news and current affairs programs are made to seem the 'best sense' of a given situation. They are, in the unfolding of television's accounts, [and in the press] categorized as 'common sense,' 'moderate public opinion,' 'rational understanding' or 'the consensus.'" Given that common sense is ideological and, as I suggest in the previous chapter, racialized and gendered, it would seem that news accounts are intended for the reasonable person, the ideal typical Canadian who shares the dominant perspectives by and large, even though s/he may on occasion exercise what Stuart Hall (1980b) has termed negotiated and oppositional readings of media accounts.[4]

Similarly, news practices influence the ways in which stories about particular groups are told and retold. Through the deployment of frames, filters, and stereotypes, the mass media, and particularly the news media, communicate a constructed social reality (Gitlin 1979, 1980). This reality consists of "strips" (Tuchman 1978) pieced together through practices of selection and combination, and framed within the parameters of the media's interpretations of objectivity, impartiality, and balance (Hackett and Zhao 1998; S. Hall 1974). In framing stories, the media utilize "persistent patterns of cognition, interpretation, and presentation, of selection, emphasis, and exclusion" (Gitlin 1980, 7), which again draw on the stock of common-sense knowledge. It is the deployment of such frames that lends coherence to media stories. The criteria used to select stories are themselves ideologically grounded and also influenced by the larger frames of meaning. What gets selected as news is thus contingent on the perceived newsworthiness of an event – newsworthiness amounting to what makes a story worth telling. These criteria include relevance, immediacy, unexpectedness, intensity, unpredictability, resonance, cultural proximity, clarity, and intelligibility (Galtung and Ruge 1973).

In his analysis of the illusion that is news, Bennett (2003) identifies four biases inherent in the production of news stories: personalization, dramatization, fragmentation, and the authority-disorder bias. He argues that through personalization, news is designed to appeal to the individual: "The news gives people a me-first view of the world in which 'my' well-being, 'my' group, and 'my' country are emphasized over social realities that differ from one's own" (2003, 63). In emphasizing the dramatic, news stories tend to focus on crises, escalations, and resolutions. The fragmented nature of the news is most evident in the way that stories are decontextualized and presented in a piecemeal fashion. And through a heavy reliance on experts and government as official sources and spokespeople responsible for restoring order, the news media manifest an authority-disorder bias.

News conventions and the criteria of newsworthiness inform the way news is organized, packaged, and made meaningful. However, these conventions and criteria lend themselves to a particular type of coverage of race-related matters and racialized groups. There appears to be a play of affinities between the discourses surrounding race and the frameworks implicit in the organizing and telling of news stories.

The personalizing tendency of the news comes through clearly in the media's attempts to locate racism in individual actions and psychopathology. The systemic nature of racism is reduced to the actions of a few individuals or to individual ignorance or pathology. This has two results. On the one hand, it secures the image of society as tolerant by relegating racist actions to a few extremists; on the other, it reduces structural phenomena to the level of personal quirks and ignorance (Guillaumin 1974). The accompanying dehistoricization of racism removes it from the broader context – the realm of history (Hartmann and Husband 1974) – into the realm of nature. Naturalized, racism is seen as being an inherent feature of all societies, and it is trivialized by its confinement to the actions of the few.

News also tends to be about disruptions in the social order and threats to social stability. Seen from the perspective of the White eye (to use Stuart Hall's term), difference that is unusual or threatening is likely to be caught in the news trap as an item worthy of reportage. Given the minoritized status of people of colour (both within the West and in the dominant global media), the general absence of racialized bodies of colour in elite circles (those representing heads of state, corporations, and the upper echelons of society) means that most news about racialized groups tends to focus only on their involvement in conflicts and conflict situations. These may be conflicts in their communities or conflicts in countries around the world. The media's focus on issues that symbolize a threat to the social order also contributes to negatively charged coverage about racialized people. The historical treatment of racialized groups has contributed to a storehouse of narrative forms that position them as aliens, invading hordes, unassimilable ethnics, and as victims (Armour 1984; Indra 1979). These narratives are consistently reactivated in news coverage about immigrants and crime.

Furthermore, newsworthiness is measured by the novelty and dramatic value of an event. In this regard, racialized people are likely to be included in news stories if they are perceived as introducing an element of novelty or drama to a given situation. Thus, when racialized individuals attain an extraordinary standard of achievement in an uncommon venue, they are likely to receive extensive media attention. The underlying expectation is that such individuals or groups are generally incapable of rising to such standards, or come from cultural traditions antithetical to the particular avenues in which they excel. Or, alternatively, their representation is used to shore up the image of the dominant society as one of tolerance, meritocracy, and equality. Of course, this does not hold true for raced bodies that stereo-typically appear most frequently in the music and sports sections of the newspaper. Here, their success is often attributed to their innate predisposition toward these activities.

The novelty or dramatic criterion of news stories also coincides with certain aspects of racialized minority cultures. Seen against a backdrop of White society, these groups offer colourful alternatives. Their fashion, music, and cuisine become objects of attention. The exotic dimension is captivated and becomes a focal point of attention in the coverage devoted to ethnic festivals and ceremonies. Conversely, cultural rites and rituals are given coverage when these are perceived and positioned as being antithetical to social norms (Youngs 1989; Thobani 1992). The persistent coverage of arranged marriages, circumcision rites, communal living arrangements, and different religious traditions contributes to images of racialized communities that cast them as being uncivilized, oppressive, and undesirable (Arat-Koc 2002; Narayan 1997).

Representing Race in the News

> Just as the noise of the "big bang" still resonates through the universe, so the overdetermined construction of world "civiliza-tion" as a product of the rise of Europe and the subjugation of the rest of us still defines the race concept.
>
> – Michael Omi and Howard Winant, "On the
> Theoretical Status of the Concept of Race"

In representing race, the news media racialize particular groups of people, demarcating them as different from the majority and imputing qualities that emphasize their difference, and then, by inferiorizing, trivializing, and exoticizing these qualities, ultimately render such differences deviant. As Omi and Winant (1993, 9) argue in the quote that opened this section, these representations are grounded in a legacy of colonialism and imperialism.

Existing studies focusing on representations of racialized minorities in mainstream Canadian television and print news media conclude that they are markedly under-represented and that the majority of these representations are stereotypical.[5] Many of the recent studies have taken the policy of multiculturalism, which requires broadcasters to reflect the multicultural and multiracial character of Canadian society as a point of departure for assessing existing representations (see Dunn and Mahtani 2001; Fleras and

Kunz 2001; Mahtani 2001). In the previous chapter, I discussed the multi-culturalism policy and its implications in shaping the discourse on gendered violence against racialized women of colour. Within the terrain of media coverage, multiculturalism is also similarly translated into the language of culture, where each cultural community seeks and is often given requisite access, with broadcasting licences and the like, to express its cultural worldviews through ethnic programming and the ethnic press. The Canadian Radio and Television Commission (CRTC) determines whether or not stations will be granted a licence, based, of course, on the perceived legitimacy of the group or the station, as evident in the licensing requirements imposed on the Al-Jazeera network. However, while the issue of ethnic media is an important one, it is the representation of racialized people rather than so-called ethnic cultures within the dominant, mainstream media that is the main point of contention. In other words, the conflation of ethnicity and race results in occluding the reality of racial barriers and works in the interests of advancing a depoliticized cultural agenda. As Frances Henry (2002, 237) observes: "The multiculturalism policy, in sum, still emphasizes culture at the expense of structure. It is still primarily focused on providing opportunities for ethno-cultural groups, community organizations, and even researchers to engage in activities that deal with ethnicity and culture rather than dismantling barriers to equal opportunity in employment, housing, and the institutional structures of Canadian society." The emphasis on culture rather than race has several implications that play out in the realm of policy. First, differences between ethnic groups are collapsed: White ethnics such as the Scottish or the English are often granted the same level of access and privilege as ethnic communities of colour;[6] second, given that communities, as Bannerji (2000) reminds us, are constructed in response to external conditions and circumstances, this makes any community organized under the banner of culture rather suspect. Which cultural interpretation is being used as the authentic and emblematic signature? And further, which individuals or group within these communities have the power to define what constitutes cultural authenticity and cultural membership?

That aside, under-representation is a significant issue because it communicates the relative absence of a particular group in the symbolic order represented by the dominant media. As Tuchman (1978) has argued, a lack of representation constitutes a symbolic annihilation (see also Gross 1991). In other words, not having representation in the symbolic landscape of the nation means that one simply does not exist. For racialized minority groups, the lack of any representation indicates that they do not matter, that they are invisible in the nation, and that, as invisible Others, they remain on the margins. Being under-represented, however, translates into minimal, marginal, and stereotypical representations. This reaffirms the minoritized status of racialized communities. It basically negates their history and contribution to the development of the nation-state and erases their ongoing participation in the social order. Through under-representation, the media continue to border these communities, casting them as Others outside the social body.

Existing studies indicate that representations of racialized minorities tend to cluster around the themes of crime and deviance, ethnic exotica, athletic prowess, and societal achievement, thereby constructing them as Others – different from "us." Within this context, there has been a controlling association between people of colour and immigration, evoking a host of negative connotations linking immigrants with fears of invasion, illegal entry, and opportunistic behaviour, all of which are seen as threatening Canadian identity and its imagined national traits. Earlier studies have documented the strength of this association, drawing on historical and contemporary examples in the news media (see, for instance, DuCharme 1986; Henry and Ginzberg 1985; Indra 1979; Scanlon 1977). What this research suggests is that immigrants constitute the Other by which Canadian national identity is reconstituted and reproduced over time. Without the Others at the borders, clamouring to get in through legal or illegal means, we would have a difficult time defining Canadian identity. In other words, *they* are a strategic necessity for self-definition to occur. In the face of their presumed proclivity to violence, *we* come across as civilized; in contrast to *their* illegal actions, *we* are tacitly, and at times explicitly, constructed as law-abiding citizens. The nation as a peaceful haven becomes contrasted to *their* countries, which are characterized by war, corruption, and instability.

In their extensive study of race and Canadian media, Fleras and Kunz (2001, 140) categorize existing representations of racialized groups into five themes: "minorities as invisible, minorities as stereotypes, minorities as problem people, minorities as whitewashed, and minorities as adornments." These stereotypes are particularly apparent in the coverage dealing with minorities as "problem people." Representations of minorities as whitewashed or assimilated are those that fail to reference cultural and racial differences or that erase the impact of these differences on the lived realities of racialized groups. Finally, representations of minorities as adornments are inherently linked to their role as exotic Others whose differences can be periodically celebrated and consumed in the style of what Fish (1997) describes as boutique multiculturalism.

Ethnic restaurants, festivals, costumes, and exotica are often celebrated as signs of difference but also as ways in which differences can be rendered more palatable as commodities to be consumed voluntarily and at leisure. Alternatively, strange foods and culinary practices are also the site of disdain and revulsion, and used as signifiers of savagery. Trinh T. Minh-ha (1989a, 57) remarks, "Exoticism can only be consumed when it is salvaged, that is reappropriated and translated into the master's language of authenticity and otherness." The translation of difference into the realm of culture is, then, rendered possible through appropriation, whereby one makes the Other one's own, divesting it of its meanings or retaining only that which secures an aura of authenticity. Thus is difference made meaningful and therefore safe for consumption.

However, more often than not, representations of racialized groups within the news media have become associated with the negative and destructive elements of social life (Dunn and Mahtani 2001; P. Li 2003; Mahtani and Mountz 2002). The association between immigrants and crime is a common strategy used to both racialize crime and criminalize racial groups. Thus, while the exotic dimension of difference can be tamed and consumed, the threatening dimension of difference tends to be condensed under the sign of criminality whereby it can be Othered, confined, and restrained discursively and incarcerated physically. These moves represent the symbolic violence of race as perpetrated by the mass media.

Fleras and Kunz (2001) attribute these categories of stereotypical representations to the media's tendency to adopt a "rapids and shallows" approach. The shallows period is marked by routine and normalized coverage, where there is an absence of a national emergency or moral panic. In contrast, "within the context of crisis or calamity, involving natural catastrophes, civil wars, and colourful insurgents," (78) the media's proclivity is to embrace a rapids approach whereby racialized minorities are quickly solicited for their views and often given heavy coverage, depending on the nature of the story. They further add that the mediacentric bias, which they define as the deployment of a double standard within newsrooms, contributes to the limited framing of racialized minorities. They note:

> Mainstream media select those race-related incidents that are atypical but deemed newsworthy, frame them in a stereotypical fashion, and contrast them with the behaviour and standards of whites – in effect reinforcing a discourse of whiteness as normal or superior and minorityness as deviant or inferior. Such a controlling effect is accomplished in different ways, namely, through (a) negative stereotypes, (b) the racializing of certain activities such as crime, (c) the assertion of Eurocentric judgements that reinforce the normalness of whites while demonizing others as substandard or irrelevant, and (d) the imposition of double standards; for example, white crime is framed as individual aberration while a black offender is defined as typical of the community at large. (43)

Inferential and Overt Racism

In the current social climate, it is difficult but not impossible for media institutions to openly subscribe to a racist viewpoint. The tendency is for media institutions to use a mode of inferential racism by which to communicate race and racism. Stuart Hall (1990a, 12-13) defines inferential racism as referring to "those apparently naturalized representations of events and situations relating to race, whether 'factual' or 'fictional,' which have racist premises and propositions inscribed in them as a set of unquestioned assumptions. These enable racist statements to be formulated without ever bringing into awareness the racist predicates on which these statements are grounded." Hence, while overtly racist statements were and could be articulated with a certain ease in a colonial context, such sentiments now tend to be camouflaged utilizing an inferential form of racism, although shock jock radio still tends to employ explicitly racist rhetoric. An example of how inferential racism is used to advance and legitimize a racist viewpoint can be seen in the coverage of the case of CHOI, a popular Quebec radio station.

In mid-July 2004, the CRTC released its decision to revoke the licence of CHOI. The station's host for the morning program, Jean-François Fillion, was known for his acerbic and derogatory commentary on racialized and other marginalized groups in society. Some of the comments that incited the CRTC's actions included the following one by co-host André Arthur: "In Muslim countries and in countries in Black Africa, the ones who are sent abroad to study are the sons of people who are disgusting ... the sons of plunderers, cannibals" (Ha 2004a, A6). Other comments, attributed to Mr. Fillion, focused on pejorative remarks about the economic "burden" of carrying psychiatric patients and women's intellectual capacities in relation to the size of their breasts.

The decision incited a flurry of responses against the CRTC's decision, reflecting the popular and populist disdain for government intervention even when such intervention is predicated on protecting the rights of minorities from the language of hate. Nonetheless, the argument in favour of CHOI, as articulated even by those who espoused progressive views within the mainstream media, was that its continued existence exemplified the freedom of Canadian society – a freedom that allows for the ranting of hate-filled speech as well as a celebration of difference. The effect of this kind of moral equivalence between hate on the one hand and tolerance and celebration on the other is that it is mythical and based on an abstract and absolute notion of freedom. The issues are positioned as two sides of a duality – both permitted by the notion of freedom. In reality, however, the freedom to choose which side is "right" is accorded only to those who have the power to *define* and decide the limits of the debate.

For racialized minorities, as with other marginalized groups in society, the power to define and decide, or even set the limits of a debate, is considerably lower than that possessed by dominant groups. Those who embrace CHOI's position (the CRTC was apparently flooded with letters of complaint from CHOI's loyal fans) constitute a highly sought-after market segment – a population between the ages of eighteen and thirty-three years, presumably male and White. They represent a dominant sector of Quebec City's population. For this group of listeners, the radio station's permissible attitude toward open and derogatory talk about minorities is acceptable, if not refreshing. However, for those who are most impacted by CHOI's derogatory language, the choices are few. As minorities, they have little power to make their voice heard, and considerably less social and cultural capital in terms of being accorded any kind of legitimacy or credibility should they articulate their complaints. Thus, in a situation of unequal power, the status of minorities is not equal to the status and legitimacy accorded to dominant groups. Consequently, even the impact of racist speech, as broadcasted by CHOI, is harsher on minority groups than on the majority dominant group that appears to embrace such talk (see Fleras and Kunz 2001). In contrast, the media reportage emphasizing the populist voice flattens out this hierarchy, suggesting a level playing field.

In the coverage of the CRTC decision, the *Globe and Mail* began its reportage of the story with a headline on the front page stating, "Free-speech fight erupts after CRTC bans station" (Ha 2004a). In the very first paragraph, the reporter, Tu Thanh Ha, writes: "In a Canadian first yesterday, federal regulators yanked the broadcasting licence of CHOI-FM, Quebec City's most popular radio station, because of a long-running pattern of offensive comments by its morning hosts." In this depiction of events, the station's licence is "yanked" and the pattern of racist and sexist comments is collapsed into the catch-all category "offensive" – minimizing its potential and actual damage to those who are victimized by such language. However, immediately after this, the reporter goes on to describe the impact on the station and then to quote Patrice Demers, the owner of CHOI. The CRTC's defence of its decision is made apparent in the fifth paragraph with a counter-quote from Charles Dalfen, the commission's chair. The *Gazette* framed this whole issue under the label "censorship debate." The transformation of this story from one dealing with a renegade station that refused to follow *its own codes*, let alone adhere to the conditions imposed by the CRTC, to an issue dealing with free speech is itself indicative of how the concerns of marginalized groups are minimized and trivialized.

Interestingly, there were no voices that directly addressed the racist, ableist, and sexist remarks represented in the coverage in either one of the papers on the day the story broke. The violence of racism is erased in these public accounts, thus illustrating the ways in which inferential racism works to advance a dominant definition of social reality. As Patricia Hill Collins (1998, 923) observes: "The hate speech of men against women, of whites against people of colour, of adults against children, of heterosexuals against gays and lesbians remains largely invisible as violence because speech and action are typically classified as two, mutually exclusive categories." Collins' comment touches on another thorny issue, namely, the difference and connection between speech and behaviour. Although speech is often regarded as removed from the plane of behaviour, speech normalizes a certain way of looking at things. Speech acts, when enshrined in common sense and articulated repeatedly and in credible contexts, contribute to discursive violence and, over time, normalize actions that emanate from a certain way of thinking. It is the normalization of racism that becomes increasingly problematic, especially for racialized minorities who bear the brunt of its effects.

Hate speech is not seen as violence but as an instance of a sacrosanct right – the right to free speech – raising the question: free for whom? More critically, the representation of hate as one predicated on freedom of speech neutralizes opposition since it converts violence into the language of individual will, ignorance, and desire for notoriety. Thus, the violence of racism becomes trivialized and dismissed, and in such a context, the complaints of marginalized groups are similarly trivialized – as arising from their insecurity, over-sensitivity, and assumed predilection for launching complaints.

Adherence to an absolute notion of the freedom of speech is permitted by news values that enshrine notions of objectivity, impartiality, and balance within the news media (Gitlin 1979, 1980). To put forward a semblance of objectivity, impartiality, and balance, the media are bound to report those values that they do not necessarily agree with but which they see as embracing a contrarian position. This is part of the media's self-defined role as the fourth estate – looking out for the interests of the masses against the power of the state. Thus, reporting on two sides of an issue – showing the "other side" – secures such an image. It also reinforces the notion of a common consensus as underlying and shaping the boundaries of the debate. The resulting effect is one where hierarchies are flattened so that opposing views appear to be equivalent – thus protecting the media from charges of bias. It is the inflection of these views, their particular privileging through accessing official sources and elites, and their utilization to promote specific explanations of a given phenomenon that further allow the media to position themselves as neutral and objective bearers of the truth while simultaneously communicating dominant and preferred interpretations.

Aside from masking issues of inequality, a primary way in which the media utilize inferential racism is through coded language: immigrants become synonymous with foreigners, illegal migrants, so-called bogus refugees, and terrorists; diversity becomes a code word to communicate racial differences with racialized groups often being referred to as multicultural Others (Karim 1993a; P. Li 2003); tolerance is presented as a kind of benevolent forbearance of difference (Mirchandani and Tastsoglou 2000); and culture becomes a way of talking race (Razack 1998a). As Omi and Winant (1993, 7) observe, "It is now possible to perpetuate racial domination without making any explicit reference to race at all. Subtextual or 'coded' racial signifiers, or the mere denial of the continuing significance of race, may suffice."

Race and Crime

The media play an instrumental role in advancing common-sense explanations of crime, explanations that resonate with the mutual stock of knowledge (Ericson 1991; Ericson, Baranek, and Chan 1989; S. Hall et al. 1978; Wortley 2002). For example, the emphasis on policing certain groups of people and certain types of crimes is reflective of the social stratification system underpinning Canadian society. Those at the bottom are considered to be most prone to crime, less credible and deserving, and are often perceived by the dominant society as the dispossessed and disposable (Dulude 2000; Jiwani 1999). Hence, a good deal of negative attention is paid to them and their demands. Henry et al. (1995) argue that the decision to police certain kinds of crime over others reflects the racism and classism inherent in elite institutions. It reflects the power of the dominant White, invisible, and middle-class society to define what constitutes crime and punishment. Thus, rather than police white-collar crime, which exacts steep economic and human costs (Snider 2002), the tendency has been to police crimes associated with the poor and with racial minority groups. It is not surprising, then, that racialized communities have consistently maintained that they are being over-policed and under-protected (Quigley, as cited in the report of the Royal Commission on Aboriginal Peoples 1996, 35-36; Williams 1996).[7]

In an interesting study tracing the links between race, media, and crime in a hundred US cities, Wortley (2002, 76) found that "increases in the Black population, accompanied with media coverage of minority crime, are much stronger predictors of police budget increases than are both the official crime rate and overall population growth." Economic motives aside, the very construction of Others as symbolic threats generates a climate of terror which then advances a law-and-order agenda (Arat-Koc 2002). And that climate of fear is nurtured and amplified by the mainstream media (S. Hall et al. 1978). Since September 2001, the anti-terrorism legislation, combined with a draconian increase in state surveillance, has resulted in fostering a domestic climate of terror, a topic I address in more depth in Chapter 7. For the present, what I wish to underscore is the amplifying role of the media in generating a moral panic. Repetitive reporting of crimes supposedly committed by a specific racialized group leads to the erroneous impression that every member that shares any kind of resemblance to this group has a proclivity to crime. Further, amplifying such reports not only creates a moral panic around particular groups and crimes but provides the fuel, often in the form of a populist outcry, propelling the state to enact measures to counter the perceived threat. One outcome of this is racial profiling (see Henry and Tator 2003).

The Discourse on Immigration

In his analysis of racist thought and talk, van Dijk (1987) found that discourse about immigrants was usually organized around the following categories of threat: threats to the social order because of their presumed proclivity to crime and deviance; threats to the cultural order because of their adherence to their own cultural traditions and their resistance to assimilation; and threats to the economic order because they drain vital social services, manipulate the system in opportunistic ways, or steal jobs from members of the dominant society. Media representations of racialized minority groups in Canada can be categorized in a similar manner.

The discourse of immigration itself has become racialized (Thobani 1998, 1999a). Hence, the term "immigrant" is popularly constructed as referring to a person of colour (Henry et al. 1995). More telling are the connotations of inferiority associated with the stereotypical immigrant who is seen as a recent arrival from a poverty-stricken Third World country, bound to a traditional culture, and unable to speak the dominant language. This stereotype seeps into and is mutually reinforced by images of the so-called developing nations, which are consistently portrayed as impoverished, war-torn, and famine-stricken areas with little or no structure of law and order (Dahlgren with Chakrapani 1982; Fleras and Kunz 2001; Hackett 1989; Kleinman and Kleinman 1996). These kinds of stereotypical representations of racialized immigrants tend to emphasize their difference and deviance, all the while evacuating any notion of how and why they are forced or coerced into fleeing their homelands. As Adrien Hart (1989, 14) remarks:

> The problem so often glossed over or ignored is that these so called "negative" images depict Third World suffering in a manner which casually jettisons the historical, political and economic context that has produced such suffering. The problem with images depicting starving African children is not so much the existence of an image but rather the absence of an adequate explanation of why the child is starving. This absence opens the door to all manner of mythical interpretations emanating from the flux of ideologies forming our individual "common sense" view of the world. Consequently, racist and ethnocentric "explanations" are inevitable amongst an audience with pre-existing assumptions about the Third World and its problems, about Black people and about the superiority of white, Western cultures.

Such representations engender feelings of moral superiority, grounded in the assumed benevolence of the Canadian state and manifested in strategic discourses of rescue that are themselves underpinned by superiority and condescension (Hage 2000). Thus, it is not surprising to see such rescue myths being mobilized to justify peacekeeping missions and to support military interventions in other countries (Razack 2004). While these actions take place "out there," immigrants who are "over here" feel the brunt of these representational discourses, albeit in a different way.

Immigrants as Moral Panics

Racialized immigrants are the media's latest moral panic, albeit a panic whose pitch varies according to international and national agendas dictated by globalization, wars, and the resulting poverty, suppression, and displacement of peoples. As threats to the social order, immigrants have often been stereotyped as transgressing normative rules by jumping the immigration queue, weakening the moral fabric of society by adhering to their own social codes, and engaging in criminal behaviours that violate the law and order of the dominant society.

In their study of the media coverage dealing with the arrival of approximately six hundred Chinese migrants on the coast of British Columbia in 1999, Hier and Greenberg trace the development of a moral panic through the media's amplification of the issue and call for public response. As they describe it (2002, 145):

> As soon as the first boat arrived off the coast of British Columbia, the migrants were racialized in the news media, prematurely branded as "illegal," and lumped into a homogenous category: the Chinese/Asian "other." Once further boats began arriving, and once rumours of still more boats began to circulate, the migrants were objectified within a racialized discourse of illegality through the use of terms such as "boat people," "human cargo," "aliens," "detainees," and "illegal Chinese." This did much to amplify the "problem" among the Canadian public: fewer than 600 people arriving on four boats over two months came to epitomize "waves" of illegal Chinese/Asian refugee claimants.

Although the media was guilty of fomenting the hysteria generated by the arrival of these migrants, its most critical role was in catalyzing an already embedded current of anti-immigrant and anti-Asian sentiments fanned by economic issues pertaining to the increased cost of real estate, high unemployment rates, increases in property taxes, and so forth (Ley 1997). Anti-Asian sentiments have been an integral part of the history of British Columbia as a White settler colony. The earliest race riots occurred in Vancouver at the turn of the nineteenth century and were aimed at expelling Asians from that city (K. Anderson 1991; Armour 1984; P. Li 1994). These anti-Asian sentiments were rooted in the fear of a so-called yellow peril. For example, writing in the 1920s in Vancouver, local commentator John Nelson observes: "British Columbia is one of the last frontiers of the white race against the yellow and the brown. It is a land where a hoary civilization meets a modern one, and where the swarming millions of ancient peoples, stung into restless life by modern events are constantly impinging on an attractive land held by a sparse thousand of whites ... a community which stands at the sea-gate of the northwest Pacific and holds it for Saxon civilization" (cited in Buchignani and Indra with Srivastava 1985, 5).

In her study of the Vancouver press from 1905-76, Doreen Indra (1979) found evidence of overt racism in the press and, further, uncovered the moral stratification system regulating the representations of different groups. Her analysis of this "domestic moral community" reveals that the Scottish and English were ranked at the top, followed by Americans, Germans, Russians, and French Canadians, who occupied the middle range. In contrast, the Chinese, South Asians, Italians, and Aboriginal groups scored the lowest. This hierarchy is reminiscent of Porter's (1965) conceptualization of Canada as vertical mosaic with privileged groups at the top and the underprivileged or non-preferred groups at the bottom (see Chapter 1, this volume).

The common thread linking previous and contemporary representations of immigrants is one of threat – more specifically, the threat of being engulfed by the Other. It is not surprising, then, that the dominant discourse of immigration relies so heavily on what van Dijk (1993) has called the "numbers game." This game, he argues, is a discursive strategy designed to elicit fear of an invasion. Consequently, when the media report on issues of immigration, they invariably cite figures indicating how many of *them* are out there, and how many more are trying to get in (see Dunn and Mahtani 2001; Henry and Tator 2002; Mahtani and Mountz 2002). The inverse of this numbers game is one often used by well-meaning advocates who use population statistics to encourage media institutions to become more diverse – in the interests of attracting the growing number of well-to-do immigrants who possess considerable purchasing power. In either case, the image is one of invasive hordes that need to be contained and controlled, if not used for the benefit of the nation through immigrant investor programs (see Henry 2002).

Racialized immigrant communities are often portrayed as bringing the politics associated with their countries of origin into Canada. As such, they are represented as participating in activities that are gang related, illegally supporting wars and warlords, and as engaging in petty and serious crimes. In an interesting study of the Montreal police's social construction of gangs,

Symons (2002) found a prevalence of racialized descriptions that police used when referring to the various kinds of gangs they encountered. Ethnic gangs were referred to by their culture or country of origin, whereas supremacist White gangs were referred to by their activities. Symons quotes one of the police officers she interviewed who, in reference to the ethnic gangs, claimed: "It's directly related to the mentality of their origin." Symons notes that police "also speak about a 'culture of violence' that the youth left behind in their 'war-torn' country of origin (immigrant status being taken for granted)" (118). She concludes that police "construct ethnocultural communities as the 'Other,' and the 'we/they' dichotomy is clearly articulated in both language and practice" (119).

Interestingly, while the Canadian nation can support the wars of others, for example, the United States and Britain, by providing troops and other resources, the presumed involvement of immigrant groups in the conflicts in their countries of origin is deemed suspect – reflecting their lack of loyalty and patriotism to the Canadian nation. Again, the we/them dichotomy that Symons mentions is apparent in media accounts, as is the double standard Fleras and Kunz (2001) identified as an organizational feature of media discourses about racialized Others. Which struggles are deemed legitimate, which groups are seen as the legitimate stakeholders, and whose connections with a homeland or with a powerful ally are seen as just causes that require little or no interrogation are defined by the media in the interests of those who have power and dominance.

Nonetheless, not all media report immigration stories in the same way. As Henry and Tator (2002) have demonstrated, papers with a more conservative orientation, such as the *National Post*, tend to represent immigration and racialized issues in particularly negative ways (see also Winter 2002). In contrast, other papers, including the *Globe and Mail*, tend to take a more polite approach – still underscoring the race "card," albeit in more subtle ways (Henry and Tator 2002; Hunter 2001; Odartey-Wellington 2004). Hence, while the media offer a discursive field of contesting interpretations, the very limits of this field are predetermined and the very terms of the debate are taken for granted.

Referring back to Stuart Hall's (1990a) example of the inherent ambivalence of these stereotypes, the counter-stereotype to the crime-prone, tradition-bound, and illegal migrant is the representation of the demanding, arrogant, undeserving immigrants or community who tend to complain ceaselessly and whose cunning guile needs to be kept under check, especially given the soft-hearted nature of benevolent "Canadians," not to mention the liberal Canadian state. Thus, when people of colour are perceived to be challenging the status quo and calling into question the government's policies, the tendency is to underline their immigrant status, their ungratefulness, and their over-demanding nature. Here, portrayals border on overt racism. A particularly poignant example of this is the national media's treatment of Sunera Thobani, former president of the National Action Committee (NAC) on the Status of Women, once the largest feminist organization in Canada. Immediately after she assumed NAC's leadership, Thobani came under fire for not being an "authentic" Canadian (see Jiwani 1998a). Subsequently, in October 2001, when she made a speech at a national Elizabeth Fry Conference in Ottawa, she was attacked by the *National Post* and the *Globe and Mail* (these "attacks" were also carried in other papers owned by the same parent companies) for calling on the government to refrain from supporting the US-led intervention in Afghanistan. By this time, Thobani was no longer NAC president.[8] Nonetheless, in the ensuing coverage, the media questioned her credentials as a Canadian and her position as a professor, and underlined her lack of gratitude to the Canadian state (see Thobani 2002b, 2003). Throughout this coverage, her immigrant status was continually emphasized. In her words (2003, 401):

> By repeatedly reconstructing my status as a non-white immigrant woman, the media reiterated – in a highly intensified manner – the historically racialized discourse of who "belongs" to the Canadian nation, and hence has a right to "speak" to it. This racialized discourse constructed me as an outsider to the nation, part of the "enemy" within its territorial boundaries, against which the ideological borders of the nation had to be defended. Repeated calls for me to be fired from my teaching position, and to have me "go back to where I came from" (and in a good number of cases for me to "go back" to Afghanistan!) reconstituted – in a moment of crisis – the vulnerable and constantly "under surveillance" status of Third World immigrants in Canada.

Thobani's experience clearly highlights the role of the media in creating and sustaining a sense of an imagined community, with racialized individuals and groups either at the outskirts of this symbolic empire or as enemies within. That she is a citizen who has lived in the country for over a decade and that her country of origin is not Afghanistan points to the conflation of race, immigration status, and cultural origin. The message from this coverage, especially when coupled with other messages from advertisers and the entertainment media, is that women of colour are tolerable, even alluring, provided they stay in their place. However, should they step out of this place, they become targets of increasing and hostile scrutiny, and of physical and symbolic acts of violence. The category of immigrant is, then, packed with loaded signifiers that connote difference and inferiority. Further, because this catch-all term dissolves and homogenizes differences,[9] those labelled immigrants are viewed as recent arrivals into the nation

– not quite a part of it and yet contained within it. They are never real Canadians, an observation typically levelled at them through daily question, such as where are you from? (J. Kelly 1998).

The coverage of the Thobani case also reflects a gendered narrative, invoking past resonances with the collective stock of knowledge defining desirable versus undesirable women, that is, those who can be recuperated in the interests of the nation and those who need to be extricated from the social body. This gendered narrative was most apparent in another story that captivated the attention of the global media, including the *Globe and Mail,* in the same period. This story focused on Yvonne Ridley, a British reporter who was held hostage by the Taliban (Matusic 2001). Ridley was captured by the Taliban sneaking into Afghanistan wearing a burqa and disguised as a Muslim woman. The story of Ridley's capture appeared in the *Globe* on 1 October. She was described as an ambitious woman, a woman too hungry for stories to care about her daughter whom she had left in the care of her mother, and as a woman who was at one time married to an ex–PLO (Palestine Liberation Organization) official. She was contaminated – a fallen woman and an imperfect mother. By 9 October, Ridley had been recuperated as a heroine. Shown to have survived the Taliban ordeal by engaging in a hunger fast and writing notes on scraps of paper, she was installed as the reporter who had made it and survived (Parkinson 2001). Her prison notes were published in the British papers but, here in the *Globe,* this was mentioned only in passing. Heather Mallick, one of the commentators, wrote about her ordeal and commended her on her survival (Mallick 2001). In the stories published on 20 October, there is no mention of Ridley's ex-PLO partner. In fact, Mallick, using Ridley as the model of the superwoman reporter, describes the pressures that women reporters face in their quest for stories and in their attempts to match or outdo the standards set by their male counterparts.

The day after the Ridley story first appeared in the *Globe,* the paper printed columns on Sunera Thobani's speech at the Elizabeth Fry Conference on violence against women (Sallot 2001). Professor Thobani was described as having "purple rhetoric" (Valpy 2001), as more extreme than Bush (Murphy 2001), and as an immigrant who is callous and doesn't know any better (Wente 2001). Even the *Globe's* editorial (2001) condemned Thobani, as did the premier of British Columbia (Armstrong 2001) and several ministers in the House of Commons. She became the irredeemable woman of colour who could not be saved and did not deserve to be saved.

The contrasting depictions of Thobani and Ridley underscore several dimensions of the gendering narratives of news coverage. Initially, both were castigated as fallen women. In particular, Ridley's status as a single mother, an ex-spouse of an ex–PLO member, and a non-nurturant or non-caring mother pursuing her career even in zones of extreme danger marked her.

Yet, Ridley is recuperated and even celebrated. Her recuperation takes place through the deployment of feminist rhetoric. She is, as Heather Mallick remarked, "audacious, 'stroppy,' strong – and her critics hate it." Ridley's feminism, though predicated on her attempts to reach the same goals of professionalism as her male counterparts, is lauded. In contrast, Thobani remains a fallen woman – irredeemable and undeserving. Thobani's feminism comes under fire from both the media and the government, as well as from the women's groups who attempted to distance themselves from the controversy (see Laghi 2001). While Ridley was caught and survived the enemy, Thobani became the enemy within.

The media are also a site of contestation among and within themselves. Nowhere is this more apparent than in the coverage following the *Toronto Star*'s extensive report on racial profiling. The investigation, carried out by two reporters, examined a database of 480,000 police-recorded incidents and approximately 800,000 charges laid by the police (Henry and Tator 2003). In a series that ran in October 2002, the *Star* found that police were engaged in racial profiling. Not only did the police treat Blacks more harshly than Whites, but they also apprehended and held them overnight more frequently. At bail hearings, Blacks were more likely to be refused bail. In short, Blacks were more likely to be ticketed, arrested, and charged. These findings echo those reached in other studies (Henry et al. 1995; Henry, Hastings, and Freer 1996; Williams 1996; Heller 1995). Not surprisingly, the *Star*'s stories generated considerable backlash, both from the policing community and from the other big media – most notably the *National Post* (Henry and Tator 2003; Wortley and Taner 2003; Melchers 2003).[10]

Henry and Tator (2003) examined the different discourses that appeared in both of the major national dailies (the *Globe and Mail* and the *National Post*) and compared them with the counter-narratives offered by other smaller, independent media. What is most interesting is the defensive reaction of columnists in the two major dailies. These columnists trivialized the issue of racial profiling and racism in general, and deflected the charge of systemic racism by focusing on individual police officers and, in some rather far-fetched instances, charging the *Toronto Star* with racial profiling simply because it chose to investigate such a story (Henry and Tator 2003). Yet, it is not as if these views were uncontested. In fact, discourses of resistance were apparent even within the same media, albeit subordinated and relegated to the back pages. Nonetheless, as Stuart Hall argues, consent and consensus are never permanent but ever shifting. The media "[establish] the 'rules' of each domain, actively ruling in and ruling out certain realities, offering the maps and codes which mark out territories and assign problematic events and relations to explanatory contexts, helping us not simply to *know more* about 'the world' but to *make sense of it*. Here the line ... between *preferred* and *excluded* explanations and rationales, between permitted and deviant behaviours, between the 'meaningless' and the 'meaningful,' between the incorporated practices, meanings and values, and the oppositional ones, is ceaselessly drawn and redrawn, defended and negotiated: indeed, the 'site and stake' of struggle" (1979, 341).

The issue of *which* community is racialized is central to the ways in which the media select particular groups and the manner in which the latter are framed. Skin colour is most often used as a sign of race, especially in North America and western European countries. The contrasting stories of immigrants and refugees from different countries of origin reveal that those who are raced and whose appearance differs from the dominant society are more likely to be subjected to racialized reporting, as opposed to those who racially blend in with the dominant society. In an analysis of the media's coverage of immigration issues in the Vancouver and Prince George newspapers, Mahtani and Mountz (2002) found that refugees from Kosovo were treated far differently from those who had arrived via boats from China. With regard to the former, they suggest that "Canadians felt good about themselves vis-à-vis the press, the actions of government, and the contributions of citizens through that immigration event" (29). The same feelings did not carry over with the Chinese immigrants, where even the government was attacked for being "too soft."

This double standard of reporting was also evident in the 1992 refugee crisis involving two separate though equally traumatic world events – Somalia's civil war and famine, and the civil war in Bosnia. In the nightly television newscasts of both events, the oppositional binaries inherent in the narratives clearly privileged the Bosnian refugees over those from Somalia, rendering the former more acceptable and hence deserving of our sympathy than the latter. There was little interrogation in the mainstream media of why and how the Canadian government could justify its differential policies of refugee acceptance by readily accepting Bosnian refugees but restricting the number of Somali refugees. Rather, the refugees from Bosnia were portrayed as White women with children, looking reasonably healthy, ecstatic over being admitted into Canada, and expressing gratitude to Canadians for letting them in. Moreover, these women were always shown inside a building, packing clothes or performing tasks. In contrast, the Somali refugees portrayed were usually males, in large numbers, protesting outside immigration offices; they were represented as ungrateful and threatening. Somali children were shown as being emaciated, and the land was frequently shown as being a site of poverty and famine.[11] The gendered nature of the representations of these two refugee groups is instructive in terms of how the discourses of rescue and aid (Razack 1998a, 2004) come into play, and further, who is considered eligible for membership in the nation and deserving of assistance. (See Chapter 7 for a more extensive discussion of the role of gender in news coverage.)

In her revealing examination of the role of the Canadian forces as peace-keepers in Somalia, Razack (2000b, 128) argues that "Canadian atrocities in Somalia disappeared into the national mythology of 'clean snows' and in-nocent peacekeepers – noble intermediaries between the superpowers. This process relied on the construction of Somalia as the opposite of Canada, as nothing but heat and dust. Somalis (both those in Somalia and those who come to Canada as refugees) have become the embodiment of disorder and dirt." In contrast, refugees from Bosnia were not perceived in the same way. Rather, their ability to blend in – an ability predicated on their skin colour – transformed them into more deserving refugees in the eyes of the media and the larger society.

These examples illustrate the various ways in which the mainstream me-dia, through the coded language of inferential racism, deploy dominant discourses to communicate the status of racialized minorities as being out-side the pale of "civilized" Canadian society. As Wortley, Macmillan, and Hagan (1997) demonstrate in their case study of the Just Desserts case – a case involving the shooting of a White woman by three Black men, whom the media described as being Jamaicans, at a restaurant in an upscale Toronto neighbourhood in 1994 – crime coverage involving racialized groups uti-lizes deviance as a form of social control. The concentration of racialized representations in the crime sections of the newspaper, particularly of Black people, exemplifies the continued criminalization of this particular group (Wortley 2002).

In his analysis of the Toronto media, Wortley (2002) demonstrates that there is a greater concentration of stories pertaining to the Jamaican com-munity in the crime section of the newspaper, arguing that these represen-tations tend to frame members of this community as perpetrators rather than as victims of crime. When Black women are victims of violence, their stories rarely make it to the front page; they are instead confined to the back pages, subordinated by stories that give greater weight and space to crimes committed by Black people. Because the audiences of most of these newspapers are White, Wortley suggests that "crimes against racial minori-ties ... just don't have the same marketability as crimes against white, middle-class people, and thus they receive significantly less coverage" (75). These representations do not simply remain in the imaginary landscape of the media but have definitive implications. Annmarie Barnes (2002) argues that the coverage of the Just Desserts shooting fuelled the passage in 1995 of section 70(5) of the Immigration Act, which permits the deportation of any persons found to be dangerous to society regardless of their status as perma-nent residents. She notes that between July 1995 and December 1997, 40 percent of those who were deported were Jamaican nationals.

On the other hand, when racial minorities are portrayed as a lucrative source of income, there is a begrudging reluctance to grant them a modicum of positive representations. The use of the occasional model minority is a case in point, where such individuals become emblematic of Canadian liberal-democratic values, values that seemingly allow racialized minorities to rise up the ladder, thereby enabling their signification as tokens of tolerance. These representations are also suggestive of who qualifies as a bona fide Canadian. The path to legitimate status comes through clearly in the coded signifiers used to prescribe and describe the ways in which legitimacy and hence belonging to the nation can be achieved, as well as in the potential and actual costs involved in deviating from this path. The example of Ben Johnson, the athlete who was stripped of his gold medal at the Seoul Olympics in 1988, attests to how when the going is good – when the racialized individual performs admirably – he is embraced and his membership in the nation is confirmed, but when caught transgressing the rules of the game, that individual becomes stigmatized and disowned by the imagined community (Cantelon 1988; Jackson 1998; Levine 1988).

"Fictions of Assimilation"
In the preceding sections, I outlined the ways in which the media exert a form of social control, by portraying racialized groups in ways that Other them through exoticization, inferiorization, and criminalization. At the same time, the examples I draw from indicate a similar structure of duality and ambivalence as inherent in colonial stereotypes – that the negative side of portrayals tends to be counterbalanced by a "positive" dimension that coheres around the assimilated, bleached racialized minority who is also a success story in terms of transcending structural barriers (the tokens of tolerance that I allude to above). Yet, negative portrayals, I argue, far outweigh the positive ones, both in sheer numbers and in the psychological, emotive weight they carry. Positive portrayals work strategically to deactivate the transgressive element of difference, thereby containing its immanent threat and facilitating its commodification as an exotic element that can be easily consumed (Beltrane 2002; Lalvani 1995). Nonetheless, in presenting these two sides (and there are many sides, of which only two tend to be chosen), the media fulfill their mandate of "balance" and effectively communicate an image of impartiality and objectivity. In so doing, they retain the power to define positive and negative representations and, more importantly, to keep intact the basis from which such judgments are made. Thus, Whiteness is quietly reconstituted as normal.

In maintaining the mythical balance between negative and positive representations, the media's coverage, both in the realm of fictional programming and news and current affairs, underscores the message of assimilation. This message bears material consequence when viewed in the context of socialization and identity development. As I have described in the previous chapter, such consequences stem from the "fictions of assimilation" (de

Jesús 1998) wherein dominant media messages influence the ways in which those of another culture seek to emulate supposed North American ideals and values. Citing the work of Dinah Eng, de Jesús notes: "Her remembrances illustrate how the Nancy Drew text functions as a site of colonization: how 'absence' (not seeing her own image), coupled with the pervasive White hegemony of American culture in general, leads to psychological conflict and self-obliteration" (240). This view has also been echoed by hooks (1992, 1994), Collins (2000), and other feminists of colour (such as Durham 2001), who suggest that the effects of media stereotypes are not linear or direct but involve complex nuances determined by social location, identity, and ways of seeing. Notwithstanding the negotiated and resistive readings that audiences may exercise in their reading of media messages (S. Hall 1980b), the dominance communicated by the mass media in their preference for the hegemonic ideal types of femininity, masculinity, racial identity, heterosexuality, and ability clearly play a role in reproducing society's hierarchies of power. As van Zoonen (1994, 39) confirms, "The power to define is intricately linked to other power relations in society, such as economic, ethnic, gender and international relations."

Conclusion: Strategies for Change

The violence of race in these representations lies in the media's ability to define racialized groups in ways that are pejorative, dismissive, and that work to Other them through inferiorization. As Fanon (1965, 18) argues, "Every colonized people – in other words, every people in whose soul an inferiority complex has been created by the death and burial of its local cultural originality – finds itself face to face with the language of the civilizing nation; that is, with the culture of the mother country." It is this inferiorization and, by corollary, internalization of the violence of the dominant culture that is in itself the most brutal and disempowering violation that can be experienced by a people. In that sense, we come "face to face with the culture of the mother country" (Fanon 1965, 18) – the culture of colonialism and, hence, White dominance. And, in internalizing the hierarchy, racialized minorities themselves work to reproduce the dominant system by distancing themselves from Others who are viewed either as "fresh off the boat" (FOB), as whitewashed, or as the unproblematic "middle" (Pyke and Dang 2003; see Chapter 5, this volume). This is the assimilated Other who still retains the colourful cultural heritage (mostly practised in private) but whose cuisine, fashions, and ornamental attributes can be utilized for consumption in the public domain and who, conversely, can act as a representation of all that can go wrong should one choose to transgress social norms.

The stigmatization, exclusion, and overall lack of a sense of belonging that result from these strategies of containment contribute to a vulnerability to fictions of assimilation and, more obviously, to a continued marginalized existence where one is constantly attempting to fit in. This process is rendered all the more difficult by the surveillance of racialized groups – as threats to the economic, social, and cultural order. Framed within the gaze of the White eye, to use Stuart Hall's term, the behaviour and comportment of racialized minority groups come under increasing scrutiny. Any transgressions are seen as reflective of an entire community. This is the "burden of representation" (Mercer, cited in Cottle 2000, 106) that racialized people of colour carry. Thus, the liability of individual acts is quickly transferred to entire communities, which are then stereotyped and criminalized (see also Fleras and Kunz 2001; Henry and Tator 2002). Given that the media are closely allied with other dominant institutions, and are also closely followed by the latter, the policy implications of this surveillance in terms of racial profiling are already noticeable in this post-9/11 era. These implications suggest that racialized groups will be increasingly marginalized and subject to legislative violations, reinforcing the reign of terror that the media have so skilfully reproduced and amplified in their role as sentinel of danger.

The media's role in the production and reproduction of race and racism is highly problematic because it advances a definition of racism that neutralizes its charge. In this forum, racism is presented as an emotional phenomenon that can be rectified with the proper amount of education, increased exposure to racial Others, and perhaps even therapy. Racism is thus psychologized as a pathological orientation. Second, racism is presented within the framework of individual expression and permitted under the guise of freedom of speech. As the example of CHOI radio station in Quebec City aptly demonstrates, racism and anti-racism become equivalent opposing phenomena, thereby neutralizing the charge of the former and deactivating or draining the oppositional power of the latter. Third, racism is often represented as a naturalized outcome of too much diversity (see Fleras and Kunz 2001; Mahtani and Mountz 2002). Here, racialized groups themselves are blamed for increasing the racism against them. This blame-the-victim approach simply serves to naturalize the inequities of power and privilege by positioning "Canadians" as those whose tolerance has been stretched to the limits and who are naturally reacting against this imposition (Henry and Tator 2002; Jiwani 1993). The discourse of denial renders as common sense the racist presuppositions underpinning mediated constructions of race and racism, enabling media organizations to deny any responsibility for perpetuating subtle and overt forms of racism (as evident in the Thobani case). What is more, these definitions normalize racism in society and, as with other structures of domination, trivialize and erase the violence of racism in terms of its power to delimit and influence the everyday lives of racialized peoples.

In the chapters that follow, I detail two sensational cases that hit the newsstands locally, nationally, and internationally. I pay particular attention to other discourses of denial – namely, the erasure of race, and the culturalization of racism, both strategic discursive moves undertaken to limit an understanding of the nature and extent of race and racism as forms of violence. But before turning to these cases, I propose proactive measures that may limit the violating nature of contemporary media representations. These measures are based on Stuart Hall's notion that a starting point for popularizing anti-racism and shifting the common-sense stock of knowledge so that it is more inclusive of the subjugated knowledge of racialized groups lies in breaking the chain of associations (or signification) that are activated every time a representation is evoked.

The very act of decoding these discourses of racial violence contributes to a mapping of the values, norms, and practices around which these discourses are organized. In so doing, possible sites of intervention can be explored, whether these afford momentary or enduring changes. On an individual level, media monitoring raises consciousness. However, a more effective strategy is likely if the monitoring is carried on by an organized group that can follow up with advocacy. A national Canadian media monitoring organization whose research focuses on racialized audiences, their representations, and reception of mainstream media messages could do just that – both by providing necessary research and by making policy recommendations for public and private media organizations.

In the more immediate reality, some measure of change can be implemented by introducing other ways of telling the story. To narrate news stories in different ways may succeed in breaking the chain of meanings that are usually activated. Legitimizing different forms of narration involves institutional commitment. It also involves the transformation of the very practices and organization of media institutions. However, this can be accomplished only in conjunction with the educational organizations that transmit journalistic know-how and that socialize reporters in performing their work within traditional paradigms (Shoemaker and Reese 1996). A final and more fruitful approach lies in supporting radical alternative media that work to centre subjugated knowledges. This is where the success of alternative media becomes an urgent matter, as it broadens the field of contestation.

While these strategies and tactics are more suited to a continuing and prolonged effort, short-term interventions include utilizing official channels or institutional bodies such as the CRTC, the Canadian Association of Broadcasters (CAB), press councils, and other agencies mandated, either by industry or government, to intervene. Although the efficacy of these official channels is highly debatable,[12] they do permit a small opening that can be utilized by groups working in coalitions. That said, these regulatory agencies support and uphold the principles of objectivity, balance, and impartiality in media organizations. As I have shown in this chapter, these principles are highly problematic. To present a racist view and then counterpoint it with an anti-racist view fulfills the criterion of balance but presupposes that the two sides are culturally, socially, and politically equivalent. If racism is recognized as a form of violence, then simply pitting a violent and a non-violent perspective side by side does not balance out the situation. Similarly, impartiality and objectivity are untenable given that stories are written from a particular viewpoint and influenced by media ownership (Hackett et al. 2000; Winter 2002), as well as constrained by routine practices.

Another immediate strategy involves utilizing a mail-back campaign. In 1984, Carol Tator and the Urban Alliance of Race Relations worked with other advocacy groups in Toronto to initiate such a campaign. They sent back all flyers they received from the major department stores on the grounds that they did not represent the communities that formed their clientele (Tator 1984). Within a few months, the stores responded by using models from different ethno-racial backgrounds. Following the Urban Alliance of Race Relations's lead, one can participate in a massive mail-back campaign but, again, this requires a broad-based effort on the part of multiple organizations working together. Time commitments as well as divergent interests and priorities, not to mention different socioeconomic backgrounds, make such coalition work difficult. Moreover, a mail-back campaign against advertisers raises the issue of whether such a strategy would simply fuel an increased commodification of difference – so that difference is made more palatable for consumption – or actually result in social change.

Boycotting is another powerful strategy that can be implemented to effect change. As profit-oriented enterprises, the media are concerned about consumer preferences and dislikes. However, this approach too requires working in solidarity with broad-based coalitions. But even within this context, divergent interests and interpretations pose significant barriers. How a person perceives and understands particular media messages is contingent on her/his social location and identity, which includes race, class, gender, sexual orientation, and ability. Minority communities that regard a particular message as injurious may not be able to find others who interpret the message in the same way. This is an especially significant obstacle when the populist culture is itself infused with racist attitudes and norms – as evident in the CHOI case.

Higher levels of employment of committed anti-racist people of colour within media organizations can be an effective vehicle for ensuring the inclusion of alternative voices and ways of seeing. Nonetheless, such a strategy cannot work in isolation but must be implemented in combination with actions designed to change the internal structure and practices of media organizations (Cottle 2000).

While these strategies are useful and require commitment, the first step in any process of change begins with an investigation of the current situation and a mapping of the terrain in order to identify the ways in which the violence of race is obscured, deflected, and erased by discourses of denial. In the following chapters, I pursue this task by focusing on two sensational media cases involving race, gender, and violence.

Part 2
Sensationalized Cases

3
Erasing Race:
The Story of Reena Virk

It's another ideological position which allows you to see what the
particular structure of one narrative is and essentially what are its
limits ... that process begins by always identifying what I would
call the silences in a particular narrative form. It is not what an
ideology says, which is what we usually think; it's in the things
that ideology always takes for granted, and the things it can't say –
the things it systematically blips out on. That represents exactly
the point of its selectivity, and that's how (if you take another
ideological position) you see where the absences and silences are,
and you can begin to interrogate the seamless web of that particular
story from the viewpoint of another story as it were.

– Stuart Hall, "The Narrative Construction of Reality"

As Hall points out, in taking another ideological position, one can discern
the absences and silences embedded in a dominant narrative. The following analysis is based on an alternative ideological position – that grounded
in the subjugated knowledges of racialized women. In the previous chapter,
I highlight the connections between racialized representations of people of
colour and their criminalization. I argue that mediated racism works by
commission and omission, the latter being communicated through inferential racism. In this chapter, I attend to the silences – the erasure of race
and racism as explanatory vehicles by which to provide an alternative understanding of a story, an understanding grounded in a critical anti-racist and
feminist perspective. Through an analysis of the murder of Reena Virk, a
young woman of colour, I demonstrate the ways in which media accounts
privileged a particular anti-feminist interpretation, which in turn erased both
racism and sexism as fundamental discourses underpinning the murder.
In recovering the elements of sexism and racism, I draw on observations

recorded during the second trial of one of the co-accused, Kelly Ellard, and conclude with an account of a collective media intervention that was initiated with the intent of changing the framing of the murder. This case analysis, then, includes insights derived from a media analysis, observations of a court watch, and a media intervention strategy.

Sexist Violence and Gendered Racism

Kimberle Crenshaw (1994, 97) notes, "Race and gender are two of the primary sites for the particular distribution of social resources that end up with observable class differences." An analysis of how racism interlocks with other systems of domination to shape the realities of racialized girls and young women requires acknowledging racism as a form of violence that is endemic and pervasive. Nevertheless, while it has become increasingly common to accept the structured inequality produced and reproduced by sexism, the same does not hold true for racism (Richie 1996). Thus, because racism is not accepted as a structure of domination, similar to sexism, and as arising from a legacy of colonialism, its reality has to be continually proven (Bannerji 1987, 1993). From an intersecting and interlocking framework, the issues that bear examination are factors that contribute to a privileging of a gendered interpretation and representation as opposed to privileging a race-based interpretation (Staunæs 2003). In other words, which aspect of identity is forefronted in the mediated discourses of representation? In the case I analyze below, the interlocking nature of racism and sexism becomes apparent. In other words, how sexism makes racism possible, and how both are evacuated in explanatory frameworks advanced in the interests of White dominance and patriarchal powers, is revealed. However, before I turn to the case of Reena Virk, I need to address the context in which violence against girls and young women of colour becomes possible and so draw upon the highlights of my discussion of this topic in Chapter 1.

Racialized Girls and Vulnerabilities to Violence

The UN-based Working Groups on Girls (WGG) notes in its report that immigrant and refugee girls experience higher rates of violence because they experience sexism from within their own communities and also experience sexism and racism from the dominant society. In addition, vulnerability to violence, it argues, results from the impact of their dislocation from their countries of origin, and the exclusion they encounter from those in their adopted society (Friedman and Cook 1995). The patriarchal values encoded in the dominant society intersect with the patriarchal values structured in their own communities. The alliance between these "scattered hegemonies" as Grewal (Grewal and Kaplan 1994) defines them, contributes to the violence of racism and sexism. As I note in Chapter 1, through the discursive regulation of their bodies, via strictures on morality and mobility, racialized girls and young women walk a tightrope negotiating and navigating between the often competing demands of their own communities and those imposed by the dominant society (see Handa 1997).

For racialized girls and young women from immigrant and refugee communities – whether these are recent or more established – "the fictions of assimilation" (de Jesús 1998), as I have described in previous chapters, play a powerful role in communicating to them their place in the social order and the actions that they need to engage in so as to fit in and gain acceptance. The degree and intensity of rejection and exclusion mediated by the mainstream society results in girls and young women seeking to conform and assimilate so as to gain at least some kind of conditional acceptance. However, the internalization of the dominant culture often leads to feelings of inferiority, negation, and self-hatred as well as a distancing from one's community. I do not mean to suggest that these girls and young women are passive recipients of the dominant ideology. Rather, my intent here is to emphasize the ways in which dominant structures of power constrain and contain them.

In an insightful study, Pyke and Johnson interviewed one hundred daughters of Korean and Vietnamese immigrants in the United States and found that

> respondents draw on racial images and assumptions in their narrative construction of Asian cultures as innately oppressive of women and fully resistant to change against which the white-dominated mainstream is framed as a paradigm of gender equality. This serves a proassimilation function by suggesting that Asian American women will find gender equality in exchange for rejecting their ethnicity and adopting white standards of gender. The construction of a hegemonic femininity not only (re)creates a hierarchy that privileges white women over Asian American women but also makes Asian American women available for white men. In this way, hegemonic femininity serves as a handmaiden to hegemonic masculinity. (2003, 51)

Pyke and Johnson's work suggests that hegemonic images of femininity exert a performative force and, when internalized over time, can result in a rejection of one's cultural community. As they suggest, the power of hegemonic femininity lies in the subordination and devaluation of racialized immigrant communities and their stereotypical portrayal as being ultrapatriarchal while negating and invisibilizing the patriarchal forces within the dominant society. Pyke and Johnson's work further suggests that the common-sense explanations of these young women and girls as being caught in a cultural or intergenerational conflict are too simplistic and ideologically grounded in a particular view of racialized communities. In other words, the very notion of these conflicts as explanations needs to be unpacked and examined more critically (a subject I address in more detail in Chapter 5).

The murder of Reena Virk, a young woman of colour, thus needs to be located within this context; a context governed by structural forms of violence and dominance as in the power of Whiteness, the coercive pressures of assimilation, and the rejection from and marginalization by dominant others.

The Murder of Reena Virk

On 14 November 1997, fourteen-year-old Reena Virk, a girl of South Asian origin, was brutally murdered in a suburb of Victoria, British Columbia. Reena was first beaten by a group of seven girls and one boy, all aged between fourteen and sixteen. She was accused of stealing one of the girls' boyfriends and spreading rumours. Her beating was framed as retaliation against these alleged actions. According to journalistic accounts, the attack began when one of the girls stubbed out a cigarette on her forehead. As Reena tried to flee, the group swarmed her, kicked her in the head and body numerous times, attempted to set her hair on fire, and brutalized her to the point where she was severely injured and bruised. During the beating, Reena reportedly cried out, "I'm sorry" (N. Hall 1999c).[1]

Battered, Reena staggered across a bridge, trying to flee her abusers, but was followed by two of them – Warren Glowatski and Kelly Ellard. The two then continued to beat her, smashing her head against a tree and kicking her to the point where she became unconscious. They then allegedly dragged her body into the water and forcibly drowned her. Reena's body was found eight days later, on 22 November 1997, with very little clothing on it. The pathologist who conducted the autopsy noted that Virk had been kicked eighteen times in the head and her internal injuries were so severe that tissue was crushed between the abdomen and backbone. She also noted that the injuries were similar to those that would result from a car being driven over a body. The pathologist concluded that Reena would probably have died even if she had not been drowned.[2]

Back in 1997, this chilling murder of a fourteen-year-old girl sparked a moral panic across the nation. Heavily reported in the local, national, and international press, the media's initial framing of the murder focused largely on girl-on-girl violence. Issues such as racism, sexism, the pressure to assimilate, and the social construction of Reena Virk as an outcast were rarely addressed. On the odd occasion when they were addressed, it was always in the language of appearance – that she weighed two hundred pounds, that she was five feet eight inches tall, that she was plain. According to media accounts, her heaviness, height, and plain looks precluded her from being accepted. The assumption regarding the validity of normative standards of beauty and appearance was significantly absent in all accounts. Rather, as with dominant frameworks of meaning that are utilized to cover stories of racialized immigrant and refugee communities, Reena's difference was underscored and inferiorized. Because she was a young woman of colour, her race and gender contributed to her lack of fit in her peer group's normative culture, and this in turn led to her marginality and vulnerability to violence. However, the issue of just what she needed to fit *into* was never explored, nor were the assumptions underlying normative standards of beauty and behaviour for teenage girls interrogated. Thus, neither the racism nor the sexism of normative standards was explored.

In the following sections, I examine how the media and the judicial system effectively evacuated race from their framing and discussion of the event, thereby privileging a particular interpretation of the crime as one involving physical girl-on-girl gang violence. This omission on the part of the media (in their reporting of the murder) and the court (in its trial of Kelly Ellard) is symbolic of a discourse of denial – for in covering up race and racism, its immediate and long-term implications were never explicated nor critically examined. The reality of racism as a form of violence communicated by processes of Othering, inferiorization, exclusion, and the framing of difference as deviance was erased.

Media Frames

In the previous chapter, I outline the ways in which Canadian mainstream media communicate notions of race and forward particular definitions of race and racism. These definitions explain racism as arising from ignorance, increased immigration, and economic downturns. Such explanations are privileged through various discursive means so that they appear to be meaningful and resonate with everyday social reality. Racists are then defined as ignorant, uneducated, and usually rural-based individuals who at times are organized into hate groups. At the same time, race is represented by allusions to cultural differences and phenotypic differences where these can be readily observed – that is, through film footage and pictures – and through binary oppositions, which underscore these differences within the footage itself or that are embedded in the narrative. In the press coverage that followed, Reena's photograph was constantly shown – often juxtaposed with that of Kelly Ellard, the co-accused. These photographs highlighted the racial differences between the victim and the accused. In portraits of the Virk family, they were often shown dressed in traditional Indian clothes, emphasizing their cultural difference. However, instead of identifying the murder as determined by the violence of race and racism, the media told a different story – one that erased the sexist and racist structures of violence that shape and influence the lives of racialized girls and young women.

As the events leading to Reena Virk's murder unfolded in the daily papers and television newscasts, the horror of what "girls do to other girls" was highlighted and quickly became the dominant frame through which the murder was explained. As such, the murder was encapsulated in terms of horizontal or relational violence (girl-on-girl violence). Reena's death was thus held up as a symbol of how girls are not immune to committing acts of violence. Story after story in the daily papers covered the issue of teen girl violence, quoting research to support the main contention that girls are just as dangerous as boys. Even though existing research clearly links the issue of teen girl violence to the *internalization* of a dominant, patriarchal culture that values sex and power (Artz 1998; Joe and Chesney-Lind 1995; Winter 2002), this connection was trivialized if not sidestepped altogether. Additionally, counter evidence which demonstrates that only 3.83 percent of violent crimes are committed by girls (Schramm 1998) failed to hit the headlines in the same manner or intensity. Nor were issues of context elaborated in the papers, as for example, the statistical increase in the number of girls being incarcerated for minor infractions (see Reitsma-Street 1999).

Headlines from the *Vancouver Sun* during this early period (November and December 1997) framed the story in this way: "Teenage girls and violence: The BC reality" (Jimenez 1997b); "Teenage girls: Facing a world where violence is always just around the corner," qualified by a second lead, "Girls' fighting marked by insults, rumours, gangs" (Jimenez 1997a); "Bullies: Dealing with threats in a child's life" (Gram 1997); "Girls killing girls a sign of angry, empty lives" (Steffenhagen 1997). The implication of this last headline seemed to be that if girls were still following normative gender roles, their lives might not be so angry and empty.

Indeed, throughout the coverage, the *Vancouver Sun* puzzled over how increasing violence among teenage girls could be happening at a time when both girls and boys were supposedly enjoying greater freedoms, access, and success. Statistics indicating the growing number of girls graduating from high school with honours, as compared with boys, were used to demonstrate this perplexing contradiction. Implicit throughout was the sense that girls had no *right* to be violent because of the privileges they were now enjoying. Further, it was advanced that girls, perhaps, were not used to the demands inherent in these privileges, rendering them unable to "cope" with their new status – a proposition that disturbingly echoed late nineteenth-century thinking and telling of feminist backlash politics (Faludi 1992). The media reported neither on the kinds of violence to which girls are generally subjected, nor on the differential impact of violence on girls and boys from different backgrounds. In fact, this kind of coverage surfaced only with the Columbine High School murders in Littleton, Colorado, and the subsequent copycat murder in Taber, Alberta.

Frames, as Gitlin (1980, 7) elaborates, are "persistent patterns of cognition, interpretation, and presentation, of selection, emphasis, and exclusion, by which symbol-handlers routinely organise discourse, whether verbal or visual." Thus, the frame organizing this story privileged an interpretation that focused on the supposedly increasing violent tendencies of girls. This frame served several strategic functions. First, it flattened all differences between girls and young women. Thus, Reena became the "same as" any other girl. Second, through the deployment of this frame, the hierarchy of race was successfully evacuated. That Reena was a Brown girl who was allegedly murdered by a White girl was an issue that was absented from the frame. In other words, what permitted a White girl to murder a Brown girl and feel that she could do so with impunity was a matter never explored in these mediated accounts. Third, the framing precluded any attention or discussion of the inherent violence of sexism that girls and young women encounter in their daily lives. Factors that contributed to the murder – the story about Reena allegedly stealing a girlfriend's address book and calling the latter's boyfriend – did not strike the media as an example of how the very act of having and keeping a boyfriend is reflective of patriarchal power, a power that is internalized given that it is seen as accruing status to those girls who have boyfriends as opposed to any of the other girls.[3] Acquiring social status as a result of demonstrating adherence to heterosexual norms and standards speaks volumes about the power of patriarchal structures and the violence of sexism in society. Yet, this was simply taken for granted, reflecting the dominance of heteronormativity.[4]

In the immediate aftermath of the event, a secondary focus became schoolyard bullying, with a sprinkling of stories about misfit children thrown in for good measure. Aside from a few opinion pieces written by individuals from the public at large (mostly of South Asian origin), none of the news articles discussed the issue of racialization as it impacts on girls who are physically different by virtue of their skin colour, or the pressures of assimilation that racialized girls experience in attempting to fit within their peer group's culture.

Subsequent coverage of the court appearances and sentencing of the six girls who were charged in connection with the murder focused on Reena's inability to find acceptance in her peer culture and, once again, emphasized her weight and height as the major factors contributing to her exclusion. In spite of her physical difference as a racialized girl, only one article mentioned racism as a possible motive for her murder. In other words, and by implication, the overwhelming message was that had she fit the normative standards of teenage girlhood, she would have been accepted. According to dominant social norms, "normal" means a body that is thin, White (or exotic and beautiful), middle class, able, heterosexual, and conforms to accepted notions of female teenage behaviour.[5] Here again, standards of normativity concerning beauty and appearance were never interrogated, the implication being that if one does not fit these normative standards, then it really is an individual problem, one which can presumably be rectified with the right amount of cosmetic surgery and dieting. Such an explanation also evacuates the significance of race, as it suggests that the raced body can be converted, through these external measures, into one that is reasonably exotic and thus acceptable and accepted.

A brief interlude in the construction of the story occurred with the revelation that Reena had allegedly been sexually abused by a close family member. This underlined once again her lack of fit – both within her familial culture and within the culture of her peers. It also implied that the family was to blame for Reena's marginalization and abuse. Allegations concerning the abuse were immediately denied in the media's detailed coverage of the eulogy delivered by an elder of the Jehovah's Witness Kingdom Hall at her funeral. The denial was underscored by her mother's comments to reporters suggesting that Reena had been a troubled child. Journalistic accounts that stressed her inability to conform to her family's values, including the strict beliefs of the Jehovah's Witnesses, reinforced her mother's statements and helped locate the issue as one of intergenerational conflict, youth rebellion, and cultural conflict (Beatty and Pemberton 1997). Though the allegations were reported again in a subsequent article that focused on a friend's disclosure of Reena's sexual abuse by a family member, they were not contextualized in terms of existing statistics on child sexual abuse and the links between violence in the home and running away from home (Kinnon and Hanvey 1996), or to the particular pressures on girls of colour not to report such abuse (Tyagi 1999).[6] What I wish to emphasize here is that despite there being commonalities – and there are commonalities in the exercise of gendered violence – these were not explored. Thus, child abuse is a prevalent issue, but this was something not addressed in the coverage dealing with Reena. Instead of attending to these commonalities, the media's framing *privileged* only one common basis of identity – that these were all girls.

Not only was Reena's racialized identity erased, but there was a significant lack of attention paid to the *possibility* that her death was racially motivated. The significant absence of any discussion or investigation of racism as a motive reflects the minimization of the violence of racism, and the extent to which it is taken for granted in our society (S. Hall 1990a; Essed 1990). Almost two years later, at the trial of one of the alleged murderers, Warren Glowatski, the issue of racism was brought up by one witness – Glowatski's former girlfriend, Syreeta Hartley. Syreeta Hartley's testimony might well have been explicit in highlighting the racial motivations of the murder, but its import was minimized both by the judge presiding over the trial and the media. In fact, Glowatski had, on the night of the murder, boasted to his friends that he had killed an Aboriginal man. Weeks later, he told his girlfriend that he had killed an "East Indian" girl whom he had never spoken to, in order to get back at other "East Indians" who had beaten him up. Despite the girlfriend's admission of this in the courtroom, her evidence of the racial motivation behind the killing was not considered by Justice Macaulay in his reasons for judgment.[7]

At no time did the local or national media make much of the fact that Warren Glowatski had once bragged about picking a fight with an Aboriginal man, nor delve into why he would select the latter as the target for his aggression. In fact, the lack of interrogation of this matter and its taken-for-grantedness suggest that it is fairly easy to beat up an Aboriginal man and get away with it (see Razack 2002). The transcript of the decision in *R. v. Glowatski* records the following conversation between Hartley and Glowatski, shortly after Reena's murder: "I [Hartley] was bugging him [Glowatski] and he said he had a hairy ass and he was just like, You think I have a hairy butt, and he's like that other, that Reena had a hairy butt too and I was like, that's great how would you know, did you pull her pants down. And he's just like, he said no but when she got dragged into the water, her pants came off" (paragraph 75).[8]

This notion of excessive hairiness is a significant racialized trope evoking a chain of connotations of animalistic connections and savagery. This trope re-emerged in the trial of Kelly Ellard. What is more significant is that neither this observation nor those dealing with the cigarette burn and the earlier victimization of an Aboriginal man were pieced together to narrate a story of racism, either by the media or by Justice Macaulay. I raise this issue because it is common for the media to report on sentencing decisions and to quote extracts from these decisions. That this was not consistently done in the reportage of this case or the Ellard trial underscores the ways in which race and racism are erased.

An interesting aspect of this coverage is that it did not activate the usual frames of racialized minorities as deviants. In part, this may have to do with the victim status of Reena Virk: in other words, her portrayal as a helpless girl simply trying to fit in made the coverage appear to be more tolerant and benevolent. However, it is equally apparent that the girl-on-girl frame was privileged above that of the victimized girl or the issue of race. In other words, the media selectively chose to tell the story in a way that resonated with populist and hegemonic concerns, that girls were receiving better treatment, education, and other social advantages than boys and, hence, the resulting and natural outcome was an equivalence in aggression and violence. This backlash discourse became the underlying paradigmatic frame within which information was organized and communicated (Winter 2002).

Two years later, a *Vancouver Sun* editorial (1999) opined that the Virk case was, like other cases such as the murders at Columbine, those at the École Polytechnique (the Montreal massacre), or the Fabrikant incident at Concordia University, simply a matter of "the ostracized, the outcast or the mentally unstable" feeling alienated. The editorial goes on to argue that the "hard teen years" combined with "teenage despair, violence-saturated media and access to guns add up to a lethal combination." Editorials carry considerable weight since they are seen to reflect the views of the newspaper as a whole and not individualized opinions or perspectives (van Dijk 1987). They summarize the dominant interpretation of the issue. Focusing on alienation, mental instability, and marginality (in a psychological sense) forwards an interpretation that psychologizes racism and sexism. Locating these issues within an individualistic framework suggests that not to feel alienated and not to be an outcast is a matter of individual choice. Medications can ameliorate mental instability and good social skills can ameliorate ostracization. In effect, such a position brackets structures of dominance – it neutralizes the violence of racism and sexism, and it absents any recognition of the power of White and patriarchal powers.

In all, Reena was erased, as were her experiences of racism. Wortley (2002) notes that victims of colour rarely receive much attention and, in this case, the life of Reena Virk was scarcely mentioned, aside from the constant messages about her lack of "fit." The following extracts from the coverage three years after the event reflect the continuity of the initial frames and demonstrate that while race is intimated, it is never fully explored:

> It's known Virk was an outsider with low self-esteem. She was big for her age – 5 feet, 5 inches tall, more than 150 pounds – which made it tough to be accepted, as did her facial and body hair and the brown skin of her South Asian heritage. She sometimes came home from school crying. (Girard 2000)

> She battled the Virk family's ethnic values and strict Jehovah's Witness faith, but appeared to be at a turning point, her mother said. (Meissner 1999)

> Reena Virk died because she was an outcast, a girl who suffered taunts and indignities from schoolyard bullies from an early age. Had Reena been White, petite and assertive, her fate might have been much different. But Reena was tormented by the ultimate curse of youth. Gentle and sensitive, she had the misfortune to be unattractive ... Tall, heavy, dark-skinned and plagued by facial hair from the time she entered adolescence at age 12, Reena was an easy target. (Horwood 2000)

> [Reena was] awkward in her own body and uncertain of her personality as she tried to make the difficult transition from child to young adult. She was picked on at school and sometimes came home crying. She told a Victoria social worker in 1996 that she had been sexually abused. At one time, she accused an unnamed relative in India; then she said it was her father; then she recanted the charge. Virk moved out of her parents' home and went into the care of foster parents. She had freedom. And she chose a rough and troubled group of children for friends, many of whom were in foster care, too. She started shooting heroin and began to fantasize, as many of the teens in her group did, about L.A. gang life ... Reena Virk's brutal death

flowed from a youth subculture that idolized gang life and sought to com-
pensate for a lack of self esteem through extreme violence. (Hume 2000)

References to descriptors such as brown skin, facial hair, South Asian heritage, ethnic values, and gangs are all racialized in this context and implicitly and explicitly contrasted to White skin, petite stature, and assertiveness.
Not fitting in translates into a lack of self-esteem but, once again, there is a
lack of interrogation as to what one fits into, let alone why the pressure to
fit in should exact such a great price. Nor is there any acknowledgment of
racism. Rather, the latter is collapsed under the rubric of bullying and problem teens. The blame is put on parents for not socializing their children,
and on education as the panacea for recuperating alienated teenagers. The
Vancouver Sun captured this sentiment in its editorial entitled, "Lessons to
be learned from the Reena Virk case," reasoning that "to prevent future
Reena Virks and Kelly Ellards, parents and the wider community must educate teens about the minimum standards of social behaviour" (*Vancouver
Sun* 2000). The editorial dichotomized the worlds of teens as constitutive of
acceptable and unacceptable behaviour, locating the latter in a "zone of
degeneracy" (Razack 2002). Drawing on the spatial metaphor, Razack (2002,
155) observes that "bodies in degenerate spaces lose their entitlement to
personhood through a complex process in which the violence that is enacted is naturalized."

For the media to explore the issue of marginality as stemming from racism would have first involved recognition of its systemic and widespread
nature. It would also have necessitated a consciousness of the hollowness of
common-sense explanations such as those advanced under the rubric of
girl violence or individual pathology stemming from ostracization. But such
a perspective requires a positioning outside the dominant ideological frame
and a standpoint grounded in critical anti-racist feminist frameworks, a standpoint that was significantly absent in these accounts.

Privileging White Innocence: Media Coverage of the Kelly Ellard Trial

In March 2000, Kelly Marie Ellard was tried for the murder of Reena Virk.
Media speculation about Ellard's role in the murder had continued throughout the two years leading up to her trial. From the beginning of January to
21 April 2000, more than a hundred local and national radio and television
newscasts and press articles focused on the Reena Virk murder. This sustained and at times heavy coverage appeared to be motivated by the desire
to advance an explanation of the crime that made "sense." The desire to
make sense of it emanated from the same cognitive dissonance that had
occurred in the case of Karla Homolka, Paul Bernardo's partner who was
charged in the murders of several young women. Like Homolka, Ellard came
from a middle-class, White family (Faith and Jiwani 2002). Although her

parents were divorced, Ellard appeared to have a close relationship with her family – an observation that motivated one judge to overturn a ruling so as to allow her to stay at home rather than be incarcerated in a youth detention centre. Her appearance did not fit her crime. As one columnist opined, "How do you match the sweet-looking teenage girl who doesn't stand five feet in her platform shoes, who's a little heavy in the hips, who speaks tremulously on the stand, with the image of an accused killer?" (McMartin 2000).[9]

From the outset of the trial, Ellard was represented as a normal-looking teenager, "with straight black hair cut just above the shoulders," and who wore "a grey sweater and black pants" (Stonebanks 2000, A1). However, these descriptions were juxtaposed with photographs of Ellard that portrayed her with a smug expression, downcast eyes, and a hint of a smile – all images that communicated the idea that this was a person who was cognizant of more than she was willing to reveal.

A number of external factors influenced the coverage of the Ellard trial. Reporters attending the trial had followed the story from its inception two years prior. Hence, they were privy to details revealed in the testimonies presented at the earlier trial of Warren Glowatski, the co-accused, and the hearings of the other young women involved in the beating. It was not uncommon to see reporters gather outside the courtroom to verify with each other what they had heard in the courtroom and identify common themes of relevancy for their particular articles and newscasts. In addition, reporters were cautioned by a preceding incident, in which one newspaper was severely chastised by a judge for revealing details of a trial before the jury went into deliberation.

In the Ellard trial, the presiding judge, Madame Justice Nancy Morrison, had decreed that the jury would not be sequestered for the length of the trial. This meant that journalists could not report on anything other than what witnesses stated in their testimonies. Thus, the reportage was extremely factual and rarely reached the level of descriptive discourse used in the Homolka case (Faith and Jiwani 2002). Nonetheless, terms such as "chilling," "gang-murder," "savage," "cold-blooded killing" and "calculated" were liberally used to describe both Ellard and the murder. Most of these terms were borrowed directly from testimony provided by witnesses.

From the testimonies, the media constructed an image of Ellard as a cold-blooded killer who had deliberately murdered Reena Virk. She was portrayed as the most aggressive youth in the group responsible for the attack on Reena, and the leader of the assault. She was also described as having bragged about the murder to her friends. Yet, throughout the trial, Ellard's composure was reported as having vacillated between tearful and calm, depending on who was on the witness stand. However, between sessions in court, the camera often captured her laughing and joking with her family and with the defence counsel.

The defence strategy was to portray Ellard as a helpless victim of a conspiracy organized by the co-accused, Warren Glowatski. Ellard and members of her family were the key witnesses for the defence. Together, they weaved a picture of middle-class normalcy and concern. Ellard was composed on the stand. She spoke softly and denied any involvement. She identified Warren Glowatski and two other young women as having committed the murder. According to news reports, Ellard cried when asked to recount why she had delivered the first blow to Reena Virk and replied, "I guess I was being like them, victimizing her" (D. Moore 2000a). A nuanced reading of the textual reports (minus the headlines) in the coverage reveals a portrayal of both Reena Virk and Kelly Ellard as two troubled teenagers – the first because of her lack of fit, and the second because of her self-esteem issues and her companionship with the wrong crowd.

On 20 April 2000, Madame Justice Morrison sentenced Kelly Ellard, convicted of the murder of Reena Virk, to life imprisonment with parole eligibility after five years. Ellard had been convicted of second-degree murder by a jury on 31 March 2000, and the jury had made no recommendations for parole eligibility. In her sentencing decision, Justice Morrison stated: "The motive was not racism." In so doing, she highlighted the narrow interpretations of racism that informed this case. Addressing Ellard, the judge added, "You are young and intelligent and have a wonderful family. They believe in you and I can only say that you should never let them down" (D. Moore 2000b). Drawing from the thirty-one letters she received in support of Ellard's character, Justice Morrison reportedly stated in her decision, "She has a special way and always had with children and the elderly" (Papple 2000).

Morrison's portrayal of Ellard as a person who loved animals, had a positive and caring relationship with her family and friends, and posed a low risk to society in general, combined with her denial of racism in the murder suggests that the judge entertained a particular construction of racists as a categorical group. By implication, the judge seemed to be suggesting that racists do not love animals, have no positive relations with others, and pose a high risk in terms of displaying overtly criminal behaviour in society. In other words, to confine racism to just this type of person removes the onus of recognizing the systemic nature of racism. It deflects attention from the inequalities and power differentials perpetuated by racism both across and within gender lines. It ultimately frames Kelly Ellard's actions as those of a White girl from a privileged class background who *just happened* to hang out with the wrong crowd. As a result of its influence, she also *just happened* to kill Reena Virk, a fourteen-year-old girl who *just happened* to be of South Asian origin. The sheer brutality of the murder was rendered insignificant by the judge's decision. The decision also reflected the judiciary's appalling lack of understanding of race and racism, despite numerous educational initiatives directed at it.

The insistence that racism was not a factor in this case was often predicated on the fact that other girls of colour were involved in the first beating. It was quickly forgotten that both Glowatski and Ellard – the two who had been instrumental in Reena's death – are White. Similarly, Reena's mother's statements about the racism Reena had endured and her suggestion that racism was indeed a factor in her tragic death were never touched on in the courtroom. Even Warren Glowatski's alleged "beef" against South Asians because of what *they* had done to one of his friends (as mentioned by a witness during his trial) and his previous attack on an Aboriginal man were cast aside as inconsequential details when it came to Kelly Ellard's trial.

In a similar manner, the lit cigarette that had been stubbed out on Reena's forehead was never considered a sign of racism. Rather, it was passed off as an act of teenage retaliation designed to punish Reena for having violated the confidentiality of one of the girls by taking her address book and making phone calls and telling stories. However, if we are to compare this act to similar acts of brutality, injuries like this one tend to be directed to those parts of the body that are either not visible to others or visible only to the person being injured. In the case of torture, for instance, cigarette burns are usually inflicted on the victim's arms, fingers, or hands – places where the victim can see the marks. In situations of intimate violence, injuries tend to be on those parts of the body that are not immediately visible to others. All this is to say that to butt a lit cigarette out on Reena's forehead was to stamp her cultural identity as a South Asian girl indelibly – and forcibly – on her. Much like the bindi that South Asian women traditionally wear, the burn on Reena's forehead significantly marked her cultural identity – as South Asian.

Court Watch Notes

The FREDA Centre, one of five Canadian centres dedicated to researching violence against women and children, and Justice for Girls Outreach Society, a relatively new organization at the time that was providing advocacy and support to girls and young women dealing with bureaucracies within the criminal justice system, were present for the duration of the seventeen-day trial, and observed the full proceedings. Their intent was to document the ways in which issues of race, class, gender, and age played out in the courtroom and influenced the ways in which the story of Reena Virk was understood and framed in a legal context. An additional objective was to observe how the court treated young witnesses, particularly women. In all, thirty-two witnesses were called and, of the 358 exhibits collected in the course of the murder investigation, 30 were presented to the jury. Of the thirty-two witnesses who testified, four were involved in the beating of Reena

Virk. In total, testimonies of sixteen young people who were either in the vicinity or present at the beating were presented in court. Experts who identified the body and provided details of injuries and weather conditions at the time of the murder, and police officers involved in the investigation, also testified.

In observing the Kelly Ellard trial, as part of the FREDA Centre's research team, it was interesting to see that although there was no mention of the racism that Reena experienced, race was an ever-present theme in the courtroom. In describing Reena's body hair, which was immaterial to this case, the Crown mentioned how excessive body hair is common to particular racial groups. The defence frequently noted how White Kelly Ellard was, her Whiteness not only standing out starkly against Reena's darkness but also an allusion to Ellard's innocence (or purity). This was in sharp contrast to identifiers used to mark some of the other young witnesses called to the stand. Fred Thomas, the only young Aboriginal man to appear as a Crown witness, was described by the defence as "drunken FT" and by Crown counsel as "a practiced drinker" (Bhandar 2000). As Bhandar insightfully notes, "the use of this phrase, in the context of the defence strategy in general, was meant to invoke the stereotype of 'the drunken Indian.'" This young man was, upon entering the stand, immediately asked by the defence how much he had drunk that night and how it might have influenced his perception of seeing Ellard wet to her waist. A young Black woman who testified was singled out for her "bad character" and past record of criminality and was constructed by the defence to be the real murderer. Yet, she was the only young woman to have had a friendship with Reena.

Credibility, as defined by the court, seemed to be based on appearance, demeanour, criminal record, professional status, the ways in which the witnesses articulated their responses, and the certainty with which they answered the questions directed to them. Legitimacy was ascribed to those behaviours and characteristics rooted in and reflective of a middle-class background. Thus, while adults were treated as credible witnesses, young people and especially young women tended to be discredited on the stand. Their records were brought up by the defence, and although many showed remorse and some had actually reformed, for the most part these witnesses were stripped of their dignity and treated rather contemptuously by both Crown and defence counsels. In one case, participating in an anger management course was construed and framed by the defence counsel as a sign of lacking credibility. The defence counsel's explicit suggestion that many of the young witnesses were liars, combined with the rigorous interrogation these witnesses were subjected to, underscored issues about the fairness of treatment and raised the question of whether such harsh cross-examination could actually facilitate the giving of a more accurate testimony.

A poignant example of this was evident in the treatment of G.O., a young woman of colour who had turned herself in after a warrant was issued for her arrest because of her non-compliance with the subpoena requiring her presence as a witness. G.O. entered the courtroom shoeless and in youth detention garb – sweats. She was clearly distressed, rocking back and forth while answering counsel's questions. She spoke softly and often inaudibly. She broke down crying, and the judge ordered a recess until the next day to give her time to look over her police statement so that she could better answer the questions. Contrast this to the presence of Ellard's mother, Sue Plakos, or her friend Tammy Brown – the defence's witnesses. Both are White and middle class. Both were well dressed in court. Both appeared composed on the stand, speaking clearly and articulately as they answered questions directed at them.

The only instances in which young people were considered credible, in fact, were those involving the defence's three young witnesses: Kelly Ellard; J.B., a young woman whom the defence described as having turned her life around; and S.L., a young man who worked part-time at a hotel. Working at a hotel, going to college, and being well dressed – these were the signs that demonstrated credibility. Interestingly, it was only on behalf of Kelly Ellard that defence counsel pointed to the stress that a young witness experienced in giving testimony. Further, the defence reminded the jury that they were to "bear in mind that she is in grade 11 because she will be cross-examined by an experienced prosecutor who has more years of experience than she has been in school" (author's trial notes). No mention of this was made with regard to the Crown's other young witnesses. Nor were aspects of their lives brought in to contextualize their behaviour.

This pattern of demeaning and tearing apart the credibility of the Crown's young witnesses was repeated in the appearance and testimony of another young woman – C.K. The Crown had alerted defence counsel one month before the trial that C.K. knew defence counsel Adrian Brooks and had negative associations about him. The Crown requested that, rather than Brooks, defence counsel Mark Jette conduct the cross-examination. On the day C.K. was to testify, the Crown discovered that Brooks was insisting that he conduct the cross-examination. The Crown appealed to Justice Morrison, claiming that Brooks' cross-examining would jeopardize the witness's ability to provide accurate testimony. The Crown presented as witness C.K.'s aunt, her foster mother. The aunt relayed that when C.K. was about six-and-a-half years old, she had witnessed her mother shooting her father. Brooks had been involved in defending the mother, and the mother had taken C.K. with her into hiding. C.K. was subsequently found in what appeared to be a drug den, ill-clothed and underfed. She had vivid memories of this and associated Brooks with what she had experienced and witnessed. Despite this telling evidence, the judge ordered Brooks to proceed with the cross-examination on the grounds that witnesses could not dictate to the court. The defence could have conducted the cross-examination in an alternative manner – for example, by having the witness in another room and the examination conducted via video camera. This, however, did not occur.

Common-Sense Explanations

The Crown's explanation of the murder fit with the common-sense explanation: this was a group of teenagers from a suburb in a small town that was bound by a code of loyalty. That code of loyalty made Ellard and Glowatski follow Reena Virk to ensure that she didn't "rat" on the others who had beaten her up. This one-dimensional explanation was countered by another one-dimensional explanation by the defence counsel, who argued that Ellard was innocent and had been framed by Glowatski in concert with others. The defence argued that, rather than Ellard, the girl who *actually* killed Reena Virk was none other than the only friend she had in that group. The Crown never put forth the position that violence is about power and dominance, and that the hierarchical relations within the group were predicated on notions of belonging and power, which in turn influenced the vulnerability of those who did not belong and had no power. Reena did not belong – she was an outsider who was visibly different – and she had no real power. Her difference, negatively valued as it was, made her an easy target, one that could be erased without fear of repercussions.

In light of the circumstantial evidence presented in this case, the perceived lack of credibility of the young people who testified, and the judge's acquiescence to defence counsel's objections and requests, it was surprising that the jury came up with a guilty verdict. The verdict undoubtedly sent a strong message that violence of this magnitude would not be condoned. Yet, one wonders how much of this was based on a law-and-order agenda, and on sexist expectations that nice girls such as Ellard don't behave in such ways.

The murder of Reena Virk is a stark symbol and reminder of how race, class, age, and sexuality intersect and interlock to make some girls and young women more vulnerable to violence than others. It also calls attention to the dynamics of violence in which power is able to assert itself in a manner that neutralizes the charge of racism, thereby erasing recognition of its impact as violence. Race, class, and gender were aspects that Justice Morrison shared with Kelly Ellard. To that extent, she was able to relate to Ellard as another human being, almost as if Ellard had been her own daughter. Ellard, herself, never related to Reena Virk in the same way – despite the commonalities of age and gender; nor did Justice Morrison for that matter.

In delivering her reasons for sentence, Madame Justice Morrison (2000, 5-6) stated:

[Ellard] got into trouble with her schooling and she was hanging out with a peer group that can only cause one to question the word "peer." She was not showing good judgment. She was into substance abuse, marijuana and some alcohol, marijuana use on an almost alarming level. She was doing poorly in school, she was stubborn and she was blaming others ... She has a special way and always has had, we are told now, with the elderly and with children. There is a lack of racism in her makeup, and whatever the motives or impetus for this terrible crime ... It was not racism on the part of Kelly Ellard ... She has never been violent. There is no history or signs of violence before this event or after. She has always had and remains having an over-whelming love of animals, gentle and caring always with them.

Barbara Trepagnier (2001, 142) argues that the category of "'not racist' has become a default category in that anyone who does not commit blatantly racist acts or make intentionally racist statements is automatically so cat-egorized." As I have mentioned previously, this kind of reasoning demon-strates how power and dominance contribute to discourses of denial, in this case, the denial of racism and sexism. Instead, the impression one is left with is that of a poor, White, innocent girl who happened to hang out with the wrong people and who remains, ultimately, a kind and caring person.

Intervening in the Virk Case: Refocusing Violence

Kelly Ellard's trial in March 2000 coincided with the FREDA Centre's public-ity campaign to raise awareness about violence against women. The case provided a unique opportunity both to educate the public about the fallacy of the media's frame of girl-on-girl violence and to foreground the intersect-ing and interlocking influences of race, gender, and violence. As director of the centre, I also saw this as an opening whereby grassroots organizations could bring their message to the media. Given that the FREDA Centre's mandate was to forge collaborative partnerships with advocates and service providers, centre staff worked with Justice for Girls Outreach Society, which was implementing the first of its internship programs in which it employed and trained young women to conduct court watches in order to gain a criti-cal insight into how the criminal justice system operates and, in the pro-cess, identify sites of intervention (for service provision) and develop recommendations for change.

The media, as I outline in Chapter 2, favour elite sources and experts. University degrees and a position within that institution provide a basis of the kind of expertise, credibility, and legitimacy acknowledged by the me-dia. In linking up with Justice for Girls, the FREDA Centre's aim was to strategically use this position of "expert" in bringing to the fore the realities and experiences of young women themselves.

With funding from Status of Women Canada and the significant assistance and guidance of Alexandra Bordon, a student from the Communications Department at Simon Fraser University, we engaged in a media strategy.[10] Together with Justice for Girls, we developed a media release, a media fact sheet on the statistics pertaining to violence against girls, and backgrounders on both the centre and Justice for Girls. Alexandra helped us develop a Q & A – a short list of questions and answers in case we were interviewed by the media. We also outlined our key messages – the messages we wanted privileged by the media in a form that resonated with the media's proclivity for sound bites. Alexandra was instrumental in training the two coordinators and the interns working for Justice for Girls, as well as in training me in conducting media interviews. Before the court trial, she sent out a media advisory alerting the media that representatives from Justice for Girls and the FREDA Centre would be attending the trial. Thus, we would be available to comment on issues emerging from the trial.

Unfortunately, or fortunately, as the case may be, the judge presiding over the trial declared a publication ban. This meant that the media were not allowed to comment on what they heard and saw in the courtroom. In one sense, this resulted in our inability to actually provide critical comments on the case simply because we could not refer to it. At the same time, it created a news hole, because the media had to fill the gap created by their inability to report on the case per se with news that was somehow associated with the case and the issues raised by it.

We changed our strategy and decided to make the most of the situation by refocusing the issue, shifting attention from a single high-profile case to one that highlighted the confluence of age, race, and gender as intersecting and interlocking variables contributing to the susceptibilities and vulnerabilities to violence in the lives of girls and young women across the board. This allowed Justice for Girls to highlight the lack of support and services available to girls and young women criminalized by the justice system, and it allowed the FREDA Centre to shift the focus to issues of race, which thus far had been erased from the publicly mediated accounts of Reena Virk's murder.

In one sense, this intervention was a success, for, by simply being present at the court throughout the trial, we were able to make ourselves available to the media. In total, we logged seventy-four interviews with local and national print, radio, and television reporters over three months. Thus, our "contrary" views were aired side by side with the narrative on girl-on-girl violence.

From an observational stance, what was most interesting about this intervention is that, rather than the key messages or the statistical sheets we had prepared, it was the informal talks with journalists that ended up influencing their retelling of the story. This was brought home to me when, after Kelly

Ellard's mother and her mother's best friend testified in court, I commented to a journalist about how the trappings of middle-class life – Ellard's mother and her friend were in the hot tub in the garden when Ellard had returned home that night – contributed to the legitimacy and credibility of these two witnesses, in contrast to the numerous young women who were revictimized on the stand by the defence counsel, with their authenticity and reliability torn to shreds in the interrogation that followed. In the reportage of the story the next day, I saw references to these middle-class trappings in the form of descriptions of white kitchen floor tiles of the Ellard home, along with other such details. So, although that particular journalist did not attribute a quote to any one of us or reference where this insight came from, the fact that it was out there in the public forum and that it infused his retelling of the story suggests future strategies on how we might work with the media to reframe a story.

Was our intervention successful? It appeared from the coverage during the trial that our intervention was indeed successful, simply because we were quoted frequently and our presence as court observers lent the trial an aura of outside scrutiny. In other words, having outside observers at the trial increased the public accountability of the process because it made the journalists, and I am sure the jury, aware that these proceedings were not immune to criticism. Justice had to be seen to be done. Consequently, the reportage was hemmed in by this scrutiny, as well as by the publication ban. These parameters undoubtedly narrowed the frame through which the story could be told while the trial was in progress. However, once Judge Morrison had decreed her decision, the media contacted us for our comments. Simply making ourselves available as observers – considered credible and legitimate because we were affiliated with a university and conducting research – ensured some of that attention. At the same time, collaborating with community organizations worked to insert an advocacy and practical front-line service provider perspective.

In terms of a discourse analysis of the content, it is difficult to assess the extent of our success. In some cases – notably in the tabloids such as Vancouver's *Province* and in the more socially critical papers such as the *Toronto Star* – our message was clearly communicated and done so in ways that suggested it was the perspective of the paper also. In radio too we received a favourable response, and one of British Columbia's lead talk shows invited us twice. In both cases, the host was supportive and once cut short an irate caller. Yet, there was always the danger that our perspective would slip into and support a law-and-order ideology – one that condemned all girls and failed to acknowledge the hierarchical order of power (based on race, class, sexuality, and ability), even within girls' peer groups.

In undertaking this intervention, one of the key issues to emerge was the necessity of monitoring the media (see also Bray 1997). This is instrumental in highlighting the routinized ways in which the media report on violence, race, teenage girls, and murders, and provides insight into the narrative structures and frames being utilized. An intervention will work only if it is mapped onto the media's terrain in this way, for by getting a sense of the media geography of an event, the spaces where intervention is possible become more apparent. Our strategy was predicated on a media analysis of how the Virk case had been reported in 1997 immediately after Reena's body had been discovered (see Jiwani 1999). Consequently, our awareness of the prior framing of the event as a girl-on-girl violence story informed our key messages, which in turn focused on the low rates of such violence and, further, highlighted how that violence could be better understood and explained through an analysis of patriarchal and racialized structures of violence. Yet, we were cognizant of the reality that the media had delimited the terms of the debate – they defined the situation in that this was a horrific case of violence perpetrated by a group of girls. As intervenors, we had to work within the limits of that debate but try to broaden its margins to include a more complex and layered analysis.

This intervention was especially instructive in demonstrating the diverse perspectives within news organizations. Reporters and journalists are by no means a monolithic group. While some share a deep concern with the democratic process and are keenly aware of the news media's responsibilities, others are not so. Similarly, while journalists may endeavour to present the complexities of a case, the routinized and hierarchical practices within news organizations often work to impede that story being published or, alternatively, the final story may be recast by having a sensational headline affixed to it. This is where developing relationships with media organizations become critical in pushing forward a social-change-oriented agenda, albeit in a limited way.

However, the long-term implications of interventions, which are designed to rupture a chain of associations, meanings, and common-sense understandings of an event, are extremely limited. For one, interventions, like the one described above, are momentary when viewed against the larger backdrop of the continuous and cumulative stock of knowledge being produced and reproduced by the media in their telling and retelling of stories. For such change to be long-lasting, the interventions must be equally consistent and persistent in challenging dominant definitions of violence. The short span of our intervention was most clearly apparent in the coverage of Ellard's second trial.

The Second and Third Trials

On the basis of a successful appeal in which the defence argued that the Crown had not maintained a position of neutrality, that is, the assumption that a defendant is innocent until proven guilty, a second trial was convened.

On 18 July 2004, this second trial resulted in a mistrial because of the jury's inability to come to a unanimous decision. Coverage of the second trial, as with the first trial and the discovery of Reena's body in 1997, reveals a persisting continuity of the erasure of race and racism as factors contributing to her death.

In the *Globe and Mail*'s coverage of the second trial, none of the articles about the case mentioned the issue of racism. Nor did the articles provide an adequate context as to the nature of the crime. Missing in all the coverage is an indication of the racial identities of the victim or the assailants – save for those clearly communicated by photographs accompanying the text. The same explanatory framework, as advanced in the earlier coverage, was reiterated in this coverage – namely, that Reena was trying to fit in, though what she was attempting to fit into was left unstated and simply taken for granted. Quoting Reena's mother saying "She was troubled" and "She was struggling to find out where she belonged" (Armstrong 2004), the reportage resolved the matter rather neatly – as one stemming from individual teenage angst (or being at the wrong place at the wrong time).

What is also interesting about the coverage of this second trial and the Glowatski trial earlier is the darkening of Kelly Ellard and Warren Glowatski. In the *Vancouver Sun*'s coverage of the trial, the court drawings of the two accused consistently portrayed them with considerably darker complexions than they actually had. These connotations, as Wortley (2002) and James (1998) suggest, cognitively and ideologically fasten the link between race and crime.

The coverage of the mistrial significantly moved away from the issue of the murder to focus instead on the legalities and expenses of convening a third trial. Despite cautionary tales of holding a third trial, Kelly Ellard was tried yet again and convicted by a jury. The coverage of this third trial tended to focus on the media's lack of access to court documents, especially those pertaining to Ellard's "pattern" of behaviour.[11] Further, much of the coverage referenced the history of the case, in some instances providing a detailed chronology of the "thrice-tried, twice-convicted 22-year-old, who is B.C.'s most famous bad girl" (Mulgrew 2005b). The focus on Ellard's past reinvoked the spectre of teen girl violence. Citing expert opinion (from two university researchers), the coverage reiterated the increasing incidents of social aggression among girls (Joyce 2005).

When the verdict was finally read (12 April 2005), Ellard's representation was discursively sealed. Now seen as a "monster," Killer Kelly, as the media dubbed her, was demonized, much like Karla Homolka was. As one headline put it, "'Killer Kelly' lacks internalized social values, doctor says" (Fowlie with Baglole 2005); another stated, "Schoolgirl presented two faces to world" (Fowlie 2005). By June, the headlines were even more negative, based on the media's increased access to background documents and records detailing Ellard's behaviour in school and the youth detention centre, and with her peers. These headlines focused on Ellard's history and her pathology: "Teen killer had history of mischief, violence" (Ivens 2005); "An ugly picture of Kelly Ellard" (Crawford 2005); "Documents detail a violent mindset" (*Times Colonist* 2005), and so forth. Toward the end, when Crown counsel Catherine Murray was asking for the maximum sentence, the media reported her as stating that the judgment rendered in the first trial was lenient because "[Justice] Morrison was under the mistaken impression Ellard was a good kid who avoided violence before and after making a single terrible mistake" (Mulgrew 2005b). That, Murray argued, was clearly not the case and she wanted the presiding judge to consider Ellard's record of behaviour.

As is evident in these headlines, Ellard's motives were never examined from within a critical perspective. Rather, her behaviours and actions were attributed to her inherent proclivity to violence, an explanation that privileged individual psychology or pathology rather than focused on the systems of power and dominance that clearly shaped who she chose as her victim and why she felt she could get away with it. Race and racism were evacuated from all accounts, save those which referenced Reena Virk's South Asian origins. Interestingly, while Ellard was demonized, Suman Virk, Reena's mother, was consistently portrayed in a positive manner, highlighting her grace and compassion toward the Ellard family (Mulgrew 2005a). Further, the trauma she had withstood for the past eight years in waiting for closure on the case was constantly reiterated as a sign of her courage. Her portrayal was more humane, based on her role as mother of the victim and her forbearance in enduring the three trials. In fact, crime reporter Joey Thompson wrote an article in the form of a letter to Suman Virk commending her on her outstanding courage, strength, and compassion (Thompson 2005). Nevertheless, the portions of Suman Virk's interviews that were cited in the media also colluded in erasing race. While she had mentioned racism in her media interviews during the first trial, by this third trial, she does not refer to race or racism at all in her media interviews. Rather, she focuses on the impact of such crimes on the families of both the victims and the accused. Her words were repeated in several news accounts: "In my mind, there is no reason why my daughter was murdered" (Baglole and Mulgrew 2005).

Conclusion

The absence of any discussion or investigation of racism as a motive reflects not only an erasure of the violence of racism but also its taken-for-granted character as a non-problematic and unrecognizable element. As Stuart Hall (1990a) and Philomena Essed (1990) point out, everyday racism is ingrained in the daily interactions of people of colour with the dominant society – it structures common-sense reality and is thereby naturalized in insidious ways.

The media's denial of racism corresponds with and reinforces hegemonic definitions of racism as an activity confined to extreme hate groups, rather than as a system and structure of domination inherent in the very fabric of society and its institutions. Furthermore, by simply accepting the sexist and heteronormative standards by which girls and young women are valued and evaluated, the media reinforce them. However, the sexist frame that was imposed in the coverage of the Kelly Ellard trials – namely, the preoccupation with girl-on-girl violence – reflected the media's backlash against feminism. As James Winter (2002, 57) remarks, "Blaming feminism for an alleged increase in aggression and violence amongst girls is one blatant aspect of the backlash against feminism." Indeed, I would argue that it was through the privileging of a sexist frame that racism was strategically erased.

The story of Reena Virk is, then, a story about a young racialized woman and the struggles she endured, as well as a story about Kelly Ellard. While both were framed as problem teenagers, their respective positioning in this case reveals the power of patriarchal and of White structures of dominance. In the recounting of the story from an alternative standpoint, we get a glimpse into the lives of racialized girls and young women and the hierarchical structures that prefer particular races, classes, abilities, and sexualities. More importantly, we learn about the normative values required for one to gain acceptance, credibility, and legitimacy. Clearly, those who are on the margins by virtue of their race, class, gender, sexual orientation, and ability are not likely to "fit in." They are unlikely to meet normative standards, whether these cohere around the notion of an ideal typical Canadian who is always seen as White or the notion of a reasonable person defined in terms of race, class privilege, and heteronormativity.

While both racism and sexism were erased in the retelling of Reena Virk's murder, such erasures are more often than not strategic. This is especially evident when one examines the typical coverage concerning racialized women who have experienced violence. Here, the tendency is to privilege a cultural frame in which information is organized in a manner that reinscribes cultural difference and, further, positions that cultural community as the Other, outside the pale of "civilized" society. Such a cultural move is made possible by the dominant society's definitions of culture. In other words, it hinges on what gets defined as culture (Razack 1998a). Moreover, it rests on which particular cultural formations stand out against the invisible backdrop of White cultural dominance. In this regard, in the coverage pertaining to Reena Virk, a cultural frame was not utilized. I suspect that part of the reason for this stemmed from the fact that although Reena's family had immigrated to Canada, they had become Jehovah's Witnesses, and the latter group is still part of the dominant Judeo-Christian tradition. Thus, explicit cultural elements were absent – there were no visible signs of cultural practices or traditions that could be blamed for Reena's marginalization and subsequent victimization – although cultural identity was apparent in the photographs accompanying the story. But more importantly, to have utilized a cultural frame would have resulted in the subordination of the girl-on-girl violence (backlash) frame. That girl violence was privileged over a cultural frame indicates how gendered representations get used to bracket out racial representations. In the following chapter, I analyze another case in which culture became the terrain on which explanations of violence were resurrected. In effect, I outline how violence becomes culturalized.

4
Culturalizing Violence and the Vernon "Massacre"

Black and *white* in some circles are becoming definite no-nos, perpetuating what some folks see as stale and meaningless binary oppositions. Separated from a political and historical context, *ethnicity* is being reconstituted as the new frontier, accessible to all, no passes or permits necessary, where attention can now be focused on the production of a privileged, commodifiable discourse in which race becomes synonymous with culture. There would be no need, however, for any unruly radical black folks to raise critical objections to the phenomenon if all this passionate focus on race were not so neatly divorced from a recognition of racism, of the continuing domination of blacks by whites, and (to use some of those out-of-date, uncool terms) of the continued suffering and pain in black life.

– bell hooks, *Yearning, Race, Gender, and Cultural Politics*

As bell hooks points out in the quote above, the privileging of ethnicity (read culture) deflects attention away from race as a structure of domination that significantly influences the lives of racialized peoples. This emphasis on culture constitutes a denial of race and racism (F. Harrison 1995). However, as hooks emphasizes, it is a strategic denial, for, by highlighting culture, difference can be commodified and, moreover, translated into "common sense" in ways that perpetuate the dominant order – the hierarchies that sustain power and dominance. The case studies in this chapter of media representations of gender-based violence underscore the way in which cultural frames get used to reproduce a grammar of race (S. Hall 1990a) whereby relations of superiority and inferiority, and the naturalization of inequalities, are accomplished (see Chapter 2).

While in the previous chapter I deal with the erasure of race, here I discuss an example of culturalized violence. Drawing from the literature, I trace the links between cultural racism and culturalized violence. I go on to provide an analysis of the *Vancouver Sun*'s coverage of the Vernon massacre, juxtaposing this coverage with that of another incident, the attempted murder of a White woman by her ex-boyfriend. Both of these cases occurred in Vernon, British Columbia, and within approximately six months of each other. In examining these cases side by side, I emphasize the media's differential and at times sensationalized coverage of them and, more particularly, their treatment of the women victims and their male abusers. I maintain that by pathologizing racialized communities and individual abusers, the media colluded in advancing explanatory frameworks that evacuated an interpretation of gendered violence as a widespread and prevalent pattern of dominance.

Cultural Racism and the Media

While earlier dominant discourses referring to racialized groups relied on the notion that there were different races in the world, more contemporary discourses use other categories to signify race.[1] In part, the reluctance to use race as a descriptive label is based on the lack of its scientific validity. Instead, there is an increasing tendency within hegemonic institutions to signify race by using terms such as "immigrants" and "foreigners," and to refer to those who are constructed as Others in terms of their language, ethnic origin and practices, or religion. British theorists such as Paul Gilroy and Stuart Hall have referred to this as cultural racism. Gilroy (1991, 60) states that in this new form of racism, "'Race' is seen instead as a cultural issue." In cultural racism, Hall (1989b, 11) observes, "differences in culture, in ways of life, in systems of belief in ethnic identity and tradition now matter more than anything which can be traced to specifically genetic or biological forms of racism." The power coordinates that Hall (1990a) describes as underpinning the old, traditional forms of racism remain intact under the guise of culture, since the aim of the discourse is to reassert the superiority of the dominant group and the inferiority of Others. Cultural differences are naturalized such that they appear as natural tendencies and proclivities rather than as fluid and dynamic social constructions that emerge in response to a particular constellation of factors; similarly, cultural differences are heightened against the backdrop of an invisible White dominance.

If modern-day or new racism revolves around culture as the defining point to legitimize unequal relations, we need to interrogate the particular definitions of culture that are being advanced in a given context and the circumstances in which cultural explanations are proffered as the reasonable and commonsensical explanations. Sherene Razack (1998a, 60) notes that "culture becomes the framework used by White society to pre-empt both racism and sexism in a process that I refer to as culturalization." This process of culturalization entails the internalization and use of the language of culture by which to refer to identities and through which to ascribe behaviours that are seen as endemic to particular groups and collectives. Culturalization has, I would argue, resonances with the colonial notions of culture, that is, the culture of Others, which is seen as being different, quaint, barbaric, traditional, and so forth, all of which reinforced unequal relations of power. It is thus instructive to examine the contemporary contexts in which the banner of culture gets evoked to explain the behaviour of racialized Others.

In her analysis of cases involving refugee claimants who are victims of gender-based violence, Razack notes a strategic use of culture that fits within the Western gaze and reinforces it. As she describes it, "Women's claims are most likely to succeed when they present themselves as victims of dysfunctional, exceptionally patriarchal cultures and states. The successful asylum seeker must cast herself as a cultural Other, that is, as someone fleeing from a more primitive culture. That is to say, it is through various orientalist and imperialist lenses that women's gender-based persecution becomes visible in the West. Without the imperial or colonial component, claims of gender persecution are less likely to succeed and asylum is denied" (1998a, 92-93). This focus on so-called primitive and on patriarchal cultures occurs against a backdrop of dominant culture that positions itself, through contrast, as progressive and egalitarian. Hence, the West is seen as being devoid of patriarchal institutions and norms, and free of any form of gender-based violence. The Others are constructed as being backward and traditional, oppressing their women in stereotypical ways as imagined by the West. In the following sections, I detail the ways in which culture was invoked as an explanatory tool by the mainstream media in their coverage of what they described as the Vernon "massacre." I argue that the media's reporting of the Vernon massacre well illustrates this process of culturalization. The news accounts that were used for my analysis appeared in the days immediately following the event and are drawn primarily from the *Vancouver Sun*.[2]

Interrogating the Vernon "Massacre"

On 5 April 1996, Mark Chahal drove to the family home of his estranged wife, Rajwar Gakhal, in Vernon, British Columbia. On reaching the driveway, he shot her father and then proceeded into the house, where he murdered eight other family members and wounded two. Those killed included immediate members of the Gakhal family as well as Rajwar's sister, Jasbir Saran, and her husband. Jasbir Saran's mother-in-law and one child were wounded. The media labelled the event the "Vernon massacre." What marked this event from other daily acts of violence against women and children is its premeditated nature and the fact that the murderer ruthlessly shot an entire family. Two aspects of the murders in Vernon captured the media's attention: the cultural background of the victims, and the magnitude and suddenness of the event.

On the day following the murders, the *Vancouver Sun*'s headline read, "Killer had threatened family: Nine die in Canada's second-largest mass murder on the eve of a Vernon wedding, and the murderer commits suicide. Killer apologizes in suicide note" (Bocking and Bolan 1996). The front-page article went on to describe the murders in greater detail. Underscoring this description are persistent references to the family's ethnicity, religious background, and immigrant origins. For instance, the article mentions the sizeable presence of the Indo-Canadian community in the area where the murders took place and refers to the upcoming wedding of one of the family members at the local temple on a religious holiday. It also provides intricate though tangential details of the Sikh religion: "Vaisakhi marks the anniversary of the formation of the Khalsa, the five symbols of Sikhism, by Guru Gobind Singh, who was the 10th and final guru of Sikhism" (Bocking and Bolan 1996). In addition to providing details about the ethnic and religious background of the family, the article refers to the immigrant origins of the estranged wife's father and his friends, stating that "Harjinder Singh Brar headed to Karnail Gakhal's home seconds after he heard of the shooting. Brar and Gakhal had been friends for 20 years since they both immigrated from India's Punjab state to B.C.'s Interior in search of a better life" (Bocking and Bolan 1996). On the same day, another article began the story with this description: "The blood on the aggregate concrete was that of Karnail Gakhal, the head of a quiet Sikh family who lived at the home" (Balcom 1996). Two days later, in another story, the victims are described as "all members of a prominent Indo-Canadian family" (Bell et al. 1996). In the same story, the reporters bring up the issue of arranged marriages as a possible reason for the tragedy: "According to people who know the family, Chahal was abusive to his arranged bride from the day they were married; on their wedding night he allegedly called her a 'slut' and beat her." The theme of arranged marriages is reiterated in another story reported on the same day. Written by Mike Bocking (1996, B2) and entitled "Step by gruesome step, one man's killing spree," the story recounts that

> only two years ago Chahal married Rajwar in the Vernon Sikh temple. Now the entire Gakhal clan was gathering in Vernon to celebrate the marriage on Saturday of his ex-wife's younger sister, Balwinder.
>
> Chahal's arranged marriage with Rajwar began to disintegrate soon after the 1994 wedding, amid charges that he abused her.
>
> In January 1995, less than a year after her wedding, Rajwar left Chahal and returned to her parents' Vernon home. At that time, she filed a complaint against Chahal for threatening her, but declined to take any further action ...
>
> [The Gakhals] are a traditional family and are founding members of the Vernon Sikh temple. The marriages of their three oldest daughters were arranged.

Within three days of the murders, the media had proffered explanations that cohered around a culturalized interpretation of the tragedy. References to the family's immigrant background, Sikh religious tradition, and the custom of arranged marriages not only located the murders on a cultural terrain but suggested that the custom of arranged marriages, close-knit community life, and religious adherence were to some extent responsible for the ensuing violence.

This privileging of a cultural explanation subsequently became an issue of contestation. The latter occurred through accessing and reporting oppositional voices, notably those of South Asian feminists and anti-violence workers. This can be seen as the media's attempt to present a balanced perspective by including a more subjugated discourse. Thus, on the day that Mike Bocking's article appeared, a smaller piece containing an oppositional perspective was run on the same page (Griffin 1996). However, even in this story that focuses on the dangers of stereotyping, reporter Kevin Griffin states that Indo-Canadian counsellors "also say that particular cultural and family values can influence how some men carry out, and women react to, domestic violence." After interviewing Sashi Assanand and Mobina Jaffer, well-known activists in the South Asian community at the time, the reporter adds, "Ten bilingual and bicultural counsellors in Assanand's organization helped 1,180 women in 1994-95, in 18 languages ranging from Cantonese and Vietnamese to Spanish and Punjabi." Once again, the women are described in cultural terms and violence is safely relocated to the cultural terrain.[3] Positioned in this way, gendered violence becomes a matter of the innate tendencies of particular racialized groups.

In the stories that followed, the *Vancouver Sun's* filter shifted to include a focus on the RCMP's role. In particular, the issue of gun control and the issuance of two gun permits to Mark Chahal became the topics of coverage. However, even within this framing, the cultural angle of the murders was retained by referring to Rajwar Gakhal's reluctance to have the police initiate any action even though she made numerous complaints, because of how it might affect her reputation in the Sikh community. The implicit suggestion was that Rajwar was to blame for not allowing the RCMP to charge Mark Chahal. By September 1996, the dominant frame of the story had shifted to the issue of gun control and to the findings of an inquest ordered by the government (after intensive advocacy by anti-violence activists and service providers), both of which were actions directly stemming from Sharon Velisek's public disclosure about her experiences, a topic I turn to below.

The focus on culture deflects attention away from the real issues at hand: power and control, and the results of challenging male authority or patriarchy. Similarly, the focus on arranged marriages is a red herring in this situation. It fails to account for the endemic nature of violence in relationships supposedly based on love. Rajwar Gakhal challenged patriarchal authority when she left her husband and filed for divorce. Yet, rather than focusing on the bravery of this woman, existing accounts simply blamed the victim by suggesting that she was remiss in not laying charges. The fear of taking such an action is dismissed, even though existing research indicates that many women are afraid to press charges for fear of retaliation from their ex-spouses (Jiwani and Buhagiar 1997). Because of this fear, many cases either do not proceed to court or result in a stay of proceedings. And it is precisely because of this fear that the BC attorney general's office issued a mandatory charging policy in 1993. According to this policy, police have to investigate a case where there is suspicion of violence in an intimate relationship, regardless of whether the woman wishes them to do so. Further, they have to report the case to Crown counsel, who then pursues it in court. But this did not occur in either the Gakhal case or the Velisek case.

By underlining the immigrant origins of the family, the media reinforced the social distance that separates *us* from *them*. Karnail Gakhal had been in Canada for twenty years. His daughter Rajwar Kaur Gakhal was barely six when she arrived, and her sister Balwinder was only one; the rest of the siblings were born in Canada. They were raised on Canadian soil, and they died on Canadian soil. That makes them Canadians for all intents and purposes. Yet, their Canadianness receded into the background and was, in fact, rendered invisible. Rather, the media's spotlight focused on the immigrant origins of the family, their cultural traditions and backgrounds, and their adherence to Sikhism.

The Sharon Velisek Story

Less than two weeks after the Vernon tragedy made headlines, Sharon Velisek, another victim of male violence, reported her story to the media. Her ex-boyfriend shot her in November 1995 and then shot himself. She had complained to the RCMP detachment in Vernon on numerous occasions but had not received an adequate response. The media reports on the Velisek case do not mention her cultural background, her ethnic community, or her religious affiliation. Instead, the stories concentrate on the events leading up to her attempted murder and highlight the lack of police action. The following example typifies the kind of reporting that the *Vancouver Sun* undertook in its coverage of the Velisek case:

VERNON – Vernon RCMP failed to act decisively on stalking complaints by a woman whose ex-boyfriend later shot and nearly killed her with a sawed-off shotgun, she has charged. Vernon resident Sharon Velisek complained seven times in a month-long period last fall that Larry Scott was following her, making nuisance phone calls and committing vandalism.

Police did not arrest Scott and on Nov. 22, he hid in the darkness behind Velisek's house and confronted her in her carport. The first blast from his sawed-off 12-gauge shotgun shattered her left arm and knocked her to the ground. He stood over her, held the shotgun to her right shoulder and shot again, blasting away four ribs and most of her right lung. Perhaps thinking he had already killed her, he turned the gun on himself and fell to the ground dead, his head slumped on Velisek's shoulder.

That night, RCMP told reporters that Velisek had complained about Scott but did not want them to do anything. That's also what Vernon RCMP say Rajwar Gakhal wanted. Her estranged husband, Mark Vijay Chahal, later obtained handgun permits from the police and killed Gakhal and eight members of her family here on Good Friday.

The police response to the Gakhal case is one of the reasons why Velisek decided to tell her story. Today she is sending a letter to Attorney-General Ujjal Dosanjh that asks for a "hard, honest look at the problems which exist in the RCMP detachment in Vernon when dealing with cases like mine."

"I don't want the action to be to figure out who's to blame here," she said in a weekend interview. "What I want is to show the real problem here is the system. It doesn't protect women." (Crawley 1996c)

The story continues describing Velisek as an active agent providing her own response to the situation. Although the report describes Velisek as a receptionist and a mother of four and provides some background to her relationship with Larry Scott, it also includes a synopsis of the escalating violence that characterized their relationship and highlights the lack of police response.

The absence of a cultural explanation as a cause of violence in the Velisek case may have to do with her unmarked appearance – she is not a racial minority belonging to a community or religious tradition that constitutes the popular and common-sense notion of a cultural Other. Rather, she embodies the stereotype of the dominant culture that remains invisible to scrutiny. But if we are to use a culturalized explanation, Sharon Velisek's experiences of violence could be seen as emblematic of Canadian culture. The media did not advance such a viewpoint on the probable grounds that it would reflect negatively on the dominant culture, thereby making visible the patriarchal powers entrenched in it. Further, in highlighting the shortcomings of the dominant culture, the media would also draw attention to the systemic barriers that underpin women's inequality and vulnerability to violence.

Contextualizing Gendered Violence in Vernon
In the days following the murders of Rajwar Gakhal and her family, the South Asian community in British Columbia and Canadian society at large

reeled from the shock of this senseless violence. The same questions kept arising: How could something like this have happened? How was it possible that a man with well-known violent intentions was allowed to get any-where close to the family that subsequently became victims of his wrath? Did this massacre have anything to do with the cultural background of the killer or of his victims? Did the criminal justice system fail the victims?

At the time, the media labelled this event the "second-largest massacre in Canadian history" – the first being the massacre of fourteen women at the École Polytechnique in Montreal in 1989. Quite apart from these large-scale and widely reported massacres are the numerous deaths of and assaults on women that take place each year in Canada.[4] Yet the focus on group mur-ders fits with the criteria of newsworthiness described in Chapter 2. It also conforms to what Marian Meyers (1994, 1997) has described as the "hierar-chy of crime" operating within newsrooms, namely, that when the crime is a murder, it receives more attention, and when numerous homicides are perpetrated by the same person, the newsworthiness increases. The Vernon murders, like the Montreal massacre, involved a number of people and, hence, the focus of attention was dramatically intense compared with mur-ders of individual women or women who are situated at the lower ends of the socioeconomic order. However, unlike the Montreal massacre where killer Marc Lépine did not have an intimate relationship with any of the fourteen female victims he shot, in the Vernon situation, Mark Chahal was the estranged husband of Rajwar Gakhal. By constantly comparing the two events as massacres, the media reinforced the equivalence between stranger-perpetrated femicide and familial (intimate) violence perpetrated by a known family member. It failed to contextualize the violence in Vernon as part of a national pattern wherein violence against women in relationships escalates when they attempt to leave or do actually leave relationships, nor in terms of the alarming rate of uxoricide (wife killing).[5]

Shifting attention away from the pressing issue of wife abuse in particular and gender-based violence in general is symptomatic of patriarchal power (see also Berns 2001; Wykes 1998). As such, in the Vernon coverage, the angle became one of an "extraordinary" event (the massacre) attributable to the ready availability of guns. But even here, the interpretation was con-tested, and the coverage mirrors this contestation in terms of how the domi-nant frame shifted between the inadequacies of the RCMP's enforcement of existing laws to the accessibility of guns resulting from the lack of gun con-trol mechanisms. The issue of culture receded into the background but was ever-present through the consistent depiction of the Gakhal and Saran fam-ily portraits, replete in Indian attire.

The Velisek and Gakhal-Saran murders also became intertwined in the subsequent coverage in the print media. However, in almost every article on the issue of the murders, gun control, and the inquest, the publication of the Gakhal family portrait reiterated and invoked a cognitive resonance linking this violence to a cultural phenomenon, a culturalized interpretation heightened by the inclusion of Sharon Velisek's experience but lack of such treatment in her case.

An analysis of fifteen press stories from 15 April 1996, when Velisek first articulated her complaints about the RCMP to the media, to an editorial in the *Province* on 6 December 1999 reveals an interesting but not unexpected pattern of reporting.[6] As detailed by Carter (1998), Meyers (1997), and Wykes (1998), the reporting of domestic violence tends to focus on singular and individualized cases. However, it was impossible for the media to limit their focus to just one of the two incidents in Vernon given that both revolved around the same issue – namely, the lack of enforcement and intervention by the RCMP – and both had occurred in the same geographical area. Thus, the twinning of the two cases remained a predominant theme but one that was often contextualized in terms of the provincial government's call for an inquest.

As the literature suggests, the focus on individual pathology dominated as the common-sense explanation of the murders (Forsyth-Smith 1995; Kidd-Hewitt 1995; Meyers 1994, 1997; Surette 1998). The following chronology reflects this kind of individualizing and pathologizing evident in the reporting of the Vernon murders:

> It is last Thursday morning and 30-year-old accountant Mark Vijay Chahal has just left his Burnaby highrise apartment to drive to Vernon.
>
> In his sporty, red Nissan Pulsar, Chahal is carrying a 12-gauge shotgun and two handguns – a Smith & Wesson .40-calibre semi-automatic pistol and a Smith & Wesson .38-calibre revolver.
>
> Although it is a cloudy day, the weather is good for driving and he should have no trouble reaching the Interior in five or six hours.
>
> He is angry. For more than a year now, he has been separated from his wife, Rajwar Gakhal, who is now living in her parents' Vernon home. (Bocking 1996)

What is also interesting about this account is the reporter's filling in of the narrative. He imagines what Mark Chahal was going through and, yet, there is no indication throughout the report that this is a fictionalized account (see Clayman 1990; Frank 1999). In essence, the reporter projects what he, as a male, might be feeling if his wife left him. Thus, the imputation of anger suggests that rage is an understandable response in such circumstances – a view clearly anchored and articulated from a patriarchal perspective.

In another article, the reporter directly quotes both the RCMP officer and a gun club manager, with the latter stating: "Handguns like the ones Chahal used are restricted to police, security guards, gun collectors and gun-club members. The permits made public Tuesday by police show Chahal was a member of the Barnet Rifle Club in Burnaby. Club manager Keith Caughlin told The Canadian Press that Chahal appeared normal and there was no indication he would ever snap. 'Guys go bonkers ... If a guy goes nuts, he goes nuts,' Caughlin said" (Crawley 1996b). Here, the murders are explained away in the language of common sense – as normalized responses to the breakup of a relationship and as expressions of rage. That it is normal to express such rage through gendered violence remains unexamined. Further-more, the patriarchal basis of this rage – as stemming from the sense of losing ownership over a woman and as a legitimate action rationalizing her murder – are not interrogated either.

In the case of Sharon Velisek, a similar individualized focus and emphasis on pathology is apparent. In one article discussing Larry Scott, the man who attempted to murder Velisek, the reporter relies heavily on the views of Scott's friends, quoting them liberally:

Larry Scott "seemed to become a different person" last fall, prompting Sharon Velisek to end their relationship. "He wasn't the person I wanted to spend my life with" Velisek, 41, testified yesterday.

But he intended to spend eternity with her. On Nov. 22, Scott ambushed Velisek in the driveway of her Vernon home, shooting her in the arm and back before turning his shotgun on himself. Velisek survived, but Scott, 51, died at the scene.

"Larry was physically and emotionally devastated and appeared, at times, more of a little boy, childlike," close friend Karen Redekop testified.

"He stopped eating, began to shake, lost weight and was not sleeping.

"Larry would listen to the answering-machine tape of Sharon breaking up with him over and over and asked me if I wanted to hear it. I thought that was insane," said Redekop.

Asked why she did not report her concerns to the police she replied: "I had mostly third-party information. I thought they would laugh it off. I never really believed he could harm anyone."

Three days before the shooting Scott moved in with a friend, Kerry Bourdon of Kelowna. "He was in his worst state," Bourdon testified. "He sat on the couch watching TV, mumbling and talking about hiring a hit man in Vancouver and shooting Sharon. I just said yeah, right. I didn't truly believe he was capable of harming a flea. The next day I called Karen Redekop and Larry's doctor and told them he just isn't right. I thought he needed a doctor's help, mostly for his shaking." The inquest continues today. (*Province* 1996)

This kind of emphasis on individual feelings and behaviour was common throughout the coverage of the Velisek case and augmented by the insertion of expert voices and opinions, notably those of a psychologist. The subordinate discourse of the gendered pattern of such violence was largely absent, and if present, relegated to the last few sentences of the coverage (see, for example, Pemberton 1997a, 1997b). What is also interesting about this coverage is that in contrast to the fictionalized account of Mark Chahal reported by Bocking, there is no filling in of the narrative here. Rather, the reporter took pains to obtain insights about Larry Scott from those who knew him.

In analyzing the place of the two women within these stories, a similar pattern of visibility/invisibility emerges. In the ensuing representations and narratives, Rajwar Gakhal disappeared in the media coverage as a person with a history and with very real concerns. In contrast, Velisek gained considerable public visibility in her call for the RCMP to improve its treatment of domestic violence cases. This focus on Velisek as the victim who lived to tell the tale is not altogether surprising but it does reinforce the individualistic bias of the coverage. In the reportage, anti-violence activists and service providers were generally collapsed under the rubric of "Women's groups" and consigned to the background even though they had consistently pressured the government to take these issues seriously. Velisek's increased credibility and appearance in the discourse may have to do with the alignment of her position with the official ideology – namely, one that emphasizes and advocates education and training as panacea for all social problems, especially those dealing with race and patriarchal power.

The emphasis on increased programmatic intervention through training was supported by the attorney general's office and the RCMP. In fact, in the ensuing coverage, one of the key issues to emerge was the lack of funding for the adequate training of RCMP officers. There was no investigation or interrogation of where funds designed for violence prevention and previously allocated to the RCMP had been spent. Moreover, the emphasis on education and training, while notable, reflect a limited understanding of the widespread and pervasive nature of gendered violence, a violence made possible by the ideology of patriarchy.

These news accounts demonstrate how the media work to degender gendered violence by decontextualizing it and personalizing it (Berns 2001). By culturalizing the focus in the first instance, the media in effect equate gendered violence with a cultural pattern of behaviour, implying that the Indian cultural traditions of the Gakhal and Saran families are responsible for the gendered violence committed against Rajwar Gakhal and her family. In the Velisek instance, gendered violence is degendered by the focus on Larry Scott's psychopathology rather than contextualizing his behaviour within an analysis of the systemic and structural patterns of gendered violence. In effect, gendered violence as a form of what Forsyth-Smith (1995) describes as domestic terrorism is translated into a naturalized though somewhat unfortunate occurrence. In other words, what both Gakhal and Velisek experienced at the hands of the men they were at one time intimately involved with is erased. Rather, in the Vernon murders, Rajwar Gakhal was indirectly blamed for not wanting the police to intervene, though she did alert them about the dangerous behaviour of her ex-husband. Blaming the victim is a strategy commonly employed by both the media and the police in order to evade responsibility for their roles in failing to protect women (see Rigakos 1995).

In analyzing the coverage, what is equally striking was the way in which the opinion pieces in the newspapers became the only sites in which a systemic focus on violence was permitted. In other words, it was through the op-ed pieces that one got a sense of how widespread woman abuse really is, and of the context surrounding both the murders of the Gakhal and Saran family members and the attempted murder of Sharon Velisek (Hightower 1996). Through the op-ed pieces, anti-violence feminist activists were able to articulate their counter interpretation and counter-framing of the event (see Jiwani 1996). The notion of balanced reporting, then, while ideologically constraining, provided an opening whereby the hegemonic construction of an event was contested, though within prescribed discursive limits.

Organizing against Violence: An Anti-Racist Feminist Perspective

The framing of the Vernon "massacre" as a cultural phenomenon and the media's attitude of blaming the victim, Rajwar Gakhal, for not pressing charges, greatly disturbed South Asian women. This, combined with the blatant failure of the RCMP to enforce the attorney general's policy on violence against women in intimate relationships, galvanized an organized response through the Coalition of South Asian Women against Violence. The latter included South Asian women's groups, as well as individual South Asian women from allied feminist organizations. In particular, the coalition was composed of the India Mahila Association (IMA), the South Asian Women's Centre, the Indo-Canadian Women's Association, the Punjabi Women's Association, and representatives from the Vancouver Status of Women (VSW), Surrey Delta Immigrant Services Society, Women against Violence against Women (WAVAW), Vancouver Rape Relief, and the Feminist Research, Education, Development and Action Centre (FREDA).

Steps in Organizing

The coalition first organized a meeting in which women from the community and supporting organizations came together to share information about the tragic events in Vernon: it was critical that everyone participating in the meeting knew the whole story, as media accounts tended to lack details that were relevant to us. This provided the opportunity to develop a collective stock of knowledge about what had transpired in Vernon. On the basis of this, we developed an action plan.

The action plan revolved around two major issues: first, the development and implementation of a strategy by which to debunk the media's portrayal of the murders as a culturally inscribed phenomenon; and second, to organize a way in which coalition members, affiliated organizations, and members of the larger community could come together to express grief about the deaths and outrage at the inadequacy of the police response that had resulted in these murders.

As a result, the coalition organized two events. The first involved a press conference; the second was a public vigil. Two committees were formed, each tasked with implementing a specific action. Both committees worked tirelessly, with volunteers and support from other feminist and women's organizations.

In *Understanding News,* John Hartley (1982) reinforces the point that timing is crucial if an issue is to get media attention. The Vernon murders occurred on Friday of the Easter weekend, 5 April 1996. The coalition met on the Monday. In the interim, the media were looking for accredited sources (with institutional authority) whom they could interview to present either an analysis of the event or a contrary view. The coalition organized a press conference on Friday, 12 April 1996, at which it relayed its key message – that the violence was not culturally based and that violence against women is a pervasive phenomenon. Representatives from allied organizations were invited to attend the conference as a sign of support. A number of groups, including the British Columbia Institute on Family Violence (BCIFV) and the Stepping Stone Society, an Aboriginal group, were present at the press conference. As well, the coalition received many letters of support from women's centres and transition houses around the province.

The press conference was heavily attended by the news media and reported on the front page of the *Vancouver Sun* and broadcast on the CTV and CBC television evening newscasts. The press conference helped displace the focus on culture by critically attacking the media's obsession with this explanatory framework, and to some extent, through that interrogation, it succeeded, albeit temporarily, in shifting attention to the prevalence of spousal violence and pattern of inaction on the part of the RCMP. The vigil, however, was not well attended. Approximately four hundred people assembled in front of the Vancouver Art Gallery. Most were members of Vancouver's South Asian communities. There were few non–South Asians.

However, despite our success in temporarily shifting the cultural frame, the issue of sexism remained a dominant paradigm marking the coverage. In this sense, the media undermined our message. For example, in the *Vancouver Sun*'s account of the press conference, the reporter focused on one of the key coalition members, stating, "Dosanjh who is married to the attorney-general, said the media never went to the Italian community for explanations of why Paul Bernado raped, tortured and murdered two Ontario schoolgirls. Nor did it delve into Clifford Olson's cultural heritage to find reasons for his killing of young children and teenagers" (Bolan 1996). While the report reflects some key points from the coalition's position, the message was undermined by positioning Dosanjh as the wife of the attorney general rather than as a founder of the India Mahila Association, one of the oldest South Asian women's organizations in Canada and long involved in anti-violence organizing and advocacy. This kind of tactic reflects the media's privileging of what they perceive as the criteria of legitimacy. But more importantly, it underscores a view of Dosanjh as a woman whose stature and status is dependent on her husband. Thus, what Dosanjh said was subordinated to her status, and although her status as the wife of the attorney general would make her a highly credible and quotable source, her position as his subordinate fixed her identity as his spouse and nothing else.

What the Coalition Asked For
The coalition delivered a well-thought-out list of actions that it asked of the government. These recommendations were not reported in totality. However, the call for an independent inquiry was relayed by the media in its coverage. Specifically, the coalition requested

> **THAT** a full and independent inquiry be ordered by the Attorney General focusing on the RCMP's lack of enforcement of the policy concerning violence in intimate relationships;
> **THAT** the inquiry be conducted by an external and independent agency;
> **THAT** there be meaningful inclusion and participation of women's groups in reviewing and amending policies dealing with violence against women in intimate relationships;
> **THAT** the media be cognizant of the reality that violence is not a culturebound phenomenon, but transcends race, class and culture;
> **THAT** the Attorney General immediately implement the recommendations of the Oppal Commission particularly with regard to enabling independent and external monitoring of all aspects of the criminal justice system as it affects women who are victims of violence;
> **THAT** the government undertake efforts to increase awareness and prevention of violence against women and children.

What the Coalition Achieved
Through collective action, the coalition was able to put forth its perspective on the tragedy in Vernon. In terms of concrete outcomes, it was unsuccessful in persuading the attorney general to call for an independent inquiry.

However, the attorney general did order an internal investigation into the RCMP's actions. He then, upon the disclosure of a second violation of policy – a violation brought forward by Sharon Velisek – ordered a coroner's inquest.

Based on this response, the coalition sent out another press release informing the media that while an inquest was a positive step in uncovering why the system had failed to protect Rajwar Gakhal, its mandate needed to be broadened to examine all aspects of the justice system. As well, the coalition called for the inclusion of anti-violence feminist groups in the appointments to the inquest. These latter demands were not met.

By this time, the story was stale, at least as far the media were concerned. It was now confined to the back pages, overshadowed by contemporary events, and the impending provincial election. Consequently, the media release did not make it to print. Nevertheless, as a momentary interruption in the hegemonic discourse of culturalized violence, the coalition's intervention provided an alternative way of understanding the event. Through news releases, press conferences, one-on-one interviews, and the distribution of the coalition members' analysis of the tragedy in the alternative press, such as *Kinesis* (a now defunct feminist national paper), this alternative perspective infused subsequent attempts at framing the event, albeit temporarily and primarily in the alternative media.

A year later, at the behest of the coalition, the FREDA Centre published a report based on the responses of women's centres around British Columbia to a survey asking for their interpretations of the effectiveness of the attorney general's Violence against Women policy (Jiwani and Buhagiar 1997). The report indicated that there were many more "Vernons" waiting to implode and that the policy was not being implemented consistently throughout the province. This report was also released at a press conference attended by coalition members and representatives from supporting organizations; they were asked to speak about their own experiences with the policy. Once again, although no concrete measures were implemented as a result of the publication of the report, the publicity generated by the press conference embarrassed the government and made it somewhat publicly accountable – to the media, if not the larger society.

The ways in which culture is used or rendered absent in these accounts demonstrate how the dominant culture sees itself through the lens of the mass media. In the case of the Vernon tragedy, the media consistently emphasized the cultural background of the victims so as to accentuate the differences between practices of arranged marriages – cast as being oppressive and strongly traditional – and the egalitarian and progressive ways in which the dominant society encourages heterosexual unions. Similarly, the constant emphasis on the immigrant backgrounds of the Gakhal-Saran and Virk families (see Chapter 3 for a discussion of the Reena Virk case) underscores their status as Others, no matter what their status as Canadians actually is. This makes them unlike "real" Canadians, who are framed as not being immigrants by virtue of being born in this country, and who are White and middle class and who are not seen to be problematic in the same way, despite the culture of violence that shapes and informs Canadian society and its institutions. Implicit in these stories is the notion that immigrants who are visibly and culturally "different" cannot fit into the invisible and dominant Canadian culture – a culture that is White, Christian, and patriarchal. In the end, their inability to fit makes them a target of violence. The responsibility for perpetuating such violence is thus strategically avoided. It is not the responsibility of the state or of Canadians at large to prevent such violence. Rather, such responsibility lies with the individual.

Racializing culture or culturalizing race enables the mainstream media to amplify differences and, through this amplification, define Others in society. It also becomes a way by which to neutralize the charge of racism. By simply pointing out cultural differences, the media can refrain from using the explicit language of race. At the same time, they can attribute pejorative connotations to culture that underscore the superiority of the dominant group and the inferiority of Others. Culture becomes a way of talking race by dismissing and erasing the notion of racism. This is particularly true in the context of modern-day racism, where groups are treated differently and denied access on the basis of their cultural differences. However, while the obsession with cultural difference is highly problematic, as evident in the Gakhal and Saran murders, the converse, where culture is erased, can be equally troubling.

Sherene Razack (2005) aptly questions the validity of entirely divorcing culture from violence. Contrasting the strategy used by the Coalition of South Asian Women against Violence (as described above) and, more particularly, the structuralist orientation of the FREDA Centre with approaches that favour a cultural explanation, Razack argues that privileging a deculturalized interpretation can erase the specific kind and form of violence experienced by particular groups of women. While this is a valid critique, especially given that it stems from a recognition of the specificities of women's experiences of violence, my interest here is in the strategic use of these explanatory frameworks by dominant powers such as the media. Thus, rather than dismissing any interpretation of the lived reality of culture, I want to suggest that cultural formations are fluid and change across time and space. By contextualizing the murders of the Gakhal and Saran families as located in a culture of arranged marriages and Otherness, the media used cultural specificities to blame the victim and her culture. Consequently, which cultural interpretations are retained and accentuated as emblematic signifiers of that culture is a matter of context and the inherent power structures within culturalized and racialized communities, as well as the dominant society.

As Razack (1998a, 59) states, "[The] risks of talking culture are particularly acute when, as so often happens, it is the dominant group that controls the interpretation of what it means to take culture into account." To be sure, a woman having hot oil thrown on her (an example Razack uses in her discussion of some South Asian women's experience with violence) or being nearly killed by a sawed-off gun (as in the case of Sharon Velisek) are two very different modalities by which violence is enacted on the gendered body. Yet, the corporeality of the body as the site of such violence remains the same. In both cases, women are victimized and suffer severely from the expression of male violence. In advancing this argument, my focus is on the power that is exercised in the framing of the gendered and racialized body: its representation in the dominant media and its construction in the language of power. In that sense, and referring back to Chapter 1, I would argue that violence is a language of power and its instantiation at the immediate level of lived reality is governed by contextual factors that include the cultural frameworks available to girls and women, and the larger maps of meaning that make violence intelligible to the dominant gaze and make its power apparent to those who are subordinated by it.

Conclusion

By contrasting news accounts of the Gakhal-Saran murders and the attempted murder of Sharon Velisek, I have endeavoured to highlight the ways in which cultural explanations of violence are used strategically to deflect attention away from the persistence of gender-based violence. In both of these cases, the core issues dealt with the RCMP's lack of adequate response to the violence experienced by these women. In one instance, the lack of response was blamed on the victim's cultural background – her concern about her standing and her family's reputation within the Sikh community. In the other instance, the RCMP had no ready explanation for its disregard of Sharon Velisek's numerous complaints. I contend that part of the dismissal of gender-based violence has to do with how women are framed in these encounters. For the RCMP not to have taken Sharon Velisek's complaints more seriously, and to abide by what they argued were Rajwar Gakhal's wishes, suggests a deeper undercurrent – one that speaks to the trivialization of gendered violence. The focus on individual psychopathology facilitates this translation of gendered violence from a collective phenomenon to an individualistic behaviour, while the focus on culture similarly removes the issue of gendered violence from the larger societal context and ascribes it to the pathology of particular cultural traditions. Racism and sexism thus work in concert to make the appearance of gendered violence an anomaly – an anomaly resulting from the pathology of cultures and individuals. Both of these pathologies are defined in relation to an implicit and unstated normative standard that speaks of an imagined and imaginary Canadian (see

Wilden 1980). To make visible the pattern and pervasiveness of gendered violence would risk unveiling this mask of civility. Hence, in this instance, as in others (see Razack 1998a), the tendency is to rely on the panacea of education and training. Such a move allows the state and its powers of enforcement (such as the police and the media) to maintain a semblance of resolving the situation.

These cases illustrate how certain cultures are racialized with the intent of differentiating them as Others and legitimizing their inferiorization, criminalization, ghettoization, and exoticization. In talking about the violence of race, it is these processes of Othering at the micro-social level, though determined by larger social structures, that need to be foregrounded and interrogated for the strategic purposes they serve, purposes that are ultimately in the interests of maintaining a hierarchy based on power and dominance.

In Part 3, I turn to the lives of racialized girls and young women with the intent of mapping some of these processes of Othering that influence and shape their daily lives and realities. My focus is on privileging the voices and lived realities of racialized girls and women in order to highlight the links between these larger structural forces and the constructed common-sense worlds of racialized girls and women.

Part 3
Voicing the Violence

5
Racialized Girls and Everyday Negotiations

"A crime of pure hatred," Crown says
ST-ANDRE-EST, Que. – Aylin Otano-Garcia was six when she
immigrated here with her mother from Cuba, and by the time
she reached her teens she had blended in. She had many friends
in high school and spoke French with no trace of an accent.
"Nobody knew she was Cuban. She was a real Quebecer," recalled
Niurka Perez, a close family friend. But somebody noticed Aylin's
unusual family name and slightly darker complexion. In what a
Crown prosecutor called a crime of "pure hatred," the pretty 15-
year-old was targeted as an immigrant, lured to a remote sandpit
and bludgeoned to death with a baseball bat last June.

– Graeme Hamilton, *National Post*

[My parents] always ask me to make Canadian friends, but you
know, it's hard. The culture is different so it's hard to make
friends with them sometimes when they speak different. They talk
slang ... I don't understand what they're talking about. So I just
remain silent.

– participant, Jump Start workshop

If the brutal murder of Aylin Otano-Garcia dramatically demonstrates the
inability of society to accept racialized girls and young women as Canadians, the quote from the young participant in the Jump Start workshop[1] for
girls of colour highlights the everyday struggles these girls face in their attempts to fit in. Both draw attention to the specific challenges faced by
racialized immigrant girls and young women – challenges which, as the
case of Reena Virk examined in Chapter 3 well illustrates, are only heightened by Canada's tendency to deny the role that race and racism play in
creating these vulnerabilities in the first place. In Reena's case, race was

erased, as were her experiences of being racialized; similarly, racist and sexist violence were evacuated, deflecting attention away from the structures of power that define and regulate the lives of those who are racialized and marginalized. In effect, the forces that put Reena Virk in a place where she could be and was subjected to violence, and that permitted the kind of violence that was inscribed on her body, were all erased. It is this violence – the structures of dominance that make violence possible and that are violent in themselves – that I wish to attend to in this chapter. However, here I focus on the expressions of this violence in the daily lives of racialized girls and young women.

Canada is perceived to be a leader in the international human rights arena. It is regarded as an egalitarian nation, motivated by a desire for justice for minorities and the underprivileged. Canada is a signatory to various international accords, conventions, and agreements upholding the rights of indigenous peoples and marginalized groups, including women and children. Yet, the rhetoric is hollow, as the recent report filed by Amnesty International (2004) on violence experienced by Aboriginal girls and women reveals. As a colonial and colonized nation, Canada puts forward a public face that is part of its own mythology – of the innocent, moderate, middle power (Razack 2004) that boasts a multicultural complexion and a multiracial workforce, a nation signified by its image of a peaceful kingdom amid the havoc and turmoil characterizing the rest of the world.

In this chapter, the public face Canada presents to the world is contrasted with the lived realities of racialized immigrant and refugee girls and young women. My intent in mapping the ways in which systemic structures of violence are translated into daily life is to decode the language of violence as it is lived by girls and young women of colour. In making the intersections and interlocking sites of violence visible to scrutiny, I hope to unpack some of the ways in which intimate and interpersonal violence are grounded in and textured by these very structures of dominance. My aim here is to establish how these different forms of violence are understood, experienced, and, most importantly, vocalized by girls and young women from racialized immigrant communities. In highlighting these voices, I draw from an extensive research project conducted under the auspices of the FREDA Centre.[2] This project was inspired by a desire to understand the conditions that endangered Reena Virk's life, and the particular risks she faced growing up as a girl of colour in a dominant White society.

In looking at the intersecting and interlocking sites of racism and sexism within the context of gendered violence, it becomes clear that the kinds of violence that racialized immigrant and refugee women and girls experience are mediated by their particular status as gendered, raced, and classed subjects whose heteronormativity is usually taken for granted. Social location, group status, cultural scripts, and accessibility to resources mediate the experience and kinds of abuse that girls and young women from different groups encounter.

Regulatory criteria governing the entrance of racialized immigrant girls and young women underpin and influence their access to services and their potentiality to respond to violent situations. As dependants of their sponsors or their family heads of households, usually the fathers, girls and young women occupy a subordinate position. When faced with violence at home, they are often reluctant to leave for fear of jeopardizing their family's ability to acquire landed or citizenship status and its financial position. Section 39 of the Immigration and Refugee Protection Act stipulates that "a foreign national is inadmissible for financial reasons if they are or will be unable or unwilling to support themselves or any other person who is dependent on them, and have not satisfied an officer that adequate arrangements for care and support, other than those that involve social assistance, have been made." Given the current laws, should a sponsored family member access social services, the sponsor becomes financially liable. This places an added strain for those girls and young women who want to leave an abusive environment but are afraid to do so because of the financial impact and loss of face for their families.

Hence, a significant aspect of the lives of immigrant and refugee girls and young women of colour is their own intersectionality: their specific positioning at the junctures of race, gender, official status, class, and age, with each of these factors interlocking in ways that contribute to their subordination and thus susceptibility to systemic, intimate, and interpersonal forms of violence.

Situating Racialized Immigrant Girls and Young Women

In 1996, 24.3 percent of the visible minority population was under the age of fifteen, and *the majority of these youths were immigrants*. One of every ten immigrants is a female under the age of fifteen years (Kobayashi et al. 1998). As I have argued in previous chapters, immigrant status confers its own connotative associations, notably those that inferiorize difference by equating it to stereotypical notions of Third World people. In the case of immigrant girls and young women of colour, these stereotypical connotations are part of the violence they encounter – both as the exotic and inferiorized Others, whose very difference becomes the site of everyday racist and sexist violence. In Chapter 1, drawing from Himani Bannerji's (2000) work, I refer to racialized immigrant communities as being constructed communities, emerging in response to state-imposed criteria and being shaped by dominant patriarchal structures from within. Formed within a context of multiculturalism where race has no validity and where culture becomes the reigning discourse by which difference is understood and consigned to a category of Other, the lives of immigrant girls and young women of colour are similarly framed within a dominant culturalist gaze. Race becomes culture, and racialized violence becomes culturalized violence (Razack 1998a).

From the perspective of the dominant society, these girls and young women become emblematic signifiers of particular cultural formations. It is in the language of cultural racism that such distinctions are made and authorized (see Chapter 1). By cultural racism, I mean the racism that is expressed and directed at groups seen to be culturally different. Within such a framework, cultural practices become the target of inferiorization, though, by association, so does the group in question. Cultural racism is the latest manifestation of racism. Given that biologically, race is empirically nonexistent and given the social climate that prohibits and disapproves of openly racist statements that are grounded on phenotypic differences such as skin colour, the tendency is to camouflage racist sentiments by focusing on the cultural terrain (see Bredström 2003; Razack 1998a; Gilroy 1991). Thus, the dominant perspective frames these girls and young women as oppressed victims by focusing on issues such as the hijab (the head covering worn by Muslim girls) (K. Bullock and Jafri 2001; Jafri 1998), arranged marriages (Imam 1999), dowry deaths (Narayan 1995), honour killings (Bredström 2003), and female infanticide. If we are to draw on Rebecca Raby's (2002) delineation of the discursive categories used to define adolescent girls, then racialized girls readily fit into the category of being at risk. Their depictions as passive victims of patriarchal cultures ensure such a categorization and engender corresponding responses from the state and social service agencies. In effect, these girls and young women are perceived as suffering from what Uma Narayan (1997) terms "death by culture" (see Chapter 1, this volume, for a further discussion).

Two dominant trajectories emanate from this kind of cultural gaze. First, the emphasis on culture becomes the hallmark of explanatory frameworks and academic studies that seek to examine the lives of racialized girls of colour. Second, this same culturalized framework is deployed to comprehend gendered violence as experienced by these girls and young women (see Chapter 4). In the first instance, the use of a cultural framework is evident in the literature on the acculturation and assimilation of racialized girls. Rooted in an immigrant adaptation framework, these studies seek to understand and highlight the situations of immigrant girls and young women of colour from diverse communities within Western societies. Numerous examples of such studies are found in the broader field of assimilation and acculturation studies (e.g., Drury 1991; Hennink, Diamond, and Cooper 1999; Hutnik 1986; Jabbra 1983; B. Miller 1995; Mogg 1991; Onder 1996). Here the focus is on explaining the variables that facilitate or impede girls' and young women's integration or assimilation through acculturation into the dominant society. Acculturation here refers to the gradual adoption of the values and normative behaviours of the dominant society, a process which is seen to culminate in assimilation whereby one loses one's attachment to an ethnic identity and becomes part of the larger society. A key finding of these studies is that the acculturation process is highly gendered, meaning that it has different outcomes for girls and boys. Second, girls and young women tend to express a higher level of dissatisfaction with their cultural communities than do boys and young men. Third, girls within these cultural groups are more closely restricted and their behaviour highly regulated compared with boys. An example of such an approach can be found in a study of Vietnamese girls in Australia by Rosenthal, Ranieri, and Klimidis (1996). They argue: "It is young girls who are likely, with exposure to Western values, to see the disadvantages of their role within a traditional Vietnamese culture. As a result, family dynamics are likely to be more disrupted for girls who may wish to adopt those values that offer them a more positive, active role in their self-development in this new environment" (89). Dissatisfied with the values and behaviours prescribed by their own community and yearning to be liberated through the embrace of Western values, these girls and young women are perceived as experiencing a "cultural conflict" or "culture clash."[3] Imam (1999) calls this the "culture deficit" model, where the dominant Western culture is seen as being emancipatory and egalitarian, while minority cultures are seen as being static and frozen. Interestingly, these explanations are also articulated by young women of colour, reflecting their internalization of the dominant hegemonic ideology, which posits the dominant Western culture as being an idyllic landscape of gender equity and freedom from gender-based discrimination and structural violence (Espiritu 2001; Pyke and Johnson 2003; Tsolidis 1990).

This view of a frozen and static culture fixes these communities as holdovers from a past. As Amita Handa (1997) argues, it converts them from dynamic and fluid entities to premodern, monolithic, and homogeneous entities. The emphasis on cultural traditions (as ways of preservation and identity formation) is construed as a sign reflecting a lack of progress. Against this, dominant Western cultures are constructed as progressive landscapes and their passports to acceptance are premised on the basis of acculturation and assimilation.

The notion of culture clash or culture conflict as the defining paradigm for explaining immigrant girls' and young women's lives is problematic for the following reasons. Brah (1997) notes that such a perspective is predicated on the assumption that the clash occurs between two homogeneous cultures of equal standing. Acculturation within this framework is based on the assumption of a linear absorption of the Other into the host culture, thereby negating any possibility of exchange or hybridization. Additionally, the assumed homogeneity of different cultural formations is erroneous given the diversity within cultural formations and their evolution in response to changing environments. No culture is static, and cultural formations, in general, are not monolithic (S. Hall 1990b; Imam 1999). As Bhatia and Ram (2001, 14) note: "To suggest that the acculturation process merely involves 'culture shedding' or 'some behavioural shift' or the 'unlearning of one's previous repertoire' implies that one can float in and out of cultures, shedding one's history or politics and replacing them with a new set of cultural and political 'behaviours' whenever needed. Advocating the strategy of 'integration' as the endpoint or the telos of the individual or the group's acculturation process overlooks the contested, negotiated and sometimes painful, rupturing experiences associated with 'living in between' cultures."

Rejecting the standard psychological view of acculturation as a linear process involving defined stages which the immigrant moves through in a gradual fashion, Bhatia and Ram (2001) posit an alternative view, one predicated on a post-colonial framework that takes into consideration the continuous movement of people across cultures and nation-states and the inequalities resulting from colonial and neo-colonial relations of power. They argue that the dominant paradigm of acculturation tends to universalize the experiences of all immigrants and fails to take into consideration issues of race, gender, and power. Immigrants of colour have been and continue to be treated differently from White immigrants. The legal requirements vary for each group, with immigrants of colour undeniably being excluded or allowed entry on conditional grounds as a result of exclusionary legislation, tightened immigration rules, and negative perceptions of their countries of origin (see also Razack 2000a). Further, many racialized communities are diasporic in nature, maintaining ties both within the hostland and the homeland. Migration, then, is not a discrete process with a beginning in one site and an ending in another. Nor can it be defined in a linear manner as progressing through stages such as integration, assimilation, and marginalization. Rather, Bhatia and Ram (2001, 3) suggest, the processes of migration within these "non-European/non-White diasporic communities bring into sharp relief the sense of constantly negotiating between here and there, past and present, homeland and hostland, self and other."

Bhatia and Ram's (2001) critique is indicative of the shortcomings of the cultural clash paradigm in that they argue that the conflation of culture and nation is highly problematic. Drawing from post-colonial theorists, they demonstrate that nation-states include all kinds of cultural groups that are often situated in an uneasy tension. Further, nation-states have been historically defined through processes of colonization and imperialism; hence, the state is inclusive of diverse cultural groups rather than being a homogeneous entity, though dominant groups within constantly attempt to erase differences. The nation is, then, an imagined community, a contested terrain in which notions of identity, belonging, and culture are continually negotiated and resisted by those who are located on its outskirts (see also S. Hall 1996a).

As indicated above, studies dealing with violence against girls and young women of colour have tended to adopt a linear model of acculturation. While some have argued that once acculturated, immigrant girls and young women are less likely to experience cultural conflicts, Debold et al. (1999) suggest otherwise. They argue that acculturation increases girls' and young women's risk to violence since those who are acculturated tend to internalize the valuations and hegemonic ideals of femininity that are ultimately damaging to their psychological and physical well-being. They contend that those who are marginal are not as likely to internalize the dominant norms and idealized images of hegemonic femininity as are girls and young women who are closer to the dominant value system. Bearing in mind the structural location of immigrant girls in terms of class, race, and gender, Debold et al. assert that acculturation represents a core dilemma. Girls and young women are forced into a dilemma in which "'success' in middle-class terms too often means a betrayal of cultural and familial connections and the terror of isolation, whereas, on the other hand, not achieving such success can mean betraying one's own and one's parents' hopes, economic marginalization, and restrictive notions of identity and social position" (1999, 183). In other words, to be a part of the larger society involves internalizing the dominant value system and hierarchy. Hence, not acculturating implies a degree of protection from the harmful values of the dominant host society. It ensures that girls are more in touch with their voices and thoughts, less affected by sexism, less susceptible to pressures to conform to the idealized body-image and sexually compliant behaviour, and more likely to access alternative role models from within their own communities (Brown, Way, and Duff 1999). In this regard, cultural identity becomes a protective force rather than a liability. Basow and Rubin (1999) note that a strong ethnic identity equips girls and young women with modes of coping with external forms of violence such as systemic racism and sexism. Drawing on an urban stress model, David Miller (1999) argues that racial socialization and racial identity enhance adolescent resilience to stresses caused by poverty and racial discrimination. And, in his review of the differential rates of depression among migrant populations, Bhugra (2004, 252) argues that, "if fluency in English is taken as one proxy measure of acculturation, then it would appear that higher levels of acculturation may lead to higher levels of psychological morbidity."

Again, while this discussion is laudable in terms of affording some recognition to the resilience afforded by an attachment to a collective ethnic or racial identity, it fails to address basic issues of power. In other words, what makes ethnic identity salient in particular contexts? What makes attachment to that identity attractive? In his study of five thousand grades 8 and 9 children in two US cities, Rumbaut (1994, 754) contends that

> youths see and compare themselves in relation to those around them, based on their social similarity or dissimilarity with the reference groups that most directly affect their experiences – e.g., with regard to such visible and socially categorized markers as gender, race, accent, language, class, religion, and nationality. Ethnic self-awareness is heightened or blurred, respectively, depending on the degree of dissonance or consonance of the social contexts which are basic to identity formation. For youths in a consonant context, ethnicity is not salient; but contextual dissonance heightens the salience of ethnicity and of ethnic group boundaries, all the more when it is accompanied by disparagement and discrimination.

Contextual dissonance and exclusion through discrimination are, then, the critical factors that need to be examined, rather than focus simply being on a colonial notion of culture. Disparagement and discrimination are inversely related to power and privilege. In a raced and gendered context that frames racialized communities of colour as dissonant Others, disparagement and discrimination translate power and privilege through a discourse of violence. The violence that Others these youth is a violence that they resist or seek to counter through a reaffirmation of their marginality. Rumbaut (1994) calls this a reactive ethnicity.

The issue of identity as a mobilizing force has also been observed by Potvin (1999) among Haitian youth in Montreal. She notes that while the first generation of immigrants tended to embrace a more integrationist stance – hoping to ameliorate their situation while waiting to return to the homeland, the second generation tends to take a more distant approach, identifying instead with Black movements in the United States, and attempting to assert an essentialist identity of Blackness as an oppositional response to the pervasive reality of racism they experience. Potvin argues that it is these experiences of racism that have become the defining moment around which mobilization and identity (re)construction takes place (see also Aujla 2000).

Gender, Age, and (Im)Migration: Tracing Multiple Violences

The migration of racialized groups undoubtedly raises issues about their acceptance into the host society and the latter's embracing of racial and cultural differences. Issues of racial and ethnic violence are significant barriers in impeding integration and sense of belonging. Combined with the influence of gender, age, and race, the impact of migration may be particularly harsh when mapped on the socio-developmental changes taking place during the transition from girlhood to adulthood (see Beiser et al. 1998; Beiser, Shik, and Curyk 1999). As a result of globalization, migration, and consumer culture, concepts of childhood and adolescence are becoming more universalized. Thus, while adolescence may mark the transition from girlhood to motherhood in some societies, the tendency in the West is to see adolescence as an extension of girlhood: a young woman in an in-between stage – not quite girl but not quite woman either. In this transition, the rituals marking the change from girlhood to womanhood are becoming increasingly complicated and imbued with contradictory meanings (Mitchell and Reid-Walsh 2005). Yet girlhood, like womanhood, is neither a universal nor an essentialized identity. Rather, it is deeply textured by race, class, sexuality, and ability; hence, its expression varies accordingly (de las Fuentes and Vasquez 1999a, 1999b).

As forces of domination, discourses of racial and gendered violence mark the lives of immigrant girls and young women. As I demonstrate in Chapter 4, racism becomes culturalized by virtue of its use of culture as the signifier of inferiorized difference (Gilroy 1991; S. Hall 1990a). Cultural norms and traditions that are perceived to be different and are negatively valued become the vehicles through which the hierarchy of preference and privilege are communicated and sustained (Dei 1999). Internalized over time, this preference structure engenders an inner group hierarchy, reflecting the "hidden injuries of race" (Osajima, cited in Pyke and Dang 2003, 151; see also Fanon 1967) – the damage resulting from internalized racism.

In her study on young South Asian women in Britain, Imam (1999) underscores their experiences of and exposure to racial violence. She argues that this exposure and experience result in feelings of exclusion and ostracization and, further, force young South Asian women and men to remain within the confines of their homes and communities (see also Brah 1997). Within the home, women become more vulnerable to patriarchal control and surveillance. Outside of the home, they are subject to patriarchal control exercised by the dominant society that not only inferiorizes and exoticizes them but also keeps them in "their place" by invoking fears of being victimized by overt and covert violence. In Imam's study, young South Asian women were also subjected to verbal and physical violence by White males and females in educational and other youth settings. These intertwining and interlocking influences of racism and sexism reflect the confluence of patriarchal forces within communities of colour as these are aligned with patriarchal forces in the dominant society. The racist exclusion and ostracization of the dominant society makes it possible for patriarchal powers within the community to exert their dominance through the imposition of moral strictures and limitations on young women's mobility (see Chapter 1).

Amita Handa's (1997) groundbreaking study of South Asian girls in Canada demonstrates how their lives are shaped by competing discourses. On the one hand, they have to negotiate pressures of assimilation in the context of school and employment. On the other, because they are signifiers of culture, there is an emphasis on protecting them from the Westernizing influence of the dominant society and ensuring their conformity to and maintenance of cultural traditions. Western traditions are perceived as weakening the moral fabric of community life. And, as with Espiritu's (2001) study of Filipina girls, discussed in Chapter 1, South Asian girls are similarly regulated in terms of their moral behaviour and their mobility. Yet, in order to belong and gain a sense of acceptance, these girls and young women have to engage with dominant Western norms and mores in the public domain. This is the site of the cultural conflict. However, Handa problematizes the notion of culture that is couched within the conflict paradigm, as static and frozen rather than dynamic and relational.

If we are to understand the ways in which racialized girls and young women negotiate the competing demands placed on them, we need to attend to how power and privilege are communicated through racialized and sexualized discourses of dominance. In this sense, we need to decode the "fictions of assimilation" (de Jesús 1998) that they are presented with as passports to acceptance and belonging. Conversely, we need to interrogate what defines acceptance and belonging.

Fitting In and Belonging

The mediated accounts of Reena Virk's murder (see Chapter 3) suggest that acceptance and belonging are obtained through fitting in. This notion of fitting in demands further scrutiny. It raises the question, fitting into what? Clearly, the dominant social values and normative expectations are part of what girls and young women feel they need to comply with as part of their way of fitting in. While these normative standards are based on an ideology of consumption, they are, more importantly, grounded in an ideology of Whiteness, heterosexuality, and ableism (see Gonick 2003). The comportment of an ideal typical Whiteness carries with it connotations of slimness, beauty, sexuality, and a certain look. Certainly, there are variations, but even these cohere around particular notions of what is considered beauty and what an ideal body type looks like. They are also assessed in terms of whether these bodies can and do attract the attention of boys and young men. Racialized girls and young women, then, face a more complex, intertwined, and powerful confluence of normative standards that are both raced and gendered and that are articulated through class privilege, heteronormativity, and able-bodiedness (see Scott 2002).

The pressure to fit in and belong is a key factor in the socialization of girls and young women. It is mediated by consumption practices encouraging girls and young women with the requisite purchasing power to obtain the same kinds of clothes, makeup, and other signifying commodities as their peers (Twine 1996). For young immigrant women of colour, poverty and lack of economic resources do not permit belonging through consumption (Blythe 2000). In their report on immigrant youth, Kunz and Hanvey (2000, 5) found that "over one-third of immigrants who have been in Canada for less than 10 years report that their household income is under $20,000, compared to 16% of those who have been in Canada for more than 10 years." The lack of fluency in the dominant language compounds immigrant youth's sense of isolation and lack of belonging. According to Kunz and Hanvey, 71.07 percent of immigrant children under the age of fifteen speak neither French nor English.[4] The resulting exclusion and Othering constitute forms of violence that dialectically feed into and reproduce internalized racism (Fanon 1967) – racism that manifests itself in a hierarchical structure of preference from within immigrant youth's own communities and peer groups.

In their study based on 184 in-depth interviews with young American adults of Korean and Vietnamese descent, Pyke and Dang (2003) elaborate on this inner group hierarchy. The oppressive forces of the dominant society influence the ways in which ethnic members within a community or peer group are perceived and in turn shape the ways they view themselves. At the one end of the resulting internal hierarchy are the whitewashed or assimilated ethnics; at the other end are the FOBs (those fresh off the boat), who are seen as being the least assimilated. In between is the normalized segment, those who are also assimilated, albeit not to the same extreme as those who are considered whitewashed. Pyke and Dang (2003, 168) argue that, "Although the construction of the identities 'FOB' and 'whitewashed' involves somewhat different 'othering' dynamics, both are constructed as an adaptive response to the racial oppression of the larger society. By discrediting coethnics who either confirm stereotypes of Asians as unassimilable or defy racial categories by attempting to merge into White society, a bicultural identity emerges that deflects stigma and defines the 'normals.' This process of intraethnic othering is an attempt to resist a racially stigmatized status; however, it does so by reproducing stereotypes and a belief in essential racial and ethnic differences between whites and Asians."

They caution that these findings do not reflect a conscious tendency on the part of those interviewed and are best understood as strategies of compliance and resistance fashioned in response to the pressures imposed by the dominant society. In Toronto, a study conducted for the Council of Agencies Serving South Asians (CASSA) and the South Asian Women's Centre (SAWC) reports that girls in the convened focus groups felt "they had strived so hard to fit in and be 'accepted' that they feared that any attempt on their part to support the newcomers might lead to exclusion from the group" (Desai and Subramanian 2000, 15).

While racialization involves the stigmatization, marginalization, and devaluation of difference, its gendered expressions often involve exoticization in ways that frame difference to make it alluring and even tolerable in small doses. For girls and young women of colour, this exoticization often results in the construction of their difference in sexual terms – as being open to or versed in particular erotic practices and as representing an Other who can be easily subjugated and exploited, sexually and otherwise (Park 2004). At the same time, the language of exoticization communicates to girls and young women the kind of differences that will be tolerated or that are perceived as being attractive and, conversely, differences regarded as revolting. In either case, the result is an objectification of the person. As one young woman of colour in Bourne, McCoy, and Smith's (1998, 61) study reported, "I've been told [by white boys] so many times, oh you're so exotic ... And it's like, am I a parrot or something?" Another commented: "Either you're so exotic or different or ... you're disgusting because you're a minority student." Either way, the discourses of difference position them outside the normative framework. As outsiders, they are often put in the position of being informants and held accountable for explaining the presumed strange and peculiar customs of their culture and community.

Reverberations of Violence

The impact of violence, whether it is intimate/interpersonal or systemic, can reverberate in subsequent generations. For example, in her study examining the effects of internment and redress among third-generation Japanese-Americans, Takezawa (1991) points to the intense shame and humiliation experienced by the children of those who were interned. She notes, however, that the movement toward redress helped restore a sense of identity. These memories of past experiences of structural violence have long-lasting reverberations, as evident in Mona Oikawa's (2002) study of Japanese women interned in Canada during the First World War. In a study of Filipino-Canadian youth in Vancouver, Geraldine Pratt (2002, 5) suggests that the "'cascade' of trauma from one generation to the next may also work through silences and evasions." For the youth who participated in her focus groups, the racist exclusion they experienced and its attendant lack of belonging forced them to re-create a sense of community and home by reviving and revitalizing links with the Philippines, both geographically and culturally. Their witnessing the deskilling of their parents also influenced their sense of exclusion. The economic violence caused by deskilling and lack of accreditation for parents of immigrant children and youth has been documented extensively. Deskilling results in an economic decline leading to poverty, and also generates hardship within the family in terms of gender role reversal and reliance on the labour of children and youth (see Chapter 6).

Bernard's (2002) discussion of African-American children reveals that growing up in a racist environment often compels the children to keep silent about the abuse they are experiencing within the home. There is, on the one hand, a supposition that such violence is normal within all Black families, and on the other, the perception that calling attention to such violence will result in a dismissal and denial of it. More importantly, the children feel torn as they are confronted with betraying their parents, whom they see as being similarly and negatively impacted by White society's racism. Hence, along with the condemnation of "race treason" (Flynn and Crawford 1998) from the community for those girls and women who call the attention of external authorities to the abuse they face at home, the girls and young women experience feelings of disloyalty as they wrestle with the guilt that emanates from their own sense of having betrayed either one or both of their parents.

This feeling of betrayal and its attendant loss of voice for fear of bringing shame on the family is a common barrier for young women of colour who are incest survivors. In her study of such young women, Smita Vir Tyagi (1999) articulates a three-tiered conceptual framework to better situate the factors that silence their voices and impede disclosure. On the global level, the framework of patriarchy ensures that male privilege and power work to subordinate women and girls and to silence any refusal or opposition; on the cultural level, prevailing attitudes and practices ensure that girls and young women conform to the standards of the culture per se, including notions of honour, saving face, and self-blame. At the third level, the community-in-context – namely, the particular subcultural group to which the individual belongs – imposes its own standards and codes. Tyagi (1999, 174) suggests,

> Communities of colour, particularly new immigrants and refugees, have subcultures that operate differently from the dominant culture, particularly if they are struggling to survive in a hostile or racist host environment. In order to deal with stresses inherent in discontinuity and change communities turn naturally to known, familiar values, behaviours, and beliefs. Many turn further inwards to their sense of ethnic identity and accompanying values in an effort to enhance community belongingness. To do so however, it is axiomatic that (a) the subculture's own cultural values be constructed as good and therefore worthy of preservation; (b) problems, dissonant ideas be externalized as a disruptive, coming from the outside, i.e., the host-culture; (c) a mythology be created that the values from the source (the motherland, country of origin) are the standard and impervious to change; (d) the only method of ethnic identity preservation is to preserve that standard; and (e) these positions be legitimized and endorsed by community leadership.

Tyagi adds that "this process creates the psychological foundation upon which entire communities can rest their denial of incest" (174). I would extend the analysis to include denials of disabilities as well as Othered forms of sexuality.

The studies outlined above raise interesting questions and suggest potential areas for research. For one, how do girls and young women from racialized communities come to know "their place" in the larger society? In other words, how are the experiences of Othering understood as such by them, and how do they discursively construct a sense of identity and belonging in the face of exclusion? Or if, as Dei (1999, 24) suggests, "race assigns, as well as, [sic] denies identity," how is this communicated and how is it understood by those whose identities are so determined? These questions assume a heightened significance in a context of globalization marked by the continual movement of people and capital, the formation of diasporic communities, and the pervasiveness of transnational media that blur the lines between homeland and hostland (Appadurai 1990; Karim 1998; Mandaville 2001; Naficy 1998). As well, these questions are increasingly salient in a context where difference, and especially racialized difference, is continually defined as a threat while simultaneously being used to project all that is antithetical to mythologies of national identity.

It can be argued that while the first generation of immigrant children and youth is beset by the trauma of dislocation, parental deskilling, and the challenges of adapting to a new milieu, for the second generation, the core issue tends to be one of acceptance. The lack of acceptance and belonging results in a second-generation attitude brought about by realization of the illusory nature of the fictions of assimilation. Andall (2002, 391-92) suggests:

> The term "attitude" encapsulates both the positive and the negative. In relation to the second generation, it can be conceptualized as the expression of an assertiveness which is different from that of their immigrant parents and which is, in fact, indicative of their ambiguous insider/outsider status as citizens (sometimes) who do not necessarily belong. Although "second generation attitude" has the potential to lead to a negative and nonconformist relationship to the wider society, more positively it can also disrupt static conceptions of identity and nationhood and contribute to the construction of social and political spaces which can accommodate hyphenated senses of belonging.

It is these spaces of disruption that I attend to next.

Recontextualizing Racialized Immigrant Girls and Young Women

In attempting to answer some of these questions, I turn to the findings of the study on the Canadian girl child conducted through the FREDA Centre in Vancouver, British Columbia. The study was a response to the murder of Reena Virk and was intended to outline factors that contribute to violence against racialized girls. It involved multiple methods, including background research papers, policy analyses, and focus groups and interviews with racialized girls and young women and with service providers. In the following sections, I draw primarily from the focus group and one-on-one interviews with racialized girls and young women to illustrate the kinds of violence they experience in their daily lives and their sense of identity and belonging.

Methodology

Elsewhere I have detailed the methodologies and the epistemological framework of this study (Jiwani, Janovicek, and Cameron 2001). For the present purposes, I highlight some of the critical issues, given that they undoubtedly influenced what the girls and young women felt they were able to articulate in the context of these interviews and focus groups.

Violence is a sensitive subject in most contexts. In the case of racialized immigrant and refugee populations, violence and particularly gender-based violence are especially contentious issues. This can be attributed in part to the general surveillance of these communities, their criminalization, and the possibilities that, having been marked as violent communities, any disclosures of violence would simply reaffirm the stereotypes circulating about them in the dominant society (Lucashenko 1996). As well, a code of silence, even within the dominant community, surrounds gender-based violence. Within minoritized communities, the imposition of this code is intensified by the above mentioned factors, fuelled by racism and the dominant society's manifest expression in the zealous and rather unequal application of laws, which often result in harsher consequences (Martin and Mosher 1995).

These factors, combined with the rather rigid standards of ethics review committees within universities, make it difficult to conduct research on girls – considered to be underage – in communities already noted for their vulnerabilities and past histories of exploitation.[5] In light of these considerations, the research that was undertaken attempted to assuage some of the ethical issues involved in conducting research with marginalized and racialized communities by (a) involving an advisory group of young women of colour at the initial stages of the development of interview and focus group questions; (b) utilizing the grounded expertise of community groups, service providers, feminist advocates, and young women of colour in conducting interviews and facilitating focus groups; and (c) conducting research in a participatory framework that recognized and affirmed the role of community groups as partners in the process.

Many of the service providers and advocates involved in this study had conducted interviews prior to this research, and many were aware of the code of silence extant within their communities with regard to issues of gender-based violence. Further, many were chosen because of their involvement in organizing and working with youth and, in some cases, being youths themselves. To reassure interviewees and focus group participants and make them feel as comfortable as possible with the process, the interviewers and facilitators were selected from racialized communities, albeit not always from the same communities as the girls and young women being interviewed. In addition, an initial list of open-ended questions prepared for the interviews and focus groups was vetted by a group of young women of colour from immigrant communities who were convened as an advisory group to the project, as well as by another advisory group consisting of policy makers, social service personnel, and researchers.

The attempt to conduct the research in a participatory fashion involved several key principles. The first dealt with issues of a power differential based on racial identity. By having interviewers and focus group facilitators who were themselves from the various communities of colour and/or of immigrant background, it was thought that the power differential that occurs between the researched and researchers could be diminished (Lather 1991; Ristock and Pennell 1996). Further, embracing a post-colonial framework required an awareness and acceptance of the impact of race, class, and gender, in terms of how these categories have been used to Other those who are different and to discount their experiences (hooks 1990, 1995). Finally, the aim was to conduct research that blurred the line between researcher and researched through a recognition that the experiences being drawn out of this study were shared – basically to harness a grounded expertise based on the knowledge of simultaneously being marginalized and serving a marginalized population (L. Smith 1999).

Through partnerships with community organizations and community researchers, fifty-two girls and young women were recruited to participate in the project. The youngest was thirteen years of age and the oldest was twenty-two; the majority were between fifteen and sixteen years old. Their countries of origin or their parents' countries of origin included Antigua, Barbados, China, Congo, Ethiopia, Fiji, India, Iran, Jamaica, Mexico, Pakistan, the Philippines, St. Kitts, Taiwan, Thailand, Trinidad, and Zaire. Seven young women participated in the Iranian focus group. Five young women from the Caribbean participated in a focus group conducted by a local Afro-Canadian support organization. Ten young women participated in the focus group for Latin American young women. A two-day focus group workshop was convened with sixteen young women of colour from a variety of countries, including China, Mexico, Pakistan, India, and countries in West Africa. This focus group utilized a theatre-of-the-oppressed model and was facilitated by Jump Start Consulting, a group which was initially involved in the project through a FREDA community partnership with SUCCESS, a Chinese-Canadian settlement service agency. The Affiliation of Multicultural Societies and Service Agencies of British Columbia (AMSSA) conducted the other two focus groups, which consisted of six participants, four of Eastern European background and two of African background.

Raced and gendered identities are highly situational (Mahtani 2002a; Matthews 1997; Räthzel 2000; Twine 1996). Hence, the articulations of experiences of violence, identity, and belonging are influenced by and indeed grounded in the particular localized circumstances in which girls and young women find themselves (Bredström 2003; Lee 2006). Most of the interviews and focus groups occurred in Vancouver, and that city's historic and contemporary climate of intolerance would undoubtedly have shaped and influenced their responses.[6] Hence, the findings of this study cannot be generalized across the board, nor are they intended to be. Rather, they highlight the ways in which race and gender work together in contributing to susceptibilities and vulnerabilities to different forms of violence. Nonetheless, these findings offer insights into the influences shaping the lives of young women like Aylin Otano-Garcia whose murder I describe at the beginning of this chapter, and to the range of everyday racist and sexist violence that Reena Virk experienced.

In talking to the girls and young women in the focus groups and interviews, it was apparent that they negotiate multiple realities. To highlight this element of negotiation, I use the term "walking the hyphen," taken from Indy Batth's illuminating thesis on South Asian girls (Batth 1998). Batth makes the point that Indo-Canadian girls are constantly negotiating between multiple subject positions and the fluidity of their identities is mediated by structural location and systemic factors. My point of departure in mapping these links between Othering, belonging, and violence in the lives of racialized girls from communities of colour rests on this process. In the sections below, I detail some of the main findings. Many of these support the existing literature but other themes emerging from the interviews and focus groups demand a more complex analysis.

Defining Violence

The majority of the girls and young women who participated in this project identified racism as the dominant and pervasive form of violence they encounter in their daily lives. They defined racism in interpersonal and systemic terms – from discriminatory treatment by teachers in schools to the minimization of their participation, the silencing of their voices, and the erasure of their histories and cultural realities in the school curriculum. They also identified racism as acts of verbal and physical abuse that cause pain and that result in their Othering, inferiorization, and exclusion.

Some of the other themes that emerged from the data revolved around their notions of belonging, how they fit within the dominant culture, the hierarchy of racism, and the ways in which they are Othered. A significant theme was the impact of the media in negating and stereotyping their communities.

Notions of Belonging

In negotiating a sense of self and their own positionality vis-à-vis their communities and the dominant society, many of the girls and young women revealed a relational identity – in other words, they would be Iranian (or whatever) in one context and Canadian in another. Overwhelmingly, they did not see themselves as Canadian when in Canada but, rather, when they were visiting their ancestral homeland or within the context of their own group. For some, their perception of authentic "Canadians" was based on the latter as being White and of European origin. As one Iranian girl noted: "I think they see me as Iranian. Like the Brown people, Moroccan, Iranian are like all one ... They don't see me as White like they call Canadian" (interview). Another stated: "They look at you and go, 'You're not Canadian. You're Persian or whatever. But you're not Canadian because you don't have blue eyes or blond hair'" (interview).

In her study of women of mixed race in Canada, Mahtani (2002a, 77) found that their notion of "an 'authentic' Canadian is of either British or French blood – those 'real' Canadians who are part of a 'capital-C Canadian' society." Aujla (2000, 41) makes the same observation about second-generation South Asian women who are made to feel "never quite Canadian enough, never quite White enough." The Whiteness of the dominant identity not only reinforces the darkening of the identity of the Other but is constitutive of the very process by which "the culturally dominant create the nation as home – in other words, as part of a home-making project of white Canadians" (G. Pratt 2002, 8n).

It is this exclusion from the ideal typical notion of Canadian identity that results, in part, in the adoption of hyphenated identities. The latter reflect the fluidity and the tenuousness of belonging. In speaking of women who share more than one basis of cultural identity, Mahtani (2002, 79) notes: "The burden of hyphenation, where one is seen as not solely 'Canadian' but 'Canadian and fill-in-your-ethnic-background' is especially heavy for women of 'mixed race,' who further trouble the hyphen by employing and intermingling two or more ethnicities in their own definitions of their identities." Yet, this very act of naming is often a forced response, compelled by the framing of the quintessential question, where are you from? As Kamala Visweswaran describes it, "To pose a question of origin to a particular subject is to subtly pose a question of return, to challenge not only temporally, but geographically, one's place in the present. For someone who is neither fully Indian nor wholly American, it is a question that provokes a sudden failure of confidence, the fear of never replying adequately" (cited in Aujla 2000, 43). Jennifer Kelly (1998) makes reference to the same issue in her study of Black youth in Canada, who are constantly subjected to the dominant gaze.

In the focus group with Afro-Caribbean young women, birthright – whether they were born here or not – was a key factor in how they defined themselves. Those who were born here felt that they were Canadians. Those who had immigrated here did not feel the same level of comfort in calling themselves Canadian, though they were often referred to as such when they visited their relatives in their country of origin. Utilizing the notion of birthright is one of the ways in which the differentiation between newly arrived communities and those that are well established is maintained. Yet, as the Filipino focus group participants in Geraldine Pratt's study indicate, birthright does not automatically grant a sense of permanence or belonging. A recurring phrase in her focus groups was, "Made in the Philippines, born in Canada" (2002, 4). Aujla makes a similar argument in articulating young South Asian women's sense of exclusion, which she suggests is worse for those born in Canada. Speaking to this issue, one of the young South Asian women interviewed stated: "I feel more Indian here. Because when you go to India, there's so much more to it. So it's like you're too much Indian here and not enough Indian there."

Acquiring a sense of belonging is indeed possible but only when one is surrounded by examples of acceptance. As one young South Asian woman stated in response to a question about her sense of identity and belonging, "I definitely did [belong] because I went to a very multicultural school, especially when I was younger. There were so many different people around me and all my friends were from different places. I think that was really good for me especially. And my mum, my whole family, always said, 'Don't ever leave one person out because they're different or anything like that.' They've always taught me that" (Jump Start workshop). Her comments reveal the mitigating influence of an accepting environment and parents who are aware of the implications of exclusion.

However, as this same young woman recounted, there was an explicit rejection of Canadian identity when it involved associations with overt racism: "My parents ... they're constantly [saying] like I'm giving my kid a better [life]. But what is better? That's not to say it doesn't happen in our countries. We hear it constantly – ethnic warfare and political strife – but they think that it's so much better here and then you hear things like [incidents with the Ku Klux Klan] and it totally breaks down your faith in humankind and Canadian nationalism and pride. I don't want to have pride in that. If that's Canadian, I don't want to be Canadian" (Jump Start workshop). This kind of critical interrogation of their identities and location was apparent in a number of interviews, but the majority saw their identity as Canadians in evolving terms – not one that was inherently theirs but one that could possibly be acquired over time via an increased facility with English, broader networks with European Canadians, and "knowing the system."

Fitting In

The aspects of fitting in that the girls and young women described were also highly influenced by systemic and everyday racism. As a young woman in the Iranian focus group reported:

> Well, they make fun of my name ... White people. Well, my name is [name]. It [sounds] like gonads. It's close to that. They make fun of it or they say that "Your name is stupid." Sometimes they say that ... Like I want my name to be what it is. I don't have to shorten it for people to make it easier for them. I mean I have to learn their way to fit in but they can't say my name properly, spell my name properly, or pronounce it properly. Like if I don't say it right, they would make fun of me. They'd be like, "Oh, you're an FOB."

Clothes – as in the wearing of trendy ones – constituted a major signifier of acceptance (see also Gonick 2003). This is something shared by all girls and young women; however, for immigrant and refugee girls of colour, the issue of poverty makes it very difficult for them to acquire clothing that would facilitate their fitting in. As well, informal knowledge about the normative values ascribed to clothes is something that they can acquire only over time. Fitting in requires fluency in the dominant language and the ability to remain silent in the face of dismissal and erasure – in other words, knowing how to stay in one's place. Many of the young women were cognizant of this implicit demand. Others saw it as a normalized response to a situation in which they had little knowledge of the rules or limited access to social resources. As one of the young Iranian women put it: "Right now, you're under a lot of pressure. You have so many things in your mind. And plus this, this whole thing, not knowing English, and trying to fit in but you're not because your appearance is not good enough, the way you dress is different, it's a different style, it's a different taste of clothing. And other things that you want to do but you can't, that's a lot of pressure and I think it's going to be very difficult. Because at this age, there's a lot of pressure you're going through" (interview). Her experiences reflect the pressures of conformity – to dress in a particular way, to satisfy the criteria of attractiveness, and to speak in the language and style of the dominant group. When these demands are mapped onto the developmental cycle of adolescence and augmented by class considerations, the result is often marginalization

– a marginalization made possible by class, race, gender, age, and the demands of living in a consumer society.

Another Iranian girl spoke of the self-policing that accompanies the internalization of dominant norms and perceptions: "Persians are loud people ... People would be looking and staring at us, White people. And I'd be like, 'Shut up. Don't speak so loud. Everybody's looking at us.' Because I don't like that kind of stuff. Like we should balance out. We don't like everybody to stare at us. We don't want everybody to say, 'Oh, those people are so loud'" (interview). Her quote confirms Foucault's (1980a, 155) insights when he describes the power of "a gaze which each individual under its weight will end by interiorising to the point that he is his own overseer, each individual thus exercising this surveillance over, and against, himself." Jennifer Kelly (1998) argues that the youth in her study live "under the gaze" of White society. Here, the White gaze has been internalized and regulates behaviour in concordance with the dictates of the dominant society.

The ultimate form of violence in the lives of these young women, and perhaps the most profound and harmful manifestation of the desire to fit in, is the negation of self. This process can occur through assimilation, internalized racism, and sexism. The young women in the focus groups and interviews revealed the self-denial and self-erasure they experience. As one Afro-Caribbean Canadian focus group participant said, "Sometimes I feel like I have to lose my true identity to fit in." Another young South Asian woman from Fiji reported: "The only time I think I would be like Indian would be when I would go to a party, or a wedding, or a Temple." Her comments illustrate the ways in which cultural identity becomes compartmentalized and privatized, relegated to the sphere of community (Peter 1981).

The Othering of girls and young women of colour is achieved through strategies in which their differences are devalued, exoticized, or distanced, largely through the dominant culture's construction of such differences. As one Afro-Caribbean young woman said: "They always ask us about our hair and they always feel our hair and it really bothers us. 'Oh, is that your real hair or is that extensions?' They come up to you on the bus and start feeling your hair without asking if they can touch your hair" (Afro-Caribbean focus group). This comment illustrates the curiosity of those in the dominant society – wanting to touch and feel the strangeness that they witness – and, further, the certitude with which private space is transgressed in the interests of satisfying a personal curiosity. That Black hair should be considered strange reflects one facet of the ethnocentric White gaze, but that one's space can be so violated demonstrates a power relation whereby those who are crossing this space in order to assuage their curiosity feel no sense of transgression because they simply take for granted the inferiority of the person whose hair they are touching.

One young Black woman noted the commodification of Black popular culture as yet another mechanism by which African-Canadians get exoticized. As she put it: "The hip hop thing going on. Most people try to dress like hip hop. And there's an issue also that a lot of other people from other races try to talk like us, do you know what I mean, in that sort of way. A lot of them sometimes feel like they belong too but, you know, I've met this Caucasian girl and she's told me she's Black ... when people say that ... I didn't say anything" (interview). Jennifer Kelly (1998) observes similar dynamics in her study of Black youth. However, in the case of the young woman quoted above, the issue she highlights is also one of appropriation – how, once a style or tradition is commodified, it is rendered more attractive and palatable for consumption (see Lalvani 1995). Transformed into commodities, these symbols or styles are then used to signify Western superiority over other cultures and traditions (Durham 2001). The process of commodification alluded to in the above quote also foregrounds the phenomenon of the wannabes – those who claim a particular heritage or group membership by virtue of appropriating the symbols of that heritage. That the White girl can assert such a claim reflects her occupation of space of power and privilege. But the Black girl who attempts to claim membership in the White group would probably be the object of derision in her group, where she would be accused of being whitewashed, and the object of ridicule in the dominant group, where she may be conditionally accepted but only through the erasure of her identity as a young Black woman.

Stereotyping and criminalizing emerged as two other key strategies by which difference is underscored and devalued. Stereotyping is the more subtle strategy of the two, and was often attributed to the media, the ignorance of peers, and authority figures. This is evident in the following exchange which occurred in a focus group with Afro-Caribbean girls and young women:

Girl: The thing is, if White folks think that Black folks are so bad, why are they trying so hard to be us?

Girl: There's this girl, she comes to me and, "I know how to talk like Black people." I'm like, "How do Black people talk?" And she's like, "What's up, mon?" I get that a lot. I tell her nobody talks like that and it's not, "What's up, mon." That's how White people say it.

Girl: And the teachers. "Where you from?" "Jamaica." "Jamaica mon, Jamaica mon."

Girl: My teacher, he's like, "I went to Jamaica and the guy was speaking English but I couldn't understand what he was saying." And then he's like laughing. He's like, "Just tell him to write it down so I could understand what he's saying."

Girl: He should write down when he's talking, too.

These comments demonstrate the derision with which other cultures are stereotyped and mockingly mimicked. But as the last statement suggests, these young women are aware of the differential power relations that are being used against them and by which they are being judged.

The strategy of criminalization was more pronounced, with young women reporting that they were often followed by employees or security guards if they were in stores, or perceived to be prostitutes if they were hanging around a street corner or waiting for a bus. In the words of one Afro-Caribbean girl: "I was in Superstore with a couple of Black people and we were talking. And this one lady that worked in the store, she walked by us like ten times. She kept on walking by and looking at us as if we're going to hijack her store or something. Who would try to hijack Superstore?" (Afro-Caribbean focus group). And in the words of another: "I was on the street. My cousins were here. And we were waiting for the bus and a police car walked by and we started showing off. And they stopped and they walked around the block and they looked at us. And they walked around the block and they came back and they walked around again. And I'm like, 'We're not prostitutes. We're waiting for the bus' (Afro-Caribbean focus group). The assumption that race is associated with crime and prostitution reflects the dominant construction of racialized groups as being prone to crime, and of racialized women as working in the sex trade; both of these activities are sites of degeneracy, as defined by the dominant society (Razack 2002) and, hence, both entail excessive scrutiny if not criminalization. Hanging around a street corner is then construed as loitering or causing trouble. The gendering of this dominant construction results in a stereotype of Black women (and other women of colour) as prostitutes or sex trade workers if they are seen in public spaces, also reflecting the dominant society's devaluation of sex work. As James (1998, 168) eloquently puts it: "White people window-shop, Black people loiter."

Inferiorization is also communicated through the institutional streaming of girls and young women of colour into ESL classes. As this young woman noted: "When I first came here, it was my second year at school. And they're like taking me to this room ... I speak English because they were going to put me in ESL. I'm like, 'I speak English. In my country, I speak English. That's the only language I know. English'" (Afro-Caribbean focus group).

As in Pyke and Dang's (2003) study discussed earlier, being accepted or being perceived as fitting in was also predicated on being defined as different from those Others – notably those immigrants who were newly arrived and who had not yet assimilated. As this young woman from the Iranian focus group said: "But I have Canadian friends too. But then they, Canadians, make fun of my friends. Like, 'Are you hanging out with those FOBs again. Come hang out with us. Why are you hanging out with those FOBs?' I'm like, 'They're not FOBs just because they can't talk English,' or ... you know? But that's just making fun. That's not really ... I don't think that's really racist." Here, the experience of differentiating between the FOBs versus the more established immigrants is not understood in terms of racism but imputed to the ignorance of members of the dominant society. Again, as this young woman's comment reveals, the distinction is hierarchical. At the top of the hierarchy of acceptance and authenticity are the "true" Canadians, defined by their skin colour and access to informal and formal social knowledges. At the bottom end of the ladder are the FOBs, defined by their newness, their lack of such cultural capital, and their cultural or racial difference. Or as one young woman described them: "FOB is like 'fresh off the boat.' It means that you're really ... geeky and you don't know how to speak and stuff. You dress stupidly or whatever, right?" (Iranian focus group). In between are the assimilated, relatively accepted but culturally or racially different girls and young women. Aujla (2000) argues that this internal hierarchy consists of those who are assimilated, the honorary Whites, and the authentic – those who have retained their cultural traditions. One young Iranian woman commented: "The ones that are new hang out with Persians, their own culture. The ones that aren't, they usually hang out with White people. They're called Whites. They pretend that they're not Persian" (interview). Facility with the dominant language is seen as the passport to achieving acceptance. One young Asian-Canadian woman reported: "Some people you meet in Canada, they look like Chinese but they were born here. They don't like Chinese people who have just come to Canada. I don't know why but if you come to Canada and your English is really good, then you can speak with them freely. But if you can still speak Chinese, they think you are no good, they think you're a bad person because you come from China. If you tell them, 'I don't know any Chinese, I don't know Cantonese, I was born here,' they'll like you" (Jump Start workshop). Thus, knowledge of the ethnic language is similarly construed as a signifier of inferiority by those who embrace the dominant society's categories of classification for acceptability. From the perspective of those within a given community, such a sign may be construed as a badge of authenticity. Nonetheless, the hierarchy resulting from this preference structure is not simply confined to an internal register of cultural identity but works in tandem with the external register of so-called Canadian identity, in which other racialized groups are ranked in order of preference and degrees of acceptance.

This hierarchy of race was most clearly expressed in terms of the inter-ethnic or racial conflict endemic in most schools. Most participants and interviewees reported witnessing considerable intergroup violence in their schools. Girls and young women noted that they often hung around with members from their own communities as a form of protection and because they could communicate more freely with those who shared their cultural affiliation (see Pugh-Lilly, Neville, and Poulin 2001). As one of the inter-viewees put it:

> Like as in right now, there's a big group of Persians and there's a big group of Koreans, and a big group of ... well White people mostly hang around with different colours or White people all together. But Persians, if you're in that group, you feel safe because there's a lot of us and if something hap-pens to one, there is a lot of people to help back the person up. But then if you're alone, people are going to make fun of you and if you have nobody, then that's definitely difficult. It's going to be really difficult.

That "White people mostly hang around with different colours" needs to be contextualized in the sense of indicating who has the freedom to choose the friends they will interact with. Those in positions of power within a hierarchy can make such choices without constraint or necessity. They can exercise a greater degree of mobility in crossing boundaries and borders.

The hierarchy of race is also implied in terms of perceptions and differen-tial treatment accorded to particular groups vis-à-vis other groups. As this Iranian young woman explains: "I know because I remember Chinese people had the day off because they had Chinese New Year. But when we asked if we could have our day off, Persian New Year, they said no, we can't. Or we wanted to have a party or something, we wanted to use a little room in our school. And we wanted to use that to just party during lunchtime for our New Year, but we couldn't do that either" (interview). Though preferential treatment was perceived as being accorded to certain groups over others, the overall sense of these girls and young women was that the White stu-dents were given more attention, allowed more privileges, and treated bet-ter than any of the students of colour. As the Iranian girl quoted above elaborated in an interview:

> And then also, I don't know what it is but my teacher, when we come in late, she starts yelling at us, she starts saying, "Why are you late again? La, la, la, la." But some White girl comes in, she goes, "Oh, where have you been." She goes, "I was out with my friends, I'm so sorry," and she starts laughing. I would be like, "What the hell was going on?" Why is she yelling at us and not her and she's not saying anything. Or assignments. You hand

them in one day late, "Oh that's a zero for you." But then Canadian people, I don't know what they do, suck up to them or whatever, and then they can get the marks.

Despite being aware of the ranking and differential privileges accorded to various groups, including the power and authority of teachers, the girls and young women who participated in the study did not perceive this as an interconnected issue. On the contrary, many attributed the interracial violence and hostility of their peers to the innate characteristics of different groups and to a competitive and violent school environment. This reflects how "common sense" works to align interpretations in ways that correspond with hegemonic values and beliefs.

Girls and young women who participated in this study attributed their peers' racism to a lack of understanding about the impact of their remarks and interpreted these remarks as being based on misconceptions about racialized cultures. Like gender-based violence, racism operates on a continuum of violence.[7] Ignorance of another person's culture and fear of diversity may not be as explicitly threatening as name-calling and bullying. However, common-sense racism is just as damaging because it reinforces the position of the dominant culture and creates an environment that allows violent racist acts (J. Kelly 1998). The following comments describe the common-sense racism girls encounter at school:

> You'll hear things down the hall. I guess there are racist things but there's not a sense of racism behind it. It's just a remark that nobody really understands. (interview with South Asian girl)

> Someone asked me if we have TV in Iran. If you see someone, and you see they're not closed-minded but because of the limitation that they have, that they don't really have a good idea of what it's like so I have to explain to them in order to get the idea. (Iranian focus group)

The girls' and young women's comments repeatedly revealed their willingness to excuse their peers' lack of knowledge about the history and customs of racialized minorities. In this sense, their own perceptions are subsumed under the dominant discourses of denial, which trivialize and dismiss the subtle and overt expressions of racism or simply refuse to name them as such. This refusal to name racism can be attributed to the lack of language by which to name the abuse. Without a history of race and any substantive discussion defining it within the school system, those who are subordinated and marginalized are not necessarily going to be able to access such language or have the power to use it. Further, given the intensity of the discourses of denial that are operative in the school, mall, and media context, there is no collective recognition of racism as a form of violence. This makes the task of naming racism an individual one, and one likely to result in a certain degree of discomfort and danger of retaliation. Thus, while they recognize the everyday and systemic nature of racism, these girls and young women do not call attention to it for fear of having it dismissed by those in positions of authority, or of invoking potential retaliation. Further, as Matthews (1997, 14) observes in her study of Asian girls and boys in an Australian school, "being too quick to label can restrict and limit your social interactions and opportunities. Here the refusal to evoke discourses of racism or sexism can be seen to involve the tactical maximization of limited opportunities and thereby relocate the sites of negotiation to other grounds."

Nonetheless, everyday racism exhibited in subtle forms of Othering and inferiorization, combined with overt expressions of racism and sexism, engenders a sense of difference and marginalization (Canadian Council on Social Development 2000; Kunz and Hanvey 2000; Mogg 1991). School staff and administrators may engage in racist actions and attitudes in their treatment of and response to racialized immigrant children and youth. And the school curriculum itself may be exclusionary in terms of lacking content that is inclusive and that addresses the reality of the different racialized communities (Capuzzi and Gross 1996; J. Kelly 1998). Anti-racist, anti-sexist, and anti-homophobic educational materials and information on human rights and fundamental freedoms are lacking in most school curricula (Dei 1999; Lonsway 1996; Randall and Haskell 2000). Echoing these findings, one of the focus group participants commented:

> In school they don't teach you anything about Black people really. They don't teach you anything about your culture or anything. And if they teach you anything they teach you about Africa. That's not the only place where Black people are from. I think they should teach you about other places, not just one area. (Afro-Caribbean focus group)

Another girl explained how her teacher's dismissal of Canadian slavery affected her:

> In school we were learning about slavery and she goes, "Oh, we all know that there was never slavery in Canada," and then it kind of made me feel bad because I know there was slavery in Canada ... I went up to the teacher and I told [her] she said there was never slavery in Canada. And the teacher said, "Yeah, there was slavery in Canada but it wasn't as big a deal as the States" ... They should check their research on it before they teach it instead of reading the school books and then teaching what it says. Because a lot of the school books about African history is not true. (interview, Afro-Caribbean girl)

Other studies have corroborated these strategic absences in school curricula (see Canadian Race Relations Foundation 2000; Wideen and Barnard 1999). However, what the above comment points to is the minimization of Canada's role in permitting slavery and the latter move simply affirms the notion of Canadian tolerance. For these young women, tolerance comes across as putting up with difference, thereby implying a hollow, conditional, and rather tenuous form of acceptance.

Access to Resources

Services available to racialized girls and young women in schools were typically limited to ESL courses. And even these tend to be concentrated in urban centres. One girl from Thailand living in a small town reported that she attended school for two weeks before her father informed the school that she did not understand English. Since there were no ESL courses available in her school, she was placed in remedial classes. A service provider from the same town in rural British Columbia described the experience of two sisters she had worked with: "At home, they were loved by their parents and the parents wanted them to learn and go to work and do everything like anybody else does. But at school, these two young girls felt very isolated. People would look at them, stare at them, and call them names ... People won't sit beside them because they felt East Indian girls were smelly. So their experience at school was very, very difficult. All they wanted to do was learn but they didn't look forward to going to school" (interview). Given that isolation is a key risk factor for violence (see Chapters 1 and 6), the situation of immigrant and refugee girls in rural areas is in a sense worse than that of their urban counterparts. Lacking peers who share their cultural background, they have to make a choice between internalizing the violence and the rejection they experience, and trying to fit into peer groups that are not always accepting of their difference.

Although less isolated than their rural counterparts, racialized immigrant girls and young women in urban communities still face a hostile school environment. The problem is exacerbated by the refusal of many principals and teachers to acknowledge racism in the schools. Many young women described their frustration with teachers who discriminate against them and with principals who dismiss them when they describe racist acts: "I wouldn't go to a principal because they would go against me, too. It has happened a couple of times that they would say, 'Oh, this is not about race.' ... Somebody in our school got suspended because she said she felt one of her teachers was really racist. She got suspended even though she didn't say who it was" (interview, Iranian girl).

Racism in the schools was perceived as being fostered by teachers and administrators who refused to speak out about it or who simply perpetuated it. As one of the focus group participants explained: "The teachers, they keep it to themselves, the principal, they always try to keep it in secret. They don't go out and say we need to deal with this issue" (Afro-Caribbean focus group). Another recounted: "I've had a teacher talk to us like – some Chinese people were talking their language – I've had teachers say, 'Hey, shut up. Talk English.' Just like that. And it's like, 'Hello? You don't say that. Obviously they're going to be scared of you now.' So they really need to deal with the situations of kids. A teacher is almost like a parent because you're with them every day, you have classes with them, they're supposed to understand you and stuff like that. And the communication is supposed to be good" (Afro-Caribbean focus group).

The girls and young women who confronted their teachers over such issues reported that their concerns were often dismissed. Likewise, their attempts to correct the misrepresentations of their cultures and histories on the grounds that these contributed to the racism they experienced on a daily basis generally went ignored. They conceded that their histories and cultures were being erased in the context of the classroom.

These comments highlight the denial and dismissal of racism by White school authorities, especially since the girls and young women who were interviewed did not mention teachers or principals of colour whom they had encountered in these ways. More than that, they demonstrate the fear that girls and young women experience in calling attention to such racism, and the potential retaliation they might experience as a result. One of the South Asian young women interviewed outlined the severe consequences that might arise for those who remain silent about racist acts and incidents: "From what I've seen, the kids fear it so they won't go and tell people about it. They'll just keep it inside. And I think that sooner or later, it's just going to make them explode. So if I could give them advice, I'd tell them, number one, go to a person who you know you can trust. I wouldn't say first to go to somebody at school" (interview). These kinds of comments suggest that schools are perceived as sites of external control rather than as *loco parentis* entrusted with the duty to care and nurture personal development.

The young women themselves identified various solutions to the tensions in the schools. When researchers asked them what they would recommend to reduce violence, they suggested programs that would bring together students from different backgrounds to unpack the social hierarchies and confront the racism that shapes day-to-day relations among peer groups: "They could have this program, if they could bring people from different groups together and take them somewhere so they had to all bind in together and understand each other and work their problems out together, come up with ideas together. That would help. You don't judge people by the way they look, the way they dress, the way they are, what their personality is" (interview, Iranian girl).

Mediated Violence

A key issue raised by the focus group participants and the girls and young women who were interviewed dealt with the media's role in disseminating stereotypical representations of their respective communities. As these participants from the Afro-Caribbean focus group noted:

> And on TV and stuff, if they're showing you about a Black place, there'll be like nice places in the country but they show you the poorest areas. I hate that because they're showing you the worst place of the country to make it look really bad.

> [TV] portrays all the bad things like it's known for marijuana or ganja or whatever drugs. They always come up to me [at school] and go, "So do you know where the drugs are?" No I don't. I don't even know what the tree looks like. So I always tell them saying, "Yes, I have some in the backyard of my house and if they want some, they can come over later." Because I'm sick of it. That's about all you hear.

Racial and cultural stereotypes in television and popular film have been noted as having a negative effect on the self-image and peer acceptance of immigrant and refugee youth (Canadian Council on Social Development 2000; Kunz and Hanvey 2000). These types of racist media images, coupled with sexist media content, can deeply influence the identity formation of the refugee and immigrant girl child. Social messages about who is and who is not desirable and what characteristics constitute beauty converge to effect the self-esteem and self-image of racialized girls and young women. The results include self-consciousness about body image, low self-esteem, and eating disorders (Basow and Rubin 1999; Sarigiani, Camarena, and Petersen 1993; Squire 2000). Schooler et al. (2004) found that Black girls who had a choice in viewing Black programming did not identify with mainstream images of White women's bodies or standards of beauty. This analysis reflects the necessity to provide alternative and community media that affirm cultural and racial identities and act as a protective force against the fictions of assimilation identified by de Jesús (1998).

Aside from this indirect influence, many of the girls and young women, by virtue of being minorities, carry with them the "burden of representation." Kobena Mercer (cited in Cottle 2000, 106) uses this term to describe Black media producers' quandary in being held accountable by their communities for representing them in the best possible light while attempting to create a product that speaks to their own truth and reflects their own interests. Here, I extend the concept to apply to those who are subjected to the same feeling of accountability for their entire group regardless of whether

that group shares any degree of homogeneity or whether they even identify with the group in question. One of the Afro-Caribbean focus group
participants provided a poignant example of this: "For example, I'm reading this book in school, *To Kill a Mockingbird*. And it was about the Black
guy, they thought he raped the girl or something. The whole time I had my
head down because maybe it's nothing big. It's just my personal feelings
because it just makes me feel like all Black people, they're the ones who are
the rapists and the killers. And I'm the only Black girl in my class, so and
then they have all these White people." An Iranian girl mentioned during
her interview that she was highly embarrassed and shamed by the teacher's
screening of a popular film, *Not without my Daughter,* which portrayed Muslim cultures as backward and brutally patriarchal. In recounting her experience, she said, "I start[ed] crying and I was so upset and I talked to my
teacher and told her this is not how it is for me. Now I realize that all the
people who are Chinese, Japanese, from all over the world, would think of
Iran based on this" (Iranian focus group). Another young woman of South
Asian origin pointed to the discrepancies between exoticized and depress-
ing representations of India, her cultural homeland. As she put it: "[The
media] shows [India] being very exotic, with Madonna and her mendhi
[henna] and saris being turned into drapes and the masala and everything
being exotic ... It's [also] shown as a welfare culture. It's the kids on the
UNICEF ad. So on one hand, it's like this big rich silk industry which does
henna on the side and on the other hand, it's the nude baby with the
overswelled tummy on the UNICEF ad" (Jump Start workshop). The burden of representation contributes to the ambassadorial role in which
racialized children and youth are commonly cast. Here they become representatives of their entire cultures and groups, and experts on whatever practices are considered peculiar and demanding of explanation (see also G.
Pratt 2002).

Though faced with what appear to be insurmountable structurally mediated forces of violence, these young women have developed their own strategies of resistance. These include the formation of tight peer groups with
members who share the same cultural ethos, asserting their own perspectives and definitions when compelled to do so, and defending their cultural
communities. As this young Iranian woman stated in an interview:

> The thing about me is I don't like to change myself. Why should I change
> myself for other people? So the thing is that if I like my culture, if I like
> whatever – now is the fasting time right? and I'm fasting – if someone calls
> me and says, "You can't fast. This is Canada." That's none of your business.
> This is my culture, this is me, I want to keep it. You can't tell me how to
> change it. So I don't change the culture because of other people. I change it

if I don't like it. Then I'll change it. I don't change it because other people tell me Persian culture sucks or whatever.

The assertion that this young woman makes is itself grounded in a cultural terrain. So rather than see the issue of imposition as one of power, she translates this into an affirmation of individual will and cultural identity. As in the news media, the language of power and conflict are culturalized and individualized.

In response to how she might be perceived by the dominant group, this young South Asian Canadian woman said: "If they don't see it, then all I can say is I'm Canadian. If they see it differently, then they see it differently. I'm not going to change whatever I am to suit their needs. If they don't see it, then that's just their problem" (Jump Start workshop). The confidence that underpins any assertion of identity needs to be grounded in a sense of self that has remained intact or that is somehow supported in the struggle to remain intact (hooks 1992). Family and community provide such anchoring and protection. As another young South Asian woman put it: "I've just become my own person I guess. I've started to realize that it's all right to be me and different. When I say different, I don't mean freakishly outcast or anything. Just different as in different backgrounds" (interview). A mark of that surety of identity comes through in this comment by a young woman in the Iranian focus group:

Like when you're talking to White girls, you talk to them and have different opinions and you're like, "Yeah, okay, you have a different opinion about something." And if there's a fight in school, my White friends are like, "Yeah, you Persian girls fight all the time." And now that upsets me because I'm with Persians. Before it was like, "Yeah, Persian girls fight. Who cares?" Now it kind of upsets me. "What do you mean Persian girls fight all the time?" Now I defend myself. I think I defend my friends of Persian [origin]. Like, "No, Persians don't fight all the time. That's the way it is." If somebody says something to me, I'm going to defend myself.

Above all, this last comment highlights the necessity of such a defence – a necessity derived from the need for solidarity in opposing violence in all its manifestations. Such solidarity is organic in terms of its evolution and its emergence in sites of support and affirmation.

Conclusion

These interviews and focus group data reveal the complexity of the negotiations that racialized girls and young women are engaged in daily, both in terms of identity formation and in securing a place for themselves in society as a whole. They also disclose a number of insights which parallel the experiences of women in violent relationships. Many of these young women articulated definitions of violence that were equated with racism. For them, racism is a significant aspect of their everyday reality. They were cognizant of the power of the authoritative structures in the school and of their symbolic absence in the curriculum. However, they were unable to perceive how the hierarchy of races that was in place serves the interests of the dominant group. Further, they often attributed racism to ignorance on the part of their peers – a reflection that reinforces elite notions of racism relayed by the media in which racism is portrayed as being due to a lack of education or the ignorance of a few loonies out there (van Dijk 1993). Like those of women who experience violence, their stories reveal that there are few services or safe places available to girls or young women from racialized communities of colour. Rather, they are often faced with little choice except to turn to their own communities – to friends and family within those communities – to deal with these issues.

The discourses of denial that are operative in the lives of these girls and young women cohere around the following axes: the denial of teachers and principals to address issues of systemic and everyday racism that these girls and young women encounter; the erasure of these issues in the curriculum; and the failure of these institutions to examine the intersections of race and gender in terms of how the latter might render girls and young women of colour more susceptible to the violence of gendered racism. Further, these discourses are apparent in the very denial of the existence of racial hierarchies within the school system, hierarchies that are maintained and reproduced in the interests of those who stand to benefit from them. The influence of these hierarchies in engendering internal stratification systems within racialized communities that differentiate Others on the basis of their immigrant status is highly problematic. That such hierarchies are glossed over or ignored by those in positions of authority and power is reflective of the dynamics of whitewashing or, inversely, of problematizing difference. In the latter case, specific groups are targeted and defined as problems that need to be expelled or contained. Finally, the continued stereotyping by the media and the unfair burden of representation that it forces racialized girls and young women to bear is itself reflective of the discourse of denial. For here the notion of individual choice – as in turning the dial or switching the channel – becomes a way in which institutional responsibility is evaded if not denied altogether.

Naming the violence and acknowledging its systemic nature would considerably ameliorate the situation of racialized girls and young women. For, as Helene Berman (1999) observes in her analysis of the children of war, by naming the war, collectively recognizing it, and collectively experiencing it, these children were in a far better position than their counterparts, who had experienced and witnessed the private war of domestic violence. If the systemic nature of racist violence is named, acknowledged, and recognized, that violence cannot be dismissed or trivialized as an individualized, pathological, and aberrant action.

Discourses of denial are apparent in other institutional contexts as well. These discourses are used strategically by elite institutions to erase, trivialize, dismiss, or contain difference. However, each institution has its own set of rules by which it sustains and perpetuates discourses of denial. In the following chapter, I continue to focus on the voices of those who have experienced violence, but shift my attention to racialized immigrant women and their encounters with the health care system.

6

Gendered Racism, Sexist Violence, and the Health Care System

A punch in the eye or a kick in the stomach is probably the same no matter what colour you are or what language is being shouted at the time.

> – Christine Rasche, "Minority Women and Domestic Violence"

The conscious or unconscious behaviours of people whose culture has the power to define service policies and practice may cause those from other cultural groups to feel powerlessness, anger and humiliation often resulting in avoidance of the service. In Maori that response is called whakam, to make things white, an emotional whiteout.

> – Irihapeti Ramsden, "Kawa Whakaruruhau"

I begin this chapter with two poignant quotes. Together, they eloquently summarize the situation of racialized immigrant women who have experienced violence, and their encounters with the health care system. On the one hand is the representation of the visceral reality of violence that knows no cultural or racial boundaries. On the other are the responses of health care providers that result in an emotional whiteout for abused women whose histories, needs, and lived experiences are trivialized, inferiorized, or erased. These two facets are indicative of the encounter between the brutal corporeal violence inflicted on the body and erasure of hierarchies of power embodied in the larger society and mirrored in the formal health care system.

Immigrant women of colour who have experienced violence are positioned at the juncture of multiple, intersecting, and interlocking systems of domination. They are located in the lower echelons of the social stratification system of the wider society because of their race, class, and gender;

they are also located at the bottom of the hierarchy of preferred clients of the health care system. They are, in effect, viewed as problem patients. Because they are women who are classed and raced, their needs and realities have been and continue to remain invisible, and their voices confined to the realm of advocacy and survival. Immigrant status confers its own subordinate positioning, which race, gender, and class accentuate in different and interlocking ways (J. Anderson et al. 1993; Bolaria and Bolaria 1994; Dossa 2004; Lee with Harrison 1999; Ng 1993a, 1993b).

In this chapter, I focus on immigrant women of colour who have experienced violence and their encounters with the health care system.[1] My intent is to uncover the power relations underpinning these encounters and through that process highlight the mechanisms by which power asserts and reproduces itself through racial stereotyping and the culturalization of violence. My aim is to demonstrate how the health care system as a hierarchical structure not only mirrors the dominant structures of violence inherent in the wider society but also perpetuates them in particular ways, ways that generate a hierarchy of preferred patients. The preferred patient is the deserving patient, as defined by Colleen Varcoe (1997) in her extensive and insightful work in this area. I argue that it is through this hierarchy that White dominance and patriarchal power are kept intact.

The Health Care System

The issue of health care is a highly sensitive one, given the cutbacks that have been implemented across provinces, and the insidious implementation of a two-tier system that allows those who can pay to obtain medical services as quickly as they wish and creates waiting lines for others. Yet, the health care system is often considered the hallmark of Canadian liberal democracy – a system originally designed to ensure the well-being of all its citizens. The dismantling of this system is often attributed to large-scale immigration, which is regarded as having unfairly burdened the system and, along with presumed immigrant abuse of its many benefits, violated the democratic intent of this system. What is often missing in this racially charged logic is the other side of the equation, namely, the numerous immigrants who are lured into the country because they possess expertise in health care but then are denied jobs on the basis of a lack of Canadian experience or lack of Canadian accreditation, as well as the migrant workers and Others who pay taxes to maintain the system. Erased from the public imagination are criteria imposed on immigrants for their access to Canadian health care.

Government policy defines immigrants as all those who are not born in Canada.[2] Even before immigrating, applicants have to demonstrate that they are in good health and that they will neither pose a risk to public health nor impose a burden on provincial health care systems. According to section

19(1a) of the Immigration Act, a foreign national will not be admitted if her/his health demands "exceed that of the average Canadian (evaluated as $2,500 per year); if their admission may displace a Canadian resident from obtaining services; or if the required services are not available and/or accessible" (Laroche 2000, 53). The more recent Immigration and Refugee Protection Act (2001) has a similar stipulation; however, it exempts those who are sponsored by a family member, those who fall in the family class, and those who are convention refugees and/or protected persons.

The popular perception of immigrants as either a danger to public safety or a drain on the nation's health care system has a long history (Beiser 1998).[3] Historically, the association of people of colour with strange and unwelcome diseases was used to rationalize a relatively closed-door immigration policy (J. Anderson and Kirkham 1998). The fear that this association generated still remains, continuing to influence policy decisions involving screening mechanisms for the detection of diseases among potential immigrants (Beiser 1998; Shroff 1996-97).

Legislation and policies on immigration have a tremendous impact on settlement and access to services. Hence, the category in which a woman immigrates – as an independent, a sponsored dependant in the family class, a convention refugee, or someone with landed status after serving time as a domestic worker or live-in caregiver – determines her subsequent status and access to services (Thobani 2000a).[4] The same applies to undocumented women, migrant workers, and foreign students, whose access to services may be further impaired by the degree of legality ascribed to their status.

As a dominant institution, the health care system is stratified. It is raced, classed, and gendered in the way in which services and labour are organized (Puzan 2003). Janitorial, kitchen, and laundry staff occupy the bottom echelons of the system, while nurses are located above them, and physicians, along with hospital administrators, account for the elite. Each level also has its own stratification system. Thus, some nurses occupy the bottom echelons of that order while others are at the top. These hierarchies are raced (Calliste 2000). This is particularly the case within the formalized health care system, which includes sites such as hospitals, clinics, and physicians' private practices. Within this tiered context, varying levels of violence are perpetrated against those who have relatively little power or control (Varcoe 1997).

Overt racism in the health care system is reflected in the unequal practices of hiring people of colour, their ghettoization in certain jobs, their lack of advancement, and their absence from decision-making positions. The reluctance to accredit medical practitioners trained in other parts of the world is another manifestation of the exclusive structure of power and privilege inherent in the medical system (see Basran and Zong 1998; Battershill 1992). Such a structure serves to exclude both people of colour and immigrants from Eastern European countries whose medical credentials are similarly devalued. Nonetheless, if we are to examine the representation of people of colour in the hierarchical structures of hospitals, it is apparent that most end up at the janitorial level – as kitchen staff, cleaners, and ward nurses. This latter point is an obvious indicator of systemic racism.

In a study focusing on Black nurses in a Toronto hospital, Das Gupta (1996) observes that their work is more heavily scrutinized, and the demands and expectations placed on them greater, than in the case of White nurses. Furthermore, Black nurses are more often sidelined for advancement. These findings corroborate those of an earlier study by Head (1986) that looked at minority nurses in Toronto hospitals. Head found that minority nurses were significantly under-represented in decision-making positions in hospitals and were not promoted at the same rate as White nurses, despite having the same or superior qualifications (cited in Henry et al. 1995). Agnes Calliste (2000, 158) observes that

> Black women were allowed into nursing as a floating reserve army of labour during the postwar expansion of industrial capitalism and severe nursing shortages. However, they were then and are today marginalized and treated as the "Other." For instance, even at the present time they are concentrated at the bottom of the gendered and racially segmented nursing labour force as staff nurses; they are also more likely than their White counterparts to be employed part-time and as casuals. Thus, they are less likely to be entitled to fringe benefits. Moreover, Black nurses who work full-time are more likely than their White counterparts to be underemployed, to be denied access to promotions and to be assigned the least desirable shifts and duties involving mostly menial work.

If the health care system reflects the dominant structures of power and privilege that inhere in the wider society, what happens to immigrant women of colour in their encounters with this system? How are they perceived and treated, and how is gendered violence against immigrant women recognized and treated? In answering these questions, the larger issues pertaining to migration and health deserve a brief mention here, given that they form the contextual background informing the lives of immigrant women of colour.

Racialized Immigrant Women and Health
Much has been written about the impact of migration on health (Bhugra 2004). In his study of the Southeast Asian boat people, Beiser (1998) observes that immigrants go through three distinct stages during their process of resettlement in Canada: euphoria, disillusionment, and adaptation. These

periods accentuate the stresses of migration that mark the lives of all immigrants, resulting in a sense of loss, helplessness, and alienation (Choi 1997; Moussa 1994; Schneller 1981; Vega, Kolody, and Valle 1987; Zulman 1996), especially for those whose migration is forced. For refugees, these stresses are intense as a result of having witnessed, or having been victimized by, violence. In the case of immigrants of colour, the harsh reality of racism makes the settlement process even more difficult – if not traumatizing. American studies have emphasized the negative health impact of racism (e.g., David and Collins 1991, as cited in Cameron, Wells, and Hobfoll 1996). Combined with the poverty resulting from deskilling, underemployment, and unemployment, the disruption of social ties, and the lack of immediate supportive networks, the health impact of migration is more severe for those who are marginalized, including immigrants of colour (Brice-Baker 1994; Dossa 2004).

For most immigrant women, their dependency on their spouses is underscored by the sponsorship requirements and reinforced by the state. Sponsorship obligations are often used as instruments of power and control by abusive spouses to reinforce their authority within the family (Agnew 1998; MacLeod and Shin 1990; Moussa 1998-99). In essence, the dependant designation subordinates women in the relationship and accentuates their dependency on sponsors to meet basic needs (Ng 1993a, 1993b). For women, this translates into a feeling of indebtedness (National Association of Women and the Law 1999), and a fear of deportation, of having their children taken away from them, and of poverty and destitution should they leave an abusive relationship. Legal status, then, defines and confines immigrant women of colour, their access to health care and social services, and their ability to leave violent situations (Abraham 1995; Calvo 1996; Choudry n.d.; Dosanjh, Deo, and Sidhu 1994; MacLeod et al. 1994; Rhee 1977).

Several key factors are identified in the literature as resulting in the increased susceptibility of immigrant women of colour to negative health outcomes. These include the impact of deskilling and ghettoization in underpaid, seasonal, unprotected, and often dangerous occupations; lack of language skills, which contributes to isolation and lack of access to adequate services; and structural barriers that impede their mobility and ability to participate fully in various domains of social life. Having said this, I do not want to suggest that immigrant women of colour are passive victims or advance a view in which, as Lutz (1995, 301) puts it, "immigrant women [and girls] appear as victims – 'puppets on a string' – doomed to follow a pre-written script, dependent on the help and leadership from others in search of a new identity." Rather, my intent is to lay out the structural constraints that operate and define immigrant women's lives, limiting the latitude and mobility they have in exercising their own agency. To this end, I concur with

Ristock and Health Canada (1995, 9) when they argue that factors such as "racism, isolation, lack of services, language barriers, geographical barriers, and religious beliefs" can amplify the impact of violence. This observation is echoed in other literature focusing on immigrant women in the United States (e.g., Brice-Baker 1994; Bohn 1993; Champion 1996; O'Keefe 1994; Raj and Silverman 2002).

Structural Violence(s)

Upon arrival in Canada, many immigrants who are selected on the basis of their qualifications and skill sets (as determined by the Canadian immigration point system) find themselves deskilled and devalued (Basran and Zong 1998; Dossa 2004; Ervin 1994; Ng 1993a, 1993b). Their qualifications are not recognized and they are required to obtain Canadian experience in order to get a job. Not having any Canadian experience because of the lack of accreditation and the reluctance of employers to hire them, they experience downward mobility (Kazemipur and Halli 2001). For racial minorities, this factor is heavily influenced by the pervasive racism in Canadian society (Akbari 1999; Reitz and Sklar 1997). Stereotypical constructions of racialized people of colour as inferior, less educated, and less capable impede their employment and occupational mobility, contributing to the stresses of migration and settlement, and undoubtedly impacting on health. In his review of the literature on migration and health, Bhugra (2004, 247) observes that "pre-existing relations between the immigrant's background and the recipient society will determine the course and outcome of migration itself." In other words, how source countries are viewed and how particular cultural backgrounds are constructed influence the ways in which immigrants from those countries are received and the degree to which they will be accepted in the dominant host society.

In constructing immigrant women as dependants of their spouses, Canadian social policy exerts a compounding factor in that it erases their social, economic, and cultural contribution to the nation (Thobani 1999a). Despite having high qualifications, many immigrant women, like immigrant men, are unable to practise in their fields because of language barriers, the lack of accreditation of their qualifications, and undervaluation, the last two of which are predicated on systemic racism (Kazemipur and Halli 2001). Further, immigrant women are often diverted from language instruction and economic integration programs on the assumption that they are not the principal breadwinners of the family (Ng 1993a, 1993b; B. Roberts 1990). Lack of skills in the dominant language results in women being streamed into low-paying, low-mobility, and seasonal jobs (Ng 1993a, 1993b; Ocran 1997). This renders them a pliant and cheap labour force, which can be easily exploited. Bolaria and Bolaria (1994) note that immigrant women tend to work in occupational areas that are dangerous and hazardous to health. Further, many of these sectors are unprotected by unions, rife with economic exploitation, and seasonal or part-time in the kind of work they offer, and render women working within them vulnerable to all forms of violence (J. Anderson 1985, 1987; Jiwani 1994; MacLeod et al. 1994; Philippine Women Centre of BC 1997; Savary 1998). This has a direct bearing on the stresses they experience, on their vulnerability to violence, and on their inability to access adequate services.

Ghettoized in particular jobs (Iyer 1997; Ocran 1997), many of these women experience gender role dislocation in the family. The deskilling and unemployment of men, combined with more rapid employment of women in low-paying jobs (Ng 1993a, 1993b) – for example, domestic work – create additional tensions in the family. In a series of focus groups convened by the MOSAIC immigrant settlement society in Vancouver, women from the Kurdish, Somali, Vietnamese, Polish, and Latin American communities discussed the gender shifts in their family and the potential for violence. The focus group participants "felt that immigration and the resulting changes in the family roles and expectations, appear to increase men's insecurity in the relationship, and that insecurity, in turn, resulted in dysfunctional behaviour" (MOSAIC 1996, 4-5).

In an insightful and sensitive study of Iranian women's migration to Vancouver, Dossa (2004, 29) reports that the individual Iranian woman has "been subject to four behavioural phases related to the veil: traditional veiling from the time of puberty; forceful unveiling following the Shah's 1936 decree; forced re-veiling in the post-revolutionary era; and the 'invisible veiling and walls' in her adopted country of Canada." Dossa's comment makes explicit the links between the physical act of veiling – voluntarily and involuntarily – and the metaphoric veiling that contains, defines, and delimits the lives of Iranian women in Canada. Joan Anderson (1987) notes that for the immigrant women in her study, loneliness and depression were daily features of life. In their study of South Asian women in the United Kingdom, Gilbert, Gilbert, and Sanghera (2004) cite evidence linking depression to having a subordinate status, entrapment, and a sense of shame.

Immigrant women, in particular, have been identified as a high-risk population when it comes to migration stress and its impact on health. Meleis (1991) suggests that their increased vulnerability stems from the multiple roles they are required to play, and the constant negotiation that results from these competing demands. This notion of role overload has been identified in US, UK, and Canadian studies as one of the key stressors in the lives of immigrant women (J. Anderson 1987; Choi 1997; N. Li and May 1997; MacKinnon and Howard 2000; MacLeod and Shin 1990; Rhee 1977). Although some authors have framed these multiple roles biculturally – that is, in terms of how immigrant women help construct a transnational community, transmit cultural knowledge, and provide support to immediate and extended kin (Alicea 1997; Ng 1993a, 1993b; Lutz 1995) – one cannot ignore that this process of negotiation occurs within a larger social context. As such, it is the way the receiving society responds to those forced to assume these many roles that plays a critical part in exacerbating (or not) role overload. Part of this societal response lies in the kinds of services and programs made available to immigrant women to facilitate their integration into the economic and cultural spheres. Yet another aspect revolves around attitudes directed at immigrant groups in general and racialized groups in particular (Bald 1995; Henry et al. 1995). In other words, role overload among immigrant women is directly linked to how their particular group is received by the larger society, and how these groups in turn react to the exclusion. Exclusion from the larger dominant society means that immigrant women's responsibility as nurturers increases, forcing them to provide a compensatory space within the home that is affirming and that provides a sense of belonging through cultural continuity and familial networks of support.

Linking Structural and Intimate Forms of Violence
In describing the situation of immigrant women in the United States, Pinn and Chunko (1997) identify isolation as another key risk factor for domestic violence. If a lack of cultural knowledge about the society in which they are living increases their sense of loneliness (Wiik 1995), exclusion from that society because of racism only exacerbates this feeling (MacLeod et al. 1994; Sidhu 1996; Rasche 1988). On a practical level, the combined effects of social, structural, and cultural isolation mean that many women do not know where to turn when they encounter violence in their homes. Even when they do know where to turn, an inability to communicate in the dominant language impacts interactions with service providers (see Spencer and Chen 2004), leading to feelings of frustration and heightened dependency on those who can translate. Too often, the interpreters are members of the family. This compromises confidentiality and engenders feelings of shame and embarrassment (MacLeod and Shin 1990; Sasso 2000). Lack of adequate and appropriate interpretation can lead to misdiagnosis, thereby endangering the lives of immigrant women (Sasso 2000). An inability to communicate in the dominant language also compounds the difficulties of negotiating with government, health care, and social service bureaucracies (Gany and Thiel de Bocanegra 1996). Given immigrant women's concentration in the lower, unprotected echelons of the labour force and the piecemeal nature of work they are required to perform, women often cannot afford to take time off to access services. Should they take time off, finding transportation and someone who can accompany them to interpret is another problem.

Interestingly, in her study of immigrant communities and their access to health care, Christensen (2000) found that the inability to speak in the dominant language was mentioned by only 27 percent of the individuals she surveyed. For her part, Joan Anderson (1987) found that immigrant women of colour who speak English fluently also experienced barriers to services based on the stereotypes that health care providers had of their particular cultural groups. Such stereotyping explains, in part, why immigrant women of colour might retreat into their own cultural communities. However, for those experiencing violence in the home, this dependency on the cultural community becomes problematic should they choose to report the abuse. Awareness of the community's subordinate position in the larger society – its exclusion and stigmatization – makes women reluctant to disclose the abuse they are experiencing. In examining African-American women's experiences of violence, Bent-Goodley (2004) refers to this as a "racial loyalty," arguing that it is predicated on the recognition, both historical and contemporary, of how the wider systems of disciplinary enforcement criminalize African-Americans if violence is disclosed. I would argue that the concept of racial loyalty can also be applied to racialized immigrants of colour who are exposed to a heightened scrutiny and for whom such disclosures of abuse are likely to result in criminalization, if not deportation. Betraying racial loyalty also results in the exclusion and stigmatization of immigrant women from their own communities. Thus, when the community is the only site where a sense of belonging is felt and self-esteem is boosted, the social cost of going public is high (Dasgupta and Warrier 1996; Health Canada 1994; Huisman 1996; Ferraro 1996; Razack 1998a). In this sense, the plight of immigrant women who experience violence parallels that of rural women whose only choice in leaving a violent relationship is to leave their community (Jiwani, Moore, and Kachuk 1998).

Encounters with Health Care Professionals

For women who are experiencing violence, the doctor's office may be the only place they can go unaccompanied. It may also be the only place where they are comfortable enough to disclose the abuse they are experiencing, but often only when asked directly about it by a concerned physician. Yet, as a study of general practitioners in Manitoba by Trute, Sarsfield, and MacKenzie (1988) reveals, most physicians do not ask questions about violence. They also found that physicians who were male and who had been practising for a long time were among the least likely to detect abuse.

While women opt to go to the hospital when there is an emergency,[5] the first line of refuge for an abused immigrant woman is likely to be the family physician – a point underscored by community-based research (e.g., Sidhu 1996).[6] Nevertheless, what anecdotal and community research also suggests is that disclosures of abuse are usually not given serious enough consideration. Sidhu's (1996) study of twenty-two immigrant women who had experienced abuse highlights how the structural dependency of these women plays into this tendency of physicians to turn a blind eye. As sponsored immigrants, many of the women rely on the same physician as their abusive partners. Not only does the family physician find herself/himself in a position of conflict – serving the abuser and victim at the same time – but the danger that the physician is more likely to believe the abuser's account makes disclosing an even riskier option for women.[7] As Sidhu (1996, 33) explains: "If [their] partners were unwilling to cooperate or expressed anger at the women for raising 'their' family problem in the public arena, the women risked more abuse from their partners." That aside, the issue of confidentiality is a major concern, with women expressing fears that physicians from their own communities would reveal their disclosures to the other members of the family whom they also treat (Gilbert, Gilbert, and Sanghera 2004).

The medical profession's response to women who have been abused has been inadequate. According to studies cited by Kinnon and Hanvey (1996), medical personnel identify only one battered woman in twenty-five. The absence of an effective response to the screening and treatment of battered women has been attributed to a lack of knowledge about violence among medical personnel, their unease with dealing with issues of violence, the implications of violence in terms of their own experiences of abuse, stereotypes about women, and preconceived notions about woman abuse. Further, identification of abuse tends to depend on the visibility of symptoms and the lack of alternative explanations by which to understand the injuries. For women whose symptoms are not visible, the possibility of effective identification and intervention is further reduced. For women who are racialized immigrants, the issue of racial stereotypes comes into play, influencing how physicians are likely to view and treat them, and how they are likely to understand and respond to the violence these women are experiencing. Notwithstanding the above, the political economy of medical care is also undoubtedly an influential variable, given that physicians are paid on the basis of the number of patients they treat. The time required to deal with an abused woman is greater than the time required to prescribe medication, and where racist and sexist stereotypes colour the interaction between physician and patient, the tendency to dismiss or medicalize the woman's symptoms is likely to be higher.

The Medicalization of Violence: Systemic Sexism and Racism

The health care system reproduces social inequalities by privileging those who have power and subordinating others. In so doing, it draws upon the dominant language of biomedicine to categorize, manage, and process patients. Symptoms become the categorical referents, which are then organized to generate the seemingly appropriate prescriptions.

In an insightful analysis of the treatment of woman abuse by the health care system, Ahluwalia and MacLean (1988) note that the medical encounter is a hierarchical one in which power inequalities between the patient and the physician are asserted and reinforced. The physician assumes the role of the expert, deciphers the symptoms of the patient, and prescribes an antidote to eliminate or control the symptoms. In keeping with the dominant ideology of capitalism and liberalism, the patient is seen as being responsible for her/his ailment and, hence, compliance becomes a way for the patient to assume responsibility. This kind of processing of patients and the commodification of their symptoms within the economic arrangements underpinning the health care system result in a management of the health effects of violence that render the patient – in this case the woman who has been abused – as responsible for her abuse. Post-traumatic stress syndrome, battered women's syndrome, and other psychiatric classifications become an avenue by which symptoms are managed and controlled. The labelling also serves another purpose – namely, to negate the social dimensions of violence against women and to translate it as an "individual problem of self-abuse" (Ahluwalia and MacLean 1988, 190).

Studies by Stark, Flitcraft, and Frasier (1979), Kurz and Stark (1988), Varcoe (1997), and Warshaw (1993) identify the specific ways in which women who are abused become labelled, and their symptoms used to generate prescriptive interventions in the form of antidepressants and referrals to psychiatric services. In a study of the treatment of abused women in one hospital, Warshaw (1993, 141) found that the very practices of the medical profession have a detrimental impact on the diagnosis of symptoms associated with gender-based violence. As she observes:

> Using the standard medical shorthand, which is an important shaper of how physicians learn to organize their thinking, we see how the subject becomes a mere descriptor. What are foregrounded are the symptoms: swelling and pain on the mouth. The physician's note uses the passive voice and focuses on the physical trauma. Even the additional statement, "hit by a fist," is structured to give information relevant to the mechanism of the injury and what damage might have been done to the body. It removes the fist from the person attached to it. In doing so, the physician, although perhaps not consciously, makes a choice that obscures both the etiology and meaning of the woman's symptoms.

These routinized practices are contingent on and informed by an ideology of scarcity (as expressed in discourses of limited resources and inadequate funding for health care) (Varcoe 1997). This overarching framework is used to make sense of and rationalize the rapid processing and turnout of emergency patients. However, who gets the requisite time and attention is also dependent on the stereotypical constructions of deserving patients. Varcoe notes that patients are assessed on the basis of their appearance and class and that the treatment provided by nurses varies accordingly. Her study reveals how nurses' perceptions of violence hinge on signs of physical abuse manifested by the women they see. Thus, their estimates of the prevalence of abuse in the women who come to emergency are much lower than indicated by the statistical evidence.

Critical analyses of the failure of the medical system to adequately address the widespread and systemic issues of violence against women have resulted in a range of interventions spanning from the introduction of screening protocols in hospitals to educational measures aimed at physicians and nurses, and the insertion of violence-related curricula in medical and dental schools (S. Berman and McLaren 1997; Coeling and Harman 1997; Grunfeld, Hotch, and MacKay 1995; J. Hamilton 1996; Hotch et al. 1995).[8] However, as Puzan (2003) observes, there are resistances against these structural changes.

As with sexism, the formal medical establishment and the health care it offers are not immune to racism. In fact, the traditional power and authority of physicians is maintained by ideological beliefs grounded in the perception of the superiority of Western medicine, and the inferiority of Other, indigenous forms of health care (Puzan 2003), a perception reflected in their views regarding preferred and deserving patients. Such a view spills into their perceptions and treatment of patients who are racialized and marginalized, and its gendered dimension comes through in treatment accorded to immigrant women of colour who have experienced sexist violence.

Raced Stereotypes and the Culturalization of Violence

> Well, from my experiences and what I hear, the principal problem is stereotyping. Like categorizing people. Let's say southern Europeans are emotional people, therefore you tend to downplay what the woman or the patient is saying because you assume that they are emotional, their verbal expressions, their body language is so much more expressive than North Americans. So the doctor tends to, "Well, okay, perhaps I should cut in half." Well, the general perception that we have of immigrants is that North Americans, that their culture and mode of culture, is superior to any other, therefore they have to educate us and to make us up to their standards. I think it's very serious if you look at the whole context and implication that brings up. And for the immigrants, it's a very serious situation because we are never looked at as equal, we are never looked at as being people who can actively contribute to this country. And when it comes to the health system, we actually run into a set of problems.
>
> – service provider, organization serving immigrant women

The problems that immigrants of colour run into, according to the service provider quoted above, are the stereotypical representations that physicians and health care professionals have of them. In a series of focus groups with physicians and patients, researchers found that physicians tended to stereo-type patients according to which cultural group they come from. Patients, for their part, acquiesced to the authority of the doctor and regarded Western medicine as superior to other forms of medicine (Cave et al. 1995). Beiser (1998, 29) has demonstrated how one's racial status influences the kind of health care one receives: Blacks are more likely to be diagnosed with schizophrenia than Whites, and "family doctors are less likely to refer non-English clientele to specialists than their English-speaking counterparts, and surgeons are less likely to perform procedures such as cardiac bypass surgery, or kidney replacement on minority, than on majority group patients" (see also Schneider, Zaslavasky, and Epstein, cited in Long et al. 2004). A recent American study found that Black patients are less likely to seek emotional assistance from professionals and more likely than Whites to be under-diagnosed for psychiatric disorders (Kosch, Burg, and Podikiju 1998). This stems in part from the reluctance of racialized and minoritized groups to seek professional health care. However, this finding has not been replicated in other studies, notably those dealing with Afro-Caribbean populations, which have found an incidence of over-diagnosis (Bhugra 2004).

Bhugra's overview of the literature suggests that immigrants tend to be either as healthy as or healthier than the native-born population. However, over time, and particularly in the second and third generation, they are likely to evidence higher rates of ill health. His analysis suggests that "environmental stress caused by living in societies where individual or institutional racism may well play a role in creating social, economic and political disadvantages" is more likely to contribute to this situation (250). Declining health among immigrants who have been in Canada more than ten years has been corroborated in other studies and attributed to the acquisition of bad health habits among the immigrant population (see Beiser 1998). In a sense, these studies seem to support Debold et al.'s (1999) contention that acculturation results in negative outcomes for immigrant racialized girls and young women (see Chapter 5).

Studies of immigrant women's access to and encounters with medical professionals consistently point to the erasure and trivialization of their health concerns. The MOSAIC (1996) service organization's consultation with immigrant women from various ethnocultural communities revealed that women felt they could not communicate with their physicians and, further, that the physicians' focus on the physical aspects of their health negated the root causes of their illness and erased the totality of their being (see also J. Anderson 1987). In other words, physicians did not employ an analysis that situated the woman in the context of her experiences and lived reality. Given the stresses and impact of migration, role overload, racist and sexist violence, and the streaming of women into dangerous and unprotected jobs, it is surprising that physicians do not take these vital aspects of immigrant women's health into account. This puts the onus for any remedy on the immigrant woman herself, evacuating any cognizance of the structures of power that contribute to her condition.

Joan Anderson (1987, 426) notes that the Indo-Canadian women in her study "continually repeated that health professionals did not understand their concerns, so in other words, there was no point in trying to communicate with them." Abraham (1995) echoes this observation, suggesting that health professionals' insensitivity and apathy toward immigrant women stems from their negative stereotypes and perceptions of particular ethnic groups. And a recent exploratory study of young women of colour and their encounters with the Canadian health care system offers similar observations (Women's Health in Women's Hands Community Centre 2003). In her analysis of the "unbearable whiteness of nursing," Puzan (2003, 197) argues that in her experience, "it was not unusual for healthcare providers to check charts to determine whether or not patients were welfare recipients, solely on the basis of appearance, with the patient's skin colour serving as a frequent cue for this behaviour."

The prevalence of stereotypes about people of colour among health care professionals has been documented extensively by Varcoe (1997). In her participant-observation study of nurses in several emergency departments, Varcoe observed that the nurses had definite notions of deserving versus non-deserving patients. Non-White, poor, and intoxicated or overdosed women were usually seen as undeserving patients. Maintaining that the health care system is organized around such discourses of deservedness, as well as those of scarcity and violence, Varcoe goes on to argue that violence can be understood within two frameworks of meaning: that of pauperization and that of racialization. Where patients are both poor and of colour, these two frameworks intersect and interlock. However, in the case of women of colour, violence was more readily associated with their culture. This culturalization of violence is reflective of the dominant Canadian discourse on race and racism, and it pervades mainstream services (MacLeod and Shin 1990; Razack 1998a; see Chapters 1 and 4, this volume).

Culturalization of violence leads to a situation of heightened visibility and scrutiny on the one hand and dismissal of women's experiences of violence on the basis of cultural membership on the other. As one nurse in Varcoe's (1997, 215) study states: "Culturally, because I have had a lot to do with a [certain group of] people in the last [few] years, I would say overall, that as a group of nurses [at this hospital] people are more suspicious of abuse in a multicultural type of patient situation than they are in an actually Caucasian situation." One can assess from this comment just how far the language of multiculturalism has permeated the thought and speech of members of the dominant society. That a multicultural type of patient exists seems rather illogical and can be understood only as a euphemism for a person of colour. In contrast, the Caucasian person is implicitly thought to be monocultural person. Further, the cultural attribution here (as in multicultural) raises suspicion about the abuse when the woman is from a different racialized community, despite the reality that many women, across the board, are victims of violence.

Within this discourse of the racial and cultural Other, the immigrant woman has already been constructed as a problem patient, as opposed to "a patient with a problem" (Kurz and Stark 1988, 263). The unwillingness of doctors and social workers to get involved with this so-called problem patient in any substantial or sustaining way is further augmented by their lack of awareness about available services – a lack of awareness that is shared, all too often, by the women concerned. Thus, language barriers, racial stereotypes, and cultural explanations deflect attention away from the root causes of violence, and instead the task becomes one of dealing with the visible signs of abuse. If gendered violence tends to be dismissed on the basis of women asking for it or women deliberately putting themselves in such a situation, culturalized violence is similarly dismissed as a pattern that is common to a particular cultural community and one that the woman, as a culturalized Other, will not willingly leave.

Another outcome of cultural racism is the inverse construction of the supposed preferred patient. Preferred patients are those who are White, middle class, and who manifest the comportment of a reasonable person – the middle-class norm. In the case of immigrant women who are being abused, the preferred patient is one who can be rescued. The difference here is that within the ranking of deservedness, a woman of colour may qualify for deserving treatment if she exhibits active agency and decides to leave the relationship with the help of the staff. In other words, making the staff feel that they are contributing to something valuable (as in rescuing the woman) elevates her status to that of a preferred patient.[9] This standard seems to be applied to immigrant women even though their financial and social dependencies on their partners are complicated and all too often sealed by legislation.

These discourses of rescue rely on the construction of the racialized immigrant woman as a raced and gendered subject – a condensed sign invoking culturalized racism and culturalized sexism (Razack 1998a) as explanatory vehicles by which to (a) privilege a cultural interpretation of race and racism, and (b) advance a viewpoint that attributes violence against women to a specific cultural trait or predisposition. In either case, power is evacuated from these explanations and the structures of dominance are obfuscated so that only the patriarchal power of racialized communities stands out and is emblematized as a traditional patriarchal structure while the patriarchal structure of White dominance is erased or remains invisible in the background. Similarly, cultural racism obscures and deflects attention away from the power of White dominance, making it seem that, against the invisible backdrop of the White society, only racialized groups have cultures that are identifiable and that are distinctly problematic.

Immigrant women of colour interviewed by Joan Anderson noted the prevalence of similar stereotypes that impacted on their ability to access appropriate health care. These stereotypes are also confronted by young women of colour (Women's Health in Women's Hands 2003). Anderson (1987, 433) suggests that "One could argue that non-white women's experiences are shaped by the history of imperialism and oppression, and are not only the result of their immigrant status. Instead, these experiences have to be understood in terms of their status as non-white immigrant women from a Third World nation. So, not only must non-white immigrant women contend with ideologies about women's roles, but they must also contend with stereotypes that are entrenched within the mainstream culture, which determine the ways they are perceived."

It is the playing out of these stereotypes and hierarchies of preference in the encounters that immigrant women of colour have with the health care system that I attend to in the section below. But first, a methodological note is in order.

Accessing Voices and Experiences

In accessing the voices of immigrant women of colour who have experienced violence and who have sought health care, a multifold methodological strategy was employed. This entailed an environmental scan consisting of telephone interviews with twenty-one organizations in British Columbia, and one-on-one interviews with six key informants working with immigrant women. In addition, focus groups with both immigrant women who had experienced abuse and bilingual and bicultural anti-violence service providers were conducted. These were supplemented with interviews with immigrant women of colour from a South Asian background, all of which were conducted in Vancouver's Lower Mainland between 1999 and 2000.[10]

Questions asked in the interviews and focus groups were developed in concert with front-line anti-violence workers and based on a literature review conducted prior to the study. Questions were semi-structured and an informal interview style was used. The six key informants, found through referrals by anti-violence workers and advocates in Vancouver, were selected on the basis of their expertise in working with women who have experienced violence, or their familiarity with issues facing immigrant women of colour in their encounter with health care service providers. These informants consisted of representatives from two immigrant settlement organizations, a hospital-based sexual assault program, a women's centre, a transition house, and a multicultural health program with one of the regional health boards. In total, twenty-seven informants and service providers working in different organizations were contacted for the environmental scan.

The focus group with immigrant women who had experienced abuse consisted of five women, from Mexico, India, China, and the Philippines. The focus group with bicultural and bilingual service providers consisted of eleven women, most of whom were immigrant women of colour from the following backgrounds: Mainland Chinese, Filipina, Vietnamese, Korean, South Asian, East African, Polish, Latin American, and Italian. To supplement the focus group data, ten one-on-one interviews with immigrant women of colour were conducted, using a snowball approach whereby the women who were interviewed would refer the researcher to other women they knew. Those interviewed were of South Asian origin. Interviewees ranged in age from early twenties to late fifties. Four of the women were in their twenties and had lived most of their lives in Canada. The average length of residence in Canada was 14.9 years, with the range spanning from 5 to 24 years. The interviews were conducted by an immigrant woman of colour researcher familiar with the issues.[11] In total, twenty-six immigrant women of colour were consulted through the focus groups and interviews.

While I have detailed the background of the women who were interviewed and the service providers who participated in the bilingual and bicultural focus group, my intention here is not to privilege an ethno-specific focus in the sense that all these interviewees and focus group participants represent different cultural traditions. Rather, I wish to define the range of backgrounds that were represented, and through the thematic analysis presented below, underline the structural commonalities that inhere in their experiences. In so doing, I recognize the limitations of an overdetermined structural approach; however, I am more keenly aware of the alternative, which may invoke a culturalist framework that once again pathologizes immigrant women of colour from different ethnic backgrounds. "Culture talk," as Razack (1994a, 896) notes, "is a double-edged sword." It can reify cultures as static entities, obscure the relations of power within and outside the cultural group, and fail to consider the relational aspects of cultural identity (Abraham 1995) as emerging from a migrant, diasporic existence (Bhatia and Ram 2001). Add to this the contextual backdrop of systemic and everyday racism and the focus on culture quickly becomes one of implicitly or explicitly comparing a backward, traditional, and oppressive cultural system to the modern, progressive, and egalitarian culture assumed of the West (Burns 1986; Lai 1986). Such an approach can result in the production of cultural prescriptions that further entrench stereotypic representations of particular ethnic groups (Razack 1998a).

Yet, while bearing these cautions in mind, I do not wish to suggest that an ethno-specific analysis would not yield a representative rendering of the issues and barriers faced by a particular group of women. However, an adequate ethno-specific analysis would have to employ interpretive methodologies grounded in a theoretical framework that would draw out the "thick" description (Geertz 1973) of immigrant women's lives (e.g., Dossa 1999, 2004). Such a methodology requires time and has its own issues with regard to representational politics (Bannerji 1987, 1993). Thus, the aim in the present context is not to tease out the skein of interpretive webs that signify the meaning of health in a particular ethnocultural context but to outline the impact of structural forces and the resulting barriers that impede and curtail racialized immigrant women's access to formal health care. In that sense, I am cognizant of collapsing the voices I present for the strategic purpose of foregrounding the larger structures of violence. The sections below draw from the one-on-one interviews with immigrant women who had experienced abuse, as well as those with the bicultural and bilingual service providers, many of whom are immigrant women of colour and many of whom have had previous experiences of intimate violence. As a caveat, it should be noted that while service providers and the women interviewed generally use the term "woman" in referring to their specific experiences, they are in effect referencing immigrant women of colour.

Caught Between a Rock and a Hard Place: Listening to Voices of Immigrant Women of Colour and Service Providers

> I didn't even realize I was in an abusive relationship until it was really bad. I didn't see any alternatives for myself. I guess if I knew I could get financial help or my immigration would not be taken away maybe I would have left before it became really bad. Now it is too late for me. Maybe if women knew it can happen to anyone.
>
> – participant, focus group

As the above quote reveals, the issue of immigration status is a major concern for immigrant women. As dependants of sponsoring spouses, many immigrant women of colour have little access to services. The sponsoring spouse or family has to demonstrate they are economically able to support the sponsored person for ten years. If the sponsorship agreement breaks down, the woman involved can obtain hardship assistance but she would have to verify her changed circumstances and inform the authorities (see Janovicek 2000). Her status would be reviewed, and she could potentially risk deportation (Dosanjh, Deo, and Sidhu 1994). Even if the sponsorship agreement is intact, should the woman's spouse be deported, she could be deported as well. The situation is often complicated by the reality that women are often involved in the joint sponsorship of their own and their spouse's extended family members. The coercive pressure to keep the family together compels women to remain in abusive relationships. Too often, this is a threat that abusers know well and use to silence women from speaking about their abuse. As this service provider observed in the focus group: "But the problem is that the sponsorship obligation is for ten years. She's tied to the man because he would threaten her and say, 'Well, I'm going to go and get social assistance so you'll be in trouble. You're going to have to pay for my apartment, my food, my clothing.'"

The legality and constraints of immigrant status have implications for how and whether women are likely to disclose abuse to their physicians. Part of the reluctance to disclose abuse stems from the fear of the consequences should abuse be revealed and confidentiality breached. As one service provider noted in the focus group: "[Women] always say to me that, 'I used to go to my doctor but I never opened up to my doctor because I thought he would tell everything to my husband or to my mother-in-law or to anyone in the in-law family.'" Immigrant women who participated in the focus group also noted how children often get used as interpreters, and stressed the need for professional cultural interpreters to be brought in to fill this role. As one focus group participant explained: "To take a child and to put him in a position like that, it's like putting my child in my situation and instead of helping my kids, I am also hurting them."

A significant factor that both the service providers and the women who were interviewed reported involved the failure of the medical professionals to ask about the abuse. As one of the women interviewed recounted:

> I went to the emergency room. But never for the real reason. Once my husband got angry with me because his cousins were visiting and I was in our room studying. He pushed me and I fell back and banged my head against the wall and fainted. He carried me downstairs and told everyone I had fainted and then banged my head. We repeated the same story at the hospital. So I was treated like any other patient. I was going to the hospital on a regular basis but no one ever asked any detailed questions about why I kept fainting or banging into things ... My only complaint is that no one stopped to say, "Why have you been here almost every month for a year and a half? That can't be normal?" But I try not to be angry anymore. What is the use?

If physicians do not spend adequate time with patients and foster a relationship of trust, and further, if they are unaware of the health effects of violence, then it is likely that women who are experiencing violence will not want to disclose that abuse. If the physician is treating the rest of the woman's family, she may not feel comfortable disclosing the violence for fear of a breach of confidentiality and retaliation from the spouse. Furthermore, when physicians do not ask about violence, many women will not want to reveal or disclose their experiences voluntarily unless they are actively seeking intervention. Even in the latter case, usually women will turn to their friends and family. As one woman who had been in a violent relationship reported in the focus group: "I went to see my doctor because I started getting nosebleeds and fainting spells. He never asked what was wrong. He did some tests but never really said you are anorexic. I didn't find out until I got pregnant. That's when he said, 'Well, you should eat more.'"

Fears that medical personnel will involve the police should violence be disclosed contributed to immigrant women of colour's trepidation. This reflects in part a general mistrust of a police force that labels communities of colour as "more violent" and subjects those communities to constant surveillance. In an environment where one is already framed as criminal, everything associated with files and records is cause for suspicion. But perhaps these women's hesitation to formalize their abuse in writing or, indeed, involve any official channels in their plight is grounded in cynicism: in the belief that the police, like the medical profession, are just not really all that interested in helping them. Such cynicism is easy to understand in light of stories such as this woman's, as recounted by the abused woman's service provider in the focus group: "And I asked her, did you ever end up calling the police? She said, 'Yeah, I did call the police but my husband told the police that I have a mental health problem. So the police didn't pay attention. But, the police did take me to the hospital because I was badly bruised and I was hurt.' And she says at the hospital again, 'The doctor did not spend time with me to ask me what was the issue, like how did I get hurt?'" What this service provider could not understand is how two systems – the police and the health care system – could ignore this woman's visible injuries and appear to believe the abusive husband.

Documentation of the abuse, and I would argue documentation of any sort, is likely to instil fears in the women because of possible breaches of confidentiality and the risk that such documentation may be used against them or their spouses. However, the lack of documentation works against immigrant women who want to press charges or seek custody of their children. As one service provider noted in the focus group: "I find that when it comes to a point where the woman is planning to leave and when I say, 'Okay, can we get some medical records because that can help your case,' then usually the women turn around and say to me, 'But I never told my doctor.' Or, on the contrary, at times I have heard from the women that, 'I told my doctor ... I don't want this to go into the record.'"

Service providers involved in our study were quick to point out how physicians' lack of knowledge about the health effects of violence, combined with their orientation toward the efficient processing of patients, contributes to the inadequacy and inappropriateness of their response to, and treatment of, women who have experienced violence. Many felt that the former reflected a lack of training that could be addressed by equipping physicians to recognize the health effects of violence and to ask the right questions.[12] However, in many of the situations identified by service providers and immigrant women of colour, physicians did not invest the time required to develop a trusting relationship with their patients. Rather, they were constantly perceived to be watching the clock, thereby contributing to the feelings of discomfort experienced by immigrant women of colour seeking their services. As one service provider reported in the focus group:

> We have to take into consideration that the medical field is not just to help people, it's a business. And so for a lot of [mentions nationality] doctors, we sort of compare what they have to lose if they start getting involved in domestic violence issues. First of all, they lose business from the community which is their main bread and butter. Some people will say, "Oh, here he is, breaking families apart." Number two, there are people in the community who will say, "It's a family matter. Why is he calling other workers, talking about this woman and this issue of domestic violence." And we have to take that into consideration. It's a business and so he doesn't want to lose business and therefore, if you start touching issues like family violence, it ruins your rapport with the community and therefore you lose business.

This economic dimension textures the quality of the health care encounter but it also points to the ways in which routinized practices and institutional norms combine with a minoritized community status whereby familiarity and status within a community work in tandem to deter any serious consideration and treatment of familial and intimate violence. In speaking to the routinized and methodical handling of immigrant women's health concerns, one interviewee commented:

> When I go to the doctor, I don't expect the doctor to give me an hour because I know it cannot be. But at least to listen. Not my whole life story but to at least have enough time for me to say, "Okay, this I what I'm feeling," and maybe for them to ask, "Do you think this could be related to something else, with a problem that you might have?" Or something like

that. But lately, when I go to the doctor, she just asks, "What are you feeling?" and then she starts writing and that's it. So I don't have time to express myself, that this is my difficulty or my consequence of whatever it was that I'm feeling. I think it would help just to have a little more time.

Again, I should point out that this is not a concern confined to immigrant women of colour. However, what is at issue here is the immigrant woman's status – her lack of fluency in the dominant language, her subordinate status within the larger system, and her racialized status, which bears on the kind of encounter she is likely to experience. This raises the question of who is likely to be listened to and attended to and who is likely to be dismissed. In the context of a racialized, gendered, classed, and above all, hierarchical encounter, signifiers of difference, especially when that difference connotes an inferiorized and subordinated status, are more likely to be treated in a dismissive fashion than when those same signifiers connote class, race, and gender privilege. Racialized immigrant women's concerns are often trivialized or erased, and they are made to feel as if they are to blame. Echoing revelations that emerge from the literature examined earlier in this chapter, this study confirmed that immigrant women of colour are constructed as problem patients. In other words, they are revictimized by the very system they turn to for assistance.

Data from the interviews and focus groups also support the contention that stereotypes about women who are victimized by violence and about specific ethno-racial groups structure the common-sense understandings of violence among health care providers. This influences the ways in which immigrant women of colour are perceived and subsequently treated. As this service provider indicated in the focus group:

> You are judged in the sense that the minute a South Asian woman walks into the emergency department, she's already judged. Okay, maybe this is what it is, maybe she has an arranged marriage, she's not going to talk about the abuse. Maybe even if she talks about it, she's not going to seek any services. Even if she goes to the transition house, she's going to go back. If the police are called in, the police will take the statement halfheartedly, thinking, "Anyway, she's not going to go through the whole process so what's the use of doing all this work?"

Such prejudging, based on stereotypes, denies the racialized immigrant woman the treatment she both deserves and needs and also results in an attitude that shifts the responsibility for the violence onto her and her cultural community. This attitude, as one service provider described it, echoes that which "the mainstream society has about women of colour" and reinforces the notion that "domestic violence is part of our culture somehow." The tendency among physicians to attribute the violence to supposedly innate cultural traits lies at the root of cultural racism and underpins many physicians' reluctance to discuss violence with racialized women. Thus, rather than focusing on the risk factors that make immigrant women vulnerable to violence, physicians tend to localize the abuse – attributing it to the immediate cultural context in which the woman lives. This reinforces the stereotype that some cultures are more violent than other cultures. It also deflects attention away from the structural forces and inequalities that contribute to immigrant women of colour's vulnerabilities to violence. Most importantly, it deflects attention away from the physicians' shortcomings and short-sightedness, and their failure to provide adequate care.

However, the cultural argument is often one used by service providers and immigrant women of colour themselves. They have internalized the discourse of the dominant society, which emphasizes difference and equates it with culture, and are exposed to the particularity of cultural formations within the domestic sphere where intimate violence occurs; as a result, it is not surprising to hear them articulate a similar argument. Witness this focus group exchange between two service providers, both immigrant women of colour who had themselves experienced violence:

Service provider 1: It took me a long time to come out and discuss my situation. I had gone through abuse when I came here and it took me a very long time because of the culture and because we're always supposed to tolerate, go through everything, then you leave. You don't dismantle the family and all those things. So it took me a very long time to leave the situation and be on my own. I find, because of my fears working with women, they leave sooner because they are aware of the system, maybe they're more assertive. I find that.

Service provider 2: I think that's the perception that people have. But in my experience, it's really encouraging to see that more and more recent immigrant women, young women, they are taking the initiative and they are saying, "Enough is enough." After a few episodes of abuse, they call and they say, "Enough is enough. I want to separate and I am separating," and they have only been in Canada for six months. I have worked with women who have only been here for three months. So it's so positive to see that women are becoming very strong and they're taking the courage to leave abusive relationships. Although I know that when I first started in this field, I used to hear that "Oh, immigrant women, they take a longer time. They can take triple the time than the mainstream community." But my experience has been different.

This exchange illustrates how culture talk is a contested terrain of interpretation but, moreover, it highlights the preconceived notions current within the health care and social services sector about immigrant women of colour. These associations imply that immigrant women of colour are bound to their cultural traditions and, because of this, less likely to leave. As the second service provider indicates, in her experience, the situation has changed but the earlier stereotypes continue to exert power.

As noted above, one implication of the cultural racism in this context is the construction of the preferred patient. As Varcoe (1997) demonstrates, preferred patients are deserving patients who can be rescued from the clutches of their cultures. The discourse of rescue is apparent here in that it mobilizes staff intervention but only under those conditions where the possibilities of the woman being rescued are fairly high. As this focus group service provider observed: "I find that if a social worker or the doctor gets the feeling that the woman is ambivalent, that the woman is not sure about separation, they don't even want to talk about it. Only the woman who will say that 'I want to separate' is the woman they'll refer, not acknowledging that even if the woman is not separating at this time, how important it is for her to connect with a support service for her future." This tendency of physicians and health care providers to brush aside anyone who is not easy to help, who does not know the code words, or who does not submit willingly to the kind of help being proffered also reflects a hierarchy of preferred patients where immigrant women of colour are positioned on the lower and less preferred end. One manifestation of this lack of preference is in how much time and attention a physician will devote to her/his patient. In cases involving immigrant women of colour, stereotypical associations of inferiority influence the interactions with physicians, quickly shifting responsibility once they have completed the task of addressing the physical injuries that a woman presented with. Statements such as "We're going to close the file" were used a lot. One focus group service provider stated: "They don't want to walk the extra step, even though they do acknowledge that immigrant women have very different needs than the women who are born and brought up in Canada. They do say it, but when it comes to actually putting that in practice, it's not being practised." Another added: "I think it's the attitude of passing the buck onto other professionals instead of that collaborative effort where they call you and we work together. It's okay, 'We're done with her. Now it's your problem.' And if something goes wrong, we've done our part." The implicit stereotype of women as complainers feeds into this overall negligence on the part of doctors. As one service provider recounted in the focus group: "Sometimes doctors tend to either dismiss it or to say, 'Oh, keep busy. This will pass.' And they don't really see that the woman is trying to say something. She doesn't want to disclose the whole situation but is trying to give some clues. In the community, they just go to the family doctor. They try to find family doctors who are from the community and they try to sort of unload their situation with the family doctor, who doesn't have the time to listen to the whole story, of course."

Data from the focus group and interviews indicate that male physicians are more likely to exhibit such behaviour than their female counterparts and female nurses. Female physicians – especially those from the same cultural communities as the immigrant women – were perceived to be more sympathetic, less judgmental, and more aware of services in the community. As one service provider noted in the focus group: "I find that in the [name of community], some of the female doctors, they're very proactive and they're doing such an excellent job. And when the women go to them, they talk about the abuse, they give out the agency's name and phone numbers and they encourage the women. [One doctor] calls me personally and says to me that 'this woman needs your help. Can you get in touch with her,' or she'll facilitate the meeting, our first meeting. And I think if more doctors can do that, it will really help the women." However, while these female physicians were more helpful, they were also likely to be targeted by patriarchal forces within the community and harassed for taking a stand against the violence. As in every society, women who challenge the normative order are subjected to punitive measures. Similarly, those who advocate for unpopular causes are subject to backlash and violence, as is evident in the cases of physicians who continue to provide abortion services. This situation echoes the kinds of dynamics that occur in small towns and enclaves when physicians take an active stance on supporting women's choices. In the case of racialized immigrant communities, however, backlash is experienced to a greater extent, given the small size of the community, its minority status, its geographic concentration, and the turning inward that has occurred as a result of the racism of the wider society (see Tyagi 1999).

Other physicians – in particular, those who belong to the same community as the immigrant woman of colour and, more importantly, who had been selected by her abusive partner – are all too aware of the consequences of their actions. These physicians were often reluctant to identify the abuse and to provide referrals and assistance, for fear of jeopardizing their own reputation within the community. As one focus group service provider stated: "The doctors who speak the same language seem to be less sympathetic and less understanding as compared to English-speaking doctors. I always find it such a struggle to get any information from [name of linguistic group]-speaking doctors because they don't want to be part of it, because they want to keep their image with the extended family, or with the husband rather than with the woman." Another service provider added that physicians in her community turned a blind eye simply because they did not want to acknowledge that violence against women was prevalent in their community.

Lack of fluency in English was not the biggest barrier facing immigrant women of colour in accessing health care. Economic constraints were seen as a far greater impediment: women's fear of not being able to have custody of the children because they were unemployed, and a lack of knowledge about systems that might offer assistance were the two most frequently cited reasons for staying with an abusive partner. Added to this, women could not afford to seek medical attention if it resulted in them having to take time off work. As one interviewee stated: "Yes, it might have helped [to have a doctor or nurse who spoke the same language]. But the money was more important, and who would have watched the children if I had to work? A Punjabi-speaking doctor could not change that for me."

The above-mentioned factors work toward silencing immigrant women of colour from disclosing the violence they are experiencing. The ensuing silence would seem to suggest to service providers and health care practitioners that these women do not want to tell their stories. Nonetheless, if the findings of this study reveal that women of colour indeed *want* to tell their stories of abuse, they also suggest that the ways in which they are asked questions about violence are of vital importance, as is having access to information that helps them to define the abuse. For instance, for many of the women interviewed, the abuse began as emotional harassment and escalated to physical violence. However, many insisted they did not recognize the early warnings as signs of abuse. As one woman stated in her interview: "I did not have any physical injuries as far as bruises and broken bones. This is always how I defined abuse until it happened to me. I didn't even realize what was happening. I am an educated woman with a career but that didn't matter."

Finding Ways Out: Toward an Equitable Model of Health Care

Some of the strategies identified in the literature for finding ways out of the troubling and traumatizing situations described above cohere around creating social networks of support (Emmott 1996); advocating critical analyses of structural issues and self-reflection (J. Hamilton 1996; Legault 1996; Lynam 1992); empowering women (Varcoe 1997; Yam 1995); taking a historical approach to understand the social location of the women (Bohn 1993); and employing a holistic approach (Sanchez, Plawecki, and Plawecki 1996). These strategies are not mutually exclusive but, rather, overlap in practice. When employed collectively, they work toward empowering the immigrant woman of colour, viewing her in context and as a person, and working with her to develop viable strategies. Underpinning all these strategies is the issue of respect and dignity – respecting different social locations, histories, and realities without inferiorizing or trivializing their import.

Ramsden (1990, 1993) offers a model of "cultural safety" which neatly encapsulates practical strategies, underpinned by a conceptual framework, that address the power inequalities inherent to the medical encounter. While Ramsden's model is grounded in the Maori reality and relationship with the White settler community in New Zealand, her observations and findings echo the lived realities of Aboriginal people and people of colour in Canada. Hence, when Ramsden (1990, 2) states that "we are not a perspective," she challenges the dominant normative model of multiculturalism, which identifies other cultures as perspectives, with the dominant culture as the central organizing principle – what Stuart Hall (1990a) refers to as the White eye.

In referring to cultural safety, Ramsden discusses what she calls cultural risk and argues from the perspective of the Maori woman who is presenting to a White health professional. She defines cultural risk as "a process whereby people from one culture believe that they are demeaned, diminished and dis-empowered by the actions and delivery systems of people from another culture" (Wood and Schwass, as cited in Ramsden 1993, 7). The Maori woman is thus at risk of being erased or having her concerns trivialized. What is most interesting about Ramsden's model is that she turns the issue of risk around so that rather than using the discourse of risk in the traditional sense of marginalized others being a risk to society, her view centres the indigenous woman, asking what risks she faces in encountering a dominant White system.

While I don't wish to equate the situation of immigrant women of colour in Canada to that of Maori women in New Zealand, I mention Ramsden's model in order to highlight possible ways in which the access to and delivery of health care can be made more equitable. Even though Ramsden is speaking in the context of nursing and in reference to Maori communities, her recommendations for reducing cultural risk are changes that health care professionals in Canada could implement. For instance, she notes that self-reflexivity and value interrogation are an essential first step for all health professionals to undertake, but that in order to implement structural change, nurses (or other health care professionals) need to be made aware of the impact of the larger structures of violence such as poverty, colonialism, and its influence on contemporary social processes. These two steps in tandem, she argues, would reduce the cultural risks that those who are marginalized face when encountering a hierarchical structure based on White dominance. Polaschek (1998, 456) elaborates on these points, arguing: "[The concept of cultural safety] makes clear the structural dimension of health care provision, that care is not simply provided for individuals but for members of groups whose care inevitably reflects the position of their groups as a whole within general society. It shows that such group interrelationships which influence health care provisions are unequal. It highlights the power dimension of ethnic relationships, from social disadvantage to explicit racism, which affect the provision of services such as health. It critiques the assumption of social consensus."

The notion of power differentials is underlined in Ramsden's work, as well as in Polaschek's elaboration of it. Polaschek notes that the definition of culture used in this conceptual framework is not the same as the anthropological definition of culture, which when used in the popular discourse is susceptible to being static and reified. Rather, the framework is grounded in the wide diversity of Maori culture, reflecting the power relations that have subordinated that indigenous community.

Conclusion

Reducing the risk to and enhancing the safety of immigrant women of colour entails recognition of the societal, systemic, and individual forms of violence they encounter. It involves a dismantling of cultural and sexist stereotypes, as well as of racist and sexist attitudes and behaviours that inform and structure social institutions. It entails an awareness of the dynamics of abuse within intimate relationships and social institutions, and of societal attitudes toward such abuse. It necessitates a dismantling of the hierarchies within the health care system which favour some patients over others on the basis of their race, class, and gender, and where the preferred patient is the one who is willing to be rescued by the system at the expense of endangering her own life and legal status.

Within the formal health care system, the tendency has to been to rectify shortcomings by employing approaches characterized as culturally sensitive. These approaches can easily succumb to a piecemeal approach to social change. In part, this is a result of the very nature of the system, predicated as it is on a Western biomedical model which defines illness in discrete terms and categories and relies on prescriptive antidotes that can help eradicate the illness or at least manage the symptoms. The conceptual framework that organizes such an approach favours tangible solutions. Cultural prescriptions in the form of services and treatments that are organized, concrete, and discrete have an affinity to the medical model. In contrast, solutions that argue for structural change involve mobilization and call for a change in attitudes, practices, and conceptual frameworks. They involve advocacy and are predicated on a social justice model of substantive equality (as opposed to formal equality). The difficulty of translating this approach into the dominant framework of Western biomedicine is apparent in the continued inadequacy of the medical professions' response to violence against women. Rather than dealing with the systemic roots of gender-based violence as grounded in the inequality and subordination of women, the system tends to focus on the physical signs of violence and treat them as if they were isolated from the larger social context. And rather than dealing with the impact of racism, both in terms of the immediate health sequelae of this form of violence and the impact of deskilling, occupational ghettoization, and increased dependency and isolation, as well as its interlocking nature with intimate forms of violence, the tendency of the health care system has been to erase these women's realities altogether. In other words, the interlocking and intersecting aspect of these structures of domination is negated.

For the immigrant woman of colour, the system's focus on physical manifestations of violence feeds into and reinforces her own notions of what constitutes abuse. The system's preference for particular kinds of patients – that is, its own hierarchy of preferences – combined with the internal stratification of the system, which positions racialized and marginalized groups at the bottom, contributes to the continued exclusion, trivialization, and containment of immigrant women of colour who present with injuries resulting from intimate violence. The ideological grease that undergirds and sustains this enactment of power lies in the culturalizing discourse of violence. For here, culture becomes a way of masking commonalities deriving from gendered violence and, at the same time, the cultural discourse permits the dismissal of these women or their categorization as victimized, oppressed Others who are most vulnerable to "death by culture" (Narayan 1997).

Dismantling inequalities within the health care system requires a more serious and committed approach. It requires recognition of alternative ways of healing, and recognition of the skills and expertise that immigrant women of colour have to offer. The harnessing of these skills and expertise would address the issue of the brain drain, while also facilitating the introduction and integration of different approaches to health care. Further, it would address the current ghettoization of people of colour in the lower echelons of the health care system and redress the power imbalances within the system. These changes necessitate a rethinking of the current model of the provision of health care services where access to the system is mediated by the care card, and services are commodified in terms of dollars and cents.[13] For immigrant women of colour who often have neither the money nor the unpaid time it takes to access services, the current system exacts social and economic costs which they can ill afford. Thus, it is the hierarchies of power and their expression in routinized practices that require transformation if proper health care is to be accessible to all.

While the health care system is one among many institutions structured in dominance, the stereotypes that exist within it and that distinguish preferred patients from those who are not preferred and hence not considered deserving of treatment are circulated by and gain their currency from the legitimizing role of the media. Consequently, in the next chapter, I return to the terrain of mediated representations, this time focusing on the contemporary moral panic generated by the war on terror.

Part 4
Mediations of Terror

7
Gendering Terror Post-9/11

> Terror is a feature of the symbolic order, the vast mesh of repre-
> sentations and narratives both official and unofficial, public and
> private, in which a culture works out its sense of itself. It affects
> that dynamic but relatively stable set of implicit parameters that
> establish a group's sense of the actual and the possible and create
> a loose but definite sense of collective identity.
>
> – Geoffrey Galt Harpham, "Symbolic Terror"

If the lived reality of violence, as I suggest in the previous chapters, textures
the lives of racialized girls and women, then the contemporary climate of
terror generated by the mass media accomplishes the enactment of this
violence on a symbolic scale.[1] In particular, while violence is enacted on a
daily basis through the use of dominant discourses of denial, discourses
that utilize strategies of cultural racism, erasure, containment, trivialization,
exoticization, criminalization, disavowal, and annulment of difference, I
would argue that the situation post-9/11 has ushered in a climate where the
strategic use of these discourses is increasingly subsumed and activated under the banner of terror. In looking at violence across the spectrum, I return
in this last chapter to a theme with which I started – the discursive violence
of representations. In the present context, however, I situate my analysis of
the representational discourses of the Other, this time the Muslim body, as
figured in the *Montreal Gazette*'s coverage of the events of 11 September
2001.

A cultivated climate of fear contributes to increased budgets for enforcement officers (see Wortley 2002); like other interlocking structures of violence, as those I describe in previous chapters, it also keeps racialized women
and men "in their place." The events of 11 September 2001 offer a point of
departure for examining this climate of fear, rendered even more potent

with the bombings in Madrid in 2004 and London in the summer of 2005. The dominant Western media's construction of and obsession with the events that occurred in New York on 11 September have gained a foothold in the public imagination, signifying an era of a war on terror. In this chapter, I trace the ways in which the dominant media offered explanatory frameworks that reproduced an Orientalist framing of the Muslim body but also, and more importantly, generated a climate of terror. In so doing, the bodies of Others were delineated in ways that once again deflected attention from White dominance, facilitating a complete erasure of the historical involvement of the West in the East. In this instance, religious differences were racialized and communicated through the signification of Muslims and those who "look like Muslims" (Grewal 2003) as the Other.

In the immediate aftermath of the horrific destruction of the Twin Towers and the attack on the Pentagon on 11 September, the public was overwhelmed by images of Osama bin Laden as the quintessential evil warlord of the East, and George Bush Jr. as the righteous sheriff of the West. While the latter was intent on establishing order, the former was portrayed as engaging in ceaseless violence bent on destroying the free world as we know it and unleashing the forces of chaos reminiscent of a tribal past. The binaries of *us* versus *them* were explicitly encoded in the representations of opposing forces: Bush versus bin Laden; West versus East; modernity versus primitive tribalism; freedom versus oppression; democracy versus totalitarianism; Christianity versus Islam – and the list goes on. How this war played out at the local and national levels of an imagined community fostered by the mass media offers insights into the particular hierarchies of power that are operating in various contexts, as well as the particular outgroups that are defined as the terrifying Others.

The Local Context

Montreal has been ranked as one of the most cosmopolitan cities in North America, boasting a European milieu with open-air cafés, a laissez-faire/savoir faire attitude, not to mention a spirited and festive atmosphere. Carrying a legacy of both French and English colonialism, the city is a remarkable site of the melding of these two dominant cultures with a medley of exoticized Other cultures thrown into the mélange. Within this environment, the war on terror assumed a particular dynamic, which I trace below. However, several aspects of Montreal need to be explicated first, especially its dominant, mainstream English press – the *Gazette*.

As the only major English daily newspaper in Montreal, the *Gazette* is rather peculiarly positioned.[2] Owned by the Asper family's CanWest Global Communications Corporation (a corporation that also owns many of Canada's largest daily newspapers), it is obviously influenced by mainstream conservative political values of the dominant groups.[3] However, in addition to serving the minority Anglophone community in Quebec, it is seen to equally represent the voice and interests of a significant number of English-speaking minority and immigrant communities. The *Gazette* is caught in the difficult position of trying to cater to both the traditional Anglophone and the more recently established English-speaking immigrant communities, as well as adhering to the conservative bias of its owners. Add the reality that the city of Montreal includes a sizable Jewish and Muslim population.[4] The city has witnessed several highly publicized clashes between groups affiliated with these two large communities.[5] The late patriarch of the Asper family was known for his criticism of the mainstream media, which he argued reflected a pro-Palestinian and anti-Jewish bias.[6] In contrast, many of the Arab communities in Montreal have been equally critical of the *Gazette,* arguing that the coverage in the paper is biased against them.

In an analysis that sheds light on the dynamics of this unusual conjuncture, Sharon Todd (1998) describes how coverage of the hijab – the head covering worn by Muslim women – in the *Gazette* and *La Presse* (the main French-language daily in Quebec) served a strategic function beyond what might have been expected from such news stories.[7] For both presses, coverage was predicated on how to demonstrate the xenophobia and intolerance of the other language group. If in the *Gazette* the story became one of how the *"pure laine"* Québécois are intolerant of other cultures and traditions, *La Presse*'s coverage revolved around refuting the label of intolerance by focusing on the necessity of nurturing a Québécois society. In both cases, the needs and desires of the Arab and Muslim communities were not pivotal but were considered purely in relation to the dominant needs of each news organization and their respective ideological positions.

The *Gazette,* like most papers owned by major conglomerates, uses local, national, and international news sources. For the latter, the paper draws from the newswire services of the international press agencies, including Reuters, Agence France-Presse, Associated Press, and United Press, and, for specifically American news stories, Hearst, Knight Rider, and other chains, selecting those stories that fit or resonate with the local framework. And, like other conglomerate-owned Canadian newspapers, the *Gazette* also prints articles that it obtains through the Canadian newswire services and that are printed in other newspapers owned by CanWest. The overall portrait of what transpired on 11 September 2001 was a collage of local, national, and international news stories selected by the *Gazette*'s editors in response to what they perceived as being relevant to their audience.

The analysis that I present here is limited to twenty days of coverage in the *Gazette* in the immediate aftermath of 11 September. A database search using the keywords "women," "veil," and "burqa" generated fifty-six articles containing one or more of these words.[8] I then examined these articles using a method of informal discourse analysis (van Dijk 1985, 1993). Key to this method are the identification of accessed voices (who gets to speak), types of description, semantic moves, and discursive strategies. Signs were scrutinized in terms of their denotative and connotative meanings (Barthes 1973), as well as their resonance with Orientalism as defined by Said (1979).

In my analysis, no differentiation is made between stories filed by regular columnists, onsite reporters, the paper's editors, or informed citizens writing opinion pieces. While recognizing that there are important differences between these categories, my principal aim here is to examine all the representations that referenced the category "women." I should also stress that even though the articles selected were chosen because of their mention or inclusion of the keyword "woman" (or "women"), the resulting analysis includes an examination of male representations insofar as these were portrayed in relation to women. The latter is predicated on the notion that gender is a relational category that derives its meanings from its contextual and social location vis-à-vis other categories. To understand the textual analysis of these fifty-six stories, we must first appreciate the contextual factors underpinning and framing representations of Muslims and Islam.

The Wider Context of Orientalism

Edward Said's significant contribution in defining the organizational features of Orientalism is a critical departure point for any study focusing on representations of Islam and the Muslim body.[9] Said (1979, 73) defines Orientalism as "a generic term ... to describe the Western approach to the Orient; Orientalism is the discipline by which the Orient was (and is) approached systematically, as a topic of learning, discovery and practice. But in addition I have been using the word to designate that collection of dreams, images and vocabularies available to anyone who has tried to talk about what lies East of the dividing line." In this sense, Orientalism describes a medley of diverse approaches and perspectives that are unified by a Western gaze and sedimented through historical references to other works that assume a coherence of sorts. In other words, Orientalism constitutes a regime of truth (Foucault 1980a, 131) based on an authoritative corpus of knowledge.

Said's definition of Orientalism is also relevant because it highlights the existence of a repository of images from which the collective stock of knowledge – everyday common-sense knowledge – continually draws on to make sense of the world (see Chapter 2). The articulation of these images reveals a degree of fluidity based on the changing circumstances to which these images are called upon to respond. Nonetheless, as instantiations fashioned and wrought by contemporary events, as well as by the inherent constraints and enabling influences of various institutions and technologies, they tend to echo elements of that collective and cumulative reservoir of knowledge (S. Hall 1990a).

The discursive regime of Orientalism overlaps with and is derived from discourses of colonialism and imperialism. Commonalities with these discursive traditions lie in the binary oppositions that form and inform the power coordinates of these regimes of truth. These include a perception of cultural practices as indicative of inherent and innate traits, a collapsing of differences between subject peoples so that they appear as monolithic entities, and taxonomies of knowledge which situate subject peoples in particular relations of inferiority that are then naturalized. In terms of the tradition of Orientalism, then, the Orient is a place of mystery and danger. The Orientalized body is discursively situated within this landscape; such a position legitimizes and naturalizes unequal power relations. The Orientalized body becomes a projection of all that the West finds alien and abhorrent, but simultaneously exotic, and alluring. In short, the Orientalized body essentializes otherness.

Said (1979) has argued that the Orient has been conceptualized as feminized terrain, weak yet dangerous and ready to be subjugated and domesticated through the civilizing forces of the progressive West. As I note in Chapter 1, within this context, women are seen in terms of their role as signifiers of culture: the boundary markers between *us* and *them* that underlie and structure the relationship of the dominant colonizers to the subordinated colonized (Fanon 1965; Lévi-Strauss 1966; Yeğenoğlu 1998). Thus, women's bodies have been used to solidify national boundaries, and to differentiate outgroups (Anthias and Yuval-Davis 1992). Bodies of women as gendered beings carry particular connotations and are located at multiple sites of discursive manipulation (Lalvani 1995). On the one hand, women are represented as the keepers of culture and the maintainers of tradition; on the other, they are represented as exchange commodities to be used to cement alliances, or as sexual objects that can be offered up to occupying forces and indigenous patriarchal institutions (see Park 2004).

The gendered discourse of power underpinning colonialism and subsequently post- and neo-colonial relations is also evident in the ways in which the news media cover stories about other nations and other peoples. As I discuss in Chapter 2, existing studies point to the numerous ways in which so-called developing nations are portrayed as backward, barbaric, traditional, and primitive (Dahlgren with Chakrapani 1982; Hackett 1989). In keeping with the Manichean allegories of colonial thought (JanMohamed 1985), the natives of these countries are also seen to be innocent, childlike, and pure relics of a distant past (Wynn Davies, Nandy, and Sardar 1993). In the case of women, dominant representations tend to exoticize them, highlighting their perceived excessive sexuality while at the same time representing them as dangerous and engulfing (Jiwani 1992b; Mohanty 1991a). A critical feature of many of these representations is their inherent ambivalence, which I discuss in Chapter 2 (see also Bhabha 1983; S. Hall 1990a).

Lalvani (1995) and others have traced the many ways in which the exotic Other was historically rendered into a consumable fetish. Through the process of commodification, and through the reification of the commodity, the fetish is conquered, its threat contained, and its use value replaced by its exchange value, which is articulated in the currency of desire (see also Leiss, Kline, and Jhally 1986). This is most clearly apparent in Hollywood depictions of the gendered, Orientalized body: from the geisha to the slave girl; from the dragon lady to the oppressed and victimized princess (see Gee 1988; Soe 1992).

Representations of Muslims and Arabs have also generated attention from academic scholars and community organizations. Said's seminal work *Covering Islam* (1981) identifies the tropes used by journalists in their coverage of nations governed by Islamic law, many of which centre around the notion of Islam as a monolithic entity stubbornly resisting the development (read rescue) efforts of the West. Shaheen (1984) has argued that the consistently negative stereotyping of Arabs in popular film and television has resulted in negative consequences for those Arabs living in the United States. The Canadian Islamic Congress (2002) has reiterated this view based on its monitoring of the mainstream media coverage of Islam and Muslims. Similarly, Jafri (1998) has underlined the pernicious effects of these representations in her analysis of Muslim women and their response to mainstream media messages, and Karim (2000) in his analysis of the Islamic peril generated by the media has followed the line of inquiry established by Said in examining the news media and the tropes that are utilized by journalists in their stories about Muslims and nations where the practice of Islam constitutes the predominant religion.

Discursive Features: Veiling and Unveiling Difference

As mentioned above, women from the East tend to be portrayed in Hollywood films, imperial literature, and travelogues as mysterious, exotic, erotic, and dangerous. Said (1979, 190) remarks that "just as the various colonial possessions – apart from their economic benefit to metropolitan Europe – were useful as places to send wayward sons, superfluous populations of delinquents, poor people, and other undesirables, so the Orient was a place where one could look for sexual experience unobtainable in Europe." In a more recent analysis, Razack (1998b) argues that the sexual exploitation of women and children in the lesser-developed countries is underpinned by the Orientalist framing of these countries and their populations. She notes that travelling East to secure exotic and forbidden sexual pleasures is part of the social construction of the region as an area of moral degeneracy. By corollary, the West is constructed as a zone of morality. Drawing on histori-cal examples, Razack illustrates how the sojourns of Victorian bourgeois men in areas of moral degeneracy helped to rejuvenate and restore within them their own sense of masculinity, and cumulatively reinforce hegemonic values. She further argues that prostitution and sexual exploitation are forms of violence that are predicated on, and that intersect with, the violence of the colonial and post-colonial encounter.

The theme of the sexualized Other is an important focal point in colonial literature about women in the East. Much of this literature highlights a preoccupation with the veil and the veiling of women, a preoccupation carried over by the mass media. As Yeğenoğlu (1998, 44) suggests:

> The veil attracts the eye, and forces one to think, to speculate about what is behind it. It is often represented as some kind of a mask, hiding the woman. With the help of this opaque veil, the Oriental woman is considered as not yielding herself to the Western gaze and therefore imagined as hiding some-thing behind the veil. It is through the inscription of the veil as a mask that the Oriental woman is turned into an enigma. Such a discursive construc-tion incites the presumption that the real nature of these women is con-cealed, their truth is disguised and they appear in a false deceptive manner. They are therefore other than what they appear to be.

If, as Fanon (1965) suggests, this leads to an overpowering desire to rend the veil and unmask the woman (a desire which can be understood in part as motivating Western media's fascination and obsession with the veil), the veil as a cover is also enticingly mysterious. A United Colours of Benetton advertisement featuring Afghani women in the burqa captures this sense of mystery, inviting the Western gaze to unveil the woman.[10] The woman is unveiled in the next page, suggesting that Benetton is able to undo in an instant what centuries of colonization could only attempt.

In contemporary Western media, the veil remains a symbol of Muslim women and their oppression by tribal, primitive, and conservative uphold-ers of Islam (Hoodfar 1993). As Anouar Majid (1998, 334) remarks, "For the Western media, the picture of the veiled woman visually defines both the mystery of Islamic culture and its backwardness." However, as she goes on to explain: "Despite its close association with Islam, the veil is in fact an old eastern Mediterranean practice that was assimilated to Islam in its early stages of expansion. In the two suras in the Qur'an that refer to the veil, not only is there no specific mention of veiling the face but certain parts of the body in fact are assumed to be visible."

Nonetheless, the association of Muslim women with the veil persists in Western popular imagination. Moreover, it feeds and fuels yet another pre-vailing feature in the discourse surrounding Orientalized women – that of their oppressed and tradition-bound existence. Within Western popular media, this feature often underpins the rescue motif. In this motif, the White male explorer seeks to rescue the imperilled woman of colour and save her from the savagery of her cultural traditions (see also Amos and Parmar 1984; Mohanty 1991b; Razack 1998a). Cooke (2002, 469) maintains that "the burka recalls suttee and the four-stage gendered logic of empire: (1) women have inalienable rights within universal civilization, (2) civilized men recognize and respect these rights, (3) uncivilized men systematically abrogate these rights, and (4) such men (the Taliban) thus belong to an alien (Islamic) system." This logic, she argues, "genders and separates subject peoples so that the men are the Other and the women are civilizable. To defend our universal civilization we must rescue the women. To rescue these women we must attack these men. These women will be rescued not because they are more 'ours' than 'theirs' but rather because they will have become more 'ours' through the rescue mission ... In the Islamic context, the negative stereotyping of the religion as inherently misogynist provides ammunition for the attack on the uncivilized brown men."

Interestingly, Western imperial feminism (at the height of Empire) has also been taken to task by feminists of colour for embracing this rescue motif (Strobel 1993). As Antoinette Burton (1992, 137) notes, "Many middle-class British feminists viewed the women of the East not as equals but as unfortunates in need of saving by their British feminist 'sisters.' By imagining the women of India as helpless colonial subjects, British feminists constructed 'the Indian woman' as a foil against which to gauge their own progress." The rescue motif is also apparent in the ways in which many Western feminists reacted to the plight of Afghan women, seeing them as victims of oppressive, barbaric men and waiting to be saved by their sisters (Kolhatkar 2002a).[11]

The focus on the veil from all these quarters thus allows for the enactment of the rescue motif. It legitimizes intervention in the name of liberation and progress. Indeed, many within Islamic nations have sought to mark progress in terms of normative or prescriptive dictates forbidding or sanctioning the wearing of the veil (Hoodfar 1993).[12] Yeğenoğlu (1998, 100) reasons: "It is no coincidence that the desire to unveil the Oriental woman coincided with the broader agenda of 'progress' and belief in the incompatibility of Islam with Western models of modernity and reason ... Conceived as the indisputable emblem of Islamic culture's essential traditionalism, the veil was consistently seen as a problem and its lifting as the most important sign of reform and modernization."

However, the veil has also functioned as a signifier for communicating militancy and a dogmatic attachment to tradition. The use of the veil as a sign of resistance, for instance, has been documented in the literature dealing with the Iranian and Algerian revolutions (Ahmed 1992; Hoodfar 1993; Rezig 1983). Yet, in keeping with the ambivalent structure of such representations, women who voluntarily wear the veil are also perceived as being brainwashed by the patriarchal structures within their communities and thus as having no agency.

It is not surprising, then, to see some of these tropes carried over in the coverage provided by the *Gazette*, coverage that reaffirmed particular Orientalist stereotypes of Muslims, both those living in the East and those residing in the West.

The World According to the *Gazette*

In examining the coverage printed by the *Gazette*, it was apparent that descriptions of Muslim men far outweighed those of Muslim women. Of the total number of stories examined, thirty-two contained explicit descriptions of Muslim men, while only twenty-three referenced women or dealt specifically with Muslim women. In most stories, women were mentioned in passing. The majority of the stories, especially those dealing with events related to Afghanistan, tended to utilize binary oppositions – pitting the oppressive, harsh, dictatorial, and barbaric characteristics of Afghanistan against the libertarian, democratic, and superior character of the United States. (I discuss this further in the "Muslim Men" section below.)

There were also significant differences in the ways in which Muslim women living in Afghanistan, Pakistan, and other parts of the Muslim world were represented, as compared with their counterparts in Canada and the United States. A significant number of stories pertaining to Muslims living in the United States or Canada focused on the threat of backlash. Further, and in contrast to Muslim women living in Afghanistan, Pakistan, and the Middle East, Muslim women living in the West tended to have a modicum of active representation in that they were interviewed, and their words were often quoted in print. Nonetheless, whether the stories dealt with the threat of violence experienced by them here in the West or the conditions of patriarchal oppression confronting them in the East, Muslim women tended to be portrayed as victims.

Overall, however, it was difficult to separate the representations of Muslim men from Muslim women, given that the two are intertwined in the coverage, with the framing of one giving meaning to the framing of the other. For analytical reasons, I have separated the main discursive themes used to represent women and men. In addition, I outline the ways in which the discursive constructions of Muslim women in the West, under the auspices of expressing concern for the backlash they might face as a result of their presence, contained women in a manner that converged with their containment in the East.

Muslim Women

Of all the stories referencing Muslim women, Orientalist themes were especially apparent in those that focused on Muslim women living directly under Islamic rule. For example, several stories used the image of women veiled in burqas – appearing mute and fleetingly in the streets – as a backdrop against which the horrors and barbarism of the Taliban were more fully described. In a sense, there is nothing new here. As indicated above, colonial and contemporary Western media have had a particular fascination with the veil and have represented it as a symbol of Muslim women and their oppression (Ahmed 1992; Jafri 1998; Hoodfar 1993). That said, in the corpus of the coverage examined, women's victimized and subordinate status was generally linked to the excessive patriarchal nature of Islam, and of Afghan men by association. The following story underscores this kind of reporting:

> It's midday in Pakistan's deeply conservative northwest. Bearded men sit in small groups sipping sweet black tea. The rare woman hidden in an enveloping head-to-toe cloak called a burqa, scurries through the dusty market.
>
> The call to prayer sounds. The voice is soothing, almost mournful. Then the cleric begins to preach. His voice changes, suddenly shrill and angry and his message violent. Bellowing from a loudspeaker atop the mosque, the voice rails against internationally financed aid organizations and their promotion of women's rights, girls' education and small home-based businesses. It hurls curses at the women who work for these groups, calling them evil handmaidens of a decadent West that wants to destroy traditions, culture and the Islamic religion. They should be punished, the voice says.
>
> Islamic clerics urge the faithful to shun women involved with such groups as prostitutes – or, alternatively, to kidnap them, force them into marriage and keep them locked away at home. "Don't allow these sinful women to enter our villages," roars Maulana Zia-ul Haq, a cleric in Banda, a village in the Dir district. "If you see any one of them, just take her home and forcibly marry her. If she is a foreigner, kill her." (Gannon 2001)

Entitled, "Where equality is 'obscene': Conservative Pakistani clerics vow to crush women's rights" and appearing just two days after the destruction in New York City, this article strategically brings together several Orientalist tropes. For instance, Orientalist imagery is evoked in the language used to describe the setting. The laziness of the natives comes through in the representation of men sitting around sipping tea while the women fearfully hurry about their business. Women are not to be seen or heard under Taliban rule (Franks 2003). Men, on the other hand, are charged with maintaining the patriarchal order, as exemplified in the role of the clerics. The clerics become the point men for the media, symbolizing fanaticism, ruthlessness, barbarity, and excessive patriarchal violence. Lazreg (1988, 95) notes that "the fetishism of the concept, Islam, in particular, obscures the living reality of women and men subsumed under it." Thus, Islam becomes the paradigm by which women's and men's lives are understood, as opposed to a force that emerges as a form of identification and mobilization in response to external circumstances and conditions. Interestingly, news stories, such as the one above, conflate or collapse the differences between Palestinians and Afghanis, or Palestinians and Pakistanis, and reflect the tendency of the dominant Western media to resort to homogeneous and totalizing representations (see also the Canadian Islamic Congress's [2002] evaluation of Western media bias).

However, contradictions abound. In the same story, the voice of one of the clerics vowing to crush women's rights is described as "shrill and angry and his message [as] violent." This loaded description offers a view of the clerics as irrational and insane in their ultra-patriarchal insistence that women remain subjugated, but also as weak and feminized given that emotion is stereotypically considered to be the province of women. Similarly, the women who are interviewed are presented simultaneously as victims and as active agents who, if somewhat deceptive by necessity, are resisting the patriarchal onslaught by organizing a shelter for women and setting up educational programs to make other women aware of their rights.

One of these so-called active women, for instance, is described as "cover[ing] her head in a large sweeping shawl." Her victimization is made evident from the inclusion of her experience of being in an abusive marriage with her first cousin whom she has not yet divorced. She is further described as being engaged in educational efforts to make other women aware of their rights. She adds "Their self-esteem is not there. *They think of themselves as something akin to animals*" (my emphasis). The victimhood of Afghani women is thus rendered complete – as animals, they need to be saved – and as stated by one of them no less.

Another young female worker at the shelter, Ruhi Tabassum, is also interviewed. "Smiling beneath the shawl," as the reporter puts it, she is quoted as saying, "They [the men] know that if their women know their rights, they won't be able to control them." The reporter includes mention of the smile to suggest Tabassum's duplicity. The overall portrayal of Afghani women in this article resonates with the colonial representation of women of colour as secretive, deceptive, and as appearing to be meek and submissive while plotting against their benevolent colonizers – or, for that matter, against their own men (Jiwani 1992b).

This profile is carried over into a story about the necessity for increased security measures at US airports (M. Smith and Philps 2001). Here, the traditional notion of Arab or Middle Eastern women as quintessential victims is shattered by the Israelis' contention that they have identified Arab women travelling alone in Israel as constituting a high risk. In contrast, Israeli or Jewish women who know some Hebrew are considered to be low risks. Others who constitute a high risk include Arab males, priests, and people "who purchase their tickets at the last minute." Foreigners are deemed to be a moderate risk. However, the paper does not define who constitutes a foreigner, leaving it to the reader to assume that these individuals would probably include those outside the immediate vicinity or outside the Middle East.

This confusing and sometimes contradictory conflation of woman as helpless victim and manipulative activist is found in another article that contrasts the innocence of those female victims who went to work in the Twin Towers on that fateful day with the callous and uncanny behaviour of the Palestinian women in Ramallah who were shown celebrating the demise of the victims (Schnurmacher 2001). Here, active agency in the form of the militancy of Palestinian women is presented in an extreme fashion by the writer, who then goes on to make nebulous links between Palestinian women, their celebration, and their commitment to a cause "beyond reason."

Such unquestioning and irrational commitment to a cause beyond reason is then harnessed to the female biological body by presenting Palestinian women as reproducers of terror – as mothers of suicide bombers. As the writer describes it, a "Canadian broadcast reporter whose coverage had always leaned strongly toward the Palestinian position recently became more even-handed after an encounter with the mother of a suicide bomber who told him she was happy with what her son had accomplished. Her only regret was she did not have other sons who could do the same thing" (Schnurmacher 2001). The revulsion expressed toward Palestinian women who give birth to suicide bombers echoes the kinds of fears put forth in colonial literature around miscegenation. In this literature, colonial officers were advised not to consort with indigenous women because of the latter's perceived fecundity, and the fear that the growth of a mixed-race population would lead to a weakening of the Empire's moral, political, and economic stronghold over its colonies (McBratney 1988; Mohanty 1991a). Inherent in this logic was the notion of tainted blood – that the blood of the colonized would weaken, contaminate, and result in a population that would overthrow colonial rule and, by virtue of being mixed with the blood of the colonizer, result in a hybrid form that was more dangerous. Here the representation that is being underscored is that of women's bodies as sites of danger, as begetters of violence: a violence that can engulf and annihilate if not contained or neutralized.

The same ambivalent framing of the victim-activist Muslim female is captured in a photograph and caption that accompanies a story on the US movement of arms to various areas in Afghanistan. The photo shows women in burqa with guns protesting at a rally in Lahore. The caption reads: "Veiled women activists of a Pakistani religious-political party hold toy guns and the Koran as they chant anti-U.S. slogans at Lahore protest rally" (Blanchfield and Mackenzie 2001b). That these women are actively engaged in protest as opposed to their usual passive behaviour (à la the stereotypical depiction of them as passive victims) should, according to the gender liberation rhetoric of the West, suggest a disruption that is progressive. However, here, the very act of holding toy guns and copies of the Koran makes their action suspect and indicative of an emergent threat. In contrast, women educating other women and setting up shelters for their sisters – in short, women who behave like *us* – are acceptable. However, women who are militant activists are not (Thobani 2003; see also Chapter 2).

In all these articles, Afghanistan and surrounding nations are gendered. The latter are portrayed as "allies of convenience" that cannot be entirely trusted, given that they are also deceptive and motivated by their own agendas (Wallace 2001; Goldstein 2001). Images of failed states and primitive technologies and peoples come through in these stories. What is implicitly understood, and what is even sometimes explicitly stated, is that these countries have failed because of their own inherent shortcomings rather than because of any involvement by the Western or Soviet imperial powers (Friedman 2001). Thus, it is the supposed failure of these countries that is deemed to be the motivating factor sparking resentment toward, and retaliation against, the West.

Dependency is another gendered term used when referring to many of the countries surrounding Afghanistan, as well as Afghanistan itself. The latter is the same country that the United States bombed "up to the Stone Age" (Dowd 2001), a comment that implies that Afghanistan was even *more* primitive before US intervention. Primitivism, then, becomes one of the discursive means by which to explain women's subordinate position (Bagnall 2001) and is signified by the rejection of leisure through consumption (e.g., the banning of television sets, music, and even kites) (Dowd 2001), as well as by the brutality of Afghani men (Gannon 2001). In contrast, America and Americans are represented as emblems of freedom, liberation, and democracy. While they might have a few failings, these are not equivalent to the crimes committed by the Taliban. As one writer concludes: "Before September 11, it might have been possible to feel pity for the men who joined the Taliban, with their feelings of dislocation after 20 years of Soviet invasion and civil war, their poverty, their desire to make sense of their world. But not now. By now we know how they intend to order their world: women under house arrest; the rest of the world their enemy" (Bagnall 2001). There is a complete erasure of history in the kinds of representations that are used to justify American intervention in Afghanistan. Moreover, the very notion of pity is suggestive of Western benevolence which, as Sherene Razack (1998a) reasons, is the underside of Western racism. Taken as a whole, these articles exemplify how these strategic representations work together to create an overall impression of an exploding situation "over there" that demands intervention from "over here" (Khan 2001).

Muslim Men

The inferiority of the Afghani men and the Taliban (which is made up of Afghani men) in particular comes through not only in the imagery of primitiveness but also in descriptions of their brutality and zeal. Several stories underline this brutality by linking it to the treatment of women, and more importantly, to fanaticism. For example, one mullah is "reputed to be so crazed that when shrapnel hit his eye in the battle with the Russians, he simply cut it out with a knife and kept going" (Dowd 2001). Another story discusses the attack on the World Trade Center in 1993, concluding that "the mastermind, Ramzi Yousef, later boasted that he had hoped to kill 250,000" (Spector 2001). Overall, the message is that primitivism leads to violent opposition of the West – an opposition that is irrational and grounded in a mixture of fear and resentment. Add poverty to this potent mix – a poverty that would seem, according to these stories, to be self-inflicted – and what we are left with is a confluence of factors that lends itself perfectly to the development of human weapons of mass destruction. These themes are exemplified in a story by a reporter who visits a madrasa in Pakistan where orphan boys and refugee men are schooled in the theological foundations and practice of one particular interpretation of Islam. He calls it a "jihad factory" populated by "poor and impressionable boys who are kept entirely ignorant of the world and largely ignorant of all but one interpretation of Islam. They are the perfect jihad machines" (J. Goldberg 2001).

Nowhere in this article is it mentioned that the type of Islam taught in this madrasa is akin to the Islam practised by the ruling elite in Saudi Arabia, a significant ally of the United States; nor is there any mention of the diversity that exists within the Islamic world, or the history of US involvement in the region. Nor why these young boys and men are orphans and refugees in the first place.

Another common trope in the coverage of Muslim men concerned their unwarranted envy of and anger against the West. As this writer argues:

And this Third World War does not pit the U.S. against another superpower. It pits it – the world's only superpower and quintessential symbol of liberal, free-market, Western values – against all the super-empowered angry men and women out there. Many of these super-empowered angry people come from failing states in the Muslim and Third World. They do not share American values, they resent America's influence over their lives, politics and children, not to mention its support for Israel, and they often blame America for the failure of their societies to master modernity.

What makes them super-empowered, though, is their genius at using the networked world, the Internet and the very high technology they hate to attack the United States. Think about it: they turned its most advanced civilian planes into human-directed, precision-guided cruise missiles – a diabolical melding of their fanaticism and American technology. Jihad Online. And think of what they hit: the World Trade Centre – the beacon of American-led capitalism that both tempts and repels them, and the Pentagon, the embodiment of American military superiority. (Friedman 2001)

This excerpt illustrates both the ambivalence inherent in these representations – the juxtapositioning of primitiveness with expertise in computer technology – and the strategic moves that underscore the differences between the West and the East. The latter includes those moves that minimize the grounds of their grievances. In other words, those grievances – regardless of how founded they might be – are simply translated into the emotions of anger, resentment, and envy. They are thus rendered as undeserving children who have no legitimate basis for their anger. However, their anger, though illegitimate, is dangerous enough to signal the advent of a third world war. In addition, the excerpt illustrates the binary of the benevolent West sharing its technologies with the primitive East, only to have the latter use it against its benefactors. The theme of betrayal is underscored in the above quote constructing the inhabitants of the "failed states" as beyond redemption and thus deserving of extreme retaliatory action.

The inferiorization of Muslim men is achieved by representing them as emotional, irrational, deceptive, resentful, untrustworthy, and above all, childlike. This latter rendering emasculates these men – reducing them to weak, vulnerable, and conquerable entities. Another part of this strategy of emasculation is to render these men more feminine. The use of emotional descriptors serves this function, as do other more explicit discursive devices. Witness, for example, the following description of Osama bin Laden offered by one of the reporters: "The image has flickered across North American television screens so many times in the last five days it will probably take years to fade – the liquid-eyed Osama bin Laden, almost girlishly pretty despite the breast-long beard, sits in the dust in flowing robes, firing an automatic weapon and smiling at the strength of its recoil. The film was shot years ago, but in the pictures, the charismatic gunman seems almost to be mocking the West and its grief" (Waters 2001). This feminized portrayal of Osama bin Laden coalesces a number of signifiers and connotations, producing an overall picture of bin Laden as the beguiling yet ultimately menacing arch-villain who is cold, calculating, ruthless, and sinister – all characteristics, incidentally, that are commonly associated with women of

Cartoon printed in the Montreal Gazette, *23 September 2001, A7.* Courtesy of Michel Garneau

colour in colonial literature and popular culture. A cartoon that appeared in the editorial page of the paper a week later (23 September 2001) also feminized bin Laden, portraying him as a woman in a burqa. What is interesting about the written portrayal and the cartoon is the use of feminized descriptives such as "liquid-eyed," "girlishly pretty," "breast-long beard" combined with his representation in a burqa complaining about how warm it was wearing such a garment. The cartoon was first printed in *La Presse* and subsequently in the *Gazette*.

The significance of these feminized portrayals of bin Laden lies in colonial relations of power whereby the feminine connotes and denotes an evil that needs to be contained by the civilizing force of masculinity (read the West), and where the subordinate and subjugated status of women demands conquest, domestication, and liberation via the prowess of masculinity. In this particular context, the implicit message likens bin Laden to a woman about to be conquered by the West – by a masculine superpower.

At this point, it should be mentioned that, in the course of the *Gazette*'s post-9/11 coverage, several reporters *do* attempt to explain Islam and its variegated nature to the Western audience but, all too often, dichotomous interpretations of Islam – as a religion of peace on the one hand and a religion advocating war on the other – are juxtaposed. These stories tend to draw heavily on the accessed voices of elite Islamic scholars in the West and the East (see Watanabe 2001). They also privilege a sense that the message of peace in Islam is particularly vulnerable to being hijacked, and that this vulnerability is itself a function of the inherent flaws of Islam's religious structure. Thus, a structure that is perceived to be without a central author- ity, without policing mechanisms, and with a kind of communal orienta- tion is seen to lend itself to a collective ethos that then becomes the antithesis of Western capitalism with its hierarchal structures and its centralization of power. Within such a framing, even the intellectual tradition of Islam is seen to be at fault for encouraging this kind of hijacking. As one reporter put it, "All of this flexibility and questioning mean that a clever leader or scholar with a bitter and often not very well-informed audience can twist Koranic ideas to his own ends. The jihad for example" (Waters 2001). This statement follows that of a Muslim advocate in the West who counters the stereotypical view of Islam by emphasizing its intellectual tradition and its encouragement of questioning and internal search. That Christianity, as Karim (2000) has suggested, has been similarly hijacked is an observation significantly missing from these articles. Thus the David Koreshs and Timo- thy McVeighs of the West are carefully occluded from any kind of compara- tive examination.

Backlash Stories
A significant number of stories printed by the *Gazette* during this period cohered around the theme of backlash, or the threat of backlash as experi- enced by Muslim communities in the United States and Canada. What is interesting about these backlash stories is that they served a dual ideologi- cal function. On the one hand, they communicate to minority groups that their interests are considered important enough to garner press coverage – in other words, they count. On the other hand, and from a somewhat cyni- cal perspective, the inclusion of backlash stories serves the strategic func- tion of balance. As Stuart Hall (1974) has argued, the codes of objectivity, balance, and impartiality are critical to the ideological functioning of the news media in their position as the fourth estate and their role in maintain- ing the hegemonic order (see Chapter 2). For the news media to appear to be partisan would detract from their credibility as the fourth estate and the voice of the nation, and make them vulnerable to boycotts, advertiser re- prisals, charges of biased reporting, and a disaffected audience.

Several interesting themes emerge in the stories about Muslim fears of a backlash. Of the fifty-six articles, thirteen deal specifically with the actual or potential threat of a backlash against the Muslim population living in the West. Of the ten such stories to appear in the first week following 9/11, two deal with the Muslims in the United States. Another is a personal ac- count of a Pakistani woman and her experience of racism upon moving to a particular part of Quebec many years ago. Two are editorials decrying the incidence of racist assaults and the targeting of Muslims in Montreal. One other story revolves around the reporter's overhearing of racist comments by non-Muslim women in the aftermath of the collapse of the Twin Towers. In many of these stories, incidents of assault – whether they are projected or fully realized – are noted. Most of these focus on women wearing the veil and their fears of doing so in the immediate aftermath of 9/11.

In the single article that focuses on an assault of a young Saudi female resident at a local hospital, the reporter makes no mention of a veil, though the assault itself is graphically described. Further, there is no mention of how the attacker identified the woman as being Saudi or a Muslim (Mac-Farlane 2001). According to the report, the woman is "a fourth year resident in obstetrics and gynaecology, described by her supervisors as a brilliant resident." Her dedication to her work is further emphasized by the mention that she stayed for most of her shift despite having being attacked and traumatized. While she is not interviewed, the dean of McGill University's Faculty of Medicine is quoted as saying, "Female Muslim residents will not be on call during nights, effective immediately." What is striking about the dean's response is that measures were not invoked to increase the protection of those who are rendered vulnerable to such assaults. Equally striking is that while the story appears to be sympathetic to the young woman and laudatory of her status, her own voice is erased.

In this story, as in the majority of the other backlash stories, the themes of fear and the possibility of retaliation emerge clearly. However, in most of them, it is the male authoritative figures (in general, key spokesmen or presidents of various organizations) who are interviewed or quoted extensively. Muslim women are directly interviewed in only three stories. An example of this trend is evident in this story, which appeared on 13 September 2001:

> In Canada, the backlash began Tuesday, said Shafiq Hudda, chairman of the Islamic Humanitarian Service, a national charitable organization based in Kitchener, Ont. "One of our lady volunteers was actually verbally assaulted on the highway," Hudda said.
>
> "Somebody called her an effing terrorist." Hudda said the woman, who is in her 50s and was wearing a head scarf, was shaken by the incident, which occurred near the downtown area of Kitchener ...
>
> The Islamic Assembly of North America, which is based in the United States but also has an office in Quebec, is advising Muslims in both countries to stay home. "All Muslims in the U.S. and Canada must take precautions and care from the possibility of retaliatory attacks," said the group's Web site. "Do not leave home unless absolutely necessary, especially women, [sic] who wear Muslim dress." (Richards 2001)

While the backlash stories serve the important function of highlighting the vulnerabilities of the Muslim population living in North America, their resulting message ends up reinforcing notions of the weakness and victim status of this particular group. This is especially evident in the references to women. The majority of the articles underline the view that women wearing the veil or the hijab are most vulnerable to attacks because they are easily identifiable (see, for instance, Fitterman 2001a, 2001b). Male spokespeople for the organizations that are contacted all caution women who wear the hijab or veil to stay at home. One Muslim woman specifically mentions how her daughter was afraid to wear her hijab to school and had to be accompanied by her brother to ensure her safety (Davenport 2001).

These words of caution, though well intentioned, end up legitimizing Muslim women's containment in the private sphere of the home. That home might well be located in the United States or Canada, but the end result is a strategy of containment, ironically reminiscent of that which the Taliban in Afghanistan had been enforcing upon women. Gendering terror, then, becomes in part about the ways in which the *threat* of violence and retaliation forces women and men to refrain from being seen, or from occupying space as legitimate citizens.

In yet another article, reference is made to a woman who now refrains from wearing the veil *precisely* because of this threat of backlash. In the same article, two female students recount their experiences of terror. One is told to "go home. You're just a terrorist." The other student states, "I do have a feeling of insecurity because of the looks I am getting of anger and suspicion" (Block 2001). In other words, fear, heightened security, and potential threats are all ways in which Muslim families and individuals are terrorized into "going home" or staying at home. The question is, where is home for a diasporic community? And what if home is here? (Aujla 2000).

In these latter stories, then, Muslim women are framed as victims who are acted upon by others, rather than as active agents who are capable of determining their own course of safety or resistance to the perceived threat from the outside. Such a framing accords with one of the main features of news reporting, namely, the tendency to create binaries between the victims and the perpetrators (Connell 1980). But interestingly, it also converges with the dominant ideology which, as evident from the controversial case of Émilie Ouimet, a French Canadian girl who chose to wear the veil, suggests that symbols such as the veil communicate a reluctance to assimilate on the part of a minority group member and hence lead to her further marginalization. Thus, the victim of discrimination is blamed for inciting discriminatory attitudes by refusing to adhere to the dominant norms (Lenk 2000).

As for Muslim men living in the West, these backlash stories tend to depict them as authoritative, reasonable, compassionate, and desperate to distance themselves from the acts of those who attacked the Twin Towers, as well as from the more fundamentalist clerics who advocate a literal and conservative interpretation of Islam. Such a social distancing is symbolic of a retreat. By distancing themselves from those who attacked the Twin Towers and those who represent the Taliban and the Afghanis, Muslim men who were interviewed in many of the *Gazette* articles are, by their very geographic location, rendered more like *us*. Such a sentiment is clearly articulated by one Muslim spokesperson – a professor at the University of Waterloo and president of the Canadian Islamic Congress – who is quoted as saying: "We are part of you and you are part of us" (Waters 2001). Yet, this social distancing and retreat also underlines Muslim men's victim status – as being at the mercy of Islamophobia and as needing intervention.

The *Gazette*'s representations also reinforce the binary of East versus West, and tradition versus liberation. By locating these Muslim men in the West, the connotation is that they are more Westernized and hence liberated. At the same time, the backlash experienced and articulated by these men underlines their subject position as members of weak and victimized minorities left to suffer the consequences of events far beyond their control. The terrorizing nature of the backlash becomes even more apparent with the subsequent forced incarceration of Muslim men in the United States and with racial profiling that singles out men who appear to be Muslim or of Arabic heritage. This subject position of Muslim men living in the West is also communicated in several stories through the juxtaposition of their voices against other White, authoritative experts who are renowned for their conservative perspectives on Islam (e.g., Professors Daniel Pipes and Samuel Huntingdon, as quoted in Waters' [2001] article).

However, despite the widespread publicity about unfair stereotyping, as well as the stigmatization and threats of physical and psychological violence against Muslim communities, there was scarcely any mention in this coverage of an active or assertive involvement of state authorities, such as the police, in working with these communities to safeguard them from acts of violence. On the contrary, the coverage seemed at times to oscillate between the backlash and racial profiling discourses, with the latter seeping into the ever-present anti-immigration discourses extant in Canadian news coverage (Henry and Tator 2002; Jiwani 1993; Mahtani 2001).

Harnessing Anti-Immigrant Sentiments

This seepage between the two dominant discourses – the anti-immigrant discourse on the one hand, and the backlash discourse on the other – is evident in several of the articles. For example, in one of the few cases where a Muslim woman is interviewed, her interview is used to support the view that Canada's refugee system should be tightened to exclude "extremists and nationalists." She herself is described as a refugee from Kyrgystan, and as an Uzbek woman (Sevunts 2001). In the same story, the reporter interviews two men, one of whose name sounds Muslim. In recounting these

men's experiences, the article emphasizes their observations of the vulnerabilities of the immigration system:

> Bakhtiar said the Immigration and Refugee Board needs not to tighten the
> screws but train real professionals. "The sad truth that I learned while inter-
> acting with other refugees," Bakhtiar said, "is that a convincing liar can
> become a refugee because the tribunal members have no way of checking
> his story. But a real refugee who is so nervous that makes one mistake might
> be denied his claim."
>
> Another man who didn't want his name used said instead of tightening
> the refugee determination system Canada might want to invest more in its
> immigration screening process. "I know a thing or two about interroga-
> tion," the man said. "And I was appalled by the security screening inter-
> view I had." "The first thing the RCMP officer asked me was whether I had
> ever killed anybody. The second question was whether I belong to any ter-
> rorist organizations. As if [had I] been a terrorist and a killer I would have
> admitted to it." The whole interview lasted no more than fifteen minutes,
> the man said. "No wonder they missed that Algerian terrorist and others
> like him. I'm sure they asked him the same questions and he said no. Now
> we all have to pay for it." (Sevunts 2001)

These men's accounts are used to underscore the weakness of the current
system, which supposedly allows terrorists to enter the country undetected.
Again, a forum intended for the open discussion of backlash stories is itself
hijacked in order to reinforce the hegemonic interests of another dominant
discourse.

Accessed Voices: Who Gets to Speak

In the stories that I analyzed, the voices of authority that were accessed to
make judgments and articulate a position on the issues at hand tended to
be male. Furthermore, most of these accessed voices belonged to men living
in the West, and in only a small number of instances were these voices
those of clerics in Pakistan. Where White male authoritative voices were
accessed, they subordinated those of the Muslim spokespeople. The predominant pattern that emerged was that men spoke for women, and this
was particularly true of Muslim men speaking on behalf of Muslim women
living in the West.

Muslim or Middle Eastern women who were quoted tended to be highly
educated or enrolled as students in recognized institutions (e.g., at McGill
University or Concordia University, or, in one case, with a doctorate from
the University of Western Ontario) (Block 2001; Fitterman 2001b; L. Moore
2001). In only one instance was a Muslim woman living in the West quoted

without these kinds of identifiers (Davenport 2001). The subtext suggests that if these women are educated, then they are credible and their stories can be believed. They are, in other words, more like us. No female activists in Afghanistan – for instance, women representing organizations such as the Revolutionary Association of Women in Afghanistan (RAWA) – were cited or quoted, despite that they have long been advocating an end to the oppressive conditions imposed by both the Northern Alliance and the Taliban (Kolhatkar 2002b; Moghadam 1999, 2001), and despite that RAWA's statement is readily available on the Internet and was printed by other Canadian newspapers, notably the *Globe and Mail*.

Interestingly, this emphasis on citing Muslim women educated and sometimes born in the West seems to strategically underscore the *Gazette's* representation of the West as the land of progress, gender equality, and liberation for women. This sets the West apart from the Taliban, who, according to one reporter and several scholarly sources, were specifically aiming their policies of containment at educated, middle- and upper-class urbanized Afghani women whom they perceived as being contaminated by Western notions of progress and liberation (Bagnall 2001; Hirschkind and Mahmood 2002; Moghadam 2001). That Afghani women are silenced in Afghanistan but allowed to speak in the West works ideologically to seal the dominant interpretation of the Western ethos of egalitarianism and its sense of superiority.

Overcomplete descriptions – descriptions filled with unnecessary but identificatory details – were also prevalent in the coverage of Muslim men and women living in the West. In one instance, a Muslim in Brooklyn was interviewed "as he stood behind a counter filled with incense sticks, surrounded by shelves of essential oils, trays of olives and jars of pistachios" (Richards 2001). In another, a reporter talking to a Muslim man living in Montreal notes his grey hair and beard, and describes him as reclining on "deep red velvet cushions atop an ornate Afghan carpet in his sparsely furnished Longueil apartment" (Montgomery 2001). These descriptors are replete with signification about the Orient: its exotic, lush colours and almost hedonistic lifestyle. In the same article, the reporter notes how this man's wife, Sabera, "laid out a plastic sheet on the floor, then proceeded to cover it with large pots full of rice, chicken stew, salad and plates of home-made flatbread." Here, the exoticization of the food and the simple manner of the serving style all work to underscore the Otherness of this family, as well as its incongruous appearance in a Western milieu.

Within the context of post-9/11 news coverage, representations of the gendered Orientalized body did not depart from the existing pool of stereotypical images. The militant martyr or suicide bomber was a constant figure (perpetuated in part by the coverage of the situation in Palestine), as were hostage takings and violent upheavals. Likewise, the veiled woman received much media attention, depicted as being both oppressed by and subjugated under Islam, as well as unable to liberate herself without the help of Western powers. With its stereotypical representations, the *Gazette* shared much in common with the rest of dominant Western media, even though it often gave such representations an interesting twist, given the demographic it serves and Quebec's unique political and linguistic climate.

Conclusion

These stories illustrate the imbricated nature of the gendered and Orientalized discourse of the news media in their coverage of the events following 9/11. Further, they demonstrate the ways in which such imagery becomes commonplace and commonsensical in terms of the kinds of explanations being proffered. Woven throughout this gendered discourse are descriptive tropes that identify one side as being evil, manipulative, and deceptive, while the other, notably the United States, is presented as moral, open, and explicit about its intentions. The ultimate rescue is presented as the liberation of the oppressed by the free world, and as the annihilation of evil by the powers of good: a belief reflected in the US government's naming of its intervention Operation Enduring Freedom, and grounded in the framework of Orientalism. In the final analysis, these news stories reinforce a sense of nationness – of us versus them – and analytically, offer insights into the ways in which contemporary forms of racism draw upon Orientalism but, in the process, reproduce it such that they "make sense" of the current political and social situation.

The particular cluster of backlash stories examined also demonstrates how the meta-narrative of Orientalism is not simply static but dynamically reproduced so that it is responsive to contemporary circumstances. In the latter situation, the ethos motivating the coverage on backlash was probably mediated by the structural and institutional constraints of the print medium – the necessity to constantly provide fresh stories, maintain continuity with previous stories, and fulfill the requirements for balance and impartiality. The latter factor is undoubtedly influenced by the *Gazette*'s readership, with the concentration of Muslims in the Montreal area, as well as by the Western tradition of liberalism informing the paper. However, and in spite of the mitigating impact of the backlash stories, that Muslim women and men in the East were represented in Orientalized ways underscores how the media constantly shift our attention to the problems *out there*, which are then represented as requiring our intervention *from here*.

What cannot be overlooked in all of this is the very real impact that the event of 9/11 and its reporting undoubtedly had on Muslims living in the United States and Canada. For many, the creation of an environment of terror resulted in heightened feelings of insecurity, a fear of retaliation, and a turning inward into the sanctuary afforded by their communities. That many sought to distance themselves from the attackers and the particular variant of Islam that those attackers adhere to is partly indicative of a response based on fear. This fear was and is grounded in the cases of incarceration, deportation, criminalization, and racial profiling that materialized later.

The gendering of terror is apparent in the targeting of women as victims of retaliation in the West and the East. While patriarchal powers compete for social, cultural, and economic resources, it is women and children who suffer the terror that ensues. Terror is gendered in the ways in which the nations involved are represented: the masculine United States versus the cowardly and dependent feminine Afghanistan. Terror is also gendered in the ways in which the Taliban are presented as excessively patriarchal, while the same patriarchal impulse and structure that underpins Western society and its allies remains unexamined (Franks 2003). As Sedef Arat-Koc (2002, 59) cogently observes:

> References to culture and religion as the cause of women's oppression are immensely useful and convenient to an imperialist project not just in justifying an otherwise destructive war as a "humanitarian" one to a Western audience, and claiming credit for what might appear to be the positive outcome of the war; but also in terms of disowning the failures, embarrassments or limitations of the war. For example, emphasis on culture as the central explanatory concept can help attribute the atrocities committed by the Northern Alliance against prisoners of war as an unfortunate outcome of the innate wildness and barbarism of "our allies." If Afghan women do not achieve any improvements in their conditions at the end of war, invasion and Western involvement in Afghan government, this again can be blamed on "our allies" not being able to overcome "tradition" in a short period.

Since September 2001, the situation of women in Afghanistan has not changed much. However, in the eyes of the Western dominant media, these women are now liberated, their liberation – as a *Gazette* headline that ran a year later would seem to imply – having been achieved through their transformation into consumers of Western beauty products (Halbfinger 2002). The implicit message here is that the enduring freedom of the capitalist world has been safeguarded against evil, and that Afghani women have now been released from the centuries-old traditions of tribal Islam and given access to a life of liberation and modernity through consumption. Over time, it is assumed, they will reassuringly become more like us.

For now, though, discourses of denial obfuscate Western responsibility in destabilizing regions of the world and catalyzing wars. "War talk" (Roy 2003) is emblematic of denial, for it simply focuses on and embellishes terrifying representations of the enemy – both within and outside the nation. These representations are strategic in maintaining a hierarchy of power, both nationally and internationally, and tactical in diverting attention away from the domestic terrorism engendered by structures of domination.

Conclusion

The violence makes both the man and the racial domination possible. Through it, he both knows and becomes himself. Through it, his nation also knows and becomes itself.

> – Sherene Razack, "From the 'Clean Snows of Petawawa'"

To place dominance under the analytic gaze is awkward and uncomfortable because it means questioning our own subjectivity, so heavily dependent on the families within which we are constituted and the language of our community, both of which are steeped in masculine ideology.

> – Maggie Wykes, "A Family Affair"

These two quotes point to the systemic, raced, and gendered nature of violence. Rather than privilege one structure of domination, either patriarchy or race, it is, I have argued, the confluence of these structures – the ways in which they intersect and interlock – that makes certain kinds of violence possible. These structures of power work to maintain hierarchical relations that are intimately connected to national mythologies, which in turn define who belongs to the imagined community of the nation and where that person stands in relation to others within the larger society.

I began this work with a mapping – my intent being to trace the contours of this landscape of violence and to uncover the varying configurations and permutations of race and gender informing this space. My aim has been to demonstrate the ways in which discourses of denial camouflage the intersecting and interlocking influences of racism and sexism and strategically deflect attention from the violence of systemic and structured inequalities. These discourses delimit definitions of gender- and race-based violence so that they either fail to take into or occlude consideration of the subterranean frameworks of meaning and common-sense knowledge that inform and perpetuate these violations. At the same time, through privileging the voices of those who experience this violence first-hand, I have sought to describe how these structures of dominance, with their attendant discourses of denial, infuse and permeate everyday common-sense understandings about the self in relation to the Other.

In stretching our common-sense understanding of violence so that it encapsulates the daily violations that texture the lives of racialized people, I have attempted to highlight the hierarchical structures of power that influence representational discourses about racialized Others, and about racialized women and girls in particular. However, as I have demonstrated through my case studies, these discourses are relational: they work in concert to maintain a structure of power. The subordination of one group – its inferiorization and the naturalization of that inferiorization – can be recognized only if it is constructed in relation to another group whose privilege and assumed superiority are either taken for granted or continually reaffirmed. It is this structured dominance that is normalized and that, through common sense, strategically casts the Other as the site of all that is disavowed. When such disavowal cannot be exercised in totality, it is disciplined, and through such taming, contained and tolerated.

The coded language of power that makes disavowal and denial possible rests on the strategic use and construction of binaries. However, these binaries of the civilized versus savage, democratic versus authoritarian, liberal versus traditional are not simply oppositional relations structured on a single level playing field. Rather, as the interlocking and intersecting approach I have utilized suggests, these binaries are structured *hierarchically*. Thus, throughout these chapters, I have maintained that it is the hierarchies of power that are structured in dominance, and it is the interrogation of these hierarchies that must be attended to if we are to map the ways in which race, gender, class, sexuality, and ability get used in the interests of maintaining dominance. Nonetheless, in emphasizing the interlocking nature of this hierarchical system of domination, I do not want to divert attention from the intersecting influences that bring race, gender, class, sexuality, and ability together in varying permutations. But rather than embracing an additive approach that would argue for the layering of these influences, as in race plus gender plus class equals a triple-layered oppression, what I have tried to show are the ways in which different kinds of oppression are foregrounded while others recede into the background. Moreover, the confluence of these structures of domination results in differential outcomes and in a constitution of difference that does not resemble an outcome that is simply additive. The additive method, as I have come to understand it, merely replicates the baseline construction of the universal woman, where the latter becomes the standard by which difference is measured. In arguing for difference, I do not want to advance an essentialist framework of difference and thereby dismantle all that has been done in terms of coalition building and solidarity around commonalities. That such structures of domination do impact women, albeit differentially, remains a material reality that cannot be denied.

In charting this landscape of violence, it is apparent that the regimes of truth, as Foucault defines them, operating within the discursive formations of racialized and gendered violence, delimit their recognition to their most extreme and physical manifestations, denying the continuation of violence that underpins the lives of women and girls who are located in the interstices of various forms of domination. Further, these regimes of truth obscure the parallels and interconnections between forms of violence, a strategy that results in pitting groups against each other, generating hierarchies of oppression within and among marginalized groups. Dominant structures of violence are similarly disinterred from the larger societal context, treated as random, individualized instances of aberrant behaviour on the part of pathological personalities or pathological cultures. In this way, they sustain hierarchies differentiating those who belong from those who are marginal and lack fit.

Race- and gender-based violence are also masked by the discourses of denial articulated and institutionalized through the discursive strategies of categorization, trivialization, and erasure. The latter are made possible by core ideological beliefs central to a liberal democracy but, more importantly, rooted in the collective imagination of White settler societies. Henry et al. (1995, 13) call this "democratic racism," identifying it as an "ideology that permits and sustains people's ability to maintain two apparently conflicting sets of values. One set consists of a commitment to a liberal, democratic society motivated by the egalitarian values of fairness, justice, and equality. Conflicting with these values are attitudes and behaviours that include negative feelings about people of colour and that result in differential treatment of them or discrimination against them." I contend that these very values of democracy are grounded in a historical tradition based on hierarchies of power that have consistently worked to exclude or accept racialized groups on conditional and delimited terms. In other words, there is nothing democratic about democracy, especially when it is defined in opposition to societies which are strategically represented as authoritarian, corrupt, and barbaric in the interests of imperial powers (Herman and Chomsky 2002; Said 1979).

Further, liberal democratic values are predicated on abstract notions; their strategic utilization and translation into common-sense understandings and institutionalized beliefs, attitudes, and practices contributes to the reproduction of inequalities. Through reliance on and the choice invocation of terms such as "zero tolerance," "colour blindness," "formal equality," "freedom of choice," "balance," "impartiality," and "objectivity," liberal democratic values are translated into discursive and symbolic violence. The violence enacted by these dominant discourses strategically neutralizes, if not erases, charges of racism and sexism. These dominant discourses are, to use Foucault's (1981a, 53) words, "secretly invested with reason." That structure of reason itself is predicated in an opposition to unreason or, in colonial discourse, the childlike emotionality and irrationality of subject races, the very traits that legitimized and naturalized their inferiorization and the very traits that feed into their construction as the criminally minded illegal refugee or immigrant, the demanding problem patient, and the ungrateful, manipulative, exotic, and erotic woman of colour.

In highlighting the violations that occur in the daily lives of racialized girls and women, I have sought to decentre the power of Whiteness as it is structured in dominance. I have attempted to make this power visible by demonstrating the discursive strategies used to maintain inequalities. More specifically, I have drawn attention to the ways in which racialized differences are inferiorized and racialized people "put in their place" through the discursive economy of violence that culminates in the denial, dismissal, trivialization, erasure, and exoticization of their lived realities. In juxtaposing these discourses as they surface in the arenas of mediated representations and the daily lived realities of racialized groups, my aim has been to underscore the ways in which they regulate racialized groups in each domain of social life. Such regulation is possible, I have argued, only through the exercise of power and through the normalization of that power in the common-sense stock of knowledge, as well as in the routinized values, behaviours, and practices intrinsic to different institutional contexts.

In speaking to the issue of gendered violence against racialized girls and women, I have argued against the typical explanatory frameworks that have been advanced. These first tend to divorce such violence from the larger context informing the lives of racialized women and girls; second, they fetishize culture so that it becomes a vehicle by which to reproduce cultural racism. Thus, as I have shown in the previous chapters, the notion of racialized women as being oppressed by ultra-patriarchal cultures, and as being victims of "death by culture," to quote Uma Narayan (1997), has strategically operated to re-entrench colonial stereotypes and to reproduce unequal relations of power. Moreover, the use of cultural discourses to either explain away the violence that racialized women experience or to privilege it as something unique to their situation shifts attention away from the widespread and pervasive patterns of gendered violence experienced by women across the board. At the same time, the discourse of simply footnoting racialized women's experiences of violence also fails to do justice to the complexities that inhere in their lives. These complexities, I have argued, are rooted in their subordinate status within the dominant society – a status made possible by law, but more importantly, undergirded and rationalized by constructions of racialized people as Others.

These constructions, I have maintained, gain their potency and currency from the dominant discourses and discursive devices – such as exnomination, universalization, and naturalization – that constitute the language of power. Within such a language, only racialized groups have culture, while the dominant White culture remains an invisible backdrop against which the perceived and constructed differences of Others are suitably celebrated or condemned as the situation demands. This language of power is facilitated by the fetishization of culture, a fetishization made possible through cultural racism. Here racism is clothed in cultural discourse and articulated with the dominant ideology of multiculturalism. Through the latter, cultures are reified and differences between culturalized groups in terms of their power and relative standing in society are levelled. Each cultural entity becomes sovereign unto itself – able to regulate its boundaries and impose its own hierarchal structures within, often at the expense of those who are marginalized within. And such boundaries, as I have indicated, congeal in ways that enable that community or cultural formation to retain a sense of identity and foster belonging when such is denied by the external, dominant society. The issues are who gets to define the community from the outside and who defines the community from within. In other words, who has the power to establish the register of cultural authenticity in terms of regulating membership in a community, and further, how does the community get defined from the outside? In arguing that racialized ethnicities assume a heightened salience under specific conditions, my intention is to underline the structural factors that make such identity possible and attractive as a resource. It is not primordiality of ethnic identity that I am interested in but, rather, the activation of that identity as a site of resistance to the onslaught of coercive pressures brought to bear upon racialized groups as they straddle the demands to fit into a society which continues to exclude them and find meaning from within their own communities, constructed though these may be.

It is the power to define that is the core issue, for how Others are defined influences how they in turn define themselves. And this is where the dominant media play a pivotal role in their circulation of images of "prescription and description" (Bannerji 1986). I do not wish to suggest that racialized people are passive audiences, blindly consuming the stereotypical fare commonly provided by the dominant media. Rather, it is the elite nature of the dominant media and how it works in concert with other elite institutions to orchestrate preferred definitions of social reality and racialized peoples that I wish to emphasize. As I have endeavoured to show in the previous chapters, those who are consistently portrayed as being outside or on the margins of the imagined community are likely to be viewed as such by the rest of the populace and, moreover, tend to internalize those definitions as well. Their marginalized status can also be used strategically by the state to advance its own preferred definitions of who can be permitted to enter, remain, permanently or conditionally, or be expelled from the nation.

In the mediated accounts of violence that I have presented, the strategic denial of race and racism erases the violence of racism as it affects and impacts on racialized girls of colour such as Reena Virk. Conversely, the heightened focus on culture rather than race absolves institutional power of its responsibility and accountability, for here, culture is used as a reason for intervening or not intervening as the case may be. Thus, in the example of Rajwar Gakhal (discussed in Chapter 4), the issue was one of non-intervention; a non-intervention rationalized on the basis of cultural factors. Thus, gendered violence itself became culturalized in that instance. In the case of Afghanistan and the so-called war on terror, the rationale supporting an intervention was predicated on rescuing Afghan women from the patriarchal violence of the Taliban. These instances demonstrate the strategic use of various discourses that ultimately deny the reality of racism and conceal power relations. To intervene or not, then, becomes a decision made by the powerful in the interests of securing dominance.

The discursive violence perpetrated by the dominant media is the ideological "glue," to use Patricia Hill Collins' term (1998), that binds these structures of domination, facilitating their interaction and interlocking expressions. Through explanatory frameworks that resonate with the common-sense stock of knowledge, the media are able to trivialize if not dismiss the violence of racism. Suggesting that racism is simply an emotive phenomenon or an irrationality expressed by a minority (the few "loonies" out there), the systemic violence of racism is evacuated. These frameworks also hinge on stereotypical constructions of racialized groups, constructions which are deeply embedded in the historical legacy of colonialism and which embrace a grammar of race that reaffirms the superiority of Whiteness and the inferiority of Others. Liberal rhetoric and coded language mark the inferential racism implicit in the dominant media.

The violence of such consignment and containment, as I have argued in this book, is accomplished both externally and internally through the interiorization of the dominant value systems. Interiorized, this violence erodes the self and subjugates it so that it fits – either in the mould of the preferred, assimilated girl or woman of colour with all the signifiers of acceptance such as body size, appearance, clothing, language, and comportment, or it fits with the description of the racialized criminal. Between these two ends of the continuum are those whose degrees of fit vary, contingent on the context and specific conditions of a given historical moment. This marks the journeys of those who "walk the hyphen" (Batth 1998), knowing what lies at each end of the spectrum, and the social costs involved in falling off this rather tenuous bridge or the rewards that might accrue if acceptance is achieved.

One can speculate that as diasporic racialized communities increase in population and as their transnational links become more solidified through migrations and global media, this bridge will grow more secure and ultimately become home (Anzaldúa and Keating 2002). Nonetheless, this doesn't detract from the power structures within communities, communities often constructed on the basis of migration but reactivated through exclusion. As I have shown in the previous chapters, hierarchies within communities often work in tandem with the hierarchical structures of power outside these racialized and minoritized communities. Such a play of affinities between different power structures demonstrates, in the case of racialized girls and women, a patriarchal alignment based on colonially inflected notions of cultural authenticity. This affinity borders girls and young women from within their communities – as signifiers of tradition and reproducers of communal, culturalized identities, and it borders them from the outside through their racialized construction as Others in need of containment or rescue.

In interrogating Whiteness as a dominant structure of power, I have attempted to show how racialized people and particularly racialized girls and women are at risk. I use the discourse of risk rather cautiously, as it is one that has been used to undermine and exclude racialized and marginalized groups. But here, I use the discourse of risk in a reverse fashion, based on Irihapeti Ramsden's work (see Chapter 6). My argument, drawn from her work, is that racialized people are at risk from the larger structures of domination that confine, regulate, and delimit their lives. And these risks, I maintain, are present both at the level of regulations governing entry and mobility and in daily life. The coercive pressures to belong – to fit in and be a part of the nation – are risky, for the potential of rejection, criminalization, and exclusion through stereotyping, stigmatization, and marginalization are ever-present. Whether it is "walking the hyphen" or navigating through the interstices of the various discourses of domination, or speaking out against violence, the risk is constant. As George Dei (1999, 20) concurs, there are even dangers in "speaking and writing race."

Isolation and dependency are two factors underpinning violence. In this context, the terror of isolation and the continued subordination through imposed dependency by governmental, institutional, and familial regulations are, as I have suggested, rooted in a patriarchal structure of power, but it is a structure also grounded in race, nationness, and identity. To define Self in relation to the Other, to define an imagined community, and to define who belongs to that community are the hallmarks of this power structured in dominance, a power that is communicated through "discourses of domination," to borrow the phrase from Henry and Tator (2002). The terror of isolation, as Debold et al. (1999) put it, is a constant fear that racialized girls and young women face, and it is a driving force compelling them to fit in. Similarly, dependency as defined and legislated by the state compels immigrant women to remain within abusive relationships. The discourses of violence fail to highlight these factors of isolation and dependency, focusing instead on the peculiarities of specific groups or individuals.

Through these dominant discourses, then, the reality of race is erased, trivialized, categorized, or culturalized. Yet, this reality continues to shape the lives of racialized peoples and texture the lived realities of girls and women of colour, making them more susceptible to other intimate and interpersonal forms of violence. Thus, systemic violence, as engendered by these dominant discourses, contributes to an increased vulnerability of racialized girls and women. The two realms – systemic and intimate/interpersonal – do not work in isolation from one another but are intricately interwoven and interdependent. In the lives of girls and young women of colour, the demarcation of a public and private realm of violence is not possible (Collins 1998; Ocran 1997). Rather, there is one domain whose structure, boundaries, and topography are deeply influenced by the dominant discourses of power, a power that is raced, classed, and gendered. This power is expressed through the continual othering of racialized groups and their ranking on a stratification system that privileges some over others through the unequal distribution of resources and rewards, and accomplished through coercion and complicity. "Fictions of assimilation" (de Jesús 1998) work through this coercion and complicity. They promise acceptance and belonging, but only conditionally and only through compliance.

The common elements underpinning these "discourses of domination" cohere around the notion of the reasonable person, the preferred immigrant, the preferred patient, and the ideal Canadian. Inversely, these are contrasted with the problem patient, the illegal immigrant or refugee, "ethnic exotica" (Peter 1981) to be periodically celebrated, and the conditional Canadian. These preferences are predicated on a hierarchy of power – the power of those who wish to retain a certain kind of imagined community. More importantly, these preferences are indicative of the deep structure of contemporary society – a structure that has its roots in the experience of colonialism, the legacy of which continues to shape contemporary discursive formations of racialized and gendered violence. It is the violence of these structures that is continually denied in the dominant discourses of society.

In drawing upon the deep structure-surface structure metaphor from structuralism (see Lévi-Strauss 1966; Morris 2002), my intent is not to fall into the trap of an agentless dominant structure that is impervious to change or that is a static monolith. While the overt discourses of race and racism (surface structures) shift in response to changing societal conditions, the grammar of race that Stuart Hall (1990a) describes as underpinning colonial discourses (the deep structure) remains intact though not unchanged. Thus, the power coordinates of this grammar, which pivot on the inferiorization of difference and the naturalization of that inferiorization, persist. However, while the hegemonic construction of common sense draws from a collective stock of knowledge that is historically grounded, its reproduction in every given instantiation (articulation) offers a space of contestation. Thus, as is evident in the coverage of the events post-9/11 (see Chapter 7), Orientalism gets reproduced over time, but this reproduction varies according to the changing circumstances, social climate, and differing constraints that operate in a given historical moment.

If violence is to be understood in its totality, its definition needs to be broadened to include processes of othering and inferiorization that constitute the technologies by which race and gender are managed and regulated in the interests of maintaining a culture of power. Unveiling the discourses of denial enveloping these regimes of truth offers one trajectory of intervention, revealing the sites and moves by which power is produced and reproduced. By positioning myself in the margins, and anchoring myself in the subjugated knowledges of those who are so marginalized, I have tried to unveil these discourses in order to draw attention to sites where oppositional and resistive discourses can be articulated, sometimes with enduring success and at other times momentarily in a fragmented way. These sites of contestation are tenuous and temporal, but as Foucault (1981a, 53) argues, "if discourse may sometimes have some power, nevertheless, it is from us and us alone that it gets it."

Notes

Introduction

1 Devlin (1995, 419) suggests that "throughout the case law on judicial bias, the reasonable person is assumed to be without age, gender, or race. But this universal figure is like no one we know or can recognize." In *R. v. Lavallée,* the Supreme Court of Canada acknowledged the androcentric nature of the reasonable person and argued for the inclusion of a gendered perspective (Bhandar 1997). Devlin suggests that race is also an important consideration that needs to be factored in a critical revision of the concept.

Chapter 1: Reframing Violence

1 The notion of such a mosaic is evident in the following statement by Canadian prime minister Wilfrid Laurier at the turn of the previous century. His vision of Canada was influenced by his observation of a cathedral in England: "The Cathedral is made of marble, oak and granite. It is the image of the nation I would like to see Canada become. For here, I want the marble to remain marble; the granite to remain granite; the oak to remain oak; and out of all these elements, I would build a nation great among the nations of the world" (cited in Weinfeld 1982, 82).

2 Henry, Tator, Mattis, and Rees (1995) call this form of democratic liberalism "democratic racism," as it is predicated on liberal assumptions that privilege particular elites and favour a particular interpretation of liberal values based on an erasure of history and unequal power relations.

3 According to a recent profile on family violence issued by Statistics Canada (H. Johnson and Au Coin 2003), 85 percent of the victims of spousal violence are women. Further, the General Social Survey on Spousal Violence (Centre for Justice Statistics 2000) indicates that the impact of violence is more severe and long-lasting for women than it is for men. The most extreme form of physical violence against women results in death. Homicide statistics reveal that over a twenty-year period (1979-98), an average of 3.4 wives were killed for every 1 husband. More recent trends reveal an average of approximately 4 women to every 1 man (Patterson 2003). The vulnerability of girls and women to violence from partners, ex-partners, and other family members is also reflected in statistics compiled by Gill and Brockman (1996) in their analysis of the impact of anti-stalking legislation. On the basis of an examination of 601 cases spanning a three-year period (1993-96) in Vancouver, Edmonton, Winnipeg, Montreal, and Halifax, Gill and Brockman found that 91 percent of the accused were men, and 88 percent of the victims were women. Further, 57 percent of the cases involved partners or ex-partners; 28 percent involved friends, acquaintances, or co-workers; and 12 percent involved strangers. More recent statistics indicate that rates of criminal harassment have increased, with three times as many women reporting being criminally harassed than men (Beattie 2003). So while physical forms of violence against women may be on the decline, other forms such as harassment continue to increase.

4 The universalization of the category woman reflects the collapsing of differences between women and essentializes gender as the primary definer, as opposed to race, class, sexual orientation, or disability.
5 According to Heise, Ellsberg, and Gottemoeller (1999, 1), "Around the world, at least one woman in every three has been beaten, coerced into sex, or otherwise abused in her lifetime. Most often the abuser is a member of her own family."
6 Considerable research exists on the vulnerabilities of Aboriginal peoples. Up to 75 percent of victims of sex crimes in Aboriginal communities are females under eighteen years of age, 50 percent of those are under fourteen, and almost 25 percent of those are younger than seven (Correctional Service of Canada, cited in McIvor and Nahanee 1998, 65). The Ontario Native Women's Association's study on violence against women in Aboriginal communities reports that 80 percent of women and 40 percent of children are abused and assaulted (Bopp, Bopp, and Lane 2003; Lynn and O'Neill 1995). In 1991, 23 percent of federally sentenced women were Aboriginal. Of these, 90 percent had backgrounds characterized by physical abuse, and 61 percent had been sexually abused (Canadian Task Force on Federally Sentenced Women, 1991, cited in Comack 1996). In addition, many of these women were adopted by non-Aboriginal families or placed in non-Aboriginal foster homes where they experienced intense racism from members of the dominant society (Shaw et al. 1991). Forced assimilation through child apprehension strategies, adoptions, residential schools, and other coercive means implemented through the Indian Act have had drastic consequences in rending apart the traditional fabric of indigenous societies. These effects have been documented extensively by the Royal Commission on Aboriginal Peoples in its many reports, as well as by researchers (for example, Backhouse 1999; McGillivray and Comaskey 1999; Maracle 1996; Monture-Angus 1995; Razack 1998a, 2002).

Chapter 2: Mapping Race in the Media

1 Hall defines an articulation as "the form of the connection that can make a unity of two different elements, under certain conditions. It is a linkage which is not necessary, determined, absolute and essential for all time. You have to ask, under what circumstances can a connection be forged or made?" (S. Hall 1996c, 141).
2 Elsewhere I detail the continuity of these colonially inscribed images in contemporary representations of Asian and Eurasian women (Jiwani 1992b, 2005b).
3 Rider Haggard's *King Solomon's Mines* was part of the standard reading in some Canadian high schools. For an insightful and critical analysis of Haggard's work, see McClintock (1995) and Stott (1989).
4 As Dahlgren (1988, 291) argues, "Meaning is also situation. Context and its appropriate discourse play a large role in structuring and delimiting meaning." Stuart Hall (1980b) delineates three possible readings of media texts: dominant, negotiated, and oppositional. The dominant reading is in parity with meanings that are preferred and intended; the negotiated reading refers to the process whereby certain aspects of the preferred meaning are accepted but are negotiated in relation to local and situated logics. As he states, "It accords the privileged position to the dominant definitions of events while reserving the right to make a more negotiated application to 'local conditions,' to its own more corporate positions. This negotiated version of the dominant ideology is thus shot through with contradictions, though these are only on certain occasions brought to full visibility" (137). In the oppositional reading, the viewer rejects the preferred meaning and recasts the information in an alternative framework.
5 See, for instance, Bannerji (1987); Dunn and Mahtani (2001); Fleras (1994); Fleras and Kunz (2001); Granzberg (1984); Henry and Tator (2002); Jiwani (1991, 1998a); Mahtani (2001); J. Miller and Prince (1994); Murray (2002); Nancoo and Nancoo (1997); Perigoe and Lazar (1992). Some of these studies have examined the issue by focusing on the language used to represent minorities and their concerns (e.g., Karim 1993a; Mirchandani and Tastsoglou 2000), others have focused on specific incidents (e.g., Henry and Tator 2002; Jackson 1998; Jiwani 1999; Todd 1998; Wortley, Macmillan, and Hagan 1997), while others still have focused on representations of particular groups in the mass media (e.g., Antonius

1986; Bannerji 1993; K. Bullock and Jafri 2001; Creese and Peterson 1996; Hay 1996; Karim 2000; Kunz and Fleras 1998; Lenk 2000; MacGregor 1997; Mahtani 2002a, 2002b).

6   This was forcefully brought home to me when I was asked to adjudicate on submissions for one of the federal department's national funding programs for multicultural films and videos. Although the program was identified as encouraging ethnocultural filmmakers, the submissions from Anglo-Canadians of British background were treated in the same way and with as much consideration as those from marginalized ethno-racial communities. When I argued against the equivalent treatment, I was told that the mandate was culture and not race, and after that, I was never invited to adjudicate the competition again.

7   Afro-Caribbean Canadian communities have consistently emphasized the stereotypical and racist treatment meted out by the local forces toward members in their communities. Between 1979 and 1997, thirteen black people were killed by police, the majority of them young black males (James 1998; see also Williams 1996). Black communities in Montreal have also drawn attention to the unequal and discriminatory treatment of the police in that metropolitan city. Saäl and Bisaillon created and produced the film *Zero Tolerance* (National Film Board, 2004), which documents the racial profiling and harassment of young people of colour in Montreal. The film elicited considerable opposition from the Montreal police.

8   I make this point because of the mainstream media's penchant for attacking feminist groups. Even when Thobani was president of NAC, the attacks on her were uncalled for and reflected the bias of the media against both feminist groups in general and immigrant women in particular.

9   The media make no distinction between immigrants and refugees even though the processes by which each group is allowed into the country are radically different.

10   Some of the furor generated by the *Toronto Star* series reopened the debate on the collection of race-based statistics, with some arguing for such statistical profiles and others arguing against them. Julian Roberts (2002) provides an insightful analysis of this debate, noting that an attempt had been made by Statistics Canada to collect such statistics but the impossibility of doing so made the exercise futile. It was difficult to categorize people on the basis of colour or origin. Nevertheless, race-based statistics are continually kept by Corrections Canada.

11   I have detailed the findings of this comparative analysis (of CTV and CBC nightly news) in my dissertation (Jiwani 1993).

12   According to a report by P. Finlay (1999), available on the website of the Department of Canadian Heritage (http://www.pch.gc.ca/progs/ac-ca/progs/esm-ms/prin3_e.cfm#reg), "between 1992-1995, the 126 complaints lodged with the BC Press Council were either abandoned or dismissed; in the Atlantic region, all 96 complaints over three years were dismissed, and in Ontario, 75 percent are abandoned yearly as people become tired of waiting for action."

Chapter 3: Erasing Race

1   This was reported by Neal Hall in the *Vancouver Sun* on 8 May 1999. Hall was a court reporter at the time and although this particular statement did not surface in any of the original 1997 or subsequent coverage, one can surmise that it was based on what Hall heard in the court proceedings for one of the accused.

2   This composite is based on the descriptions of the event provided by various newspapers and magazines over a two-year period (1997-99). The analysis that follows is based on coverage published in the *Vancouver Sun* during November and December 1997, and then again in May 2000, when the first Ellard trial occurred. In addition, an electronic search of all articles appearing in Canadian newspapers and dealing with the decision in Warren Glowatski's trial was conducted and the resulting articles examined.

3   The coverage of the third trial suggests that Reena was beaten because she had spread a rumour involving the boyfriends of two of the girls: that the boyfriend of one had slept with the girlfriend of the other (Bains 2005, A9).

4 For an insightful analysis of the erasure of White violence in the Virk murder, see Batacharya (2004). Batacharya contends that the violence directed at Reena was partly mediated by prevailing conceptions of Asian girls as desexualized and passive. That Reena was presumably neither made her a victim of violence.

5 In their study of girls and young women in Canadian schools, Bourne, McCoy, and Smith (1998) found that the South Asian girls in their focus group reported that they were often more accepted and attractive to boys because of their "exotic" appearance.

6 In their review of the literature on violence against women, Kinnon and Hanvey (1996, 7) note that "60 to 70% of runaways and 98% of child prostitutes have a history of child abuse."

7 In his *Vancouver Sun* article, Neal Hall (1999a) states, "Syreeta Hartley said her former boyfriend told her that his involvement [in Reena's murder] was partly motivated by racism. Virk was Indo-Canadian."

8 Date: 19990602 Docket: 95773 Registry: Victoria in the Supreme Court of British Columbia Her Majesty the Queen against Warren Paul Glowatski Reasons for Judgment of the Honourable Mr. Justice Macaulay Counsel for the Crown: S. Lowe/R. Picha Counsel for the Accused: J. Carr/D. Marshall Place and Dates of Hearing: Victoria, B.C. 12-16 April 1999; 19-23 April 1999; 26-29 April 1999; 3-4 May 1999; 10 May 1999. For an interesting analysis of the fiction of judicial impartiality, see Omatsu (1997).

9 For a more extensive discussion of this case, as well as others involving White women, see Faith and Jiwani (2002).

10 Many people were involved in the implementation of this media strategy. Primary among these was Bruce Kachuk, whose instrumental role in fielding media calls, logging media interviews, and providing continuous support throughout the trial and afterward actually made this intervention possible. As well, Lorraine Cameron's constant support and advice were essential. The volunteers at the FREDA Centre also deserve recognition for their support and involvement in this project, as do those supporters who came into the courtroom and sustained our courage and affirmed our position while we heard the horrific details of the events leading to the murder of Reena Virk.

11 My reading of this coverage is based on 112 articles collected by way of a keyword search of the Canadian Newsstand database on Proquest. The search focused on articles printed from 1 April 2005 to 20 June 2005 inclusive. I would especially like to thank Marie-Claire MacPhee and Trish McIntosh for their collating and preliminary analysis of the news accounts pertaining to Ellard's third trial.

Chapter 4: Culturalizing Violence and the Vernon "Massacre"

1 For a more extensive discussion of the historical evolution of the concept of race and its various euphemisms, see D.T. Goldberg (1993), Karim (1993a, 1993b), and Miles (1989).

2 I focus on this newspaper given that it is the leading paper in the province where the murders occurred. Further, because the *Vancouver Sun* was part of the Southam newspaper chain at the time, its coverage was reported in other papers throughout the country.

3 This culturalized explanation of the murders resulted in a submission to the *Vancouver Sun* that highlighted the pervasive and endemic nature of gender-based violence in Canadian society. See Yasmin Jiwani (1996).

4 The statistical profile on family violence in Canada indicates that in 2002, sixty-seven female spouses were murdered as a result of family violence as compared with sixteen male spouses (Centre for Justice Statistics 2004, 35).

5 Wilson, Johnson, and Daly (1995, 340) found that between 1974 and 1990 "5.6 per million co-resident wives and 28.6 per million separated wives" were the victims of uxoricides (murder by spouse).

6 I am particularly indebted to Felix Odartey-Wellington for conducting this search of the news media archives for me. The electronic search covered all Canadian papers dealing with the Sharon Velisek case from 15 April 1996 to 6 December 1999.

Chapter 5: Racialized Girls and Everyday Negotiations

1 The Jump Start workshop was a two-day event organized around the use of participatory theatre and involving young women of colour as participants. The event was designed and

facilitated by members of the Jump Start Consulting group who were also settlement service providers affiliated, at the time, with SUCCESS, a well-known Chinese immigrant
settlement agency in Vancouver.

2 The project was funded by Status of Women Canada (SWC) and the Social Sciences and
Humanities Research Council (SSHRC). My role included the conception, design, and management of the project in Vancouver, as well as the submission of a final report to SWC. An
earlier version of this chapter was published in *Violence against Women* 11, 7 (2005): 846-75.

3 Such a perspective is reminiscent of the kind of views being advanced to explain the current geopolitical conflict between the West and the so-called Muslim world, namely, that it
emerges in response to a clash of civilizations (see Karim 2000).

4 This figure accounts for immigrant children under fifteen years who arrived in the country
as dependants. For those who arrived as principal immigrants, the statistics are similar at
71.58 percent speaking neither French nor English.

5 For more information on dealing with the ethics requirements, see the final report on the
Girl Child project submitted to SWC (Jiwani, Janovicek, and Cameron 2001).

6 Vancouver has a historical tradition of xenophobia and racism and continues to evince
these same sentiments in contemporary times. The over-reporting of Asians in the Vancouver
press (Bula 1989), combined with the focus on monster houses (P. Li 2003) and on the
murders of various racialized persons, attests to the particularly negative signification of
race in that city and in British Columbia.

7 See Kelly (1987) for an explication of the gendered continuum of violence.

Chapter 6: Gendered Racism, Sexist Violence, and the Health Care System

1 The study reported in this chapter was funded by the Status of Women Canada (Pacific
region), the Vancouver Foundation, and the BC Centre for Excellence for Women's Health,
and was conducted through the auspices of the FREDA Centre. I am especially grateful to
the funders for supporting this investigation.

2 According to Ng (1993a, 1993b), the technical definition of an immigrant is one who has
not received citizenship. Yet, recent policy documents, such as the report on Health Canada's
contribution to the Metropolis project, define immigrants as those not born in Canada
(see Kinnon 1999). This reflects a shift in policy and in keeping with the historical exclusion of people of colour, their continued otherness, in contemporary Canadian society.

3 This perceived threat has, in recent times, generated considerable empirical analysis focusing on the health expenditures of immigrants. Chen, Ng, and Wilkins (1996) found that
immigrants tend not to suffer from chronic illnesses or diseases, and further have lower
levels of physician visits. The exceptions occurred for those who were in the low-income
brackets and for women who reported more frequent physician contacts (Dunn and Dyck
1998).

4 According to the 1976 immigration legislation, immigrants can come into the country
under three categories: independent, family class, or refugee. The independent category
consists of those who have the necessary skills, or who are willing to invest, or those who
can show their economic self-sufficiency. The family class refers to those persons who are
sponsored by a family member or who are dependent on the independent applicant.

5 In a survey conducted by Statistics Canada several years ago, 40 percent of the women who
had experienced violence reported being physically injured and requiring medical attention (Centre for Justice Statistics 2000). The 1993 Statistics Canada Survey on Violence
against Women revealed that 45 percent of the victims of spousal violence had been physically injured (H. Johnson 1996). In 21 percent of the cases, the abuse took place during
pregnancy (Varcoe 1997). Injuries among women who have been abused include burns,
cuts, or scratches in 33 percent of the cases, and miscarriages and internal injuries in 10
percent of the cases (Wilson 1998). According to Archer (1994, 975), "Seventy percent to
eighty percent of women who are psychiatric inpatients have a history of physical or
sexual abuse. Fifteen to 30 percent of women presenting to emergency rooms have a
history of current abuse." The Domestic Violence Program at the Vancouver General
Hospital reported a 15 percent disclosure rate among women presenting to the emergency department (Chambers 1998). As Chambers notes, most women do not disclose

the violence to the police or other authorities. Rather, they tend to confide in friends and family. Nevertheless, the health impact of chronic stress and violence compels many women to seek medical attention.

6 The Violence against Women Survey (Marshall and Vaillancourt 1993) found that only 23 percent of the women who had been injured by a male partner had approached a doctor. L. Bullock et al. (1989) found that 8.2 percent of the women who had visited the four Planned Parenthood sites in their study were victims of physical violence.

7 In an interesting study on patient-physician pairing, Gray and Stoddard (1997) found, after controlling for socioeconomic factors, that minority patients tended to choose minority physicians. While there are methodological shortcomings to their analysis, the preference for physicians from the same racial or ethnic group is observable among Canadian immigrants and may be predicated on issues of language barriers, social networks, and cultural comfort.

8 These interventions have produced valuable tools for medical practitioners by which to improve the treatment of women who have experienced violence and who are presenting at emergency rooms, clinics, and doctors' offices.

9 Elsewhere, I have made the argument that the only time women of colour are deemed to be acceptable by dominant, normative standards is when they show signs of assimilation or when the dominant society can perceive itself to be in a benevolent situation as in rescuing Third World women from their oppressive conditions (Jiwani 1992a).

10 I am especially indebted to Kelly D'Auoust, Suki Grewal, Benita Bunjun, Harjit Kaur, and Tracy Conley for their assistance in conducting this research.

11 One-on-one interviews were conducted by Suki Grewal.

12 The health effects of violence are manifold and complex. The more common include posttraumatic stress syndrome, which includes a range of symptoms (Abbott et al. 1995; Archer 1994; Argüelles and Rivero 1993; Chuly 1996; Ristock and Health Canada 1995); bronchitis and upper respiratory infections (Abbott et al. 1995); depression, anxiety, fear, mood swings, and dissociative states (Argüelles and Rivero 1993); chronic pain, fibromyalgia, chronic pelvic pain, headaches, gastrointestinal disorders, irritable bowel syndrome, and pelvic inflammatory disease (Radomsky 1995); sleep disorders, sexual dysfunction, anxiety disorders, alcohol and substance abuse, low self-esteem, suicide ideation, and obsessive-compulsive disorders. Archer (1994) notes that in a study of women who had attempted suicide, 83 percent had experienced intimate violence. Kurz and Stark (1988) found that women who had experienced intimate violence were five times more at risk of committing suicide. Women who are sexually assaulted are eight times more likely to commit suicide, six times more likely to attempt suicide, and five times more likely to have a nervous breakdown (Boychuk Duchsher 1994). While this list identifies some of the longer-term health sequelae of violence, it does not locate these within a socio-ecological model (Perilla, Bakeman, and Norris 1994) that outlines the intersections and compounding factors of race, class, sexuality, and ability or disability, as well as the larger and more immediate social context of the individual and group (Stark, Flitcraft, and Frasier 1979).

13 It has been estimated that the medical- and health-related costs attributed to violence against women amount to $408,357,042 nationally (Greaves, Hankivsky, and Kingston-Riechers 1995). These include the costs of emergency visits, consultations with doctors, ambulance services, psychiatric ward care, and some treatments. They do not include the costs to patients, such as transportation, prescription drugs, time off work, childminding, or anything else that is required to obtain medical services.

Chapter 7: Gendering Terror Post-9/11

1 The original version of this chapter was published in *Critique: Critical Middle Eastern Studies* 13, 3 (2004): 265-91. See http://www.tandf.co.uk.

2 The *Gazette* was founded in 1778 and has a readership of over half a million on the weekends, and between 360,000 and 380,000 on weekdays.

3 Canada is one of the few countries that has a major media concentration problem. The media are primarily owned by less than a handful of conglomerates. For more information on the media concentration monopoly, see Finlay (1999) and Lavoie and Dornan (2001).

4 According to Statistics Canada 2001 census results (Statistics Canada 2003), up to 100,200 Muslims live in the Montreal area.

5 The organized visit of Benjamin Netanyahu to Concordia University on 9 September 2002 resulted in one such clash: it made the front pages of the local, national, and international media.

6 As Irwin Block (2002) reported in the *Gazette,* "Pervasive anti-Israel bias in the media is a 'cancer' that is destroying much of the media's credibility and eroding support for the Jewish state, CanWest Global founder Israel Asper says."

7 The controversy over the hijab pertained to the right of a student to wear the head covering to school. On one side of the debate were those who believed that allowing minority groups to engage in such behaviour would probably result in the further marginalization of the student concerned and, further, dilute a sense of national identity. The other side was marked by a language of tolerance, namely, that the ethos of multiculturalism guaranteed such rights to all and that minority groups should be allowed the right to retain their cultural/religious heritage (see Lenk 2000).

8 The database was designed by Professor Ross Perigoe, Department of Journalism, Concordia University. I am indebted to Ross for sharing his database and for his encouragement in pursuing this particular line of research.

9 Said's analysis has been critiqued by feminists on the grounds that it does not adequately address the issue of sexuality and that it tends to be a totalizing discourse devoid of any spaces of resistance or counter discourses (see, for instance, Karim 2000; Lalvani 1995; Yeğenoğlu 1998).

10 See http://www.benetton.com/press, accessed June 2003.

11 In the same article, Kolhatkar recounts her experience of being interviewed by feminist Helen Caldicott, who seemed more interested in the reasons underlying the "barbarity" of Afghan men than in discovering information about the resistance of Afghani women. See also Naber's (2002) interesting discussion of the challenges of coalition building post-9/11, and Jiwani (2005a) for a note on imperial feminism as it textures these news accounts.

12 Hoodfar provides an insightful case analysis of the disastrous impact of deveiling in Iran. The forced measure imposed by the state resulted in a dramatic decline in women's independence and, by corollary, an increased dependence on men in the family. Women could no longer participate in the social rituals that brought them together or in the public domain of economic activity because of the societal shame that deveiling engendered.

Bibliography

Abbott, Jean, Robin Johnson, Jane Koziol-McLain, and Steven R. Lowenstein. 1995. "Domestic Violence against Women: Incidence and Prevalence in an Emergency Department." *Population Journal of the American Medical Association* 273 (22): 1763-67.

Abraham, Margaret. 1995. "Ethnicity, Gender, and Marital Violence: South Asian Women's Organizations in the United States." *Gender and Society* 9 (4): 450-68.

Abu-Laban, Yasmin. 1998. "Keeping 'Em Out: Gender, Race, and Class Biases in Canadian Immigration Policy." In *Painting the Maple: Essays on Race, Gender, and the Construction of Canada*, ed. Veronica Strong-Boag, Sherrill Grace, Avigail Eisenberg, and Joan Anderson, 69-82. Vancouver: UBC Press.

Agnew, Vijay. 1996. *Resisting Discrimination: Women from Asia, Africa, and the Caribbean and the Women's Movement in Canada.* Toronto: University of Toronto Press.

–. 1998. *In Search of a Safer Place: Abused Women and Culturally Sensitive Services.* Toronto: University of Toronto Press.

Ahluwalia, Seema, and Brian D. MacLean. 1988. "The Medicalization of Domestic Violence." In *Sociology of Health Care in Canada*, ed. B. Singh Bolaria and Harley D. Dickinson, 183-97. Toronto: Harcourt Brace Jovanovich.

Ahmed, Leila. 1992. *Women and Gender in Islam: Historical Roots of a Modern Debate.* New Haven, CT: Yale University Press.

Akbari, Ather H. 1999. "Immigrant 'Quality' in Canada: More Direct Evidence of Human Capital Content, 1956-1994." *International Migration Review* 33 (1): 156-75.

Aldarondo, Etiony, Glenda Kantor Kaufman, and Jana L. Jasinski. 2002. "A Risk Marker Analysis of Wife Assault in Latino Families." *Violence against Women* 8 (4): 429-54.

Alicea, Marixsa. 1997. "'A Chambered Nautilus': The Contradictory Nature of Puerto Rican Women's Role in the Social Construction of a Transnational Community." *Gender and Society* 11 (5): 597-626.

Amnesty International. 2004. "Stolen Sisters, Discrimination and Violence against Indigenous Women in Canada. A Summary of Amnesty International's Concerns." http://web.amnesty.org/library/Index/ENGAMR200012004?open&of=ENG-CAN.

Amos, Valerie, and Pratibha Parmar. 1984. "Challenging Imperial Feminism." *Feminist Review* 17: 3-19.

Andall, Jacqueline. 2002. "Second-Generation Attitude? African-Italians in Milan." *Journal of Ethnic and Migration Studies* 28 (3): 389-407.

Anderson, Benedict. 1983. *Imagined Communities: Reflections on the Origin and Spread of Nationalism.* Rev. ed. London: Verso.

Anderson, Joan M. 1985. "Perspectives on the Health of Immigrant Women: A Feminist Analysis." *Advances in Nursing Science* 8 (1): 61-76.

–. 1987. "Migration and Health: Perspectives on Immigrant Women." *Sociology of Health and Illness* 9 (4): 410-38.

Anderson, Joan M., Connie Blue, Angela Holbrook, and Miriam Ng. 1993. "On Chronic Illness: Immigrant Women in Canada's Work Force – A Feminist Perspective." *Canadian Journal of Nursing Research* 25 (2): 7-22.

Anderson, Joan M., and Sheryl Reimer Kirkham. 1998. "Constructing Nation: The Gendering and Racializing of the Canadian Health Care System." In *Painting the Maple: Essays on Race, Gender, and the Construction of Canada,* ed. Veronica Strong-Boag, Sherrill Grace, Avigail Eisenberg, and Joan Anderson, 242-61. Vancouver: UBC Press.

Anderson, Kay J. 1991. *Vancouver's Chinatown: Racial Discourse in Canada, 1875-1980.* Montreal: McGill-Queen's University Press.

Anthias, Floya, and Nira Yuval-Davis. 1992. *Racialized Boundaries: Race, Nation, Gender, Colour and Class and the Anti-Racist Struggle.* London: Routledge.

Antonius, Rachad. 1986. "L'information internationale et les groupes ethniques: Le cas des Arabes." *Canadian Ethnic Studies* 18 (2): 11-129.

Anzaldúa, Gloria E., and Analouise Keating, eds. 2002. *This Bridge We Call Home.* New York and London: Routledge.

Appadurai, Arjun. 1990. "Disjuncture and Difference in the Global Cultural Economy." *Theory, Culture and Society* 7: 295-310.

Arat-Koc, Sedef. 1995. "The Politics of Family and Immigration in the Subordination of Domestic Workers in Canada." In *Gender in the 1990s: Images, Realities, and Issues,* ed. Adie (E.D.) Nelson and Barrie Robinson, 413-42. Toronto: Nelson.

–. 2002. "Hot Potato: Imperial Wars or Benevolent Interventions? Reflections on 'Global Feminism' Post September 11th." *Atlantis* 26 (2): 433-44.

Archer, Lynda A. 1994. "Empowering Women in a Violent Society: Role of the Family Physician." *Canadian Family Physician* 40: 974-85.

Argüelles, Lourdes, and Anne M. Rivero. 1993. "Gender/Sexual Orientation Violence and Transnational Migration: Conversations with Some Latinas We Think We Know." *Urban Anthropology and Studies* 22 (3-4): 259-75.

Armour, Monica. 1984. "The Historical Context of Racism in Canada." *Currents* 2 (1): 8-13.

Armstrong, Jane. 2001. "Campbell Rebukes Thobani for Speech." *Globe and Mail,* 3 October: A12.

–. 2004. "Family Revisits Grief at Virk Murder Trial." *Globe and Mail,* 15 June: A11.

Artz, Sibylle. 1998. *Sex, Power, and the Violent School Girl.* Toronto: Trifolium Books.

Aujla, Angela. 2000. "Others in Their Own Land: Second Generation South Asian Canadian Women, Racism, and the Persistence of Colonial Discourse." *Canadian Woman Studies* 20 (2): 41-47.

Backhouse, Constance. 1999. *Colour-Coded: A Legal History of Racism in Canada, 1900-1950.* Toronto: University of Toronto Press.

Baglole, Joel, and Ian Mulgrew. 2005. "Third Jury Ends Ellard Trial Saga: 22-Year-Old Found Guilty of Murdering Reena Virk." *Calgary Herald,* 13 April: A3.

Bagnall, Janet. 2001. "Tale of the Taliban: Once, You Could Feel Sorry for the Dispossessed Men, but No Longer." *Montreal Gazette,* 27 September: B3.

Bains, Camile. 2005. "Kelly Ellard Guilty." *St. John's Telegram,* 13 April: A9.

Balcom, Susan. 1996. "'Small-Town' Vernon in Shock over Massacre." *Vancouver Sun,* 6 April: A3.

Bald, Suresht R. 1995. "Coping with Marginality: South Asian Women Migrants in Britain." In *Feminism/Postmodernism/Development,* ed. Marianne H. Marchand and Jane L. Parpart, 119-26. London: Routledge.

Bannerji, Himani. 1986. "Now You See Us/Now You Don't." *Video Guide* 8 (40): 1-4.

–. 1987. "Introducing Racism: Towards an Anti-Racist Feminism." *Resources for Feminist Research* 16 (1): 10-12.

–, ed. 1993. *Returning the Gaze: Essays on Racism, Feminism, and Politics.* Toronto: Sister Vision Press.

–. 2000. *The Dark Side of the Nation: Essays on Multiculturalism, Nationalism and Gender.* Toronto: Canadian Scholars' Press.

Bannerji, Himani, Linda Carty, Kari Dehli, Susan Heald, and Kate McKenna. 1991. *Unsettling Relations: The University as a Site of Feminist Struggles*. Toronto: Women's Press.

Bannerji, Himani, Shahrzad Mojab, and Judith Whitehead, eds. 2001. *Of Property and Property: The Role of Gender and Class in Imperialism and Nationalism*. Toronto: University of Toronto Press.

Barnes, Annmarie. 2002. "Dangerous Duality: The 'Net Effect' of Immigration and Deportation on Jamaicans in Canada." In *Crimes of Colour: Racialization and the Criminal Justice System in Canada*, ed. Wendy Chan and Kiran Mirchandani, 191-203. Calgary: Broadview Press.

Barot, Rohit, and John Bird. 2001. "Racialization: The Genealogy and Critique of a Concept." *Ethnic and Racial Studies* 24 (2): 601-18.

Barthes, Roland. 1973. *Mythologies*. Trans. Annette Lavers. London: Paladin.

Basow, Susan A., and Lisa R. Rubin. 1999. "Gender Influences on Adolescent Development." In *Beyond Appearance: A New Look at Adolescent Girls*, ed. Norine G. Johnson, Michael C. Roberts, and Judith Worell, 25-52. Washington, DC: American Psychological Association.

Basran, Gurcharn S., and Li Zong. 1998. "Devaluation of Foreign Credential as Perceived by Visible Minority Professional Immigrants." *Canadian Ethnic Studies* 30 (3): 6-24.

Bataille, Gretchen, and Charles L.P. Silet. 1980. "The Entertaining Anachronism: Indians in American Films." In *The Kaleidoscopic Lens: How Hollywood Views Ethnic Groups*, ed. Randall M. Miller, 36-53. Englewood, NJ: Ozer.

Battershill, Charles. 1992. "Migrant Doctors in a Multicultural Society: Policies, Barriers, and Equity." In *Deconstructing a Nation: Immigration, Multiculturalism and Racism in '90s Canada*, ed. Vic Satzewich, 243-75. Halifax and Saskatoon: Fernwood Publishing and Social Research Unit, Department of Sociology, University of Saskatchewan.

Batth, Indy. 1998. "Centering the Voices from the Margins: Indo-Canadian Girls' Sports and Physical Activity Experiences in Private and Public Schools." MA thesis, University of British Columbia.

Beattie, Sara. 2003. "Criminal Harassment." In *Family Violence in Canada: A Statistical Profile 2003*, ed. Holly Johnson and Kathy Au Coin, 8-13. Ottawa: Canadian Centre for Justice Statistics.

Beatty, Jim, and Kim Pemberton. 1997. "Slain Teen Recanted Claims of Abuse Says Church Elder." *Vancouver Sun*, 29 November: A3.

Beiser, Morton. 1998. *Towards a Research Framework for Immigrant Health*. 23-32. Ottawa: Minister of Public Works and Government Services Canada.

Beiser, Morton, Feng Hou, Ilene Hyman, and Michael Tousignant. 1998. *Growing Up Canadian: A Study of New Immigrant Children*. Ottawa: Human Resources and Development Canada.

Beiser, Morton, Angela Shik, and Monika Curyk. 1999. *New Canadian Children and Youth Study Literature Review*. Toronto: Metropolis/Ceris Centre.

Bell, Stewart, Lindsay Kines, Mike Bocking, and Petti Fong. 1996. "How Did Killer Get Gun Permit? Family and Friends Ask That Question, Saying Police Already Knew Mark Chahal Had Made Threats to His Estranged Wife: Wife 'Was Too Terrified' to Press Charges." *Vancouver Sun*, 8 April: A1.

Beltrane, Mary C. 2002. "The Hollywood Latina Body as Site of Social Struggle: Media Constructions of Stardom and Jennifer Lopez's 'Cross-over' Butt." *Quarterly Review Film and Video* (19): 71-86.

Bennett, Lance W. 2003. *News: the Politics of Illusion*. 5th ed. White Plains, NY: Longman.

Bent-Goodley, Tricia B. 2004. "Perceptions of Domestic Violence: A Dialogue with African American Women." *Health and Social Work* 29 (4): 307-16.

Berger, John. 1972. *Ways of Seeing*. London and Harmondsworth: British Broadcasting Corporation and Penguin.

Berman, Helene. 1999. "Stories of Growing Up amid Violence by Children of War and Children of Battered Women Living in Canada." *Image: Journal of Nursing Scholarship* (31): 57-63.

Berman, Sandra, and Norma-Jean McLaren. 1997. *Multicultural Change in Health Service Delivery*. Resource manual 1 and 2. Vancouver: Chara Health Care Society and Multiculturalism BC.

Bernard, Claudia. 2002. "Giving Voices to Experiences: Parental Maltreatment of Black Children in the Context of Societal Racism." *Child and Family Social Work* 7: 239-51.

Berns, Nancy. 2001. "Degendering the Problem and Gendering the Blame: Political Discourse on Women and Violence." *Gender and Society* 15 (2): 262-81.

Bhabha, Homi. 1983. "The Other Question: The Stereotype and Colonial Discourse." *Screen* 24 (6): 18-36.

Bhandar, B. 1997. "Race, Identity and Difference in the Courts: Overcoming Judicial 'Bias.'" Paper presented at the BC Provincial Court Judges' Conference, Vancouver.

–. 2000. *A Guilty Verdict against the Odds: Privileging White Middle-Class Femininity in the Trial of Kelly Ellard for the Murder of Reena Virk*. Vancouver, BC: FREDA Centre.

Bhatia, Sunil, and Anjali Ram. 2001. "Rethinking 'Acculturation' in Relation to Diasporic Cultures and Postcolonial Identities." *Human Development* 44 (1): 1-18.

Bhattacharyya, Gargi, John Gabriel, and Stephen Small. 2002. *Race and Power: Global Racism in the Twenty-First Century*. London and New York: Routledge.

Bhugra, Dinesh. 2004. "Migration and Mental Health." *Acta Psychiatrica Scandinavica* 109: 243-58.

Bird, Elizabeth S., and Robert W. Dardenne. 1988. "Myth, Chronicle, and Story: Exploring the Narrative Qualities of News." In *Mass Communication as Culture: Myth and Narrative in Television and the Press*, ed. James Carey, 67-87. Beverly Hills, CA: Sage.

Blanchfield, Mike, and Hilary Mackenzie. 2001a. "US Flexes Muscle: Warplanes Ordered to Gulf Bases; Bush to Address His Nation Tonight." *Montreal Gazette*, 20 September: A1.

–. 2001b. "Saudis in a Squeeze: US Bid for Air Base Runs Contrary to Policy, Sentiment." *Montreal Gazette*, 23 September: A1.

Block, Irwin. 2001. "City Muslims Appeal for Calm: We Thank God until Now There Is No Acceleration (of Violence) in the Montreal Area." *Montreal Gazette*, 14 September: A17.

–. 2002. "CanWest Chief Attacks 'Cancer' in the Media. Anti-Israel Bias 'Destroying Credibility.' Fundamental Precepts of Honest Reporting Have Been Abandoned, Israel Asper Says." *Montreal Gazette*, 31 October: A3.

Blythe, Kathryn Everett. 2000. "Latina Identity and the Perils of Femininity." *Agora* 1 (1), http://www.tamu.edu/chr/agora/summer00/everett.pdf.

Bocking, Mike. 1996. "Step by Gruesome Step, One Man's Killing Spree." *Vancouver Sun*, 8 April: B2.

Bocking, Mike, and Kim Bolan. 1996. "Killer Had Threatened Family: Nine Die in Canada's Second-Largest Mass Murder on the Eve of a Vernon Wedding, and the Murderer Commits Suicide. Killer Apologizes in Suicide Note." *Vancouver Sun*, 6 April: A1.

Bohn, Dianne K. 1993. "Nursing Care of Native American Battered Women." *AWHONNS Clinical Issues Perinatal Women's Health Nursing* 4 (3): 424-36.

Bolan, Kim. 1996. "Police 'Didn't Follow Policy on Violence' in Vernon: Women's Groups Say Cases of Domestic Abuse Are Supposed to Be Investigated." *Vancouver Sun*, 13 April: A1.

Bolaria, B. Singh, and Rosemary Bolaria. 1994. "Immigrant Status and Health Status: Women and Racial Minority Immigrant Workers." In *Racial Minorities, Medicine, and Health*, ed. B. Singh Bolaria and Rosemary Bolaria, 149-68. Halifax: Fernwood.

Bolaria, B. Singh, and Peter S. Li. 1988. *Racial Oppression in Canada*. Toronto: Garamond Press.

Bonnycastle, Kevin, and George S. Rigakos, eds. 1998. *Unsettling Truths: Battered Women, Policy, Politics and Contemporary Research in Canada*. Vancouver: Collective Press.

Bopp, Michael, Judie Bopp, and Phil Lane. 2003. "Aboriginal Domestic Violence in Canada." Ottawa: Aboriginal Healing Foundation.

Bourne, Paula, Liza McCoy, and Dorothy Smith. 1998. "Girls and Schooling: Their Own Critique." *Resources for Feminist Research* 26 (1-2): 55-68.

Bowes, Alison. 1996. "Evaluating an Empowering Research Strategy: Reflections on Action-Research with South Asian Women." *Sociological Research Online* 1 (1).

Boychuk Duchsher, Judy E. 1994. "Acting on Violence against Women." *Canadian Nurse* 90 (6): 21-25.

Brah, Avtar. 1997. *Cartographies of Diaspora*. London and New York: Routledge.

Bray, Robert. 1997. "How to Get Better Coverage." In *We the Media,* ed. Don Hazen and Julie Winokur, 204-5. New York: New Press.

Bredström, Anna. 2003. "Gendered Racism and the Production of Cultural Difference: Media Representations and Identity Work among 'Immigrant Youth' in Contemporary Sweden." *NORA: Nordic Journal of Women's Studies* 11 (2): 78-88.

Brice-Baker, Janet R. 1994. "Domestic Violence in African-American and African-Caribbean Families." *Journal of Social Distress and the Homeless* 3 (1): 23-38.

Brown, Lyn Mikel, Niobe Way, and Julia L. Duff. 1999. "The Others in My I: Adolescent Girls' Friendships and Peer Relations." In *Beyond Appearance: A New Look at Adolescent Girls,* ed. Norine G. Johnson, Michael C. Roberts, and Judith Worrell, 205-25. Washington, DC: American Psychological Association.

Browne, Angela. 1997. "Violence in Marriage: Until Death Do Us Part?" In *Violence between Intimate Partners,* ed. Albert P. Cardarelli, 48-69. Needham Heights, MA: Allyn and Bacon.

Buchignani, Norm, and Doreen Indra, with Ram Srivastava. 1985. *Continuous Journey: A Social History of South Asians in Canada.* Toronto: McClelland and Stewart.

Bula, Frances. 1989. "Accessing the Media." Paper presented at the In the News Media and Race Relations Seminar Proceedings, Vancouver.

Bullock, Katherine H., and Gul Joya Jafri. 2001. "Media (Mis)Representations: Muslim Women in the Canadian Nation." *Canadian Woman Studies* 20 (2): 35-40.

Bullock, Lina, Judith McFarlane, Louise H. Bateman, and Virginia Miller. 1989. "The Prevalence and Characteristics of Battered Women in Primary Care Setting." *Nurse Practitioner* 14: 47-56.

Burns, Mary C., ed. 1986. *The Speaking Profits Us.* Seattle: Center for the Prevention of Sexual and Domestic Violence.

Burton, Antoinette M. 1992. "The White Woman's Burden, British Feminist and the 'Indian Woman,' 1865-1915." In *Western Women and Imperialism: Complicity and Resistance,* ed. Nupur Chaudhuri and Margaret Strobel, 137-57. Bloomington and Indianapolis: Indiana University Press.

Calliste, Agnes. 2000. "Nurses and Porters: Racism, Sexism and Resistance in Segmented Labour Markets." In *Anti-Racist Feminism, Critical Race and Gender Studies,* ed. Agnes Calliste and George J. Sefa Dei, 143-68. Halifax: Fernwood.

Calliste, Agnes, and George J. Sefa Dei, eds. 2000. *Anti-Racist Feminism.* Halifax: Fernwood.

Calvo, Janet M. 1996. "Health Care Access for Immigrant Women." In *Man-Made Medicine: Women's Health, Public Policy, and Reform,* ed. Kary L. Moss, 161-81. Des Moines, IA: Drake University Press.

Cameron, Rebecca P., Jennifer D. Wells, and Stevan E. Hobfoll. 1996. "Stress, Social Support and Coping in Pregnancy." *Journal of Health Psychology* 1 (2): 195-208.

Canada, Citizenship and Immigration. 2001. "Immigration and Refugee Protection Act Introduced." News release, Citizenship and Immigration Canada, Ottawa, March.

Canadian Council on Social Development. 2000. *Unequal Access: A Canadian Profile of Racial Differences in Education, Employment and Income.* Ottawa: Canadian, Race Relations Foundations.

Canadian Islamic Congress. 2002. "Anti-Islam in the Media: Summary of the Fifth Annual Report." http://www.canadianislamiccongress.com/rr/rr_2002_1.php.

Canadian Race Relations Foundation. 2000. *Racism in Our Schools: What to Know about It; How to Fight It.* Ottawa: Canadian Race Relations Foundation.

Cantelon, Hart. 1988. "How Television Tracked Ben." *Content* 9-10.

Capuzzi, David, and Douglas R. Gross, eds. 1996. *Youth at Risk: A Prevention Resource for Counselors, Teachers, and Parents.* 2nd ed. Alexandria, VA: American Counseling Association.

Carraway, Chezia G. 1991. "Violence against Women of Colour." *Stanford Law Review* 43 (July): 1301-9.

Carter, Cynthia. 1998. "When the 'Extraordinary' Becomes 'Ordinary': Everyday News of Sexual Violence." In *News, Gender and Power,* ed. Cynthia Carter, Gill Branston, and Stuart Allan, 219-32. London and New York: Routledge.

Carty, Linda. 1991. "Black Women in Academia: A Statement from the Periphery." In *Unsettling Relations: The University as a Site of Feminist Struggles,* ed. Himani Bannerji, Linda Carty, Kari Dehli, Susan Heald, and Kate McKenna, 13-44. Toronto: Women's Press.

Cave, Andrew, Usha Maharaj, Nancy Gibson, and Eileen Jackson. 1995. "Physicians and Immigrant Patients." *Canadian Family Physician* 41 (October): 1685-90.

Centre for Justice Statistics. 1994. *Statistics Canada Report: Family Violence in Canada, Current National Data.* Ottawa: Department of Justice.

–. 2000. *General Social Survey on Spousal Violence.* Ottawa: Statistics Canada.

–. 2001. *Family Violence in Canada: A Statistical Portrait, 2001.* Ottawa: Department of Justice Canada.

–. 2003. *Family Violence in Canada: A Statistical Portrait, 2003.* Ottawa: Department of Justice Canada.

–. 2004. *Family Violence in Canada: A Statistical Portrait, 2004.* Ottawa: Department of Justice Canada.

Chambers, Susan. 1998. *An Analysis of Trends concerning Violence against Women: A Preliminary Case Study of Vancouver.* Vancouver: FREDA.

Champion, Jane Dimmitt. 1996. "Woman Abuse, Assimilation, and Self-Concept in a Rural Mexican American Community." *Hispanic Journal of Behavioural Science* 18 (4): 508-21.

Chan, Anthony B. 1981. "'Orientalism' and Image Making: The Sojourner in Canadian History." *Journal of Ethnic Studies* 9 (3): 37-46.

Chaudhuri, Nupur, and Margaret Stroble, eds. 1992. *Western Women and Imperialism: Complicity and Resistance.* Bloomington and Indianapolis: Indianapolis University Press.

Chen, Jianjian, Edward Ng, and Russell Wilkins. 1996. "The Health of Canada's Immigrants in 1994-5." *Health Reports* 7 (4): 33-45.

Chin, Ko-Lin. 1994. "Out of Town Brides: International Marriage and Wife Abuse among Chinese Immigrants." *Journal of Comparative Family Studies* 25 (1): 53-69.

Choi, Gil. 1997. "Acculturative Stress, Social Support, and Depression in Korean American Families." *Journal of Family Social Work* 2 (1): 81-97.

Choudry, Salma. n.d. "Pakistani Women's Experiences of Domestic Violence in Great Britain: *Research Findings.*" London: Home Office Research and Statistics Directorate.

Christensen, Carol. 2000. "Barriers to Health Care: Perceptions of Women Who Are Immigrants and Refugees." Paper presented at Ending Violence against Women: Setting the Agenda for the Next Millennium, 10th International Nursing Conference, Vancouver.

Chuly, Phyllis. 1996. "Women's Health Notes, for Remarks to Women and the Law Conference." In *Ten Years Later: The Charter and Equality for Women – A Publication from a Symposium Assessing the Impact of the Equality Provisions on Women in Canada,* ed. Margaret A. Jackson and N. Kathleen Sam, with the assistance of Krista Robson Banks, 160-68. Vancouver: Simon Fraser University.

Citizenship and Immigration Canada, Strategic Policy, Planning and Research. 2000. *Facts and Figures: Immigration Overview: 1999.* Ottawa: Minister of Public Works and Government Services Canada.

Clayman, Steven E. 1990. "From Talk to Text: Newspaper Accounts of Reporter-Source Interactions." *Media, Culture and Society* 12 (1): 73-103.

Coeling, Harriet V., and Gloria Harman. 1997. "Learning to Ask about Domestic Violence." *Women's Health Issues* 7 (4): 263-68.

Cohen, Patricia. 2001. "Like Feuding Brothers: Arab Intellectuals in the West Are Split over How to Present the Attack." *Montreal Gazette,* 29 September: D19.

Cohen, Stanley, and Jock Young, eds. 1973. *The Manufacture of News: A Reader.* Beverly Hills, CA: Sage.

Colebourn, John. 2000. "They Called Her Killer Kelly." *Vancouver Province,* 2 April: A8.

Collins, Patricia Hill. 1990. *Black Feminist Thought: Knowledge, Consciousness, and the Politics of Empowerment.* Boston: Unwin Hyman.

–. 1998. "The Tie That Binds: Race, Gender and US Violence." *Ethnic and Racial Studies* 21 (5): 917-38.

–. 2000. "Gender, Black Feminism, and Black Political Economy." *Annals of the American Academy* (568): 41-53.

Comack, Elizabeth. 1996. *Women in Trouble: Connecting Women's Law Violations to Their History of Abuse.* Halifax: Fernwood.

Combahee River Collective. 1994. "The Combahee River Collective Statement." In *Theorizing Feminism: Parallel Trends in the Humanities and Social Sciences,* ed. Anne C. Hermann and Abigail J. Stewart, 26-33. Boulder, CO: Westview Press.

Connell, Ian. 1980. "Television News and the Social Contract." In *Culture, Media, Language,* ed. Stuart Hall, Dorothy Hobson, Andrew Lowe, and Paul Willis, 139-56. London: Hutchinson in association with the Centre for Contemporary Cultural Studies, Birmingham.

Cooke, Miriam. 2002. "Saving Brown Women." *Signs* 28 (1): 468-70.

Cottle, Simon. 2000. "A Rock and a Hard Place: Making Ethnic Minority Television." In *Ethnic Minorities and the Media,* ed. Simon Cottle, 100-17. Buckingham and Philadelphia: Open University Press.

Crawford, Tiffany. 2005. "An Ugly Picture of Kelly Ellard." *Kingston Whig-Standard,* 3 June: 11.

Crawley, Mike. 1996a. "RCMP 'Could Have Denied Gun Permits.'" *Vancouver Sun,* 9 April: A1.

–. 1996b. "Police Fielded 4 Complaints about Killer: The RCMP Says That Despite Hearing of Threats, It Was Told Not to Charge a Man Who Would Later Murder 9 People in Vernon." *Vancouver Sun,* 10 April: A1.

–. 1996c. "Shooting Victim 'Let Down' by Vernon RCMP: Shooting Victim Isn't Looking to Blame Police, but Wants Protection for Women." *Vancouver Sun,* 15 April: A1.

Creese, Gillian, and Laurie Peterson. 1996. "Making the News, Racializing Chinese Canadians." *Studies in Political Economy* 51: 117-45.

Crenshaw, Kimberle. 1994. "Mapping the Margins: Intersectionality, Identity Politics, and Violence against Women of Color." In *The Public Nature of Private Violence: The Discovery of Domestic Abuse,* ed. Martha A. Fineman and Roxanne Mykitiuk, 93-118. New York: Routledge.

–. 2000. "The Intersectionality of Race and Gender Discrimination." http://www.isiswomen. org/womenet/lists/apgr-list/archive/msg00013.html.

Dahlgren, Peter. 1988. "What's the Meaning of This? Viewers' Plural Sense-Making of TV News." *Media, Culture and Society* 10: 285-301.

Dahlgren, Peter, with Sumitra Chakrapani. 1982. "The Third World on TV News: Western Ways of Seeing the 'Other.'" In *Television Coverage of International Affairs,* ed. W.C. Adams, 45-65. Norwood, NJ: Ablex.

Darnton, Robert. 1975. "Writing News and Telling Stories." *Daedalus* 104 (2) Spring: 175-94.

Das Gupta, Tania. 1996. "Racism in Nursing." In *Racism and Paid Work,* 69-91. Toronto: Garamond Press.

–. 1999. "The Politics of Multiculturalism." In *Scratching the Surface: Canadian Anti-Racist Feminist Thought,* ed. Enakshi Dua and Angela Robertson, 187-205. Toronto: Women's Press.

Dasgupta, Das Shamita, and Sujata Warrier. 1996. "In the Footsteps of 'Arundhati': Asian Indian Women's Experience of Domestic Violence in the United States." *Violence against Women* 2 (3): 238-59.

Davenport, Jane. 2001. "Muslims Wary of Reprisals: 140 at Mosque Denounce Terror Attacks." *Montreal Gazette,* 16 September: A3.

Davis, Angela. 1983. *Women, Race and Class.* New York: Vintage Books.

–. 1990. *Women, Culture and Politics.* New York: Vintage Books.

–. 2000. "The Color of Violence against Women." In *Colorlines: Race Culture Action,* www.arc.org/C_Lines/CLArchive/story3_3_02.html.

de Jesús, Melinda L. 1998. "Fictions of Assimilation: Nancy Drew, Cultural Imperialism, and the Filipina American Experience." In *Delinquents and Debutantes: Twentieth-Century American Girls' Cultures,* ed. Sherrie A. Inness, 227-46. New York and London: New York University Press.

de las Fuentes, Cynthia, and Melba J.T. Vasquez. 1999a. "Immigrant Adolescent Girls of Colour: Facing American Challenges." In *Beyond Appearance: A New Look at Adolescent Girls,* ed. Norine G. Johnson, Michael C. Roberts, and Judith Worell, 131-50. Washington, DC: American Psychological Association.

–. 1999b. "American-Born Asian, African, Latina, and American Indian Adolescent Girls: Challenges and Strengths." In *Beyond Appearance: A New Look at Adolescent Girls,* ed. Norine G. Johnson, Michael C. Roberts, and Judith Worell, 151-73. Washington, DC: American Psychological Association.

Debold, Elizabeth, Lyn Mikel Brown, Susan Weseen, and Geraldine Kearse Brookins. 1999. "Cultivating Hardiness Zones for Adolescent Girls: A Reconceptualization of Resilience in Relationships with Caring Adults." In *Beyond Appearance: A New Look at Adolescent Girls,* ed. Norine G. Johnson, Michael C. Roberts, and Judith Worell, 181-204. Washington, DC: American Psychological Association.

Dei, George J. Sefa. 1999. "The Denial of Difference: Reframing Anti-Racist Praxis." *Race Ethnicity and Education* 2 (1): 17-37.

DeKeseredy, Walter S., and Katherine Kelly. 1995. "Sexual Abuse in Canadian University and College Dating Relationships: The Contribution of Male Peer Support." *Journal of Family Violence* 10 (1): 41-52.

DeKeseredy, Walter S., and Linda MacLeod. 1997. *Woman Abuse: A Sociological Story.* Toronto: Harcourt Brace.

Dell, Colleen Anne. 2002. "The Criminalization of Aboriginal Women: Commentary by a Community Activist." In *Crimes of Colour: Racialization and the Criminal Justice System in Canada,* ed. Wendy Chan and Kiran Mirchandani, 127-37. Calgary: Broadview Press.

Desai, Sabra, and Sangeeta Subramanian. 2000. "Colour, Culture and Dual Consciousness: Issues Identified by South Asian Immigrant Youth in the Greater Toronto Area." CERIS Working Paper Series.

Devlin, Richard F. 1995. "We Can't Go on Together with Suspicious Minds: Judicial Bias and Racialized Perspective in R.V.R.D.S. (Case Comm.)." *Dalhousie Law Journal* 18: 408-35.

Dosanjh, Raminder, Surinder Deo, and Surjeet Sidhu. 1994. *Spousal Abuse in the South Asian Community.* Vancouver: FREDA Centre for Research on Violence against Women and Children.

Dossa, Parin. 1999. *The Narrative Representation of Mental Health: Iranian Women in Canada.* Working Paper Series 99-18. Vancouver: Vancouver Centre of Excellence for Research on Immigration and Integration in the Metropolis.

–. 2004. *Politics and Poetics of Migration: Narratives of Iranian Women from the Diaspora.* Toronto: Canadian Scholars' Press.

Dowd, Maureen. 2001. "History Throws Knuckleball to Bush." *Montreal Gazette,* 25 September: B3.

Drury, Beatrice. 1991. "Sikh Girls and the Maintenance of an Ethnic Culture." *New Community* 17 (3): 387-99.

Dua, Enakshi. 1999. "Canadian Anti-Racist Thought: Scratching the Surface." In *Scratching the Surface: Canadian Anti-Racist Feminist Thought,* ed. Enakshi Dua and Angela Robertson, 7-31. Toronto: Women's Press.

DuCharme, Michele. 1986. "The Coverage of Canadian Immigration Policy in the *Globe and Mail* (1980-1985)." *Currents: Readings in Race Relations* 3 (3): 6-11.

Duffy, Ann. 1995. "The Feminist Challenge: Knowing and Ending the Violence." In *Feminist Issues: Race, Class, and Sexuality,* ed. Nancy Mandell, 152-84. Scarborough, ON: Prentice Hall Canada.

Duffy, Ann, and Julianne Momirov. 1997. *Family Violence: A Canadian Introduction.* Toronto: James Lorimer.

Dulude, L. 2000. *Justice and the Poor.* Ottawa: National Council of Welfare.

Dunn, James, and Isabel Dyck. 1998. *Social Determinants of Health in Canada's Immigrant Population: Results from the National Population Health Survey.* Working Paper Series 98-20. Vancouver: Vancouver Centre of Excellence for Research on Immigration and Integration in the Metropolis.

Dunn, Kevin, and Minelle Mahtani. 2001. *"Adjusting the Colour Bars": Media Representations of Ethnic Minorities under Australian and Canadian Multiculturalisms.* Working Paper Series 01-06. Vancouver: Vancouver Centre of Excellence for Research on Immigration and Integration in the Metropolis.

Durham, Meenakshi Gigi. 2001. "Displaced Persons: Symbols of South Asian Femininity and the Returned Gaze in U.S. Media Culture." *Communication Theory* 11 (2): 201-17.

Dyck, Isabel. 1992. "Managing Chronic Illness: An Immigrant Woman's Acquisition and Use of Health Care Knowledge." *American Journal of Occupational Therapy* 46 (8): 696-705.

Emmott, Sue. 1996. "'Dislocation,' Shelter and Crisis: Afghanistan's Refugees and Notions of Home." *Gender and Development* 4 (1): 31-38.

Ericson, Richard V. 1991. "Mass Media, Crime, Law, and Justice." *British Journal of Criminology* 31 (3): 219-49.

Ericson, Richard V., Patricia M. Baranek, and Janet B.L. Chan. 1989. *Negotiating Control: A Study of News Sources*. Milton Keynes, UK: Open University Press.

Ervin, Alexander M. 1994. "'Service Providers' Perceptions of Immigrant Well-Being and Implications for Health Promotion and Delivery." In *Racial Minorities, Medicine and Health*, ed. B. Singh Bolaria and Rosemary Bolaria, 225-43. Halifax: Fernwood.

Espiritu, Yen Le. 2001. "'We Don't Sleep Around Like White Girls Do': Family, Culture, and Gender in Filipina American Lives." *Signs: Journal of Women in Culture and Society* 26 (2): 415-40.

Essed, Philomena. 1990. *Everyday Racism: Reports from Women of Two Cultures*. Trans. Cynthia Jaffe. Claremont, CA: Hunter House.

Faith, Karlene. 1993. *Unruly Women: The Politics of Confinement and Resistance*. Vancouver: Press Gang.

Faith, Karlene, and Yasmin Jiwani. 2002. "The Social Construction of 'Dangerous Girls' and Women." In *Marginality and Condemnation: An Introduction to Critical Criminology*, ed. Bernard Schissel and Carolyn Brooks, 83-107. Halifax: Fernwood.

Faludi, Susan. 1992. *Backlash: The Undeclared War against American Women*. New York: Anchor.

Fanon, Frantz. 1965. *Studies of a Dying Colonialism*. Trans. Haakon Chevalier. New York: Grove Press.

–. 1967. *Black Skin, White Masks*. Trans. Charles Lam. New York: Grove Press.

Ferraro, Katherine J. 1996. "The Dance of Dependency: A Genealogy of Domestic Violence." *Hypatia* 11 (4): 77-91.

–. 1997. "Battered Women: Strategies for Survival." In *Violence between Intimate Partners: Patterns, Causes, and Effects*, ed. Albert P. Cardarelli, 124-40. Needham Heights, MA: Allyn and Bacon.

Finlay, P. 1999. *Concentration of Ownership in the Media: A Review of Principal Issues*. Ottawa: Minister of Public Works and Government Services Canada.

Fish, Stanley. 1997. "Boutique Multiculturalism, or Why Liberals Are Incapable of Thinking about Hate Speech." *Critical Inquiry* 23: 378-95.

Fiske, John. 1996. *Media Matters: Race and Gender in U.S. Politics*. Rev. ed. Minneapolis and London: University of Minnesota Press.

Fiske, John, and John Hartley. 1987. *Reading Television*. London and New York: Routledge and Kegan Paul.

Fitterman, Lisa. 2001a. "Hate Hits Canada: Muslims, Even Sikhs, Targets of Backlash." *Montreal Gazette*, 15 September: A24.

–. 2001b. "Montreal's Pakistani Muslims Feel the Heat: 'We Are Here, We Are Not the Terrorists.'" *Montreal Gazette*, 21 September: A13.

Fleras, Augie. 1994. "Media and Minorities in a Post-Multicultural Society: Overview and Appraisal." In *Ethnicity and Culture in Canada: The Research Landscape*, ed. John W. Berry and J.A. Laponce, 267-92. Toronto: University of Toronto Press.

Fleras, Augie, and Jean Leonard Elliot. 1996. *Unequal Relations: An Introduction to Race, Ethnic and Aboriginal Dynamics in Canada*. 2nd ed. Scarborough, ON: Prentice Hall.

Fleras, Augie, and Jean Lock Kunz. 2001. *Media and Minorities: Representing Diversity in a Multicultural Canada*. Toronto: Thompson Educational.

Flynn, Karen, and Charmaine Crawford. 1998. "Committing 'Race Treason': Battered Women and Mandatory Arrest in Toronto's Caribbean Community." In *Unsettling Truths: Battered Women, Policy, Politics and Contemporary Research in Canada*, ed. K.D. Bonnycastle and G.S. Rigakos, 91-102. Vancouver: Collective Press.

Folson, Rose Baaba. 2004. "Representation of the Immigrant." In *Calculated Kindness: Global Restructuring, Immigration and Settlement in Canada,* ed. Rose Baaba Folson, 21-32. Halifax: Fernwood.

Forsyth-Smith, Debi. 1995. "Domestic Terrorism: The News as an Incomplete Record of Violence against Women." In *Constructing Danger: The Mis/Representation of Crime in the News,* ed. Chris McCormick, 56-73. Halifax: Fernwood.

Foucault, Michel. 1980a. "Two Lectures." In *Power/Knowledge: Selected Interview and Other Writings, 1972-1977,* ed. Colin Gordon, 78-108. New York: Pantheon.

–. 1980b. *The History of Sexuality, Volume 1: An Introduction.* New York: Vintage Books/ Random House.

–. 1981a. "The Order of Discourse, Inaugural Lecture at the Collège de France." In *Untying the Text: A Post-Structuralist Reader,* ed. Robert Young, 48-78. Boston: Routledge and Kegan Paul.

–. 1981b. "Truth and Power." In *French Sociology: Rupture and Renewal since 1968,* ed. Charles C. Lemert, 293-307. New York: Columbia University Press.

Fowlie, Jonathan. 2005. "Schoolgirl Presented Two Faces to World." *Victoria Times Colonist,* 13 April: A1.

Fowlie, Jonathan, with a file from Joel Baglole. 2005. "'Killer Kelly' Lacks Internalized Social Values, Doctor Says." *Vancouver Sun,* 13 April: A5.

Frank, Russell. 1999. "'You Had to Be There' (and They Weren't): The Problem with Reporter Reconstructions." *Journal of Mass Media Ethics* 14 (3): 146-58.

Franks, Mary Ann. 2003. "Obscene Undersides: Women and Evil between the Taliban and the United States." *Hypatia* 18 (1): 135-56.

Freeman, Alan, and Miro Cernetig. 2001. "Second Reporter in Burqa Arrested." *Globe and Mail,* 10 October: A8.

Friedman, Sara, and Courtney Cook. 1995. *Girls: A Presence at Beijing.* New York: NGO Working Group on Girls.

Friedman, Thomas L. 2001. "It's World War III: America Will Have to Fight on Several Fronts, and Need All Its Will to Win." *Montreal Gazette,* 14 September: B3.

Gabriel, John. 1998. *Whitewash: Racialized Politics and the Media.* London and New York: Routledge.

Galtung, Johan, and Mari Ruge. 1973. "Structuring and Selecting News." In *The Manufacture of News: A Reader,* ed. Stanley Cohen and Jock Young, 62-72. Beverly Hills, CA: Sage.

Gannon, Kathy. 2001. "Where Equality Is 'Obscene': Conservative Pakistani Clerics Vow to Crush Women's Rights." *Montreal Gazette,* 13 September: C7.

Gans, Herbert J. 1979. "Symbolic Ethnicity: The Future of Ethnic Groups and Cultures in America." *Ethnic and Racial Studies* 2 (1): 1-19.

Gany, Francesa, and Heike Thiel de Bocanegra. 1996. "Overcoming Barriers to Improving the Health of Immigrant Women." *Journal of the American Medical Women's Association* 51: 155-60.

Gazette (Montreal). 2001. "Good vs. Evil." 15 September: B6.

Gee, Deborah. 1988. *Slaying the Dragon.* Video. San Francisco: NAATA/Cross Current Media.

Geertz, Clifford, ed. 1973. *The Interpretation of Cultures.* New York: Basic Books.

Gilbert, Paul, Jean Gilbert, and Jasvinder Sanghera. 2004. "A Focus Group Exploration of the Impact of Izzat, Shame, Subordination and Entrapment on Mental Health and Service Use in South Asian Women Living in Derby." *Mental Health, Religion and Culture* 7 (2): 109-30.

Gill, Richard, and Joan Brockman. 1996. *A Review of Section 264 (Criminal Harassment) of the Criminal Code of Canada: Working Document.* Ottawa: Department of Justice Canada.

Gilroy, Paul. 1991. *There Ain't No Black in the Union Jack: The Cultural Politics of Race and Nation.* Chicago: University of Chicago Press.

Girard, Daniel. 2000. "'She Wanted to Fit In.'" *Toronto Star,* 2 April: A8.

Gitlin, Todd. 1979. "News as Ideology and Contested Area: Toward a Theory of Hegemony, Crisis and Opposition." *Socialist Review* 9 (6): 11-54.

–. 1980. *The Whole World Is Watching.* Berkeley: University of California Press.

–. 1986. "'We Build Excitement': On Car Commercials, *Miami Vice* and Ideological Style in the Reagan Age." In *Watching Television,* ed. Todd Gitlin, 1-35. New York: Pantheon.

Globe and Mail. 2001. "Just Another Chance to Berate the Americans." 3 October: A16.
Goldberg, David Theo, ed. 1990. *Anatomy of Racism.* Minneapolis and Oxford: University of Minnesota Press.
–. 1993. *Racist Culture, Philosophy and the Politics of Meaning.* Massachusetts and Oxford: Blackwell Publishers.
Goldberg, Jeffrey. 2001. "Taking Courses at Jihad School: All-Islamic Classes." *Montreal Gazette,* 15 September: B1.
Goldstein, Steve. 2001. "Ex-Soviet States Will Be Key for U.S.: Most of the 'Stans' Have Muslim Majorities." *Montreal Gazette,* 29 September: B1.
Gonick, Marnina. 2003. *Between Femininities.* Albany: State University of New York Press.
Gram, Karen. 1997. "Bullies: Dealing with Threats in a Child's Life." *Vancouver Sun,* 5 December: F1.
Granzberg, Gary. 1984. "The Portrayal of Visible Minorities by Canadian Television during the 1982 Prime-Time Season." *Currents: Readings in Race Relations* 2 (2): 23-26.
Gray, Bradley, and Jeffrey J. Stoddard. 1997. "Patient-Physician Pairing: Does Racial and Ethnic Congruity Influence Selection of a Regular Physician?" *Journal of Community Health* 22 (4): 247-59.
Greaves, Lorraine, Olena Hankivsky, and JoAnn Kingston-Riechers. 1995. "Selected Estimates of the Cost of Violence against Women." London, ON: Centre for Research on Violence against Women and Children, University of Western Ontario.
Greenberger, Allen J. 1969. *The British Image of India: A Study in the Literature of Imperialism 1880-1960.* London: Oxford University Press.
Grewal, Inderpal. 1996. *Home and Harem: Nation, Gender, Empire, and the Cultures of Travel.* Durham and London: Duke University Press.
–. 2003. "Transnational America: Race, Gender and Citizenship after 9/11." *Social Identities* 9 (4): 535-61.
Grewal, Inderpal, and Caren Kaplan. 1994. "Introduction: Transnational Feminist Practices and Questions of Postmodernity." In *Scattered Hegemonies: Postmodernity and Transnational Feminist Practices,* ed. Inderpal Grewal and Caren Kaplan, 1-33. Minneapolis and London: University of Minnesota Press.
Griffin, Kevin. 1996. "'Violence against Women Isn't Cultural': Counsellors Who Deal with Domestic Violence Worry That Stereotyping Will Obscure an Issue That Affects 'All Canadians.'" *Vancouver Sun,* 8 April: B2.
Gross, Larry. 1991. "Out of the Mainstream: Sexual Minorities and the Mass Media." In *Gay People, Sex and the Media,* ed. Michelle A. Wolf and Alfred P. Kielwasser, 19-46. New York and London: Harrington Park Press.
Grunfeld, Anton, Deborah Hotch, and Kathleen MacKay. 1995. *Identification, Assessment, Care Referral and Follow-up of Women Experiencing Domestic Violence Who Come to the Emergency Department for Treatment. Final Report.* Vancouver: Vancouver Hospital and Health Sciences Centre.
Guillaumin, Colette. 1974. "Changes in Inter-Ethnic 'Attitudes' and the Influence of the Mass Media as Shown by Research in French-Speaking Countries." In *Mass Media and the Race,* ed. James D. Halloran, 55-87. Paris: UNESCO.
Ha, Tu Thanh. 2004a. "Free-Speech Fight Erupts after C.R.T.C. Bans Station: Top Quebec City Radio Outlet Is Ordered to Shut Down over Hosts' Offensive Antics." *Globe and Mail,* 14 July: A1, A6.
–. 2004b. "C.H.O.I.-F.M. Renews Fight to Remain on the Air." *Globe and Mail,* 3 August: A11.
Hackett, Robert A. 1989. "Coups, Earthquakes and Hostages? Foreign News on Canadian Television." *Canadian Journal of Political Science* 22 (4): 809-25.
Hackett, Robert A., Richard Gruneau, Donald Gutstein, Timothy A. Gibson, and News Watch Canada. 2000. *The Missing News: Filters and Blind Spots in Canada's Press.* Ottawa: Canadian Centre for Policy Alternatives/Garamond Press.
Hackett, Robert A., and Yuezhi Zhao with Satu Repo. 1998. *Sustaining Democracy? Journalism and the Politics of Objectivity.* Toronto: Garamond Press.
Hage, Ghassan. 2000. *White Nation: Fantasies of White Supremacy in a Multicultural Society.* New York and Australia: Routledge and Pluto Press.

Hagedorn, Jessica. 1997. "Asian Women in Film: No Joy, No Luck." In *Facing Difference: Race, Gender, and Mass Media,* ed. Shirley Biagi and Marilyn Kern-Foxworth, 32-37. Thousand Oaks, CA: Forge Press.

Halbfinger, David. 2002. "Make-over Rush after the Burqa." *Montreal Gazette,* 3 September: A1.

Hall, Neal. 1999a. "Virk's Killing Motivated by Racism, Witness Says." *Vancouver Sun,* 15 April: A5.

–. 1999b. "Court Hears Tape of Accused's Girlfriend Recalling Confession." *Vancouver Sun,* 22 April: A5.

–. 1999c. "Reena Virk: A Disposable Kid to Cruel Attackers." *Vancouver Sun,* 8 May: A10.

Hall, Stuart. 1974. "Media Power: The Double Bind." *Journal of Communications* 24 (4): 19-26.

–. 1979. "Culture, the Media and the 'Ideological Effect.'" In *Mass Communication and Society,* ed. James Curran, Michael Gurevitch, and Janet Woollacott, 315-47. London: E. Arnold in association with the Open University Press.

–. 1980a. "Race, Articulation and Societies Structured in Dominance." In *Sociological Theories: Race and Colonialism,* ed. UNESCO, 305-45. Paris: UNESCO.

–. 1980b. "Encoding/Decoding." In *Culture, Media, Language,* ed. Stuart Hall, Dorothy Hobson, Andrew Lowe, and Paul Willis, 128-38. London: Hutchinson in association with the Centre for Contemporary Cultural Studies, University of Birmingham.

–, as interviewed by John O'Hara. 1984. "The Narrative Construction of Reality: An Interview with Stuart Hall." *Southern Review* (17): 2-17.

–. 1989a. "Ideology and the Communication Theory." In *Rethinking Communication.* Vol. 1. *Paradigm Issues,* ed. Brenda Dervin, Lawrence Grossberg, Barbara J. O'Keefe, and Ellen Wartella, 40-52. London: Sage.

–. 1989b. Convocation Address at the University of Massachusetts at Amherst.

–. 1990a. "The Whites of Their Eyes, Racist Ideologies and the Media." In *The Media Reader,* ed. Manuel Alvarado and John O. Thompson, 9-23. London: British Film Institute.

–. 1990b. "Culture Identity and Diaspora." In *Identity: Community, Culture, Difference,* ed. Jonathan Rutherford, 222-37. London: Lawrence and Wishart.

–. 1992. "Our Mongrel Selves." *New Statesman Society* (special suuplement): 6-8.

–. 1996a. "Introduction: Who Needs 'Identity'?" In *Questions of Cultural Identity,* ed. Stuart Hall and Paul Du Gay, 1-17. London: Sage.

–. 1996b. "Ethnicity; Identity and Difference." In *Becoming National: A Reader,* ed. Geoff Eley and Ronald Grigor Suny, 339-49. New York: Oxford University Press.

–. 1996c. "On Postmodernism and Articulation: An Interview with Stuart Hall." In *Critical Dialogues in Cultural Studies,* ed. David Morley and Kuan-Hsing Chen, 131-50. London and New York: Routledge.

–, ed. 1997. *Representation: Cultural Representations and Signifying Practices.* London: Sage in association with the Open University.

Hamilton, Graeme. 2001. "'A Crime of Pure Hatred,' Crown Says: Teen Beaten to Death for Being an Immigrant. Two Classmates Accused." *National Post,* 12 May: A1.

Hamilton, Janice. 1996. "Multicultural Health Care Requires Adjustments by Doctors and Patients." *Canadian Medical Association Journal* 155 (5): 585-87.

Hamilton, Roberta. 1996. *Gendering the Vertical Mosaic: Feminist Perspectives on Canadian Society.* Toronto: Copp Clark.

Hammond, Dorothy, and Alta Jablow. 1977. *The Myth of Africa.* New York: Library of Social Sciences.

Hampton, R., William Oliver, and Lucia Magarian. 2003. "Domestic Violence in the African America Community: An Analysis of Social and Structural Factors." *Violence against Women* 9 (5): 533-57.

Handa, Amita. 1997. "Caught between Omissions: Exploring 'Cultural Conflict' among Second Generation South Asian Women in Canada." PhD thesis, University of Toronto.

Hanvey, Louis, and Dianne Kinnon. 1993. *The Health Care Sector's Response to Woman Abuse: A Discussion Paper for the Family Violence Prevention Division, Health Canada.* Ottawa: National Clearinghouse on Family Violence.

Harpham, Geoffrey Galt. 2002. "Symbolic Terror." *Critical Inquiry* 28 (2): 573-79.

Harris, Angela. 1997. "Race and Essentialism in Feminist Legal Theory." In *Critical Race Feminism: A Reader,* ed. Adrien Katherine Wing, 11-18. New York and London: New York University Press.

Harrison, Deborah. 1985. "The Terry Fox Story and the Popular Media: A Case Study in Ideology and Illness." *Canadian Review of Sociology and Anthropology* 22 (4): 496-514.

Harrison, Faye V. 1995. "The Persistent Power of 'Race' in the Cultural and Political Economy of Racism." *Annual Review of Anthropology* 24 (1): 47-74.

Hart, Adrian. 1989. "Images of the Third World." In *Looking beyond the Frame,* ed. Michelle Reeves and Jenny Hammond, 12-17. Oxford: Links.

Hartley, John. 1982. *Understanding News.* London and New York: Methuen.

Hartmann, Paul, and Charles Husband. 1974. *Racism and the Mass Media.* London: Davis-Poynter.

Hay, Sheridan. 1996. "Blacks in Canada, the Invisible Minority." *Canadian Dimension* 30 (6): 14-17.

Head, Wilson. 1986. *Black Women's Work: Racism in the Health System.* Toronto: Human Rights Commission.

Health Canada. 1994. *Report on an Information Session with Ethnocultural Communities on Family Violence.* Ottawa: Health Canada, 19-20 March.

Heise, Lori, Mary Ellsberg, and Megan Gottemoeller. 1999. *Ending Violence against Women: Population Reports.* Baltimore: Johns Hopkins University School of Public Health, Population Information Program.

Heller, David J. 1995. "Language Bias in the Criminal Justice System." *Criminal Law Quarterly* 37: 344-83.

Hennink, Monique, Ian Diamond, and Philip Cooper. 1999. "Young Asian Women and Relationships: Traditional or Transitional." *Ethnic and Racial Studies* 22 (5) September: 867-91.

Henry, Frances. 2002. "Canada's Contribution to the 'Management' of Ethno-Cultural Diversity." *Canadian Journal of Communication* 27 (2-3): 231-42.

Henry, Frances, and Effie Ginzberg. 1985. *Who Gets the Work: A Test of Racial Discrimination in Employment.* Toronto: Urban Alliance on Race Relations and Social Planning Council of Metropolitan Toronto.

Henry, Frances, Patricia Hastings, and Brian Freer. 1996. "Perceptions of Race and Crime in Ontario: Empirical Evidence from Toronto and the Durham Region." *Canadian Journal of Criminology* 38 (4): 469-76.

Henry, Frances, and Carol Tator. 2002. *Discourses of Domination: Racial Bias in the Canadian English-Language Press.* Toronto: University of Toronto Press.

–. 2003. Racial Profiling in Toronto: Discourses of Domination, Mediation, and Opposition. Toronto: Canadian Race Relations Foundation.

Henry, Frances, Carol Tator, Winston Mattis, and Tim Rees. 1995. *The Colour of Democracy: Racism in Canadian Society.* Toronto: Harcourt Brace.

Herman, Edward S., and Noam Chomsky. 2002. *Manufacturing Consent.* New York: Pantheon.

Herman, Edward S., and Robert W. McChesney. 1997. "Alternatives to the Status Quo?" In *The Global Media: New Missionaries of Global Capitalism,* ed. Edward S. Herman and Robert W. McChesney, 189-205. Washington, DC: Cassell.

Hier, Sean, and Joshua Greenberg. 2002. "News Discourse and the Problematization of Chinese Migration to Canada." In *Discourses of Domination: Racial Bias in the Canadian English-Language Press,* ed. Frances Henry and Carol Tator, 138-62. Toronto: University of Toronto Press.

Hightower, Jill. 1996. "The Vicious Circle of Violence: We Must Educate Kids from the Cradle Onward If We're Ever to Stop the Battering and Killing." *Vancouver Sun,* 26 November: A13.

Hirschkind, Charles, and Saba Mahmood. 2002. "Feminism, the Taliban, and the Politics of Counter-Insurgency." *Anthropological Quarterly* 75 (2): 339-54.

Hoodfar, Homa. 1993. "The Veil in Their Minds and on Our Heads: The Persistence of Colonial Images of Muslim Women." *Resources for Feminist Research* 22 (3-4): 5-18.

hooks, bell. 1982. *Ain't I a Woman: Black Women and Feminism.* Boston: South End Press.

–. 1990. *Yearning, Race, Gender, and Cultural Politics.* Toronto: Between the Lines.
–. 1992. *Black Looks: Race and Representation.* Toronto: Between the Lines.
–. 1994. *Outlaw Culture: Resisting Representations.* New York: Routledge.
–. 1995. *Killing Rage, Ending Racism.* New York: Henry Holt.
Horwood, Holly. 2000. "She Sought Friends and Found Death." *Vancouver Province,* 2 April: A9.
Hotch, Deborah, Anton Grunfeld, Kathleen MacKay, and Leigh Cowan. 1995. *Domestic Violence Intervention by Emergency Department Staff.* Vancouver: Vancouver Hospital and Health Sciences Centre.
Huisman, Kimberly. 1996. "Wife Battering in Asian American Communities." *Violence against Women* 2 (3): 260-83.
Hume, Mark. 2000. "Virk's Self-Esteem Battle Led Her to Rough Crowd." *National Post,* 1 April: A8.
Hunter, Patrick. 2001. "The *National Post* on Immigrants and Refugees: A Review." *Canadian Race Relations Foundation Perspectives* (Autumn-Winter): 4.
Hutnik, Nimmi. 1986. "Patterns of Ethnic Minority Identification and Modes of Social Adaptation." *Ethnic and Racial Studies* 9 (2): 150-67.
Huttenback, Robert A. 1976. *Racism and Empire: White Settler and Coloured Immigrants in the British Self-Governing Colonies: 1830-1910.* Ithaca and London: Cornell University.
Imam, Umme Farvah. 1999. "South-Asian Young Women's Experiences of Violence and Abuse." In *Good Practice in Working with Violence,* ed. Hazel Kemshall and Jacki Pritchard, 128-48. London and Philadelphia: Jessica Kingsley Publishers.
Indra, Doreen. 1979. "South Asian Stereotypes in the Vancouver Press." *Ethnic and Racial Studies* 2 (2): 164-87.
–. 1981. "The Invisible Mosaic: Women, Ethnicity and the Vancouver Press, 1905-1976." *Canadian Ethnic Studies* (13): 63-74.
Ivens, Andy. 2005. "Teen Killer Had History of Mischief, Violence." *Calgary Herald,* 3 June: A6.
Iyer, Nitya. 1997. "Some Mothers Are Better Than Others: A Re-Examination of Maternity Benefits." In *Challenging the Public/Private Divide: Feminism, Law and Public Policy,* ed. Susan B. Boyd, 168-94. Toronto: University of Toronto Press.
Jabbra, Nancy. 1983. "Assimilation and Acculturation of Lebanese Extended Families in Nova Scotia." *Canadian Ethnic Studies* 15 (1): 54-72.
Jackson, Steven J. 1998. "A Twist of Race: Ben Johnson and the Canadian Crisis of Racial and National Identity." *Sociology of Sports Journal* 15 (1): 21-40.
Jafri, Gul Yoya. 1998. "The Portrayal of Muslim Women in Canadian Mainstream Media: A Community Based Analysis." http://www.fmw.org/.
James, Carl E. 1998. "'Up to No Good': Black on the Streets and Encountering Police." In *Racism and Social Inequality in Canada: Concepts, Controversies and Strategies of Resistance,* ed. Vic Satzewich, 157-76. Toronto: Thompson Educational.
JanMohamed, Abdul R. 1985. "The Economy of Manichean Allegory: The Function of Racial Difference in Colonial Literature." *Critical Inquiry* 12: 59-87.
Janovicek, Nancy. 2000. *On the Margins of a Fraying Social Safety Net: Aboriginal, Immigrant and Refugee Women's Access to Welfare Benefits.* Vancouver: FREDA Centre for Research on Violence against Women and Children.
Jewell, K. Sue. 1993. *From Mammy to Miss America and Beyond: Cultural Images and the Shaping of US Social Policy.* London: Routledge.
Jimenez, Marina. 1997a. "Girls' Fighting Life Marked by Insults, Rumours, Gangs." *Vancouver Sun,* 1 December: B8.
–. 1997b. "Teenage Girls and Violence: The BC Reality." *Vancouver Sun,* 11 December: A1.
Jiwani, Yasmin. 1991. "The Symbolic Mediation of Inequality: Visible Minorities in Canadian News Media." In *Beyond the Printed Word,* ed. Richard Lochead, 300-9. Kingston, ON: Quarry Press.
–. 1992a. "To Be and Not to Be: South Asians as Victims of Oppressors in the *Vancouver Sun.*" *Sanvad* 5 (45): 13-15.
–. 1992b. "The Exotic, the Erotic and the Dangerous: South Asian Women in Popular Film." *Canadian Woman Studies* 13 (1): 42-46.

–. 1993. "By Omission and Commission: Race and Representation in Canadian Television News." PhD diss., Simon Fraser University.

–. 1994. "Women of Colour and Poverty." *Occasional Working Papers Series, Centre for Research in Women's Studies and Gender Relations* (University of British Columbia) 3 (1): 1-15.

–. 1996. "Violence Is Bigger Than ..." *Vancouver Sun,* 13 April: A25.

–. 1998a. "On the Outskirts of Empire: Race and Gender in Canadian TV News." In *Painting the Maple: Essays on Race, Gender, and the Construction of Canada,* ed. Veronica Strong-Boag, Sherrill Grace, Avigail Eisenberg, and Joan Anderson, 53-68. Vancouver: UBC Press.

–. 1998b. *Violence against Marginalized Girls: A Review of the Literature.* Vancouver: FREDA Centre for Research on Violence against Women and Children.

–. 1999. "Erasing Race: The Story of Reena Virk." *Canadian Woman Studies* 19 (3): 178-84.

–. 2001a. *Mapping Violence: A Work in Progress.* Vancouver: FREDA Centre for Research on Violence against Women and Children.

–. 2001b. *Intersecting Inequalities: Immigrant Women of Colour Who Have Experienced Violence and Their Encounters with the Health Care System.* Vancouver: FREDA Centre for Research on Violence against Women and Children.

–. 2004. "Gendering Terror: Representations of the Orientalized Body in Quebec's Post-September 11 English-Language Press." *Critique: Critical Middle Eastern Studies* 13 (3): 265-91.

–. 2005a. "War Talk – Engendering Terror: Race, Gender and Representation in Canadian Print Media." *International Journal of Media and Cultural Politics* 1 (1): 15-21.

–. 2005b. "The Eurasian Female Hero(Ine): Sydney Fox as the Relic Hunter." *Journal of Popular Film and Television* 32 (4): 182-91.

–. 2005c. "Walking a Tightrope: The Many Faces of Violence in the Lives of Racialized Immigrant Girls and Young Women." *Violence against Women: An International and Inter-disciplinary Journal* 11 (7): 846-75.

Jiwani, Yasmin, and Lawrence Buhagiar. 1997. *Policing Violence against Women in Relationships: An Examination of Police Response to Violence against Women in British Columbia.* Vancouver, BC: FREDA Centre for Research on Violence against Women and Children.

Jiwani, Yasmin, Nancy Janovicek, and Angela Cameron. 2001. *Erased Realities: The Violence of Racism in the Lives of Immigrant and Refugee Girls of Colour.* Vancouver: FREDA.

Jiwani, Yasmin, Shelley L. Moore, and Patricia Kachuk. 1998. *Rural Women and Violence: A Study of Two Communities in British Columbia.* Vancouver: FREDA Centre for Research on Violence against Women and Children. http://www.harbour.sfu.ca/freda/articles/rural00.htm.

Joe, Karen A., and Meda Chesney-Lind. 1995. "Just Every Mother's Angel: An Analysis of Gender and Ethnic Variations in Youth Gang Membership." *Gender and Society* 9 (4): 408-31.

Johnson, Holly. 1996. *Dangerous Domains: Violence against Women in Canada.* Scarborough, ON: Nelson.

Johnson, Holly, and Kathy Au Coin, eds. 2003. *Family Violence in Canada: A Statistical Profile 2003.* Ottawa: Canadian Centre for Justice Statistics.

Johnson, Norine G., Michael C. Roberts, and Judith Worrell, eds. 1999. *Beyond Appearance: A New Look at Adolescent Girls.* Washington, DC: American Psychological Association.

Joyce, Greg. 2005. "Ellard Appeal Likely." *Vancouver Sun,* 14 April: B5.

Karim, Karim H. 1993a. "Constructions, Deconstructions, and Reconstructions: Competing Canadian Discourses on Ethnocultural Terminology." *Canadian Journal of Communication* 18 (2): 197-218.

–. 1993b. "Reconstructing the Multicultural Community in Canada: Discursive Strategies of Inclusion and Exclusion." *International Journal of Politics, Culture and Society* 7 (2): 189-207.

–. 1998. "From Ethnic Media to Global Media: Transnational Communication Networks among Diasporic Communities." International Comparative Research Group, Strategic Research and Analysis, Canadian Heritage, June.

–. 2000. *Islamic Peril*. Montreal: Black Rose Books.

Kazemipur, Abdolmohammad, and Shiva S. Halli. 2001. "The Changing Colour of Poverty in Canada." *Canadian Review of Sociology and Anthropology* 3 (2): 217-38.

Kelly, Jennifer. 1998. *Under the Gaze: Learning to Be Black in White Society*. Halifax: Fernwood.

Kelly, Liz. 1987. "The Continuum of Sexual Violence." In *Women, Violence and Social Control*, ed. Jalna Hanmer and Mary Maynard, 46-60. London: Macmillan.

–. 1988. *Surviving Sexual Violence*. Minneapolis: University of Minnesota Press.

Khan, Shahnaz. 2001. "Between Here and There: Feminist Solidarity and Afghan Women." *Genders* 33. http://www.genders.org/g33/g33_kahn.html.

Kidd-Hewitt, David. 1995. "Crime and the Media: A Criminological Perspective." In *Crime and the Media: The Post-Modern Spectacle*, ed. David Kidd-Hewitt and Richard Osborne, 1-24. London: Pluto Press.

Kinnon, Dianne. 1999. *Canadian Research on Immigration and Health: An Overview*. Ottawa: Health Canada.

Kinnon, Dianne, and Louise Hanvey. 1996. *Health Aspects of Violence against Women: A Canadian Perspective*. http://hwcweb.hwc.ca/canusa/papers/canada/english/violenab.htm.

Kleinman, Arthur, and Joan Kleinman. 1996. "The Appeal of Experience: The Dismay of Images: Cultural Appropriations of Suffering in Our Times." *Daedalus* 125 (1): 1-23.

Kobayashi, A., E. Moore, and M. Rosenberg. 1998. "Healthy Immigrant Children: A Demographic and Geographic Analysis." http://www.hrdc-drhc.gc.ca/.

Kolhatkar, Sonali. 2002a. "'Saving' Afghan Women." *Women in Action* 34 (3) April.

–. 2002b. "The Impact of US Intervention on Afghan Women's Studies." *Berkeley Women's Law Journal* 17: 12-30.

Kosch, Shae Graham, Mary Ann Burg, and Shifa Podikiju. 1998. "Patient Ethnicity and Diagnosis of Emotional Disorders in Women." *Family Medicine* 30 (3): 215-19.

Kunz, Jean Lock, and Augie Fleras. 1998. "Visible Minority Women in Mainstream Advertising: Distorted Mirror or Looking Glass?" *Atlantis* 22 (2): 27-38.

Kunz, Jean Lock, and Louise Hanvey. 2000. *Immigrant Youth in Canada*. anadian Council on Social Development.

Kurz, Demie, and Evan Stark. 1988. "Not-So-Benign Neglect: The Medical Response to Battering." In *Feminist Perspectives on Wife Abuse*, ed. Kersti Yllö and Michelle Bograd, 249-66. New York: Sage.

Laghi, Brian. 2001. "Reaction to Thobani Threatening, Women Say." *Globe and Mail*, 5 October: A10.

Lai, Tracy A. 1986. "Asian Women: Resisting the Violence." In *The Speaking Profits Us: Violence in the Lives of Women with Colour*, ed. M.C. Burns, 8-11. Seattle: Center for the Prevention of Sexual and Domestic Violence.

Lakeman, Lee. 2000. "Why 'Law and Order' Cannot End Violence against Women; and Why the Development of Women's (Social, Economic and Political and Civil) Rights Might." *Canadian Woman Studies* 20 (3): 24-33.

Lalvani, Suren. 1995. "Consuming the Exotic Other." *Critical Studies in Mass Communication* 12 (3): 263-86.

Laquian, Eleanor, Aprodicio Laquian, and Terry McGee, eds. 1997. *The Silent Debate: Asian Immigration and Racism in Canada*. Vancouver: Institute of Asian Research, University of British Columbia.

Laroche, Mireille. 2000. "Health Status and Health Services Utilization of Canada's Immigrant and Non-Immigrant Populations." *Canadian Public Policy* 26 (1): 51-73.

Lather, Patti. 1991. *Getting Smart, Feminist Research and Pedagogy with/in the Postmodern*. New York and London: Routledge.

Lavoie, Marie-Hélène, and Chris Dornan, under the direction of Florian Sauvageau, Centre d'études sur les médias. 2001. *Concentration of Newspaper Ownership, an "Old," and Still Unresolved Problem*. Ottawa: Department of Canadian Heritage, Minister of Public Works and Government Services Canada.

Lazreg, Marnia. 1988. "Feminism and Difference: The Perils of Writing as a Woman on Women in Algeria." *Feminist Studies* 14 (1): 81-107.

Leacock, Eleanor. 1980. "Montagnais Women and the Jesuit Program for Colonization." In *Women and Colonization: Anthropological Perspectives*, ed. Mona Etienne and Eleanor Leacock, 25-42. New York: Praeger.

Lee, Jo-Anne. Forthcoming. "Locality, Participatory Action Research, and Racialized Girls' Struggles For Citizenship." In *Girlhood: Redefining the Limits*, ed. Yasmin Jiwani, Candis Steenbergen, and Claudia Mitchell, 89-108. Montreal: Black Rose Books.

Lee, Jo-Anne, with the assistance of Cheryl Harrison. 1999. *Immigrant Settlement and Multiculturalism Programs for Immigrant, Refugee and Visible Minority Women: A Study of Outcomes, Best Practices and Issues*. Victoria, BC: BC Ministry Responsible for Multiculturalism and Immigration, June.

Legault, Gisèle. 1996. "Social Work Practice in Situations of Intercultural Misunderstandings." *Journal of Multicultural Social Work* 4 (4): 49-66.

Leiss, William, Stephen Kline, and Sut Jhally. 1986. *Social Communication in Advertising: Persons, Products and Images of Well-Being*. New York and Toronto: Methuen.

Lenk, Helle-Mai. 2000. "The Case of Emilie Ouimet: News Discourse on Hijab and the Construction of Quebecois National Identity." In *Anti-Racist Feminism*, ed. Agnes Calliste and Sefa George J. Dei, 73-88. Halifax: Fernwood.

Lenton, Rhonda L. 1995. "Power versus Feminist Theories of Wife Abuse." *Canadian Journal of Criminology* 37 (3): 305-30.

Levine, Meredith. 1988. "Canadian Secretly Relieved at Johnson's Fall." *New Statesman Society* 1 (18): 8.

Lévi-Strauss, Claude. 1966. *The Savage Mind*. Chicago: University of Chicago Press.

Ley, David. 1997. "The Rhetoric of Racism and the Politics of Explanation in the Vancouver Housing Market." In *The Silent Debate: Asian Immigration and Racism in Canada*, ed. Eleanor Laquian, Aprodicio Laquian, and Terry McGee, 331-48. Vancouver: Institute of Asian Research, University of British Columbia.

Li, Nancy, and Patrick May. 1997. "A Tale of Two Communities – HIV/AIDS Education in Asian Women." Report prepared for the Asian Society for the Intervention of AIDS, Vancouver.

Li, Peter S. 1994. "Unneighbourly Houses or Unwelcome Chinese: The Social Construction of Race in the Battle over 'Monster Homes' in Vancouver, Canada." *International Journal of Comparative Race and Ethnic Relations* 1 (1): 14-33.

–. 2003. "Social Inclusion of Visible Minorities and Newcomers: The Articulation of 'Race' and 'Racial' Difference in Canadian Society." Paper presented at the Conference on Social Inclusion, Ottawa, organized under the auspices of Canadian Council on Social Development.

Long, Judith A., Virginia W. Chang, Said A. Ibrahim, and David A. Asch. 2004. "Update on the Health Disparities Literature." *Annals of Internal Medicine* 141 (10): 805-12.

Lonsway, Kimberly. 1996. "Preventing Acquaintance Rape through Education: What Do We Know?" *Psychology of Women Quarterly* 20: 229.

Lorde, Audre. 1983. "An Open Letter to Mary Daly." In *This Bridge Called My Back*, ed. Cherríe Moraga and Gloria Anzaldúa, 94-101. New York: Kitchen Table/Women of Color Press.

Lucashenko, M. 1996. "Violence against Indigenous Women: Public and Private Dimensions." *Violence against Women* 2 (4): 378-90.

Lule, Jack. 2002. "Myth and Terror on the Editorial Page: The *New York Times* Responds to September 11, 2001." *Journalism and Mass Communication Quarterly* 79 (2): 275-93.

Lutz, Helma. 1995. "The Legacy of Migration: Immigrant Mothers and Daughters and the Process of Intergenerational Transmission." *Comenius* 15 (3): 304-17.

Lynam, Judith. 1992. "Towards the Goal of Providing Culturally Sensitive Care: Principles upon Which to Build Nursing Curricula." *Journal of Advanced Nursing* (17): 149-57.

Lynn, Marian, and Eimear O'Neill. 1995. "Families, Power, and Violence." In *Canadian Families: Diversity, Conflict and Change*, ed. Nancy Mandell and Ann Duffy, 271-305. Toronto: Harcourt Brace.

McAllister, Kirsten Emiko. 1992. "Asians in Hollywood." *CineAction* (30): 8-13.

Macaulay, Judge Malcolm. 1999. "Reasons for Judgment in *R. v. Warren Paul Glowatski*." Supreme Court of British Columbia, Docket 95773.

McBratney, John. 1988. "Images of Indian Women in Rudyard Kipling: A Case of Doubling Discourse." *Inscriptions* 3 (4): 47-57.

McClintock, Anne. 1995. *Imperial Leather: Race, Gender and Sexuality in the Colonial Context*. New York and London: Routledge.

MacFarlane, John. 2001. "Medical Resident Tells of Assault." *Montreal Gazette*, 18 September: B6.

McGillivray, Anne, and Brenda Comaskey. 1999. *Black Eyes All of the Time: Intimate Violence, Aboriginal Women, and the Justice System*. Toronto: University of Toronto Press.

Macgregor, Robert M. 1997. "The Distorted Mirror: Images of Visible Minority Women in Canadian Print Advertising." In *The Mass Media and Canadian Diversity*, ed. Stephen E. Nancoo and Robert S. Nancoo, 77-91. Mississauga, ON: Canadian Educators' Press.

McIvor, Sharon D., and Teressa A. Nahanee. 1998. "Aboriginal Women: Invisible Victims of Violence." In *Unsettling Truths: Battered Women, Policy, Politics, and Contemporary Research in Canada*, ed. K.D. Bonnycastle and G.S. Rigakos, 63-70. Vancouver: Collective Press.

McKenna, Katherine M.J., and June Larkin, eds. 2002. *Violence against Women: New Canadian Perspectives*. Toronto: Inanna Publications and Education.

MacKinnon, Marian, and Laura Lee Howard. 2000. "Affirming Immigrant Women's Health: Building Inclusive Health Policy. Final Report." Maritime Centre for Excellence for Women's Health.

MacLeod, Linda, and Maria Y. Shin. 1990. *Isolated, Afraid and Forgotten: The Service Delivery Needs and Realities of Immigrant and Refugee Women Who Are Battered*. Prepared for the National Clearinghouse on Family Violence. Ottawa: Health and Welfare Canada.

MacLeod, Linda, and Maria Y. Shin in collaboration with Queenie Hum, Jagrup Samra-Jawanda with Shalen Rai, Maria Minna, and Eva Wasilewska. 1994. *Like a Wingless Bird: A Tribute to the Survival and Courage of Women Who Are Abused and Who Speak Neither English nor French*. Ottawa: National Clearinghouse on Family Violence.

McMartin, Pete. 2000. "Shock of Virk Trial Is Ordinary Appearance of Accused Teen." *Vancouver Sun*, 23 March: A6.

Mahtani, Minelle. 2001. "Representing Minorities: Canadian Media and Minority Identities." *Canadian Ethnic Studies* 33 (3): 93-133.

–. 2002a. "Interrogating the Hyphen-Nation: Canadian Multicultural Policy and 'Mixed Race' Identities." *Social Identities* 8 (1): 67-90.

–. 2002b. "What's in a Name? Exploring the Employment of 'Mixed Race' as an Identification." *Ethnicities* 2 (4): 469-90.

Mahtani, Minelle, and Alison Mountz. 2002. *Immigration to British Columbia: Media Representations and Public Opinion*. Working Paper Series 02-15. Vancouver: Vancouver Centre of Excellence for Research Centre on Immigration and Integration in the Metropolis.

Majid, Anouar. 1998. "The Politics of Feminism in Islam." *Signs: Journal of Women in Culture and Society* 23 (2): 321-61.

Mallick, Heather. 2001. "Ridley Is Audacious, 'Stroppy,' Strong – and Her Critics Hate It." *Globe and Mail*, 20 October: F6.

Mandaville, Peter. 2001. "Reimagining Islam in Diaspora: The Politics of Mediated Community." *Gazette: The International Journal for Communication Studies* 63 (2-3): 169-86.

Maracle, Lee. 1996. *I Am Woman: A Native Perspective on Sociology and Feminism*. Vancouver: Press Gang.

Marshall, Pat Freeman, and Marthe Asselin Vaillancourt. 1993. *Changing the Landscape: Ending Violence – Achieving Equality*. Final Report of the Canadian Panel on Violence against Women. Ottawa: Minister of Supply and Services.

Martin, Dianne L., and Janet E. Mosher. 1995. "Unkept Promises: Experiences of Immigrant Women with the Neo-Criminalization of Wife Abuse." *Canadian Journal of Women and the Law* (8): 3-44.

Matthews, Julie Mariko. 1997. "A Vietnamese Flag and a Bowl of Australian Flowers: Recomposing Racism and Sexism." *Gender, Place and Culture* 4 (1): 5-18.

Matusic, Karen. 2001. "Taliban Holds Journalist Who Sneaked into Country." *Globe and Mail,* 1 October: A5.

Meissner, Dirk. 1999. "Teen Found Guilty in Death of Reena Virk." *Toronto Star,* 3 June: 1.

Melchers, Ron. 2003. "Do Toronto Police Engage in Racial Profiling?" *Canadian Journal of Criminology and Criminal Justice* 45 (3): 347-66.

Meleis, Afaf I. 1991. "Between Two Cultures: Identity, Roles and Health." *Health Care for Women International* 12: 365-77.

Meyers, Marian. 1994. "News of Battering." *Journal of Communication* 44 (2): 47-63.

–. 1997. *News Coverage of Violence against Women: Engendering Blame.* Thousand Oaks, CA: Sage.

Miles, Robert. 1989. *Racism.* London and New York: Routledge.

Miller, Barbara D. 1995. "Precepts and Practices: Researching Identity Formation among Indian Hindu Adolescents in the United States." *New Directions for Child Development* (67): 71-85.

Miller, David B. 1999. "Racial Socialization and Racial Identity: Can They Promote Resiliency for African American Adolescents?" *Adolescence* 34 (135): 493-501.

Miller, John, and Kimberly Prince. 1994. *The Imperfect Mirror: Analysis of Minority Pictures and News in Six Canadian Newspapers.* Toronto: School of Journalism, Ryerson Polytechnic University.

Minh-ha, Trinh T. 1989a. "Black Bamboo." *CineAction!* 18: 56-60.

–. 1989b. *Woman, Native, Other: Writing Postcoloniality and Feminism.* Bloomington: Indiana University Press.

Mirchandani, Kiran, and Evangelia Tastsoglou. 2000. "Towards a Diversity beyond Tolerance." *Studies in Political Economy* (61): 49-78.

Mitchell, Claudia, and Jacqueline Reid-Walsh, eds. 2005. *Seven Going on Seventeen.* New York: Peter Lang.

Mogg, Jean M. 1991. "The Experience of Bicultural Conflict by Vietnamese Adolescent Girls in Greater Vancouver." MA thesis, Simon Fraser University.

Moghadam, Valentine M. 1999. "Revolution, Religion, and Gender Politics: Iran and Afghanistan Compared." *Journal of Women's History* 10 (4): 172-95.

–. 2001. "Afghan Women and Transnational Feminism." *Middle East Women's Studies Review* 16 (3-4).

Mohanty, Chandra Talpade. 1991a. "Under Western Eyes: Feminist Scholarship and Colonial Discourses." In *Third World Women and the Politics of Feminism,* ed. Chandra Talpade Mohanty, Ann Russo, and Lourdes Torres, 53-80. Bloomington: Indiana University Press.

–. 1991b. "Introduction: Cartographies of Struggle: Third World Women and the Politics of Feminism." In *Third World Women and the Politics of Feminism,* ed. Chandra Talpade Mohanty, Ann Russo, and Lourdes Torres, 1-47. Bloomington: Indiana University Press.

Molotch, Harvey, and Marilyn Lester. 1974. "News as Purposive Behavior: On the Strategic Use of Routine Events, Accidents, and Scandals." *American Sociological Review* 39: 101-12.

Montgomery, Sue. 2001. "Loss Felt among Local Afghans: Rights Activist Hopes Level Heads Will Prevail as U.S. Mulls Retaliation." *Montreal Gazette,* 18 September: B1.

Monture-Angus, Patricia. 1995. *Thunder in My Soul: A Mohawk Woman Speaks.* Halifax: Fernwood.

Moodley, Kogila Adam. 1983. "Canadian Multiculturalism as Ideology." *Ethnic and Racial Studies* 6 (3) July: 320-31.

Moore, Dene. 2000a. "Accused Teen Killer Says She Wasn't There When Virk Killed." *Sympatico NewsExpress National News,* web-posted 23 March.

–. 2000b. "Teen Convicted of Killing Reena Virk to Spend at Least Five Years in Prison." *Vancouver Sun,* web-posted 21 April.

Moore, Lynn. 2001. "Learning the True Nature of Islam: Mosques Educating Non-Muslims." *Montreal Gazette,* 24 September: A4.

Morley, David. 1980. *The Nationwide Audience: Structure and Decoding.* London: British Film Institute.

Morris, Nancy. 2002. "The Myth of Unadulterated Culture Meets the Threat of Imported Media." *Media, Culture and Society* 24 (3): 712-27.

Morrison, Madame Justice Nancy. 2000. "*R. v. Kelly Marie Ellard.*" Supreme Court of British Columbia, Docket CC981593.

MOSAIC. 1996. *Immigrant Women's Health: A Community Consultation Project.* Vancouver: MOSAIC.

Moussa, Helene. 1994. *Challenging Myths and Claiming Power Together: A Handbook to Set Up and Assess Support Groups for and with Immigrant and Refugee Women.* Toronto: Education Wife Assault.

–. 1998-99. "Violence against Refugee Women: Gender Oppression, Canadian Policy, and the International Struggle for Human Rights." *Resources for Feminist Research* 26 (3-4): 79-111.

Mulgrew, Ian. 2005a. "There but for the Grace – Virk's Mother Extends Rare Sympathy to Killer's Family." *Vancouver Sun,* 15 April [final ed.]: A11.

–. 2005b. "Justice Delayed Again in Kelly Ellard's Sentencing." *Vancouver Sun,* 20 May: B4.

–. 2005c. "Where There Is No Publicity, There Is No Justice." *Vancouver Sun,* 28 May: B5.

–. 2005d. "Portrait of a Violent Mind." *Vancouver Sun,* 3 June: B2.

Murphy, Rex. 2001. "Girded with Irony for Times of War." *Globe and Mail,* 6 October: A21.

Murray, Catherine. 2002. "Silent on the Set: Cultural Diversity and Race in English Canadian TV Drama." Prepared for the Strategic Research and Analysis (SRA), Strategic Policy and Research Department of Canadian Heritage.

Naber, Nadine. 2002. "So Our History Doesn't Become Your Future: The Local and Global Politics of Coalition Building Post Sept. 11th." *Journal of Asian American Studies* 5 (3): 217-42.

Naficy, Hamid. 1998. "Narrowcasting in Diaspora: Middle Eastern Television in Los Angeles." In *Living Color: Race and Television in the United States,* ed. S. Torres, 82-96. Durham and London: Duke University Press.

Nancoo, Stephen E., and Robert S. Nancoo, eds. 1997. *The Mass Media and Canadian Diversity.* Mississauga, ON: Canadian Educators' Press.

Narayan, Uma. 1995. "Male-Order Brides: Immigrant Women, Domestic Violence and Immigration Law." *Hypatia* 10 (1): 104-19.

–. 1997. *Dislocating Cultures: Identities, Traditions and Third World Feminism.* London and New York: Routledge.

National Association of Women and the Law (NAWL). 1999. "Gender Analysis of Immigration and Refugee Protection Legislation and Policy." NAWL Ad Hoc Committee on Gender Analysis of the Immigration Act, Submission to Citizenship and Immigration Canada.

Ng, Roxana. 1993a. "Sexism, Racism, Canadian Nationalism." In *Returning the Gaze: Essays on Racism, Feminism and Politics,* ed. Himani Bannerji, 223-41. Toronto: Sister Vision Press.

–. 1993b. "Racism, Sexism, and Immigrant Women." In *Changing Patterns: Women in Canada,* ed. Sandra Burt, Lorraine Code, and Lindsay Dorney, 279-301. Toronto: McClelland and Stewart.

Nichols, Bill. 1990-91. "Embodied Knowledge and the Politics of Power." *CineAction!* (23): 14-21.

Ocran, Amanda Araba. 1997. "Across the Home/Work Divide: Homework in Garment Manufacture and the Failure of Employment Regulation." In *Challenging the Public/ Private Divide: Feminism, Law and Public Policy,* ed. Susan B. Boyd, 144-67. Toronto: University of Toronto Press.

Odartey-Wellington, Felix. 2004. "The Al-Qaeda Sleeper Cell That Never Was: The Canadian News Media, State Security Apparatus, and 'Operation Thread.'" MA thesis, Concordia University.

Oikawa, Mona. 2002. "Cartographies of Violence: Women, Memory, and the Subject(S) of the 'Internment.'" In *Race, Space, and the Law: Unmapping a White Settler Society,* ed. Sherene H. Razack, 71-98. Toronto: Between the Lines.

O'Keefe, Maura. 1994. "Racial/Ethnic Differences among Battered Women and Their Children." *Journal of Child and Family Studies* 3 (3): 283-305.

Omatsu, Maryka. 1997. "The Fiction of Judicial Impartiality." *Canadian Journal of Women and the Law* (9): 1-16.

Omi, Michael, and Howard Winant. 1993. "On the Theoretical Status of the Concept of Race." In *Race, Identity, and Representation in Education,* ed. Cameron McCarthy and Warren Crichlow, 3-10. New York: Routledge.

Onder, Zehra. 1996. "Muslim-Turkish Children in Germany: Socio-Cultural Problems." *Migration World Magazine* 24 (5): 18-24.

Palumbo-Liu, David. 1999. *Asian/American Historical Crossings of a Racial Frontier.* Stanford, CA: Stanford University Press.

Papple, Sarah. 2000. "Maybe Judge Knows Something We Don't. Let's Hope So." *Vancouver Province,* 21 April: A3.

Park, Hijin. 2004. "Racialized Sexual Harassment within a National and Global Context: Regulating the Presence of the 'Oriental Woman.'" In *Calculated Kindness: Global Restructuring, Immigration and Settlement in Canada,* ed. Rose Baaba Folson, 84-101. Halifax: Fernwood.

Parkinson, David. 2001. "Journalist Freed, Aid Staff Still Held." *Globe and Mail,* 9 October: A3.

Patterson, Julienne. 2003. "Spousal Violence." *Family Violence in Canada: A Statistical Profile 2003:* 4-20.

Pemberton, Kim. 1997a. "Inaction Legacy of Vernon Massacre: One Year after Mass Killings, Inquest Recommendations Still Haven't Been Acted Upon." *Vancouver Sun,* 4 April: A1.

–. 1997b. "Police Failed to Prevent Shotgun Attack by Stalker: Sharon Velisek Is Lobbying the Provincial Government to Do More to Prevent Domestic Abuse and Killings." *Vancouver Sun,* 4 April: A16.

Pemberton, Kim, and Jim Beatty. 1999. "Accused in Virk Drowning to Be Tried in Adult Court." *Vancouver Sun,* 14 May: A3.

Perez, Beverly Encarguez. 2003. "Woman Warrior Meets Mail-Order Bride: Finding an Asian American Voice in the Women's Movement." *Berkeley Women's Law Journal* 18: 211-36.

Perigoe, Ross, and Barry Lazar. 1992. "Visible Minorities and Native Canadians in National Television News Programs." In *Critical Studies of Canadian Mass Media,* ed. Marc Grenier, 259-72. Markham, ON: Butterworths.

Perilla, Julia L., Roger Bakeman, and Fran Norris. 1994. "Culture and Domestic Violence: The Ecology of Abused Latinas." *Violence and Victims* 9 (4): 325-39.

Peter, Karl. 1981. "The Myth of Multiculturalism and Other Political Fables." In *Ethnicity, Power and Politics,* ed. Jorgen Dahlie and Tissa Fernando, 56-67. Toronto: Methuen.

Philippine Women Centre of BC. 1997. *Trapped: "Holding on to the Knife's Edge" – Economic Violence against Filipino Migrant/Immigrant Women.* Vancouver: FREDA Centre for Research on Violence against Women and Children.

Pinn, Vivian W., and Mary T. Chunko. 1997. "The Diverse Faces of Violence: Minority Women and Domestic Abuse." *Academic Medicine* 72 (1): S65-S71.

Polaschek, N.R. 1998. "Cultural Safety: A New Concept in Nursing People of Different Ethnicities." *Journal of Advanced Nursing* (27): 452-57.

Porter, John. 1965. *The Vertical Mosaic: An Analysis of Social Class and Power in Canada.* Toronto: University of Toronto Press.

Potvin, Maryse. 1999. "Second-Generation Haitian Youth in Quebec: Between the 'Real' Community and the 'Represented.'" *Canadian Ethnic Studies* 31 (1): 43-73.

Pratt, Geraldine. 2002. *Between Homes: Displacement and Belonging for Second Generation Filipino-Canadian Youths.* Working Paper Series 02-13. Vancouver: Vancouver Centre of Excellence for Research on Immigration and Integration in the Metropolis.

Pratt, Mary Louise. 1992. *Imperial Eyes: Travel Writing and Transculturation.* London and New York: Routledge.

Province (Vancouver). 1996. "Woman Tells Inquest of Stalker: Shooting Stunned Friends." 20 September: A2.

–. 2000. "For Kelly, Killer in Custody." 4 April: A12.

Pugh-Lilly, Aalece O., Helen A. Neville, and Karen L. Poulin. 2001. "In Protection of Ourselves: Black Girls' Perceptions of Self-Reported Delinquent Behaviours." *Psychology of Women Quarterly* 25: 145-54.

Puzan, Elayne. 2003. "The Unbearable Whiteness of Being (in Nursing)." *Nursing Inquiry* 10 (3): 193-200.

Pyke, Karen, and Tran Dang. 2003. "'F.O.B.' and 'Whitewashed': Identity and Internalized Racism among Second Generation Asian Americans." *Qualitative Sociology* 26 (2): 147-72.

Pyke, Karen D., and Denise L. Johnson. 2003. "Asian American Women and Racialized Femininities: 'Doing' Gender across Cultural Worlds." *Gender and Society* 17 (1): 33-53.

Raby, Rebecca C. 2002. "A Tangle of Discourses: Girls Negotiating Adolescence." *Journal of Youth Studies* 5 (4): 425-48.

Radomsky, Nellie A. 1995. *Lost Voices: Women, Chronic Pain, and Abuse*. Binghampton, NY: Haworth Press.

Raj, Anita, and Jay Silverman. 2002. "Violence against Immigrant Women, the Roles of Culture, Context, and Legal Immigrant Status on Intimate Partner Violence." *Violence against Women* 8 (3): 367-98.

Ramsden, Irihapeti. 1990. "Cultural Safety." *New Zealand Nursing Journal: Kai Tiaki* 83 (110): 18-19.

–. 1993. "Kawa Whakaruruhau: Cultural Safety in Nursing Education in Aotearoa (New Zealand)." *Nursing Praxis in New Zealand* 8 (3): 4-10.

Randall, Melanie, and Lori Haskell. 2000. *Gender Analysis, Sexual Inequality and Violence: The Lives of Girls*. London, ON: Centre for Research on Violence against Women and Children.

Rasche, Christine E. 1988. "Minority Women and Domestic Violence: The Unique Dilemmas of Battered Women of Colour." *Journal of Contemporary Criminal Justice* 4-3: 150-71.

Räthzel, Nora. 2000. "Living Differences: Ethnicity and Fearless Girls in Public Squares." *Social Identities* 6 (2): 119-42.

Razack, Sherene. 1994a. "What Is to Be Gained by Looking White People in the Eye? Culture, Race, and Gender in Cases of Sexual Violence." *Signs* 19 (4): 894-923.

–. 1994b. "From Consent to Responsibility, from Pity to Respect: Subtexts in Cases of Sexual Violence Involving Girls and Women with Developmental Disabilities." *Law and Social Inquiry* 19 (4): 891-922.

–. 1998a. *Looking White People in the Eye: Gender, Race, and Culture in Courtrooms and Classrooms*. Toronto: University of Toronto Press.

–. 1998b. "Race, Space, and Prostitution: The Making of the Bourgeois Subject." *Canadian Journal of Women and the Law* 10 (2): 338-76.

–. 2000a. "Your Place or Mine? Transnational Feminist Collaboration." In *Anti-Racist Feminism*, ed. Agnes Calliste and George J. Sefa Dei, 39-53. Halifax: Fernwood.

–. 2000b. "From the 'Clean Snows of Petawawa': The Violence of Canadian Peacekeepers in Somalia." *Cultural Anthropology* 15 (1): 127-63.

–. 2002. "Gendered Racial Violence and Spatialized Justice." In *Race, Space, and the Law: Unmapping a White Settler Society*, ed. Sherene H. Razack, 121-56. Toronto: Between the Lines.

–. 2004. *Dark Threats and White Knights: The Somalia Affair, Peacekeeping and the New Imperialism*. Toronto: University of Toronto Press.

–. 2005. "A Violent Culture or Culturalised Violence? Feminist Narratives of Sexual Violence against South Asian Women." *Studies in Practical Philosophy* 3 (1): 80-104.

Reitsma-Street, Marge. 1999. "Justice for Canadian Girls: A 1990's Update." *Canadian Journal of Criminology* 41 (3): 335-64.

Reitz, Jeffrey G., and Sherrilyn M. Sklar. 1997. "Culture, Race, and the Economic Assimilation of Immigrants." *Sociological Forum* 12 (2): 233-77.

Rezig, Inger. 1983. "Women's Roles in Contemporary Algeria: Tradition and Modernity." In *Women in Islamic Societies, Social Attitudes and Historical Perspectives*, ed. Bo Utas, 192-210. London: Curzon Press; Atlantic Highlands, NJ: Humanities Press.

Rhee, Siyon. 1977. "Domestic Violence in the Korean Immigrant Family." *Journal of Sociology and Social Welfare* 24 (1): 63-77.

Richards, Sarah. 2001. "Islam Is against This Kind of Act." *Montreal Gazette*, 13 September: B4.

Richie, Beth E. 1996. *Compelled to Crime: The Gender Entrapment of Battered Black Women*. New York and London: Routledge.

Rigakos, George S. 1995. "Constructing the Symbolic Complainant: Police Sub-Culture and the Non-Enforcement of Protection Orders for Battered Women." *Violence and Victims* 10: 227-47.

–. 1998. "The Politics of Protection: Battered Women, Protection Orders, and Police Sub-culture." In *Unsettling Truths: Battered Women, Policy, Politics, and Contemporary Research in Canada,* ed. Kevin D. Bonnycastle and George S. Rigakos, 82-92. Vancouver: Collective Press.

Ristock, Janice L., and Health Promotion and Programs Branch Mental Health Division, Health Canada. 1995. *The Impact of Violence on Mental Health: A Guide to the Literature.* Discussion Papers on Health/Family Violence Issues, 3. Ottawa: National Clearinghouse on Family Violence.

Ristock, Janice L., and Joan Pennell. 1996. *Community Research as Empowerment: Feminist Links, Postmodern Interruptions.* Toronto, Oxford, and New York: Oxford University Press.

Roberts, Barbara. 1990. *Immigrant Women: Triple Oppression, Triple Jeopardy.* Paper presented at the opening meeting of the Simone de Beauvoir Institute Research Seminar (1987-88): Immigrant Women/La femme immigrante. Collection Working Papers/Inédits. Montreal: Publications de L'Institut Simone de Beauvoir.

Roberts, Julian V. 2002. "Racism and the Collection of Statistics Relating to Race and Ethnicity." In *Crimes of Colour: Racialization and the Criminal Justice System in Canada,* ed. Wendy Chan and Kiran Mirchandani, 101-12. Calgary: Broadview Press.

Rosenberg, Emily S. 2002. "Rescuing Women and Children." *Journal of American History* 89 (2): 456-65.

Rosenthal, Doreen, Nadia Ranieri, and Steven Klimidis. 1996. "Vietnamese Adolescents in Australia: Relationships between Perceptions of Self and Parental Values, Intergenerational Conflict, and Gender Dissatisfaction." *International Journal of Psychology* 31 (2): 81-91.

Roy, Arundhati. 2003. *War Talk.* Cambridge, MA: South End Press.

Royal Commission on Aboriginal Peoples. 1995. *Choosing Life: Special Report on Suicide among Aboriginal People.* Ottawa: Ministry of Supply and Services.

–. 1996. "Current Realities." In *Bridging the Cultural Divide: A Report on Aboriginal People and Criminal Justice in Canada,* 26-81. Ottawa: Minister of Supply and Services Canada.

Rumbaut, Ruben G. 1994. "The Crucible Within: Ethnic Identity, Self Esteem, and Segmented Assimilation among Children of Immigrants." *International Migration Review* 28 (4): 748-94.

Said, Edward W. 1979. *Orientalism.* New York: Vintage Books.

–. 1981. *Covering Islam: How the Media and Experts Determine How We See the Rest of the World.* New York: Pantheon Books.

Sallot, Jeff. 2001. "Fry Assailed for Remaining through Anti-U.S. Speech." *Globe and Mail,* 2 October: A11.

Sanchez, Tony R., Judith A. Plawecki, and Henry M. Plawecki. 1996. "The Delivery of Culturally Sensitive Health Care to Native Americans." *Journal of Holistic Nursing* 14 (4): 295-307.

Sarigiani, Pamela A., Phame M. Camarena, and Anne C. Petersen. 1993. "Cultural Factors in Adolescent Girls' Development: The Role of Ethnic Minority Group Status." In *Female Adolescent Development,* ed. Max Sugar, 138-56. New York: Brunner/Mazel.

Sasso, Angela. 2000. *Interpreter Services in Health Care: A Call for Provincial Standards and Services.* Vancouver: Multicultural Health Committee, Affiliation of Multicultural Societies and Service Agencies of BC.

Savary, Rosalind. 1998. "What Does Gender Have to Do with It? An Environmental Scan on Women's Health Issues." Prepared for the Adult Health Team, Health Promotions and Programs Branch, Health Canada, BC/Yukon Regional Office.

Scanlon, Joseph. 1977. "The Sikhs of Vancouver." In *Ethnicity and the Media,* 193-261. Paris: UNESCO Press.

Schissel, Bernard. 1997. *Blaming Children: Youth Crime, Moral Panics and the Politics of Hate.* Halifax: Fernwood.

Schneller, Debora Podolsky. 1981. "The Immigrant's Challenge: Mourning the Loss of Homeland and Adapting to the New World." *Smith College Studies in Social Work* 5I (2): 95-125.

Schnurmacher, Tommy. 2001. "Images of Celebration Tell the Story." *Montreal Gazette,* 14 September: A19.

Schooler, Deborah, L. Monique Ward, Ann Merriwether, and Allison Caruthers. 2004. "Who's That Girl? Television's Role in the Body Image Development of Young White and Black Women." *Psychology of Women Quarterly* 28: 38-47.

Schramm, Heather. 1998. *Young Women Who Use Violence: Myths and Facts.* Calgary: Elizabeth Fry Society of Calgary.

Scott, Kimberly A. 2002. "'You Want to Be a Girl and Not My Friend': African-American Black Girls' Play Activities with and without Boys." *Childhood* 9 (4): 397-414.

Sevunts, Levon. 2001. "Refugees Fear Mood Change." *Montreal Gazette,* 14 September: A19.

Shaheen, Jack. 1984. *The TV Arab.* Bowling Green, OH: Bowling Green State University Popular Press.

Shaw, Margaret, Karen Rogers, Johanne Blanchette, Tina Hattern, Lee Seto Thomas, and Lada Tamarack. 1991. *Survey of Federally Sentenced Women: Report to the Task Force on Federally Sentenced Women on the Prison Survey.* Corrections Branch User Report 1991-04. Ottawa: Solicitor General of Canada, Ministry Secretariat.

Shoemaker, Pamela J., and Stephen D. Reese. 1996. *Mediating the Message: Theories of Influences on Mass Media Content.* White Plains, NY: Longman.

Shohat, Ella, and Robert Stam. 1994. *Unthinking Eurocentrism: Multiculturalism and the Media.* London and New York: Routledge.

Shroff, Farah M. 1996-97. "Walking the Diversity Talk: Curriculum within First Year Midwifery Education." *Health and Canadian Society* 4 (2): 389-444.

Sidhu, Surjeet. 1996. "Perspectives of Women Who Have Experienced Violence in Relationships and Their Children." Research initiated and conducted by the Richmond Coordinating Response Committee to End Violence against Women, 13 November.

Smith, Linda Tuhiwai. 1999. *Decolonizing Methodologies: Research and Indigenous Peoples.* London and New York: Zed Books; Dunedin, New Zealand: University of Otago Press.

Smith, Michael, and Alan Philps. 2001. "Delta Force to Ride Planes: U.S. Anti-Terrorism Squad in New Role." *Montreal Gazette,* 14 September: A4.

Snider, Laureen. 2002. "'But They're Not Real Criminals': Downsizing Corporate Crime." In *Marginality and Condemnation: An Introduction to Critical Criminology,* ed. Bernard Schissel and Carolyn Brooks, 215-33. Halifax: Fernwood.

Soe, Valerie. 1992. *Picturing Oriental Girls: A (Re) Educational Videotape.* San Francisco: NAATA, Cross Current Media.

Spector, Norman. 2001. "Déjà vu for Israelis: Scenes of Destruction and Pain Are Familiar to People Who Are Used to Being Attacked for Who They Are." *Montreal Gazette,* 12 September: B3.

Spelman, Elizabeth V. 1988. *Inessential Woman: Problems of Exclusion in Feminist Thought.* Boston: Beacon Press.

Spencer, Michael S., and Juan Chen. 2004. "Effect of Discrimination on Mental Health Service Utilization among Chinese Americans." *American Journal of Public Health* 94 (5): 809-914.

Squire, Corinne, ed. 2000. *Culture in Psychology.* London and Philadelphia: Routledge.

Stark, Evan, Anne Flitcraft, and William Frasier. 1979. "Medicine and Patriarchal Violence: The Social Construction of a 'Private' Event." *International Journal of Health Services* 9 (3): 461-93.

Statistics Canada. 2003. "Quebec: Largest Proportion of Roman Catholics." Ottawa: Government of Canada.

Staunæs, Dorthe. 2003. "Where Have All the Subjects Gone? Bringing Together the Concepts of Intersectionality and Subjectification." *Nordic Journal of Women's Studies* 11 (2): 101-10.

Steffenhagen, Janet. 1997. "Girls Killing Girls a Sign of Angry Empty Lives." *Vancouver Sun,* 25 November: A1.

Stonebanks, Roger. 2000. "The Last Accused in Reena's Death: Families Gather to Witness Final Trial in Teen Tragedy." *Victoria Times Colonist,* 7 March: A1.

Stott, Rebecca. 1989. "The Dark Continent: Africa as Female Body in Haggard's Adventure Fiction." *Feminist Review* (32): 68-89.

Strobel, Margaret. 1993. *Gender, Sex, and Empire.* Pamphlet for the American Historical Association's series Essays on Global and Comparative History (1992). Reprinted in *Islamic and European Expansion: The Forging of a Global Order,* ed. Michael Adas, 345-75. Philadelphia: Temple University Press.

Surette, Ray. 1998. "The Construction of Crime and Justice in the News Media." In *Media, Crime, and Criminal Justice: Images and Realities,* 52-84. Albany, NY: West/Wadsworth.

Symons, Gladys L. 2002. "Police Constructions of Race and Gender in Street Gangs." In *Crimes of Colour: Racialization and the Criminal Justice System in Canada,* ed. Wendy Chan and Kiran Mirchandani, 115-25. Calgary: Broadview Press.

Takezawa, Yasuko I. 1991. "Children of Inmate: The Effects of the Redress Movement among Third Generation Japanese Americans." *Qualitative Sociology* 14 (1): 39-56.

Tator, Carol. 1984. "Mail Back Campaign." *Currents: Readings in Race Relations* 2 (2): 15-17.

Taylor, Georgina, Jan Barnsley, and Penny Goldsmith. 1996. *Women and Children Last: Custody Disputes and the Family 'Justice' System.* Vancouver: Vancouver Custody and Access Support and Advocacy Association.

Thobani, Sunera. 1992. "Culture Isn't the Cause of Violence." *Vancouver Sun,* 26 September: A12.

–. 1998. "Nationalizing Citizens, Bordering Immigrant Women: Globalization and the Racialization of Women's Citizenship in Late 20th Century Canada." PhD diss., Simon Fraser University.

–. 1999a. "Sponsoring Immigrant Women's Inequalities." *Canadian Woman Studies* 19 (3): 11-16.

–. 1999b. "Closing the Nation's Ranks: Canadian Immigration Policy in the 21st Century." In *Reclaiming the Future, Women's Strategies for the 21st Century,* ed. Somer Broadribb, 75-96. Charlottetown: Gynergy Books.

–. 2000a. "Nationalizing Citizens: Bordering Immigrant Women in the Late Twentieth Century." *Canadian Journal of Women and the Law* 12 (2): 279-312.

–. 2000b. "Closing Ranks: Racism and Sexism in Canada's Immigration Policy." *Institute of Race Relations* 42 (1): 35-55.

–. 2002a. "Closing the Nation's Doors to Immigrant Women: The Restructuring of Canadian Immigration Policy." *Atlantis* 24 (2): 16-26.

–. 2002b. "War Frenzy." *Atlantis* 27 (1): 5-11.

–. 2003. "War and the Politics of Truth-Making in Canada." *Qualitative Studies in Education* 16 (3): 399-414.

Thompson, Joey. 2005. "Mom Finds Justice after Silent Wait: Suman Virk Bore Ellard's Defiant Testimony with Grace." *Vancouver Province,* 13 April: A6.

Times Colonist (Victoria). 2005. "Inside a Troubled Mind." 3 June: A1, A2.

Timmins, Leslie, ed. 1995. *Listening to Thunder: Advocates Talk about the Battered Women's Movement.* Vancouver: Women's Research Centre.

Todd, Sharon. 1998. "Veiling the 'Other,' Unveiling Our 'Selves': Reading Media Images of the Hijab Psychoanalytically to Move beyond Tolerance." *Canadian Journal of Education* 23 (4): 438-51.

Trepagnier, Barbara. 2001. "Deconstructing Categories: The Exposure of Silent Racism." *Symbolic Interaction* 24 (2): 141-63.

Trute, Barry, Peter Sarsfield, and Dale A. MacKenzie. 1988. "Medical Response to Wife Abuse: A Survey of Physicians' Attitudes and Practice." *Canadian Journal of Community Mental Health* 7 (2): 61-71.

Tsolidis, Georgina. 1990. "Ethnic Minority Girls and Self-Esteem." In *Hearts and Minds: Self-Esteem and the Schooling of Girls,* ed. Jane Kenway and Sue Willis, 53-69. London, New York, and Philadelphia: Falmer Press.

Tuchman, Gaye. 1978. *Making News: A Study in the Construction of Reality.* New York: Free Press.

Twine, France Winddance. 1996. "Brown Skinned White Girls: Class, Culture and the Construction of White Identity in Suburban Communities." *Gender, Place and Culture* 3 (2): 205-24.

Tyagi, Smita Vir. 1999. "Tell It Like It Is: Incest Disclosure and Women of Colour." *Canadian Woman Studies* 19 (3): 173-77.

Valpy, Michael. 2001. "The Public Good, Thobani Is Not Alone." *Globe and Mail*, 6 October: F9.

van Dijk, Teun A., ed. 1985. *Discourse and Communication*. New York: de Gruyter.

–. 1987. *Communicating Racism: Ethnic Prejudice in Thought and Talk*. Newbury Park, CA: Sage.

–. 1992. "Discourse and the Denial of Racism." *Discourse and Society* 3 (1): 87-118.

–. 1993. *Elite Discourse and Racism*. Race and Ethnic Relations 6. Newbury Park, CA: Sage.

van Zoonen, Liesbet. 1994. *Feminist Media Studies*. Thousand Oaks, CA: Sage.

Vancouver Sun. 1999. Editorial. "A Lethal Combination for Our Young People." 23 April: A16.

–. 2000. Editorial. "Lessons to Be Learned from the Reena Virk Case." 4 April: A10.

–. 2003. Editorial. "Hard Cases, and the Long Road to Justice in Virk Murder." 2 June: A10.

Varcoe, Colleen Marie. 1997. "Untying Our Hands: The Social Context of Nursing in Relation to Violence against Women." PhD thesis, University of British Columbia.

Vega, William A., Bohdan Kolody, and Juan Ramon Valle. 1987. "Migration and Mental Health: An Empirical Test of Depression Risk Factors among Immigrant Mexican Women." *International Migration Review* 21 (3): 512-29.

Walker, James W. St. G. 1997. *"Race," Rights and the Law in the Supreme Court of Canada*. Toronto: Osgoode Society for Canadian Legal History; Waterloo, ON: Wilfrid Laurier University Press.

Wallace, Bruce. 2001. "West Anxiously Courting a Willing Iran: With Its Leader's 'Remarkable' Conversation, Islamic State Opens Door to a New Relationship." *Montreal Gazette*, 22 September: A13.

Warshaw, Carole. 1993. "Limitations of the Medical Model in the Care of Battered Women." In *Violence against Women: The Bloody Footprints*, ed. Pauline B. Bart and Eileen Geil Moran, 134-46. Newbury Park, CA: Sage.

Watanabe, Teresa. 2001. "Extremists Distort Holy Tenets to Justify War." *Montreal Gazette*, 27 September: B1.

Waters, Paul. 2001. "Twisting the Faith: Islam Is a Serene Religion, but Can Be Warped into a Form of Totalitarianism." *Montreal Gazette*, 15 September: B1.

Weber, Max. 1958. *The Protestant Ethic and the Spirit of Capitalism*. Trans. Talcott Parsons. New York: Scribner.

Weinfeld, Morton. 1982. "Myth and Reality in the Canadian Mosaic: 'Affective Ethnicity.'" *Canadian Ethnic Studies* 13 (3): 80-100.

Wente, Margaret. 2001. "Two Reasons to Thank Sunera Thobani." *Globe and Mail*, 4 October: A19.

Whitehead, Judith, Himani Bannerji, and Shahrzad Mojab. 2001. "Introduction." In *Of Property and Propriety*, ed. Himani Bannerji, Shahrzad Mojab, and Judith Whitehead, 3-33. Toronto: University of Toronto Press.

Wideen, Marvin, and Kathleen A. Barnard. 1999. *Impacts of Immigration on Education in British Columbia: An Analysis of Efforts to Implement Policies of Multiculturalism in Schools*. Vancouver: Vancouver Centre of Excellence on Research in Immigration and Integration.

Wiik, Maija-Liisa. 1995. "Immigrant Women and Wife Abuse: A Phenomenological Exploration." MA thesis, University of British Columbia.

Wilden, Tony. 1980. *The Imaginary Canadian*. Vancouver: Pulp Press.

Wilkins, Karin, and John Downing. 2002. "Mediating Terrorism: Text and Protest in Interpretations of *The Siege*." *Critical Studies in Media Communication* 19 (4): 419-37.

Williams, Toni. 1996. "Report of the Commission on Systemic Racism in the Ontario Criminal Justice System: Summary of Key Findings." Paper presented at the background notes for the Ontario Court of Justice (Provincial Division) annual convention.

Wilson, Laurene J. 1998. "Patient Satisfaction and Quality of Life: A Study of Women with Abusive Male Partners Treated in an Emergency Department." PhD diss., Simon Fraser University.

Wilson, Margo, Holly Johnson, and Martin Daly. 1995. "Lethal and Non-Lethal Violence against Wives." *Canadian Journal of Criminology* 37 (3): 331-61.

Winter, James. 1997. *Democracy's Oxygen: How Corporations Control the News*. Montreal: Black Rose.

–. 2002. *Media Think*. Montreal, London, and New York: Black Rose Books.

Women's Health in Women's Hands Community Centre. 2003. *Racial Discrimination as a Health Risk for Female Youth: Implications for Policy and Healthcare Delivery in Canada*. Ottawa: Canadian Race Relations Foundation.

Wortley, Scot. 2002. "Misrepresentation or Reality? The Depiction of Race and Crime in the Toronto Print Media." In *Marginality and Condemnation: An Introduction to Critical Criminology*, ed. Bernard Schissel and Carolyn Brooks, 55-82. Halifax: Fernwood.

Wortley, Scot, Ross Macmillan, and John Hagan. 1997. "Just Des(S)Erts? The Racial Polarization of Perceptions of Criminal Injustice." *Law and Society Review* 31 (4): 637-76.

Wortley, Scot, and Julian Tanner. 2003. "Data, Denials, and Confusion: The Racial Profiling Debate in Toronto." *Canadian Journal of Criminology and Criminal Justice* 45 (3): 367-89.

Wu, Judy Tzu-Chun. 2003. "Asian American History and Racialized Compulsory Deviance." *Journal of Women's History* 15 (3): 58-62.

Wykes, Maggie. 1998. "A Family Affair: The British Press, Sex, and the Wests." In *News, Gender and Power*, ed. Cynthia Carter, Gill Branston, and Stuart Allen, 233-47. London and New York: Routledge.

Wynn Davies, Merryl, Ashis Nandy, and Ziauddin Sardar. 1993. *Barbaric Others: A Manifesto on Western Racism*. London: Pluto Press.

Yam, Marylou. 1995. "Wife Abuse: Strategies for a Therapeutic Response." *Scholarly Inquiry for Nursing Practice* 9 (2): 147-58.

Yeğenoğlu, Meyda. 1998. *Colonial Fantasies: Towards a Feminist Reading of Orientalism*. Cambridge and Melbourne: Cambridge University Press.

Youngs, Tim. 1989. "Morality and Ideology: The Arranged Marriage in Contemporary British-Asian Drama." *Wasafiri* 9: 3-6.

Yousif, Ahmad F. 1994. "Family Values, Social Adjustment and Problems of Identity: The Canadian Experience." *Journal of Muslim Minority Affairs* 15 (1-2): 108-20.

Zulman, Arthur. 1996. "The Hidden Trauma of Immigration." *Australian Family Physician* 25 (11): 1707-10.

Index

Printed and bound in Canada by Friesens
Set in Stone by Artegraphica Design Co. Ltd.
Copy editor: Judy Phillips
Proofreader: Deborah Kerr
Indexer: Patricia Buchanan